Pierre Bourdieu, Organisation, and Management

Pierre Bourdieu, the French sociologist, philosopher, and anthropologist, has been widely studied and analysed in academic circles, particularly in sociology, where his ideas about power relations in social life helped to define the contemporary field. While many other sociological theories and figures have been extensively discussed and analysed within the contexts of organisation studies and management, Bourdieu's ideas have, until recently, been largely ignored. Offering an authoritative evaluation of Bourdieu's work, this book provides readers with conceptual frameworks, empirical examples, and methodological considerations for advancing theory and research in management and organisation studies.

This book presents an in-depth review of the relevance of Bourdieu's social theory for organisation and management studies, outlining the key aspects of Bourdieu's approach and situating his work in its historical and intellectual context of the time. An outline of the treatment of Bourdieusian theory by management and organisation scholars and a critique of the selective reception of his work are offered. The first edited collection to explore the benefits of Bourdieusian sociology for a management audience, this book is relevant for theory, research, and practice, and will appeal to an international scholarly audience of academics and research students.

Ahu Tatli is a reader in international human resource management in the School of Business and Management at Queen Mary, University of London, UK. Her research interests are in the field of equality and diversity with a particular focus on disadvantage and privilege in organisational settings, and inequality and discrimination in employment. She has published a large number of papers in edited collections, practitioner and policy outlets, and peer-reviewed journals. She has co-authored (with M. Özbilgin) a research monograph, *Global Diversity Management: An Evidence-Based Approach*.

Mustafa Özbilgin is a professor of organisational behaviour at Brunel Business School, Brunel University, London, UK, and the co-chair of Management et Diversité, Université Paris-Dauphine, France. His research focuses on equality, diversity, and inclusion at work from comparative and relational perspectives. His most recent book, *Equality, Diversity and Inclusion*, brings together papers from over 30 scholars in the field, and his other text, *Global Diversity Management* (co-authored with Ahu Tatli), provides evidence from international field studies. He has authored and edited 10 books and is widely published in journals.

Mine Karatas-Özkan is a senior lecturer in strategy and entrepreneurship at the Faculty of Business and Law at the University of Southampton, UK. Her research focuses on social and diversity dimensions of entrepreneurship. She serves on the editorial boards of the *British Journal of Management*, *International Journal of Gender and Entrepreneurship*, *Journal of Entrepreneurship and Public Policy*, and *International Journal of Business and Globalisation*.

Routledge Studies in Management, Organizations and Society

For a full list of titles in this series, please visit www.routledge.com

This series presents innovative work grounded in new realities, addressing issues crucial to an understanding of the contemporary world. This is the world of organised societies, where boundaries between formal and informal, public and private, local and global organisations have been displaced or have vanished, along with other 19th-century dichotomies and oppositions. Management, apart from becoming a specialised profession for a growing number of people, is an everyday activity for most members of modern societies.

Similarly, at the level of enquiry, culture and technology, and literature and economics, can no longer be conceived as isolated intellectual fields; conventional canons and established mainstreams are contested. *Management, Organisations, and Society* addresses these contemporary dynamics of transformation in a manner that transcends disciplinary boundaries, with books that will appeal to researchers, students, and practitioners alike.

19 **Managing Corporate Values in Diverse National Cultures**
The challenge of differences
Philippe d'Iribarne

20 **Gossip and Organizations**
Kathryn Waddington

21 **Leadership as Emotional Labour**
Management and the 'managed heart'
Edited by Marian Iszatt-White

22 **On Being At Work**
The social construction of the employee
Nancy Harding

23 **Storytelling in Management Practice**
Dynamics and implications
Stefanie Reissner and Victoria Pagan

24 **Hierarchy and Organisation**
Toward a general theory of hierarchical social systems
Thomas Diefenbach

25 **Organizing Through Empathy**
Edited by Kathryn Pavlovich and Keiko Krahnke

26 **Managerial Cultures**
A comparative historical analysis
David Hanson

27 **Management and Organization of Temporary Agency Work**
Edited by Bas Koene, Christina Garsten, and Nathalie Galais

28 **Liquid Organization**
Zygmunt Bauman and organization theory
Edited by Jerzy Kociatkiewicz and Monika Kostera

29 **Management and Neoliberalism**
Connecting policies and practices
Alexander Styhre

30 **Organizations and the Media**
Organizing in a mediatized world
Edited by Josef Pallas, Lars Strannegård and Stefan Jonsson

31 **Sexual Orientation at Work**
Contemporary Issues and Perspectives
Edited by Fiona Colgan and Nick Rumens

32 **Gender Equality in Public Services**
Chasing the dream
Hazel Conley and Margaret Page

33 **Untold Stories in Organisations**
Edited by Michal Izak, Linda Hitchin, and David Anderson

34 **Pierre Bourdieu, Organisation, and Management**
Edited by Ahu Tatli, Mustafa Özbilgin, and Mine Karatas-Özkan

Other titles in this series:

Contrasting Involvements
A study of management accounting practices in Britain and Germany
Thomas Ahrens

Turning Words, Spinning Worlds
Chapters in organizational ethnography
Michael Rosen

Breaking through the Glass Ceiling
Women, power and leadership in agricultural organizations
Margaret Alston

The Poetic Logic of Administration
Styles and changes of style in the art of organizing
Kaj Sköldberg

Casting the Other
Maintaining gender inequalities in the workplace
Edited by Barbara Czarniawska and Heather Höpfl

Gender, Identity and the Culture of Organizations
Edited by Iiris Aaltio and Albert J. Mills

Text/Work
Representing organization and organizing representation
Edited by Stephen Linstead

The Social Construction of Management
Texts and identities
Nancy Harding

Management Theory
A critical and reflexive reading
Nanette Monin

Pierre Bourdieu, Organisation, and Management

Edited by Ahu Tatli, Mustafa Özbilgin, and Mine Karatas-Özkan

NEW YORK AND LONDON

First published 2015
by Routledge
711 Third Avenue, New York, NY 10017

and by Routledge
2 Park Square, Milton Park, Abingdon, Oxon OX14 4RN

First issued in paperback 2018

*Routledge is an imprint of the Taylor & Francis Group,
an informa business*

© 2015 Taylor & Francis

The right of the editors to be identified as the author of the editorial material, and of the authors for their individual chapters, has been asserted in accordance with sections 77 and 78 of the Copyright, Designs and Patents Act 1988.

All rights reserved. No part of this book may be reprinted or reproduced or utilized in any form or by any electronic, mechanical, or other means, now known or hereafter invented, including photocopying and recording, or in any information storage or retrieval system, without permission in writing from the publishers.

Trademark Notice: Product or corporate names may be trademarks or registered trademarks, and are used only for identification and explanation without intent to infringe.

Library of Congress Cataloging-in-Publication Data
Pierre Bourdieu, organisation and management / edited by Ahu Tatli,
   Mustafa Özbilgin and Mine Karatas-Özkan.
      pages cm. — (Routledge studies in management, organizations and society ; 34)
   Includes bibliographical references and index.
   1. Bourdieu, Pierre, 1930–2002. 2. Organizational sociology.
3. Management. 4. Industrial sociology. I. Tatli, Ahu. II. Özbilgin, Mustafa. III. Karatas-Özkan, Mine
   HM479.B68P545 2015
   302.3′5—dc23
   2014048794

ISBN 13: 978-1-138-33997-2 (pbk)
ISBN 13: 978-0-415-73726-5 (hbk)

Typeset in Sabon
by Apex CoVantage, LLC

Contents

List of Figures	ix
List of Tables	xi
Foreword by Jean-François Chanlat	xiii
List of Contributors	xix

Introduction: Management and Organisation Studies
Meet Pierre Bourdieu   1
AHU TATLI, MUSTAFA ÖZBILGIN, AND MINE KARATAS-ÖZKAN

PART I
New Frontiers in Research and Theory

1 Careers as Sites of Power: A Relational Understanding of
  Careers Based on Bourdieu's Cornerstones   19
  THOMAS M. SCHNEIDHOFER, MARKUS LATZKE, AND
  WOLFGANG MAYRHOFER

2 Change and Inertia in (re)Formation and Commodification
  of Migrant Workers' Subjectivities: An Intersectional Analysis
  across Spatial and Temporal Dimensions   37
  BARBARA SAMALUK

3 Bourdieu's 'Carnal Theorising' in Organisations and
  Management: Bridging Disembodiment and Other
  Old Dichotomies   55
  KANELLOS-PANAGIOTIS NIKOLOPOULOS AND KATERINA NICOLOPOULOU

4 "Turning the Lens on Ourselves": Bourdieu's Reflexivity
  in Practice   70
  BORIS H.J.M. BRUMMANS

PART II
Empirical Insights

5 Reintroducing Power and Struggles within Organisational Fields: A Return to Bourdieu's Framework   97
KARIM HAMADACHE

6 Bourdieu, Representational Legitimacy, and Pension Boardrooms: A Contested Space?   119
SUSAN SAYCE

7 Of Trump Cards and Game Moves: Positioning Gender Equality as an Element of Power Struggles in Universities   139
JOHANNA HOFBAUER, ANGELIKA STRIEDINGER, KATHARINA KREISSL, AND BIRGIT SAUER

8 Illusio in the Game of Higher Education: An Empirical Exploration of Interconnections between Fields and Academic Habitus   162
LUCY TAKSA AND SENIA KALFA

9 Exploring Different Forms of Capitals: Researching Capitals in the Field of Cultural and Creative Industries   187
BARBARA TOWNLEY

10 Strategies of Women Managers in Sport Organisations: A Way of Subversion or Reproduction of the Existing Gendered Field?   207
MUSTAFA ŞAHIN KARAÇAM AND CANAN KOCA

Index   229

Figures

7.1 Players and Their Stakes in the Tenure Track
    Implementation   154
9.1 Researching Capitals in the CCI Field   201

Tables

2.1	Research Map	43
5.1	The Issues of Orphan Drugs	107
6.1	Pension Trustee Profile	124
7.1	Data Collection—Interviews in Four Case Study Universities	146
8.1	Participant Profile	171
10.1	Interviewee Profiles	213

Foreword*

The work of Pierre Bourdieu is recognised globally. He is one of the most cited authors regardless of the database consulted in the social sciences, notably Google Scholar (Wacquant, 2014; Chanlat, 2014). It is therefore no wonder that researchers in management and organisation have interested themselves for some time in the work of this French sociologist, translated in numerous languages, especially in English. This book that I have the honour and pleasure to preface is one such exemplary illustration.

The work of Pierre Bourdieu is considerable and fundamental: considerable because he has published numerous books, chapters of books, and articles greatly cited today throughout the world in numerous scientific fields—sociology, anthropology, sciences of education, management and organisational studies, philosophy, ethnology, sciences of language, and so forth—and fundamental for it is founded upon simultaneously theoretical and empirical contributions, which take into account social intelligence while exceeding classic dichotomies—actor-structure, micro-macro, social-historical order (Wacquant, 2013, 2014).

His work is also part of an intellectual lineage that goes back to the founding fathers of sociology: Marx, Weber, and Durkheim, especially in the French school, embodied by Durkheim and Mauss, who sought to develop an integrated and broad vision of social life. As he says himself, "*The real is relational*: it exists in the social world, these are relationships—not intersubjective interactions or relationships between agents, but objectives relationship 'independently of consciences and individual wills' as Marx said." He adds further, "The real object of social sciences is neither individual, this *ens realissimun* naively celebrated as the reality of all realities by all 'methodological individualists', nor groups as concrete sets of individuals sharing a position and condition, but the relationship between two realizations of historical action in the body and in things" (Bourdieu and Wacquant, 2014: 175).

His work is also indebted to his philosophical culture, forgetting not that Pierre Bourdieu has indeed trained in philosophy, like many other great figures of French sociology, which differentiates him from the many Anglo-Saxon sociologists of his generation, including those in the US (Wacquant,

2013). He thus supported both Bachelard and Canguilhem for the philosophy of science, and the contributions of German philosophy, especially Husserl and Cassirer.

Compared to the work of Giddens, who researched in the field of English, he too surpassed the classical opposition evident in structuration theory (1984, 1987), drawing on the work of many secondary data; Bourdieu's theoretical contribution relies on its own empirical data. From his first ethnological accounts of Kabyle culture, Bourdieu has continued to conduct great sociological surveys in order to explain and understand the articulation of social life in various fields: culture, art, education, the university, the elites, consumption, housing, and so forth (Bourdieu and Wacquant, 2014).

In this book, *Bourdieu, Organisation, and Management*, edited by our colleagues, Ahu Tatli, Mustafa Özbilgin, and Mine Karatas-Özkan, the different contributors, while all certainly recalling Bourdieu's key concepts, clearly demonstrate how they are powerful for studying certain managerial practices and organisational dynamics. In the case of the field of organisational and management studies, the value of Bourdieu's work has a multiplying effect.

First, it offers a great theoretical interest. Through many developed concepts—field, capital, habitus, doxa, illusio—all interrelated, Bourdieu provides us with conceptual tools of great strength. As he says himself, "the concepts have no other definition than systemic and are built *to be empirically implemented systematically*; notions such as habitus, field and capital can be defined within the theoretical system they represent, and not in isolation" (Bourdieu and Wacquant, 2014: 140). He explained further: "To think in terms of the field, is to *think relationally*" (141), and stresses that this mode of thought is the same relational feature of contemporary social science, found in works as diverse as those of Cassirer, Lewin, Elias, Sapir, Jakobson, Dumézil, or Levi-Strauss (Bourdieu and Wacquant, 2014). It should also be noted that the authors present in this volume all respect this relational imperative, unlike many other researchers who use Bourdieu less stringently, as has been shown by Emirbayer and Johnson in their article devoted to Bourdieu and organisational analysis (2008) and Jost Sieweke on the dissemination of Bourdieusian thinking in the management field (2011).

In the case of management, Bourdieu therefore makes a number of contributions. As the chapters in this book have shown, he makes it possible to include managerial practices in a social field and to understand the strategies of social actors in the field concerned (acceptance, resistance), especially through power relations and symbolic domination, in particular gender, exerted within organisations. He forces us to revisit the concept of bounded rationality put forward by Herbert Simon, showing that there is another limit, registered as such—namely, that "the human mind is socially limited, socially structured" (Bourdieu and Wacquant, 2014: 175). It also helps to remember the importance of history in an often short-sighted field: "social agents are the *product of history*, the history of the entire social space and accumulated experience in the course of a path determined in the relevant field" (Bourdieu and Wacquant, 2014: 186). He also offers a critique of economics and the concept of interest, which is based on his anthropological and historical knowledge: "Far from being an anthropological invariant, he writes that interest is an *historic arbitrary*, a historical construction that can not be known through historical analysis, *ex post*, through empirical observation, not derived *a priori* from a fictional design and very ethnocentric course of 'Man'"(Bourdieu and Wacquant, 2014: 164). Here he joined the seminal work of Marcel Mauss and Karl Polanyi, those of contemporary economic anthropology (Marshall Salhins, Maurice Godelier), or still those francophone colleagues grouped around the magazine of Mauss since 1980, whose object is to defend an anti-utilitarian anthropology (Caillé, 2009). He also emphasises the importance of the body, the habitus of being socially incorporated. Finally, he helps to fight against what he calls the doxa—namely, "the unquestioned acceptance of the world lived everyday" (117)—which plays an indispensable role in the acceptance of social dominance.

As we just mentioned briefly, if Pierre Bourdieu provides a conceptual range, now well known and mobilised here by various contributors, a range that renews social analysis, he also defends the use of singular works. As he writes, "The 'theories' are research programs that do not call for 'theoretical debate', but a practical implementation susceptible to their refute and generalization, or better, of specifying and differentiating their claim to generality. Husserl taught that we must immerse ourselves in the particular to discover the invariant . . . A well-built particular case ceases to be a particular case" (Bourdieu and Wacquant, 2014: 121).

The work of Bourdieu not only opens theoretical horizons but also offers a certain epistemological interest through this notion of permanent reflexivity that is at the heart of his work, if not its permanent epistemic concern; fundamentally anti-narcissistic (Bourdieu and Wacquant, 2014), this reflexive process addresses both how the researcher builds his or her research and analyses the data, and the place that the researcher occupies in the field concerned. As he wrote it, "*Reflexivity is a tool intended to produce more science and not to reduce the scope or destroy the ability of science. It is not intended to discourage scientific ambition but to make it more realistic. In contributing to the progress of science and, thus, to the progress of knowledge of the social world, reflexivity, makes possible a more responsible political action both in science and in politics. Bachelard said that 'there is only science of what is hidden' (1938)*" (Bourdieu and Wacquant, 2014: 251). From this point of view, his reflection on language is particularly illuminating of the social games that accompany the expression of the word of each one, reminding us at the same time that "*linguistic relations are always symbolic power relations*" (Bourdieu and Wacquant, 2014: 193).

His work also has a practical interest. As he writes, "As long as sociology remains at a very abstract and formal level, it is not used much. But when it comes down to the ordinary details of real life, it is a tool that people can apply to themselves for quasi clinical purposes. Sociology gives us a small chance to understand the game we play and to reduce the influence of the forces of the field in which we operate as that of the embedded social forces that operate within us" (Bourdieu and Wacquant, 2014: 255). In other words, sociology, by revealing the logic in which social actors involved, allows them, including us, to be more aware, more reflexive, and therefore more able to see the freedom of movement that exists in order to arrive at a political and ethical project that is liberating. This he expressed in a brief formula recalled by Wacquant: "Escape your structures" (Bourdieu and Wacquant, 2014: 339).

Bourdieu's work refers finally to an ethical politic. Wacquant has successfully summed up in his introduction to the new French edition of their meetings as follows: "The Sociology of Pierre Bourdieu can also be read as political in the sense that it gives to this term: a collective effort to transform the principles of vision and division by which we construct the social world and on which we can hope to reshape the world in the sense of reason and justice" (Wacquant, 2014: 100). In other words, between an untraceable revolution and the maintenance of an established social order, Bourdieu advocates for a reasoned utopia.

As this work reveals interest in the work of Bourdieu for management researchers and organisational studies, it also illuminates one of the challenges of our scientific field—namely, the role of language and translation in its diffusion (Wacquant, 1993, 2013; Chanlat, 2014). As shown by numerous studies, translation, if it is necessary for the distribution of a work, is not completely sufficient. It is also necessary that the ideas indeed have a resonance in the other linguistic universe (Chanlat, 2014). Of this, Bourdieu was well aware. He has shown that one of the barriers to the diffusion of foreign works in a scientific field and given linguistic resides in the fact that they are interpreted in the light of national schemas of understanding that remain unconscious most of the time to translators (2002).

Bourdieu has indeed experienced a differentiated reception (Wacquant, 1993; Sieweke, 2011). While many researchers in organisational studies seem interested in his work today, it must be remembered that this is not new, since the early work of Di Maggio and Powell. Indeed, scholars had already drawn on Bourdieu's work without always having give him thereafter the place which he deserved. We see at work, again, the logic of field, well identified by Bourdieu, where American work has overshadowed other work from different linguistic horizons, translation errors, or resonance in the American field (Chanlat, 2014), a phenomenon that can be also be observed in English works from Europe (Battilana, Anteby, and Sengul, 2010; Grey, 2010; Meyer and Boxembaum, 2010) or elsewhere (Clegg, Ibarra Colado, and Bueno, 1999; Ibarra-Colado, 2006; Chanlat, 2014). We must therefore pay homage to authors who have led this work, and each of the contributors, for having played the role of frontier runners, essential to the intellectual dialogue between fields.

In this respect, it is interesting to note, for a French-language researcher, that almost all of the authors of this book refer to the English editions of Bourdieu; we can see the power of translation, without which the thinking of Bourdieu would not have known such distribution in the field of English language. This confirms once again that the international language is translation, and in particular that of Europe, as was so well defended by Umberto Eco (2007). Many other interesting works receive multiple translations, as Bourdieu himself shortly predicted before his death (2001).

In conclusion, I would like to stress again with what great interest I read this book and saw how each contributor complied with both the spirit and letter of the work of Pierre Bourdieu. I have only one wish today: that all potential readers, whether students or faculty members in organisational studies and management, interested in critical thinking and the work of Pierre Bourdieu, can read it.

Regarding the major socio-economic challenges that we face today, reading this book will not only enable future readers to participate in this social reflexivity in our field, as defended by Pierre Bourdieu, but also to pay tribute to the one of the most important body of sociological works of the second half of the 20th century, whose wealth is a constant source of inspiration for many social scientists in the world.

As francophone researchers, therefore, we cannot but welcome such a publication in English. This is indeed the surest way to maintain rich conversations between the different traditions in which we live today, both in the world of social sciences and in the world of organisational studies and management, and to contribute, as Bourdieu tried to do it, to remodelling the world in the direction of both reason and justice.

Jean-François Chanlat
Professor
Dauphine Recherche en Management
(DRM)-CNRS UMR 7088
P.S. L Université Paris-Dauphine

NOTE

* We would like to thank Tarani Merriweather Woodson for her translation of this foreword from the French.

REFERENCES

Battilana, J., Anteby, M., and Sengul, M. (2010) The circulation of ideas across academic communities: When locals re-import exported ideas. *Organization Studies*, 31: 695–713.

Bourdieu, P., et al. (2001) Quelles langues pour une Europe démocratique?. *Raisons pratiques*, 2: 41–64.

Bourdieu, P. (2002) Les conditions internationales de la circulation des idées. *Actes de la recherche en sciences sociales*, 145: 3–8.
Bourdieu, P., and Wacquant, L. (2014) *Invitation à la sociologie reflexive*. Paris: Seuil.
Caillé, A. (2009) *Théorie anti-utilitariste de l'action: Fragments d'une sociologie générale*. Paris: la Découverte.
Chanlat, J-F. (2014) Language and thinking in organization studies: The visibility of the French OS production in the Anglo-Saxon OS field. *International Journal of Organizational Analysis*, 22(4): 504–533.
Clegg, S., Ibarra-Colado, E., and Bueno, L. (1999). *Global management: Universal theories and local realities*. London: SAGE.
Di Maggio, P. J., and Powell, W. W. (1983) The iron cage revisited. In W. W. Powell & P. J. Di Maggio (eds.), *The new institutionalism in organizational analysis*. Chicago: Chicago University Press, 41–62.
Eco, U. (2007) *Dire presque la Même chose: Expériences de la Traduction*. Paris: Grasset.
Emirbayer, M., and Johnson, V. (2008) Bourdieu and organizational analysis. *Theory and Society*, 37(1): 1–44.
Giddens, A. (1984) *The constitution of society: Outline of the theory of structuration*. Cambridge: Polity Press.
Giddens, A. (1987) *La constitution de la société*. Trans. M. Audet. Paris: PUF.
Grey, C. (2010) Organization studies: Publications, politics and polemic. *Organization Studies*, 31: 677–694.
Ibarra-Colado, E. (2006). Organization studies and epistemic coloniality in Latin America: Thinking otherness from the margins. *Organization*, 13(4): 463–488.
Meyer, R., and Boxembaum, E. (2010) Exploring European-ness in organization research. *Organization Studies*, 31(6): 737–755.
Sieweke, J. (2011) *The dissemination of Pierre Bourdieu's theory of practice in management and organization studies*. Working paper. Social Sciences Network.
Wacquant, L. (1993) Bourdieu in America: Notes on the transatlantic importation of social theory. In C. Calhoun, E. LiPuma, and M. Postone (eds.), *Bourdieu: Critical Perspectives*, 235–261. Chicago: University of Chicago Press.
Wacquant, L. (2013) Bourdieu 1993: A case study in scientific consecration. *Sociology*, 47(1): 15–29.
Wacquant, L. (2014) A la porte de l'atelier sociologique, préface à la nouvelle edition. In P. Bourdieu and L. Wacquant (eds.), *Invitation à la sociologie reflexive*. Paris: Seuil, 7–20.

Contributors

Boris H.J.M. Brummans (PhD, Texas A&M University) is an associate professor in the Département de Communication at the Université de Montréal in Canada. His research interests include the communicative constitution of organisations, mindful organising, organisational conflict, and organisational ethnography. He has contributed chapters to several edited books, and his articles appear in journals such as *Communication Monographs*, *Human Relations*, *Information, Communication & Society*, *Journal of International and Intercultural Communication*, *Management Communication Quarterly*, *Qualitative Inquiry*, and *Qualitative Research in Organizations and Management*.

Karim Hamadache holds a pharmacy degree from Algiers University and a PhD in management from Paris-Est University. He is a lecturer at Sorbonne-Paris-Cité University and a member of the Centre for Research in Economics of Paris-Nord (CEPN). He was a visiting researcher at Brunel Business School, London, and a consultant and lecturer on strategy and knowledge management at the Higher Institute for Management and Planning (ISGP), Algiers. He also worked at the CIPA (Centre for Small Animal Imaging) on a project aiming to improve the competitiveness of research centres and companies located in the "Centre" region of France in the biopharmaceutical sector through the exploitation of strategic capabilities available in small animal imaging. He has conducted extensive research on the emergence of the orphan drug field in the US and Europe. His research is mainly focused on institutional change, innovation, particularly in the biopharmaceutical industry, firms' political strategies, and criticism as strategic opportunity for firms.

Johanna Hofbauer is a professor of sociology at the Department of Socioeconomics, Vienna University of Economics and Business. She teaches students of management studies, economics, and socio-economics, covering theory-making and current topics in the fields of economic sociology, sociology of work, and social and economic sustainability. Her research focus lies in issues of power and domination in work organisations, with a particular emphasis on the theories of Pierre Bourdieu. She attempts to further elaborate a Bourdieuan notion of organisation as 'field within fields', as well as a praxeological view of organisation and organising. Her general concern for issues of gender inequality has more recently caused her to investigate public sector reform in the fields of labour market agency (www.affectivelabor.org/index.php/de/) and higher education (http://genderchange-academia.eu/). A key issue of this research is the impact of managerialism on performance and career conditions. Both studies emphasise the need to account for the complexity of power games within the boundaries of organisations and beyond, including the political, bureaucratic, or scientific field. Recent publications include the co-editing of "Envisioning *Inclusive Organizations*: Theory-Building and Corporate Practice", a special issue of the journal *Equality, Diversity and Inclusion* (2014, vol. 33, no. 3).

Senia Kalfa is a lecturer in the Department of Marketing and Management, Faculty of Business and Economics. She holds a PhD from the University of New South Wales and an MSc in Human Resource Management from Aston Business School, Birmingham (UK). She has researched and published on the impact of managerialism in higher education; the impact of management practices on the productivity of Australian medical manufacturing firms; and non-union employee voice. Concurrently, she is also working on a project with Professors John Boyages, Paul Gollan, and Lucy Taksa which explores the social and economic impact of living with lymphoedema, a side effect of breast-cancer treatment. Further, she is involved in a project examining leadership in clinical settings. She is a reviewer for a number of top-tier scholarly journals, such *Organization Studies*, *Human Resource Management Journal*, and *Studies in Higher Education*. She is also a contributor on workplace issues for the *Australian Financial Review* and *The Conversation*.

Mustafa Sahin Karacam is a third-year MA student at the Faculty of Sport Sciences, Hacettepe University, Ankara, Turkey. His MA thesis is an ethnographic study titled "The Construction of Masculinity in Bodybuilding and the Role of Supplement Use", and he is at the stage of thesis defence. His research interests are gender, masculinity, body, culture, and doping. He writes newspaper articles on sport, gender, and doping in addition to his academic studies. He is a member of the Turkish Association of Sport and Physical Activity for Women (KASFAD) and the Social Sciences and Sport Research Group (STOAG) at the Faculty of Sport Sciences.

Canan Koca is an associate professor in the Faculty of Sports Sciences, Hacettepe University, Ankara. She received her doctorate from Hacettepe University, Ankara, Turkey. In 2007–2008, she worked as a research associate at Edinburgh University, Scotland. Her research examines body, gender, and physical activity with sociocultural perspectives. She has published widely in refereed journals such as *Sex Roles, Sport Education and Society, Gender and Education, Gender Work and Organization,* and *Journal of Leisure Research*. Her current research, funded by the Turkish Academy of Sciences, is titled *Analysis of Physical Activity Participation of Turkish Migrants in England and Germany with Respect to Gender and Acculturation* and *Physical Activity Participation of Three Generations of Women in Terms of Socioecological Model and Cultural Feminism*, which were awarded by Koç University KOÇ-KAM Center of Gender Studies. In 2011, she was named Outstanding Young Scientist by the Young Scientists Award Programme of the Turkish Academy of Sciences (TUBA). Koca is the president of the Turkish Association of Sport and Physical Activity for Women (KASFAD) and executive board member of International Association of Physical Education and Sport for Girls and Women (IAPESGW).

Katharina Kreissl is a PhD student and junior researcher at the University of Vienna and the Vienna University of Economics and Business. Her research focuses on inequality and gender studies, discourse theory, and processes of subjectivation and emancipation. She is currently part of a research project, 'GENIA ñ gender in academia', in which she investigates the gendered effects of new public management on the personnel structures in academia.

Markus Latzke is an assistant professor at the Interdisciplinary Institute of Management and Organisational Behaviour, Department of Management, WU Vienna (Vienna University of Economics and Business), Austria. He received his diploma and doctoral degrees in business administration from WU. His teaching assignments encompass undergraduate, graduate, and executive levels and have led him as a visiting scholar to several international universities. His research was published in various academic (*Journal of Vocational Behavior*) and practitioner journals. On the one hand, he conducts research in the field of safety culture and climate in health care organisations, where he, for example, investigates the role of patient engagement and the potential of interventions like critical incident reporting systems for organisational learning. On the other hand he focuses on career studies, where his current research centres on Bourdieu's theory of practice, which he mainly applies in the context of a longitudinal study on changes in managerial careers (Vienna Career Panel Project).

Wolfgang Mayrhofer is a full professor and head of the Interdisciplinary Institute of Management and Organisational Behaviour, Department of Management, WU Vienna (Vienna University of Economics and Business), Austria. He previously held full-time research and teaching positions at the University of Paderborn, Germany, and at Dresden University of Technology, Germany, after receiving his diploma and doctoral degrees in business administration from WU. He conducts research in comparative international human resource management, careers, and systems theory and management and has received several national and international rewards for outstanding research and service to the academic community. He authored, co-authored, and co-edited 27 books, more than 110 book chapters, and 70 peer reviewed articles. He is a member of the editorial board of several international journals and an associate at the Centre for Research into the Management of Expatriation (Cranfield, UK), a research fellow at the Simon Fraser University Centre for Global Workforce Strategy (Vancouver, Canada), and a member of the academic advisory board of AHRMIO, the Association of Human Resource Management in International Organisations. His teaching assignments both at the graduate and executive level and his role as visiting scholar have led him to many universities around the globe.

Katerina Nicolopoulou is a senior lecturer with Strathclyde Business School's Hunter Centre for Entrepreneurship. Her research interests are in the interface of entrepreneurship, management, sustainability, and diversity, and her current research focus is the topic of cosmopolitanism and its application for entrepreneurship, innovation, and sustainable cities. She has chaired tracks for international conferences as well as professional development workshops in her fields of expertise and has been active within major management conferences, such as EURAM, AoM, and BAM. She is the subject co-ordinator for the Entrepreneurial Management and Leadership core module for the Strathclyde MBA. She has co-edited three books with E. Elgar and, most recently, Routledge, as well as five special issues with journals such as *Entrepreneurship and Regional Development* and, most recently, *Organizations & Environment*. She is a member of editorial review boards of *European Management Review*, *Journal of Small Business Management*, and *Corporate Governance*. Her research appears in journals such as the *Journal of Small Business Management*, *International Journal of Human Resource Management*, and the *Journal of Social Entrepreneurship*.

Kanellos-Panagiotis Nikolopoulos has 18 years professional experience in the field of foreign language teaching and vocational training. He co-directs the family business, Nikolopouleio Schools of Foreign Languages and Vocational Studies (www.nikolopouleio.gr), which specialises in the aforementioned fields as well as in online education for Greek and overseas markets. At the same time he is at the final (exit) stage of his PhD at the Open University of the Netherlands (Open Universiteit Nederland) in the field of culture and entrepreneurship. His research interests include cross-cultural management, cosmopolitanism and entrepreneurship, and global knowledge workers' social networks. He presented a workshop and a discussion paper in two High Technology Conferences for SMEs in Turin and Manchester in 2007, a doctoral colloquium paper in Vienna in 2010, and a working academic research paper in the International Small Business Entrepreneurship Conference in Sheffield in 2011. He also contributed a book chapter to a special edition on global knowledge workers by Edward Elgar in 2011.

Barbara Samaluk, PhD, is a postdoctoral research fellow in the Work and Employment Research Unit at the University of Greenwich Business School. She received her PhD at Queen Mary, University of London, researching the commodification of migrant labour from post-socialist central and eastern Europe (CEE) in the UK labour market. Her areas of expertise include transnational labour migration and staffing agencies, cultural political economy, commodification and marketisation processes within the postcolonial and post-socialist order, equality and diversity, and anti-discrimination. Currently, she works on a research project exploring the effects of marketisation on societies, where her specific focus is on the post-socialist CEE context. She has published articles in academic journals, book chapters, reports, strategies, and commentaries. She co-edited a special issue called *Critical Whiteness Studies Methodologies* (2012). Her research and academic attainment are underpinned by several years of active engagement with systemic advocacy for human rights and anti-discrimination in various CEE countries.

Birgit Sauer is a full professor of political science in the Department of Political Science, University of Vienna. She studied political science and German literature at the University of Tuebingen and at the Free University of Berlin. She was one of the founders of the section Gender and Politics in the German Political Science Association and director of the graduate school Gender, Violence and Agency in the Era of Globalisation (GIK). Since 2014 she has been a speaker for the research network 'Gender and Agency' at the University of Vienna. Her research fields include gender and governance, gender equality policies, gender and emotions in organisations, gender, religion, and democracy, right-wing populism and racism, and theories of state and democracy. Recent publications include: *A Man's World? Political Masculinities in Literature and Culture* (Cambridge Scholar, 2014; ed. with Kathleen Starck) and *Politics, Religion and Gender: Framing and Regulating the Veil* (Routledge, 2011; ed. with Sieglinde Rosenberger).

Susan Sayce is a senior lecturer at the University of East Anglia in the UK. Her research interests are diversity and pension trusteeship. She has received two Canadian faculty scholarships to explore the topic of diversity and expertise in four provinces in Canada. In the UK her work on pension trusteeship, gender, and retirement has been widely published in *Economy, and Industrial Democracy*, *HRM Journal*, and others, as well as practitioner journals. Other publications focus on employment relations and gender and include a Bourdieuan analysis of industrial relations. Current projects include exploring wasta in Jordan, gendered employment relations in Russia, and career advancement in the UK and Pakistan. She is also a co-editor with Dr Kate Sang of a new open access journal, *Interdisciplinary Perspectives in Equality and Diversity: An International Journal*.

Thomas M. Schneidhofer is a full professor of HR and organisation at the University of Seeburg Castle, Austria. He previously held full-time research and teaching positions at the WU Vienna, Austria, the University of Hamburg, Germany, and the Leibniz University Hannover, Germany, after receiving his diploma and doctoral degrees in business administration from WU. His research interests encompass careers and HRM, with special emphasis on the development of the theory of practice inspired by Pierre Bourdieu. Consequently, he has embarked on topics such as power and domination, to which he would probably not have turned unless he had been compelled to do so by the whole logic of his research. On an empirical level, he has planned and conducted longitudinal panel studies (e.g. the Vienna Career Panel Project, ViCaPP). On a theoretical level, he is interested in relational, multi-level conceptualisations of organisations and individuals. He has published in peer-reviewed journals, such as the *Journal of Occupational and Organisational Psychology* and the *Journal of Vocational Behavior*, as well as in practitioner journals and qualitative newspapers.

Angelika Striedinger is a PhD student and junior researcher at the University of Vienna and the Vienna University of Economics and Business. Her research focuses on institutional theory of organisations, gender equality, and higher education. In her PhD thesis, she investigates the institutional work of equality agents in the context of a changing university landscape. Furthermore, she currently is part of a research project, 'GENIA ñ gender in academia', in which she investigates the gendered effects of new public management on the personnel structures in academia.

Lucy Taksa has been a professor of management and the head of the Department of Marketing and Management at Macquarie University since 2009, after 18 years at the University of NSW. She has undertaken research and published on: the impact of scientific management on the Workers Educational Association, technical, management, and business education and employability; migrant employment, Australian multiculturalism, and diversity management; the impact of gender culture on women's career trajectories; the history of safety management and industrial nursing; and misbehaviour and nicknaming at work. She is currently working on a number of projects focused on identity: one with Associate Professors Ellie Vasta and Fei Guo, funded by the Australian Research Council, entitled 'Affinities in Multicultural Australia', and another with Professors John Boyages, Paul Gollan, and Dr Senia Kalfa (CI), funded by industry partners and Macquarie University, entitled 'Exploring the Social and Economic Impact of Living with Lymphoedema'. She is a member of the Australian Research Council College of Experts, an associate editor of the *European Management Review*, and the economic and labour relations review area editor for *Gender*. Previously she was a member of the Equal Opportunity Division of the NSW Administrative Decisions Tribunal (1996–2007, 2003–2007) and chair of the board of New South Wales State Archives (2007–2012).

Barbara Townley is the chair of management at the Management School, University of St Andrews. After gaining her PhD at the London School of Economics, she has taught at the Universities of Lancaster, Warwick, Alberta, Canada, and Edinburgh. She has published widely in journals in management and organisation in Europe and North America, including *Academy of Management Review*, *Academy of Management Journal*, *Administrative Science Quarterly*, *Organization Studies*, *Journal of Management Studies*, *Human Relations*, and *Organization*. Her work has been reprinted several times and translated into French, German, and Portuguese. She has been associate editor of *Human Relations*, served on a number of editorial boards, and held a number of ESRC and AHRC grants. Her current research interests are in the creative industries. With colleagues, she is researching the role of IP in creative SMEs and micro organisations; the role of design in fledgling business start-ups; and strategies of distinction in the Scottish fashion and textile industry.

Introduction
Management and Organisation Studies Meet Pierre Bourdieu

Ahu Tatli, Mustafa Özbilgin, and Mine Karatas-Özkan

> Writers, artists, and especially researchers must breach the 'sacred boundary' inscribed in their minds between scholarship and commitment in order to break out of academic microcosm and to enter resolutely into sustained exchange with the outside world instead of being content with waging the 'political' battles, at once intimate and ultimate, and always a bit unreal, of the scholastic universe. Today's researchers must innovate an improbable but indispensable combination: scholarship with commitment.
>
> (Bourdieu, 2003a: 24)

Pierre Bourdieu is well recognised for his lifelong endeavour to overcome dichotomies that have hijacked the social science debates since the late 19th century—the dichotomies of agency versus structure, individual versus society, subjectivism versus objectivism, to name a few. Yet, his commitment to tackling the silent agreement on the separation of scholarly and political actions is often overlooked. This very advocacy for recognising the intrinsically political nature of our scholarship is at the heart of the potential contribution of Bourdieu's sociology to the development of organisation and management studies as a rigorous discipline of social sciences with strong theoretical, empirical, and philosophical roots. Bourdieu (1998a, 1999, 2003a) emphasised that social scientists must engage in a permanent critique of the policy of depoliticisation and must restore political thinking and action. He believed that this responsibility is even greater in the face of the increasingly cruel neo-liberal hegemony: "It seems to me that scholars have a decisive role to play in the struggle against the new neoliberal doxa" (Bourdieu, 2003a: 23). For us, scholars of management and organisation studies, scholarship with commitment requires battling the neo-liberal, individualistic, and depoliticising tendencies in our discipline. There is a need for proliferation of critical research on organisational and managerial practices and discourses in the way they shape and affect everyday experiences of workers. There is a need for more research, which uncovers the hidden assumptions and reasoning in the domain of management and organisational studies scholarship that may help legitimise and naturalise asymmetries of power, and relations of oppression and domination. There is a need for more research on the outcomes of managerial practices for the 'ordinary' workers in order to bring experiences of dominated groups into the agenda. And there is a need for more research into the agency of different groups of organisational actors, who are caught in the midst of a process of symbolic domination in which organisational power holders forever attempt to extend their hegemony at the workplace by doxic representations of employment relations from neo-liberal and individualistic visions of the world and work. In our journeys to understand management and organisations, in their varied forms and expressions, we may gain much from questioning the disciplining duality between scholarship and commitment, a duality that is often imposed upon our work under the disguises of scientific value and worth, objectivity and rigour. Following Bourdieu's footsteps, 'scholarship with commitment' (Bourdieu, 2003a: 24) is at the heart of this collection, which brings together contributions that reveal and unpack machinations of power, identity, meaning, interaction, and domination in organisations.

Bourdieu is one of the most cited social scientists, who inspired scholars from a wide array of disciplines, including sociology, education, journalism and media studies, gender studies, anthropology, and cultural studies. With his unceasing capacity "to shuttle between levels of abstraction, with ease and with clarity", Bourdieu was an exceptional example of an "imaginative and systematic thinker", which Mills (1959: 43) called for in *Sociological Imagination*. Bourdieu offered us a theory of practice, of which he formed the foundations in *Outline of Theory of Practice* (1977), and which he further developed through his two subsequent theoretical works *The Logic of Practice* (1990a) and *Practical Reason: on the theory of action* (1998b). He was exposed to intellectual currents of the time as such he studied Marx and Weber, and was influenced by philosophers such as Husserl, Heidegger, Merleau-Ponty, and Durkheim. The quest for the meaning of individual and social and for understanding the bundles of shifting social relations among interdependent people, positions, and institutions within a wider society led Bourdieu to investigate unfolding social configurations and distributions of power resources (Paulle, Heerikhuizen, and Emirbayer, 2012) and to develop his relational theory of society.

Bourdieu's work has a global audience crossing geographic and disciplinary boundaries. Commenting on the value of Bourdieu's body of work, Lash (1993: 193) argues that Bourdieu's sociology is "not only the best, but . . . the only game in town". Similarly, Fowler (1997: 13) states that Bourdieu "has superseded various problems that have perennially plagued sociology as a critical social theory and that, at the present moment, this is the most original and cogent modelling of the social world that we have". Bradbury and Lichtenstein (2000) draw our attention to the power of Bourdieu's framework in uncovering the interplay of agency and structure, and interdependencies between different forms of capital and social space. On a similar note, Lounsbury and Ventresca (2003) argue that Bourdieu's notion of field provides a systematic approach for researchers to explore structure and agency in a single framework. Yet, the uptake of Bourdieusian theory has been comparably new in management and organisation studies. Nevertheless, the body of management and organisation research utilising Bourdieu's concepts has been exponentially growing in recent years (e.g. Al Ariss and Syed, 2011; De Clerg and Voronov, 2009; Golsorkhi, Leca, Lounsbury, and Ramirez, 2009; Grugulis and Stoyanova, 2012; Kamoche, Kannan, and Siebers, 2014; Karatas-Ozkan, 2011; O'Mahoney, 2007; Prieto and Wang, 2010; Srinavas, 2013; Tatli, 2011; Tatli and Özbilgin, 2012; Townley, Beech, and McKinlay, 2009). With this collection, we aim to contribute to the continuing proliferation of organisation and management scholarship that is inspired by Bourdieusian sociology.

A RELATIONAL THEORY OF PRACTICE

Bourdieu theoretically constructed his notion of human agency and social world, through key concepts of the field, *habitus*, capitals, strategies, doxa, and symbolic violence, which together form the spatial and historical universe of practice that is relational and situated. Bourdieu's relational sociology sets out "not simply to combine, articulate or join agency and structure but, more fundamentally, to dissolve the very distinction between these two seemingly antinomic viewpoints of social analysis" (Wacquant, 1993: 3). Bourdieu urges for the necessity of simultaneous and interconnected investigation of objective and subjective dimensions of the research subject:

> (Individuals) exist as agents—and not as biological individuals, actors or subjects—who are socially constructed as active and acting in the field under consideration by the fact that they possess the necessary properties to be effective, to produce effects, in this field ... People are at once founded and legitimised to enter the field by their possessing a definite configuration of properties. One of the goals of the research is to identify these active properties, these efficient characteristics, that is these forms of specific capital. There is thus a sort of hermeneutic circle: in order to construct the field, one must identify the forms of specific capital that operates within it, and to construct the forms of specific capital one must know the specific logic of the field.
> (Bourdieu and Wacquant, 1992: 107–108)

In Bourdieu's theory the emphasis is on the cogenerative relationship between micro and macro levels of social reality—that is, between capitals and the field. The social science endeavour is, then, marked by a circular investigation of the logic of the field and the different forms of capital that operate within the field (Bourdieu, 1987). Yet, Bourdieu has been criticised for presenting a deterministic conception of social life (Vandenberghe, 1999). These critiques posit that in Bourdieu's vision individuals are passive agents, which are pulled and pushed into various actions and positions in life by structural forces. As a result, it is argued, there is no scope for individual choice and possibilities of individual emancipation from circumstances. For instance, Burkitt (2002: 220) suggests that habitus is insufficient in making sense of "those moments when habits break down or when habits clash and the self is forced to reflexively monitor itself and the context in which it is acting in order to meaningfully reconstruct with others both self and situation". Yet, Bourdieu's model explicates tendencies created by historical and social structures rather than offering deterministic causalities. Bourdieu's caution against formulating rigid causalities in explaining social life is evident, for example, in how he describes the interplay of habitus, structure, and agency:

> Just as we should not say that a window broke because a stone hit it, but that it broke because it was breakable . . . one should not say that a historical event determined a behaviour but that it had this determining effect because a *habitus* capable of being affected by that event conferred that power upon it.
> (Bourdieu, 2000: 148–149)

Thus, for Bourdieu the relationship between agentic and structural forces is not unidirectional, and neither is it deterministic. Although the notions of habitus and field may at first glance seem to dictate a rigid and static order over actions of agents, what is central to Bourdieu's sociological endeavour is to explore the interplay between capitals, field, and habitus, which exist in interdependency and relationality with each other (Özbilgin and Tatli, 2005). Notwithstanding the fact that capitals are generated and legitimised by the logic of habitus and the field, equally, field and habitus owe their existence to the actions of individuals, who strategically deploy different forms of capital. The concept of strategies, which are employed by individuals while they compete for capital accumulation, further highlights the non-deterministic dimension of Bourdieu's theory (Nash, 2003).

Within Bourdieu's sociological universe, the field denotes the universe of partly pre-constituted objective historical relations between positions (Bourdieu and Wacquant, 1992: 16). Social and organisational fields as the defining principles of the allocation of power positions in the society and organisations draw the boundaries of individual agency. Habitus, which is the subjectification and deposition of field in the individual bodies (Bourdieu and Wacquant, 1992), is a key construct in bridging structure and agency (Grenfell and James, 1998). Bourdieu (1977: 72, 95) defines habitus as

> the strategy generating principle enabling agents to cope with unforeseen and ever-changing situations . . . a system of lasting and transposable dispositions which, integrating past experiences, functions at every moment as a matrix of perceptions, appreciations and actions and made possible the achievement of infinitely diversified tasks.

Individuals are positioned in the field with respect to different forms of capital at their disposal and employ several strategies to reconfigure the amount of capitals they own in order to enhance their power position within the field (Bourdieu and Wacquant, 1992: 129). Capitals and strategies that are available to individual agents are governed by the logic of the field and embodiment of this logic through habitus. In other words, capitals as potential sources of power and influence become functional only in relation to a specific field and habitus. They become efficient "like the aces in a game of cards" only if actors know the "rules of the game" and register to these rules (Bourdieu and Wacquant, 1992: 101). At the same time field and habitus owe their existence to the actions of individuals since they are reproduced by those actions which are realised within the matrix of different forms of capital and strategies.

To summarise, Bourdieu's sociology is, in essence, relational and contextual, as it is only through the mediation of habitus and field that different forms of capital gain their value. In effect, different forms of capital owned by individuals are not free-floating entities with generic value independent of the very framework in which they are generated and reproduced (Bourdieu and Wacquant, 1992). However, this structural embeddedness does not mean that agents are deprived of voluntary action. Instead, Bourdieu's theory of human agency acknowledges social agents' potential to transform their settings and circumstances—that is, field and habitus—as well as explaining how social structures and mechanisms are reproduced by the repetitive enactment of habitus by the individual agents in their everyday actions and interactions (Bourdieu and Wacquant, 1992). Social agents utilise strategies to allocate and distribute their volume of capital between different forms, which, in turn, not only determine the boundaries of their agency but also shape, reinforce, and transform the logic of the field within which they are situated. In recognising both structural and strategic aspects of social practice, Bourdieu's theory allows us to understand human agency in organisations as simultaneously active, dynamic, situated, and constrained.

UNDERSTANDING THE SOCIAL WORLD BEYOND DUALITIES

Bourdieu's contribution to our understanding of the social world can be best captured through an exploration of its power to transcend a number of dualities that have taken social sciences hostage. Bourdieu's sociology is firmly embedded in the late 1950s' French social science field, which was dominated by tension between the objective structuralism of Levi-Strauss and the subjective existentialism of Sartre (Özbilgin and Tatli, 2005). Within that context, Bourdieu has defined his project as seeking to overcome that binary opposition through a "structuralist constructivism or constructivist structuralism" (Bourdieu and Wacquant, 1992: 11). Grenfell and James

(1998: 1–2) argue that Bourdieusian sociology presents us with "an epistemological and methodological third way", establishing "an alternative to the extremes of post-modernist subjectivity and positivist objectivity" of his time. Similarly, Nash (2003: 49) draws our attention to Bourdieu's continuous emphasis on moving beyond "the sterile opposition of the old debate (conscious/unconscious, explanation by cause/explanation by reason, mechanical submission to social constraints/rational and strategic calculation, individual/society and so on)". In the next section, we briefly introduce the key dualities Bourdieusian sociology could help us to transcend in researching and theorising organisations.

Duality of Subjectivism and Objectivism

Defining objectivism as the reproduction of the world via structures and subjectivism as the reproduction of the world by individuals, Bourdieu (1977) highlights the importance of transcending the methodological dualism between objectivism and subjectivism. Bourdieu (2000) maintains that although subjectivist approaches contribute to the knowledge of human agency by acknowledging the importance of primary experience, they lack the methodological and theoretical means to account for it. At the other end of the spectrum, objectivism adopts a mechanistic view of human conduct, ignoring the extent to which social life is a practical achievement by competent actors (Bourdieu, 1977: 22–23) and their agency plays a crucial role in shaping social practices.

Critiquing objectivist and subjectivist methodologies, Bourdieu tasks social researchers with transcending what Emile Durkheim called preconceptions (Bourdieu, 1999, 2003b). Reflexivity is a key component of Bourdieu's (1977) notion of 'epistemological break' from preconceptions. Bourdieu (1990) is critical of the myopic tendency of social scientists when it comes to exploring their own scientific practice. He insists that sociologists must engage in a 'sociology of sociology' in order to expose the impact of their personal stories, stakes, and dispositions, on ontological, epistemological, and theoretical preconceptions that they often implicitly hold onto (Bourdieu, 1984). Researchers are positionally embedded in academic and social fields, and bring their habitus into the research setting, as much as their research participants do. As a result, epistemological break involves two levels of rupture, the first from the primary experience of the research participants and the second from the presuppositions of the researcher. The idea of a two-step process of epistemological rupture also embodies the seeds of the basic principles of a methodological tool developed by Bourdieu (2003b) in his later works— that is, participant objectivation, which engenders the reflexive and relational methodological ground for social research. Epistemological ruptures and the resultant methodological reflexivity in Bourdieusian research refer to relentless self-questioning of method itself in the very movement whereby it is implemented. This stipulates an organic relation between theory and method (Bourdieu, 1999, 2003b). According to Bourdieu (1999), every act of research is simultaneously empirical and theoretical. For him, it is important to bear in mind that theory inheres not in discursive propositions but in the generative dispositions of the habitus of social scientists (Bourdieu and Wacquant, 1992). Understanding habitus as a system of acquired dispositions enables us to understand that organisational and managerial responses and practices stem from organisational actors' prediscursive familiarity with the field they inhabit. Equally, this applies to academic fields and our practice of academic work as management and organisation scholars.

Duality of Agency and Structure

Bourdieu's theory offers us a renewed vision to examine the interplay between structure and agency. Structure (the field) denotes the domain of social relations, which are not produced in a vacuum but emerge as an outcome of power relations between agents (Özbilgin and Tatli, 2011; Karatas-Ozkan and Chell, 2015). Commenting on Bourdieu's position with respect to the duality of structure and agency, Sulkunen (1982: 103) argues,

> His (Bourdieu's) methodological point of view is at the one and the same time anti-functionalist, anti-empiricist and anti-subjectivist. The cultural forms of the practices of everyday life cannot be reduced to 'needs' of the individuals any more than to the functional imperatives of the collectivity. They take the form of irreducible symbolic expressions, the meanings of which are not directly apparent to the subjects. Yet the subjects are not determined by the collective institutions in their practices. The central concept, *habitus*, aims at combining the subjective and the culturally determined collective elements in these practices.

Bourdieu's effort to overcome the traditional dualism of agentic versus structural approaches has parallels with that of Giddens (1984) in the Anglo-Saxon tradition (see also Archer, 1995; Layder, 1993). Similar to Bourdieu, Giddens (1984) also proposed an alternative theoretical framework to investigate the complex and interwoven nature of social reality, through his theory of structuration, which purports that the social structures and human agency and action co-evolve by reaffirming and reconstituting one another. However, Bourdieusian formulation offers greater explanatory power in revealing the role of individual agency in the process of social and institutional change. Although the structuration theory suggests that structural changes result from changes in repetitive forms of individual and collective acts, Bourdieu has gone further to explain the kinds of varied resources (capitals) that individuals draw on in order to enact their strategies and how their strategies are both negotiated in and shaped by the logic of the field—that is, the social structures—which in turn is altered through enactments of human agency. In this way, Bourdieu's relational theory of society accounts not only for structural and agentic forces but also, more importantly, for the interplay between these two. For Bourdieu, it is only through this interplay that structural and agentic domains and related social practices are constructed, reproduced, sustained, and changed.

Duality of Continuity and Change

Bourdieu's concepts of habitus and field denote a social world, which protects its own boundaries. This has been a source of critique. In this critique, habitus is seen as a source of inertia as it imprints systemic mechanisms in agents' existence and practices. Habitus refers to "generative principles of distinct and distinctive practices such as what the worker eats, and especially the way he eats it, the sport he practices and the way he practices it" (Bourdieu, 1998b: 8). The emphasis is on the socially inherited dispositions of agents, predisposed ways of thinking, acting, and moving (Srinavas, 2013); in other words, habitus is a cultural grammar for action (Swartz, 1997). The interdependency and relationality between structural and agentic aspects of social phenomena form the heart of Bourdieu's theory (Tatli et al., 2014).

The power of habitus lies in the fact that agents are not conscious of its existence nor of its effects. Practice is neither unconscious nor conscious; individuals draw from doxa, their doxic experience—that is, "taken for granted world beyond reflection" (Bourdieu, 1977). It is such a system that self-contains its conditions of reproduction and existence. Consequently, the critique is that there exists no enforcement mechanism in the system to influence change. Yet, Bourdieu recognises individual agents' collective power and capacity to create change in capital endowment and conversion (Nentwich, Özbilgin, and Tatli, 2014). In that sense, Bourdieu draws our attention to long-term, sustained, and systemic change in the logic of the field and rules of the game.

Duality of Mind and Body, and Symbolic and Material Domains

Bourdieu's theory has the potential to bring meat on the skeletal framing of organisations, work, and management. Bourdieu's understanding of individual agents is not limited to their processes of thought, perception, and reason. Instead, he emphasises the importance of embodiment in enabling both agentic practices and structural processes. Breaking with Cartesian thinking, which affirms the dichotomy of mind and body and focuses on mind as the primary attribute of humans as social beings, carnal theorising through Bourdieusian lens transcends the duality of body and mind. Bourdieu emphasised the interwoven nature of the body and mind, and the social and corporeal through his use of habitus.

Similarly, the Bourdieusian notion of capitals aims to overcome the duality between the material and symbolic aspects of social life. Contrary to the human capital theories' focus on individual skills and qualifications obtained through education, training, and experience in explaining workplace careers and agency (Becker, 1975), Bourdieu (1977, 1984, 1987, 1990, 1998b) offers a relational theory of capitals. Bourdieu's notion of capital goes far beyond the simplistic conception of merit-based human capital theories, which serve to legitimise the inequalities and hierarchies in organisations (Crompton, 1986; Witz, 1992). Borrowing from the Marxist terminology, he defines capital as "accumulated labour (in its materialised form or its 'incorporated', embodied form) which, when appropriated on a private, i.e. exclusive, basis by agents or groups of agents, enables them to appropriate social energy in the form of reified or living labour" (Bourdieu, 1986: 241). However, Bourdieu expands the Marxist conception of the capital by bringing in the interplay between the material and symbolic into his notion of capitals. Possession of material resources through the means of production does not suffice to explain power and domination in society (see Townley, this volume). In addition to cultural, social, and economic capitals, Bourdieu introduced symbolic capital, which is the most complex form of capital, and is the form that other capitals take once they are recognised and legitimised within a given field (Bourdieu, 1990). Consequently, Bourdieu's conception of capitals has a potential to shed light onto the material and symbolic resources that shape organisational life as well as to bridge the gap between the material and symbolic domains of human agency.

Using Bourdieusian sociology, the contributions in this collection tackle the fundamental dichotomies between objectivism and subjectivism, agency and structure, continuity and change, body and mind, and material and symbolic that dominate not only social sciences in general but also the research and thinking in our discipline of management and organisation studies.

THE CONTENTS OF THE BOOK

Bourdieu's theory offers a significant potential of expansion for organisation and management studies as it yields a far-reaching and powerful vision to reflect on organisational life by providing us with new conceptual, theoretical, and methodological avenues. This edited volume provides a reference source for organisation and management scholars to navigate the complex and innovative ideas and concepts developed by Bourdieu. In this way, we hope to illustrate the ways in which Bourdieu's work can contribute further to theoretical, conceptual, and methodological expansion of organisation and management studies.

Part I of the book focuses on theory building and methodological reflexivity. Firmly grounded in the review and critique of the existing literature, this part brings Bourdieu's ideas into theoretical and methodological debates in management and organisation studies. Recently, there has been a growing recognition that there is a theoretical stagnation in the field, and many scholars called for new ways of theorising, including multi-level explorations and embodied framing of management and organisational issues. This part of the book provides robust ways forward in theory building in the field to overcome much implored dualistic orthodoxies, which hinder conceptual and empirical advancement in management and organisation research. The chapters in this part also pay particular attention to explaining how the theoretical and abstract ideas that they present could be applied in the context of field research. Four chapters in combination illustrate theoretical benefits of Bourdieusian sociology for promoting management and organisation research, which is capable of capturing the space, the history of, and the interplay between layered organisational realities.

Chapter 1, authored by Schneidhofer, Latzke and Mayrhofer, presents a relational and multi-level theorising of careers as results of practices for and with career-related capital within a career field. The authors reconstruct careers as sites of power games, for which habitus serves as an embodied sense of, and boundary for, playing the game. Habitus and hence the acquisition strategies and conversion rates of capitals are the results of power dynamics. By delineating careers on three levels, the authors transcend the tension between individual agency and social determinism. On the macro level they emphasise the context of careers (fields); on the micro level they highlight the content of career capital; and on the meso level, they stress the importance of linking the two through habitus. In addition to this theoretical contribution, the authors offer insights for practice by raising awareness that individual behaviour cannot be reduced to structures and they should not be seen as solely responsible for their behaviour.

A further contribution to multi-level theorising with the emphasis on the complex interplay between structural and agentic mechanisms is offered in Chapter 2 by Samaluk. Her chapter offers a theoretical and methodological toolkit for a complex intersectional analysis uncovering change and inertia in (re)formation and commodification of migrant workers' subjectivities across spatial and temporal dimensions. Samaluk argues that the usefulness of the Bourdieusian framework lies in conceptualisation of social class as a multidimensional social space that encompasses cultural, economic, and political elements and that is able to transcend objectivist and subjectivist divide. This allows for critical exploration of both structural and agentic mechanisms and symbolic and material practices that operate in the racialised class formation across spatial and temporal dimensions.

Chapter 3 offers an understanding of carnal theorising from a Bourdieusian perspective. The main thrust of the chapter, which is authored by Nikolopoulos and Nicolopoulou, is the conceptualisation of the body as a social construct, which is mediated through habitus that is defined as an embodiment of social, cultural, and gender-related aspects. Habitus and capitals are viewed as central constructs in defining and problematising embodied culture in organisations. The authors emphasise the importance of bridging between sociological approaches and insights from organisation and management studies. The chapter highlights the implications of carnal theorising specifically for the fields of international management and diversity management. Contemporary organisations operate in a transnational globalised environment, which is viewed by the authors as a complex matrix of cross-national fields in interaction with social actors' habitus, consisting of multiple cultural, institutional, and structural features, schemas, and resources. This forms the domain in which managers formulate strategies and develop their practices and hence it makes this theorising relevant for diversity management, cross-cultural management, marketing, and international entrepreneurship.

In the last chapter of Part I, in Chapter 4, Brummans turns our attention to the importance of reflexivity, which forms the core of Bourdieu's methodological approach. Management and organisation scholars infrequently turn the lens through which they study others upon themselves. To exemplify the importance of practicing reflexivity, this chapter examines how organisational communication scholars constitute a relationship of ontological complicity with their field through their textwork. Drawing on data collected by interviewing 12 prominent organisational scholars about their textwork practices, this chapter reveals that these scholars constitute their complicities through textwork games that enable them to legitimise first their expressive interests within organisational communication studies; second, their expressive interests within other fields; and third, their overall practice of research. Thus, this chapter provides valuable theoretical and empirical insights into the practice of academic reflexivity as Bourdieu envisioned it.

The underlying rationale of the chapters in this part is to promote a robust and sophisticated, yet accessible, theorising in management and organisational studies. Adopting a Bourdieusian approach, the chapters open up new theoretical frontiers in this relatively young discipline of social sciences through presenting novel theoretical lenses to transcend artificial dualities, as presented earlier. In summary, this part demonstrates that Bourdieu's theory, if adopted by management and organisation researchers, will offer three benefits: first, situating management and organisational issues in space and time; second, explicating the relational and embodied nature of organisational realities; and third, offering a conceptual toolbox to empirically investigate managerial and organisational phenomena as complex, multifaceted, and layered.

Part II of the book is devoted to chapters which use Bourdieu's theory in framing and analysis of original empirical evidence from different geographies. The chapters demonstrate robust research design and evidence base and novel insights with significant implications for knowledge and practice. The chapters explore various dimensions and facets of managerial and organisational phenomena. The Bourdieusian concepts that are empirically elaborated on in this part include field, illusio and doxa, habitus, different forms of capitals and strategies, as highlighted in the preceding section.

Chapter 5 is the first chapter of this part and is authored by Hamadache. The chapter sets out to demonstrate that the concept of organisational field, as developed in neo-institutional theory (following DiMaggio and Powell, 1983), underplays relations of power and domination between agents. Hamadache returns to the Bourdieusian conception of fields in order to tackle this oversight in researching and theorising organisations in their varied forms. The chapter illustrates the field construction process as a political and strategic activity through a case study of the construction of the orphan drug field in the United States. This chapter not only makes an empirical contribution as such but also relates Bourdieusian concepts to the debates around oft-cited new-institutionalism in organisation studies.

Chapter 6, authored by Sayce, takes us to the UK pension boardrooms with an objective to extend the debates about concepts of legitimacy and representation drawing on Bourdieusian social theory. Sayce's research demonstrates that the field of board management has its own norms and behaviours where actions and manners are reproduced through generations of boardroom activity. Using the conceptual tools of field, habitus, practice, capital, illusio, and doxa, the legitimacy that more diverse pension board members bring to the field of the boardrooms is investigated in this chapter in order to show how board diversity is being reshaped into a board image that fits with the dominant norms, expectations, and attitudes of the boardroom. Linked to the debate on continuity and change and structure and agency, this chapter specifically addresses how changes in the field, such as new regulation, offer the potential for transformation of the field while also acknowledging that existing patterns of social practice continue.

Given the emphasis on representational legitimacy and the regenerative nature of boards in Chapter 6, Hofbauer, Striedinger, Kreissl, and Sauer draw our attention to the gendering of careers in academia in Chapter 7. They discuss the role of gender equality policies as elements of field-specific power struggles in Austrian universities. Similar to Sayce's chapter, their focus is on change and, in particular, structural layers that need to be distinguished in order to assess the scope and nature of change and the role of agency in processes of change. Building on an empirical study in four universities, the authors focus on power games around implementation of the tenure track model. They note that Austrian higher education has seen major reforms during the past 10 years and universities responded differently to those reforms. In accordance with the notion of "organization as field-within-a-field" (Emirbayer and Johnson, 2008), this chapter explores the ways external regulations translate into internal rules of the game. To account for the different approaches of universities towards the implementation of equal opportunity measurements, the authors argue for conceiving universities both as collective actors whose strategies depend on the relative position taken in the academic field and as a locus of internal power games, which decide upon the relative influence that equality agents may have upon decision making and the establishment of the university's equality culture.

In another context of higher education, Chapter 8 continues with an empirical exploration of interconnections between fields and academic habitus. Taksa and Kalfa's chapter demonstrates the benefits of using the concept of habitus to tease out the interconnections between managerialism in higher education and the employability imperative. To this end, the chapter examines the adoption of pedagogies designed to help students develop transferable skills in the general context of an increasingly managerialised Australian higher education sector. Through a qualitative case study, the chapter empirically explores the relationship between the 'economic' field and the field of higher education and illustrates how the doxa of the economic field is encroaching on the doxa of the academic field, through the rise of managerialism. The crux of the argument is that the concepts of habitus and illusio allow us to highlight staff members' collective dispositions towards assessment practices aimed to develop students' transferable skills. The authors argue that on a meso level of analysis habitus bridges the concepts of field, doxa, and cultural capital, shedding much needed light on what guides academic action and how staff cope with demands placed upon them from government and industry associations and representatives for 'employable' and 'work-ready' graduates. Their data indicate that the concept of illusio provides a valuable frame for developing a more nuanced analysis of staff claims of commitment to the development of generic 'employability' skills and their adoption of assessments designed to achieve this end, while simultaneously continuing to retain the traditional goals of higher education, notably students' engagement with the relevant disciplinary knowledge.

Following this chapter focusing on habitus, in Chapter 9, Townley offers an account of how another core concept of Bourdieu, capitals, can be explored within the field of cultural and creative industries. The emphasis in the chapter is on the relationship of capitals to Bourdieu's other thinking tools. Townley offers an examination of how Bourdieu used capitals in his various empirical studies and considers some criticisms that have been levelled at this use, including criticism that it is inappropriately applied and neglects the material. The chapter then considers the adoption of Bourdieu's use of capitals in management and organisation studies, particularly social capital, and the extent to which this use conforms to Bourdieu's understanding of the term. The value of the use of the concept of capitals is demonstrated by exploring the functioning of the creative industries. The author identifies the range of factors that have to be addressed in any analysis of a cultural and creative endeavour, which focuses on how dimensions of capital are understood in a field—the balances that have to be sought and accommodated between various forms of capitals. Townley highlights the crucial role played by symbolic cultural capital as depicted in specific case analyses of creators, the habitus of practitioners, and the field in which they operate. The chapter also outlines policy and practice implications for a range of stakeholders and intermediaries in cultural and creative industries.

Final chapter of the book is Chapter 10, authored by Karaçam and Koca. The objective of their study is to examine the experiences of women managers in Turkish sport organisations by the use of Bourdieu's theory and thus to contribute to an explanation of the marginalisation of women in management positions of sport organisations, where gender inequality is an institutionalised practice. The authors argue that Bourdieu's relational approach provides a multilayered and relational analysis that positions sport organisation within its wider social and institutional context, while acknowledging its micro-level realities. Building on qualitative data, the chapter explores sport organisations as social fields in order to better understand the women managers' gendered experiences as well as their strategies of capital accumulation and legitimacy. Through this empirical application, they discuss thoroughly how their individual strategies locate them within this field and whether their strategies contribute to the reproduction of the existing gendered field.

REFERENCES

Al Ariss, A., and Syed, J. (2011) Capital Mobilization of Skilled Migrants: A Relational Perspective. *British Journal of Management*, 22, 286–304.
Archer, M. (1995) *Realist Social Theory: The Morphogenetic Approach*. Cambridge: Cambridge University Press.
Becker, G. S. (1975) *Human Capital*. Chicago: University of Chicago Press.
Bourdieu, P. (1977) *Outline of Theory of Practice*. Cambridge: Cambridge University Press.
Bourdieu, P. (1984) *Distinction: A Social Critique of the Judgement of Taste*. London: Routledge.
Bourdieu, P. (1986) The Forms of Capital. In Richardson, J. G. (ed.), *Handbook of Theory and Research for the Sociology of Education*. New York: Greenwood, 241–258.
Bourdieu, P. (1987) What Makes a Social Class? On the Theoretical and Practical Existence of Groups. *Berkeley Journal of Sociology*, 32, 1–18.
Bourdieu, P. (1990) *The Logic of Practice*. Stanford: Stanford University Press.
Bourdieu, P. (1998a) *Acts of Resistance: Against the Tyranny of the Market*. New York: New Press.
Bourdieu, P. (1998b) *Practical Reason: On the Theory of Action*. Cambridge: Polity Press.
Bourdieu, P. (1999). Understanding. In Bourdieu, P. et al. (eds.) *The Weight of the World: Social Suffering in Contemporary Society*. Stanford: Stanford University Press, 607–626.
Bourdieu, P. (2000) *Pascalian Meditations*. Cambridge: Polity Press.
Bourdieu, P. (2003a) *Firing Back: Against the Tyranny of the Market, Volume 2*. New York: New Press.
Bourdieu, P. (2003b) Participant Objectivation. *Journal of Royal Anthropological Institute*, 9, 282–294.
Bourdieu, P., and Wacquant, L. (1992) *An Invitation to Reflexive Sociology*. Cambridge: Polity Press.
Bradbury, H., and Lichtenstein, B.M.B. (2000) Relationality in Organizational Research: Exploring the Space Between. *Organization Science*, 11, 551–564.
Burkitt, I. (2002) Technologies of the Self: Habitus and Capacities. *Journal for the Theory of Social Behaviour*, 32, 219–237.
Crompton, R. (1986). Women and the 'Service Class'. In Crompton, R., and Mann, M. (eds.), *Gender and Stratification*. Cambridge: Polity Press, 119–136.

De Clercq, D., and Voronov, M. (2009) The Role of Domination in Newcomers' Legitimation as Entrepreneurs. *Organization*, 16, 799–827.
DiMaggio, P. J., and Powell, W. (1983) The Iron Cage Revisited: Institutional Isomorphism and Collective Rationality in Organizational Fields. *American Sociological Review*, 48, 147–160.
Emirbayer, M., and Johnson, V. (2008) Bourdieu and Organizational Analysis. *Theory and Society*, 37, 1–44.
Fowler, B. (1997) *Pierre Bourdieu and Cultural Theory: Critical Investigations*. Thousand Oaks: SAGE.
Giddens, A. (1984) *The Constitution of Society: Outline of a Theory of Structuration*. Cambridge: Polity Press.
Golshorki, D., Leca, B., Lounsbury, M., and Raminez, C. (2009) Analysing, Accounting for and Unmasking Domination: On Our Role as Scholars of Practice, Practitioners of Social Science and Public Intellectuals. *Organization*, 16, 779–797.
Grenfell, M., and James, D. (1998) *Bourdieu and Education: Acts of Practical Theory*. London: Falmer Press.
Grugulis, I., and Stoyanova, D. (2012) Social Capital and Networks in Film and TV: Jobs for the Boys?. *Organization Studies*, 33, 1311–1331.
Kamoche, K., Kannan, S., and Siebers, L. Q. (2014). Knowledge-Sharing, Control, Compliance and Symbolic Violence. *Organization Studies*, 35, 989–1012.
Karatas-Ozkan, M., and Chell, E. (2015) Gender Inequalities in Academic Innovation and Enterprise: A Bourdieuan Analysis. *British Journal of Management*, 26, 109–125.
Karatas-Ozkan, M. (2011) Understanding Relational Qualities of Entrepreneurial Learning: Towards a Multi-layered Approach. *Entrepreneurship & Regional Development*, 23, 877–906.
Lash, S. (1993) Pierre Bourdieu: Cultural Economy and Social Change. In Calhoun, C., Postone, M., and LiPuma, E. (eds.), *Bourdieu: Critical Perspectives*. Cambridge: Polity Press, 193–211.
Layder, D. (1993) *New Strategies in Social Research*. Cambridge: Polity Press.
Lounsbury, M., and Ventresca, M. (2003) The New Structuralism in Organizational Theory. *Organization*, 10, 457–480.
Mills, C. W. (1959) *Sociological Imagination*. Oxford: Oxford University Press.
Nash, R. (2003) Social Explanation and Socialisation: On Bourdieu and the Structure, Disposition, Practice Scheme. *Sociological Review*, 51(1), 43–62.
Nentwich, J., Özbilgin, M., and Tatli, A. (2014) Change Agency as Embodiment and Performance: Exploring the Possibilities and Limits of Butler and Bourdieu. *Culture and Organization*. DOI: 10.1080/14759551.2013.851080
O'Mahoney, J. (2007) Constructing Habitus: The Negotiation of Moral Encounters at Telekom. *Work Employment and Society*, 21, 479–496.
Özbilgin, M., and Tatli, A. (2011) Mapping Out the Field of Equality and Diversity: Rise of Individualism and Voluntarism. *Human Relations*, 64, 1229–1258.
Özbilgin, M., and Tatli, A. (2005) Book Review Essay: Understanding Bourdieu's Contribution to Organization and Management Studies. *Academy of Management Review*, 30, 855–877.
Paulle, B., Heerikhuizen, B. V., and Emirbayer, M. (2012) Elias and Bourdieu. *Journal of Classical Sociology*, 12, 69–93.
Prieto, L., and Wang, L. (2010) Strategizing of China's Major Players: A Bourdieusian Perspective. *Journal of Organizational Change Management*, 23, 300–324.
Srinavas, N. (2013) Could a Subaltern Manage? Identity Work and Habitus in a Colonial Workplace. *Organization Studies*, 34, 1655–1674.
Sulkunen, P. (1982) Society Made Visible: On the Cultural Sociology of Pierre Bourdieu. *Acta Sociologica*, 25(2), 103–115.
Swartz, D. (1997) *Culture and Power: The Sociology of Pierre Bourdieu*. Chicago: University of Chicago Press.

Tatli, A. (2011) A Multi-layered Exploration of the Diversity Management Field: Diversity Discourses, Practices and Practitioners in the UK. *British Journal of Management*, 22, 238–253.

Tatli, A., and Ozbilgin, M. (2012) An Emic Approach to Intersectional Study of Diversity at Work: A Bourdieuan Framing. *International Journal of Management Reviews*, 14, 180–200.

Tatli, A., Özbilgin, M., Vassilopoulou, J., Forson, C., and Slutskaya, N. (2014) A Bourdieuan Relational Perspective for Entrepreneurship Research. *Journal of Small Business Management*, 52, 615–632.

Townley, B., Beech, N., and McKinlay, A. (2009) Managing in the Creative Industries: Managing the Motley Crew. *Human Relations*, 62, 939–962.

Vandenberghe, F. (1999) 'The real Is Relational': An Epistemological Analysis of Pierre Bourdieu's Generative Structuralism. *Sociological Theory*, 17(1), 32–67.

Wacquant, L. (1993) On the Tracks of Symbolic Power: Prefatory Notes to Bourdieu's 'State Nobility'. *Theory, Culture and Society*, 10, 1–17.

Witz, A. (1992) *Professions and Patriarchy*. London: Routledge.

Part I
New Frontiers in Research and Theory

1 Careers as Sites of Power

A Relational Understanding of Careers Based on Bourdieu's Cornerstones

Thomas M. Schneidhofer, Markus Latzke, and Wolfgang Mayrhofer

INTRODUCTION

Careers take place at the "intersection of societal history and individual biography" (Grandjean, 1981: 1057) linking micro and macro frames of references (Schein, 1978). They might be defined as patterns of movements through a space (social, occupational, or organizational) within time (Gunz & Mayrhofer, 2011), such that the "movement is contextualized, anchored in a specific social space" (Collin, 2006). However, contemporary careers research emphasizes the micro level of referencing, culminating in a "strong bias toward treating career as an individual phenomenon to be analysed psychologically rather than as a social phenomenon involving economics, political science, anthropology and sociology" (Schein, 2007: 573). The metaphors of boundaryless careers (Arthur, 1994; Tams & Arthur, 2010) or protean careers (Hall, 1996, 2003) may serve as paradigmatic cases of this: in spite of the plethora of influencing factors that individuals do not, or only to a certain extent, control (e.g. access to educational systems and achieving success within them, entry to or advancement within organizations or fields, appropriate compensation for efforts, etc.), these concepts underemphasize both the relevance of contextual issues to the study of careers (Mayrhofer et al., 2007) and the interplay of the two (Mayrhofer & Schneidhofer, 2009). Underpinning both concepts is an ideology based on unfettered individualism and free choice, and a theory at once undersocialized and depoliticized (Arnold & Cohen, 2008: 15–16). However, they only stand *pars pro toto* for careers research in general: what is missing to a greater extent is acknowledging the power dynamics that arise in the course of one's trajectory (for exceptions, see El-Sawad, 2005; Fournier, 1998; Savage, 1998), without throwing out the baby (the remaining *possibility* of individual effort and will) with the bath water (introducing a determinism of structures instead). Consequently, the lack of theoretical models accounting for both structure and agency to the same extent for explaining the genesis of careers is subject to recurring calls (e.g. Inkson et al., 2012). Bourdieu's sensitizing devices are well suited for answering these.

Applying a development of Bourdieu's economy of practices (Bourdieu, 1977; Bourdieu & Wacquant, 1992) to the subject of careers, we present an alternative to this literature and answer this call. Linking the idea of career fields (Iellatchitch et al., 2003) with a multi-level reading of Bourdieu's oeuvre (Özbilgin & Tatli, 2005), we reconstruct careers as sites of power. More specifically, we see careers as results of relational practices, or serious games, for and with career-related capital within a career field, for which career habitus serves as an embodied sense of, and boundary for, playing the game (Schneidhofer, 2013). Habitus—and thus the acquisition strategies and playing tactics of capital on the one hand, and conversion rates on the other—is the result of power dynamics, making the career game a serious one both for and over power. Outlining this idea, the remainder of this conceptual chapter contributes to the book in three ways: (1) With the focus on careers, we add an important subject having its roots in management and organization studies (Moore et al., 2007). Although careers research increasingly loses touch with its roots—for example, the very term 'career' disappeared from the *Oxford Handbook of Human Resource Management* (Boxall et al., 2007) in favour of the term 'talent management' (Inkson et al., 2012: 328)—it nevertheless represents an important facet therein with its own tensions, one of which being the dialectic metatheme of individual agency versus social determinism. (2) With a relational perspective inspired by Bourdieu, we transcend this tension with a both-and solution (Bradbury & Bergmann Lichtenstein, 2000) and delineate careers on three levels (Özbilgin & Tatli, 2005): (a) on the macro level, emphasizing the context of careers (fields); (b) on the micro level, emphasizing the content of careers (capital); and (c) on the meso level, emphasizing the linking-pin for both (habitus). (3) Because these three levels are relationally intertwined, we reconstruct careers eventually as sites of power, as serious games (Ortner, 2006) for and over power, with recursive consequences for the agents' bodies and the social structures within which they operate.

To this end, we will start with outlining our understanding of power. Subsequently, we will translate this understanding to the subject of careers, beginning with the context of careers (fields), followed by the content (capital) and completed with the connection between both (habitus). Finally we will delineate why careers are sites of power and what the consequences of this perspective might be.

ON THE ISSUE OF POWER

To Bourdieu, issues of power and domination are pervasive, even if agents do not necessarily recognize that on a conscious level (Golsorkhi et al., 2009). Although he did not have a classical sociology of power and domination in mind (in contrast to e.g. Max Weber), his theoretical cornerstones (field, capital, habitus) are interfused with both concepts (König & Berli, 2012): There are dominant and dominated agents within each field; there are agents with a lot of (and a viable structure of) capital, and agents with a less favourable capital portfolio; there are agents with a sense of the game, incorporated with a viable habitus, and agents lacking thereof. These three constructs, which may be conceived of as different levels of analysis (Özbilgin & Tatli, 2005), are relationally intertwined (Emirbayer, 1997): they make sense only together and for each other. And their relation is one of power: agents with the best established position-takings will possess the most favourable distribution of capital and the most viable sense for the game, able to make the rules of the game in order to keep making the rules. On top of this, agents develop an unconscious social belief in this hierarchy.

Consequently, Bourdieu's understanding of power is different from viewpoints perceiving it as a property (be that as a property of individuals as with e.g. Pfeffer, 2010; as a property of interactions as with e.g. French & Raven, 1959; or as a property of structures as with e.g. Hellriegel & Slocum, 1978). Similarly, it differs from considerations of power and domination in terms of its visibility to outsiders (e.g. Lukes, 2005). In this point he is close to Foucault (see e.g. 1983: 116; 1982: 777), who considered power to be non-subjective yet intentional. Bourdieu conceptualized power as a process embedded in relations. The outcome (and, strictly speaking, the antecedent) is called practice, referring to what agents actually do. These practices depend heavily on two things: First, on the context within which agents operate—this represents the macro level of analysis, which shows a fundamental divide between agents who 'have' power, and those who 'have not'. Second, they depend on the possibilities agents have, owing to both their genetical heritage and educational development. This is the other side of the same coin, referring to the micro level of analysis. Agents with a lot of, and a favourable composition of, capital may make the rules and thus ensure that they keep making the rules. Both aspects of practice are beyond structural determination on the one hand, or free will on the other. Due to the fact that power is embodied in the body and the brain of agents, their practices are logical to the point at which being logical would cease being practical (Bourdieu, 1990: 79), and set strategically without strategic intentions (Bourdieu, 1990: 11–12). Agents do not have to be aware of it, but they always act with respect to power in the course of their practices.

The result of vocationally oriented practices might be called a career. As a serious game for and with career-related capital within a career field, it is facilitated or aggravated by career habitus. The game is a political one—for and over power. And it is played in a social arena, called field, to which we will turn our focus first.

THE STATE OF THE FIELD(S)

The prominence of the field idea is linked to the debate in social sciences of how social institutions emerge, gain stability, and change. Despite substantial differences regarding most, if not all, important elements in this discussion, there is also some common ground: the interest is in local social order which emerges, is sustained, and changes through the social relation between agents in a defined social space; the construction and reproduction of social institutions depend on various power sources—that is, pre-existing rules about interaction and resource distribution; and the institutions both constrain and enable social agents—for those benefiting from the existing rules, the enabling aspect is key, and for those at a disadvantage, the constraining aspect dominates (Fligstein, 2008). Field theories (Martin, 2003) in general seek to explain individual action patterns by recourse to agents' position-*takings* vis-à-vis one another. Fields refer to the macro level of analysis (Özbilgin & Tatli, 2005). Note, though, that the micro-meso-macro differentiation is relative to the overall frame of thinking and there are different estimates about where to locate fields as "constructed *meso*level social orders" (Fligstein & McAdam, 2011: 9; italics by the authors) where individual action takes place.

There are three different understandings of Bourdieu's field concept in the literature. The first originated in organization studies, particularly in institutional theory (Lounsbury, 2002; Lounsbury & Kaghan, 2001; Lounsbury & Ventresca, 2003). In contrast to using Bourdieu's theory as a relational sociology of the individual (Lahire, 2003), its emphasis remains at the macro level of analysis. Therefore (competing) institutional logics and questions of work structuration come into focus. Nevertheless, corresponding research on the genesis and development of fields is important for the understanding outlined in the remainder of this chapter.

For the second understanding, coming from sociology, Huppatz and her colleagues (2009; Huppatz & Goodwin, 2013; Ross-Smith & Huppatz, 2010) conceptualize occupational fields. They draw on feminists' rereadings of Bourdieu's theories (Lovell, 2000; McCall, 1992; Skeggs, 2004). Although they do not refer to careers literature explicitly, their development of (gendered) capital has significant consequences for a relational understanding of careers as well. In their view, fields combine agents of a specific occupation (e.g. nurses, managers, or hairdressers). This certainly offers interesting insights in processes of occupational choice, discrimination, or segregation.

Standing for the third understanding of Bourdieu's field concept, Tatli (2010) describes diversity managers' agency influenced by three semi-autonomous fields: first, the institutional field of diversity management, within which the question regarding 'good diversity management' is at stake (see also Tatli, 2011); second, the business field, dealing with questions regarding the business case; and third, the cultural field, highlighting marginalization. Attempting to explain the careers of diversity managers, Schneidhofer et al. (forthcoming) pick up this idea, arguing that a career field of diversity managers emerges at the intersection of these three fields. The intersection provides the setting where the careers of managers in charge of diversity management are at stake.

This understanding is related to the career-focused view of fields by Iellatchitch et al. (2003), on which we draw subsequently. They conceptualize four career fields emerging from the interplay of tight or loose coupling of agents within a field (an idea borrowed from Orton & Weick, 1990) with stable or instable configurations (inspired by Perrow, 1984, and finally borrowed from Kelley, 1967, and Herkner, 1980). As a result, four career fields emerge (company world, free-floating professionalism, self-employment, and chronic flexibility). Agents seek to advance within such fields. By cross-cutting organizations, occupations, or professions, career fields thus represent the context for making a career. However, both the starting positions and the development possibilities are not the same for all players.

More precisely, each and every field is characterized by a fundamental hierarchy which is based on capital distributions (an idea which we will delineate in the section "Concepts of Capital"). On the one hand, the orthodoxy operates topologically at the centre of the field. The closer agents approximate this analytical category, the more they are able to make the rules of the game. They then have the potential to determine who may enter the field, what is necessary to advance within the field, and how exclusion may be performed. To be sure, fields are only semi-autonomous by nature, meaning that the field's orthodoxy depends on relational obligations to other fields with which they operate. It might be the case that agents representing orthodoxy in one field may represent heresy in another (as in the case of intellectuals, whom Bourdieu depicts as the "dominated fraction of the dominating class"; Bourdieu, 2000a).

On the other hand heresy is closer to the margin of the field. Agents approximating heresy may play as well, but only according to (or in rebellion against) the rules the orthodoxy has imposed. Both forces, which have only analytic character (and are thus not to be thought of as corporal agents, or sources of collective conspiracy), develop and embody a belief in this hierarchy by the commitment to engage in this game, called doxa. This belief is pre-reflexive and mostly unconscious to agents. However, it is the basis (and the consequence) of the strategies and tactics that agents may develop.

Both ends of the spectrum—orthodoxy as well as heresy—derive their strategies and tactics not only from the objective structure of the field. There is also a subjective correspondence to the position-taking in the field, which enables/restricts strategies, tactics, and investments. In order to play the game, agents need capital, and that is what is at stake in the course of a career. In other words, the content of the career game is found on the micro level of analysis ('as above so below'). Unfortunately, the very term 'career capital' is variously used in the contemporary literature.

CONCEPTS OF CAPITAL

Capital is most prominently displayed in the mainstream concept of 'the three ways of knowing' (DeFillippi and Arthur, 1994). In times of 'boundaryless careers' (Arthur, 1994) these career competencies should help to respond to changing contextual demands and are claimed to have mutual advantages for both the individual and organizations (Arthur et al., 1995). *Knowing why* relates to career motivation, personal meaning, identification, and self-concept. *Knowing how* encompasses job-related knowledge and career-relevant skills acquired in formal education, on-the-job training, and informal learning activities (see the concept of human capital; Becker, 1962). *Knowing whom* relates to career-relevant social networks, such as inter-firm communication, relationships with key customers and suppliers, and contacts drawn from personal interaction with family, friends, and colleagues. The concept is widely used in empirical studies either as a predictor of career success (e.g. Eby et al., 2003) or as an outcome of various career investments (e.g. Sturges et al., 2003) and especially with a focus on global careers (e.g. Suutari & Mäkelä, 2007) and expatriates (e.g. Dickmann & Doherty, 2008).

Earlier publications on the three ways of knowing primarily addressed the individual, since careers have been regarded as 'personal property' making each of us 'a knowledge capitalist' (Inkson & Arthur, 2001: 51). Likewise Forrier et al. (2009: 742) introduced the notion of 'movement capital' in their theoretical model of career mobility and assigned it explicitly to the agency perspective as it "encompasses the individual skills, knowledge, competencies, and attitudes". More recently, Parker et al. (2009) show potential connections between the three ways of knowing and shift the focus slightly away from just the individual by acknowledging that some of the links involve relations between the individual and the social arena. Several authors go further by criticizing the overemphasis on agency in this career capital concept (e.g. Duberley & Cohen, 2010). Consequently we will delineate an alternative concept of career capital, putting more emphasis on the complex relationship between the social structure and individual agency, based on a Bourdieusian notion of capital (see also Latzke et al., forthcoming).

Originally, Bourdieu (1986) distinguishes three basic forms of capital, of which *economic* capital—like income and property rights—is only the most obvious manifestation. *Cultural* capital, as "the accumulated result of educational and cultural effort, undertaken either by the agent or by his/her ancestors" (Mayrhofer et al., 2002: 14), can exist in three forms: objectified, institutionalized, and embodied. In its objectified state, cultural capital appears in the form of cultural products like books, art, or machines. Institutionalized cultural capital encompasses academic titles and degrees. The acquisition of embodied cultural capital in the form of long-lasting dispositions of the body and mind consumes time and is personalized. It has a distinctive value and remains marked by its earliest conditions of acquisition, like pronunciation. Both basic guises of capital—economic and cultural— serve as a basis, and a consequence, of *social* capital, "the aggregate of the actual or potential resources which are linked to possession of a durable network of more or less institutionalized relationships of mutual acquaintance and recognition . . ." (Bourdieu, 1986: 51). The volume of social capital depends on the network size and the ability to mobilize these connections. It may be legitimized and institutionalized by family, group, or class membership or title of nobility.

Bourdieu used the concept in his work *Distinction* (1984), investigating social class, and stated that it is a product of individual agency and not simply deterministic. Furthermore, the role of the educational system in the reproduction of power relations is stressed in this regard (for France, see Bourdieu & De Saint Martin, 1987; for Germany, Hartmann, 2000). Savage et al. (2005) reviewed various concepts that address how the effects of class are produced through individual action drawing on capital, assets, and resources. They conclude that Bourdieu's concept of capital offers convincing advantages compared to theories of exploitation in Marxist perspectives, as it does recognize but does not overrate the importance of the economic facet and it enriches thinking with other forms of capital.

Capital always has to be related to a specific field, and it works in different ways in various fields. That becomes especially clear when investigating symbolic capital, which is "recognized as legitimate competence" (Bourdieu, 1986: 49), and as such it is always contingent on the rules of the field. Hence the concept does not imply universality for a capital portfolio, but acknowledges restrictions due to the role of context (Duberley & Cohen, 2010: 196) and the course of time (Bourdieu & Wacquant, 1992: 101). The history and the rules—that is, the power relations in the field—specify which combination of the basic forms of capital will be authorized as symbolic capital.

Bourdieu himself suggested the evolutionary potential of his framework, and he proposed that each form has subtypes (Bourdieu & Wacquant, 1992: 119). One such further development is the notion of career capital in career fields. According to Iellatchtich et al. (2003: 735) career capitals "are those capitals used by the agent for work related activities that are valued by the career fields." In contrast to simple games of chance like roulette, the games of society, including careers, follow different logics (Bourdieu, 1986: 246). In roulette each round is absolutely independent of the previous one and the winnings can be betted and lost at every new spin. In a field, on the contrary, the history of the game plays a vital role regarding the opportunities of agents. Accumulation, acquisition, and especially conversion rates point to the relatedness of investments and outcomes to a certain field and its inherent power relations.

One possibility to investigate career capital in action is to look at transitions, as they are able to elucidate the relationship of the individual and the social order (Duberley et al., 2006). Against this backdrop a study with Austrian business school graduates focused on transitions within and across career fields (Latzke et al., 2013). The relational nature of career capital was displayed in the various functions within different fields, like economic capital, which was regarded either as a motivator or reward (Company World) or as a starting prerequisite (Self Employment). Furthermore, the field of departure plays a major role—for example, transitions from the field of Self Employment to the field of Company World proved difficult due to little organizational knowledge and the non-accessibility of headhunters. Also applying a Bourdieusian capital concept, Duberley and Cohen (2010) investigated careers of female academic scientists. They identified all three basic forms as helpful, be it receiving grants (economic), considering a PhD as a kind of access card to mobility to other universities (cultural), or personal contacts that help when starting a research project (social). In addition they found that the area of scientific expertise itself varied in value, depending on the political and social context. A core finding was that career capital was strongly gendered: what is an asset for a man may actually be an impediment for women. For example, having access to mostly male networks and being in a relationship proved to be more advantageous for men and obstructive for women.

Picking up the second understanding of the field concept mentioned in the section "The State of the Field(s)", the conceptualization of gender (McCall, 1992) and ethnicity (Erel, 2010) as forms of embodied cultural capital proved insightful. Accordingly, Huppatz (2009) performed her study in a field which is feminized due to its numerical domination by women and to the meanings assigned to it: the field of paid caring work. Results showed that female capital (sex category) and feminine capital (gender) privilege women with access to and development within the field. Nevertheless, senior posts within the field are mainly occupied by men and the forms of gender capital seem to have limited conversion when an agent moves outside of those fields. The unfavourable conversion rate of female/feminine capital into economic capital arises because 'caring for others' is not so highly valued in the social space within which the field is embedded. Bourdieu (2001: 67) compares that to a double-bind situation. If a nurse acted like a manager, she would lose prestige within the professional field, and if she behaved in a manner highly valued in the field, she would appear incapable and unfit for the managerial job. Either way, the conversion rate for economic capital is different for agents equipped with a high amount of female/feminine capital compared to agents investing their embodied masculine/male capital. In another study men working in gendered industries (construction/retail vs. hairdressing/nursing) were interviewed, and the relevance of maleness, masculinity, and femininity as capital was investigated (Huppatz & Goodwin, 2013).

Also in migration studies the value of applying a Bourdieusian understanding of capital has been recognized by using the concept of 'ethnic capital'. In contrast to a traditional 'rucksack approach' migrants not only unpack their forms of capital from their rucksack, but also create new forms of capital in the countries of residence and engage in developing mechanisms of validation for their capitals. The study of Erel (2010), who interviewed immigrants from Turkey in the UK, revealed intragroup hierarchical distinctions (e.g. based on language) as a salient marker for validation. Moreover, the role of migrants' organizations in the UK helped them to validate (approbation) cultural resources. Quite similarly the mobilization of different forms of capital of skilled migrants from Lebanon who worked in Paris was researched (Al Ariss & Syed, 2011). The authors point to the advantage of the concept which allows accounting for the agency of skilled migrants in navigating the structural barrier to their international career mobility. Thus a prior knowledge of the French culture, French language skills, and academic qualifications proved to be valid cultural capital. Social capital in the form of family, friends, and professional networks helped them to acquire the needed economic capital, be it through family support or scholarships.

Summing up, the individual capital portfolio boosts or decreases the chances of an agent within a specific field. The power relations of the field are crucial in determining which and how various forms of capital count, creating status and prestige within a field. Although a lack of symbolic capital may reduce the probability of success, it still might enable agents to play successfully. Powerful (orthodox) agents may introduce forms of 'positive' discrimination, like affirmative action or quota regulations, in order to increase the value of certain embodied cultural capitals, like sex category, ethnicity, or disability, but even the least advantaged (heretic) agents may creatively play with their assets. They either can play in accordance with the implicit rules or may challenge the existing conversion rates to increase the value of their capital portfolio—for example, by drawing on a discourse of potential contribution. "They can, for instance, work to change the relative value of tokens of different colours, the exchange rate between various species of capital, through strategies aimed at discrediting the form of capital upon which the force of their opponents rests (e.g. economic capital) and to valorise the species of capital they preferentially possess" (Bourdieu & Wacquant, 1992: 99). Boogaard and Roggeband (2010), for example, showed how ethnic minority agents within the Dutch police force emphasize their cultural and linguistic knowledge in a specific context and thereby turn their disadvantage into an asset. Similar is the case of South Asian doctors in the UK, who could not access high-status specialities due to a lack of social capital and found their niche in less popular areas, such as geriatrics, and became influential figures in that field (Raghuram et al., 2010).

However, even if a less powerful player understands the rules of the game and invests 'rationally' in the symbolic capital most highly valued at a certain time (e.g. in the case of academia, focusing mainly on quick publishing instead of sustainable contributions, let alone focusing on teaching), a change of the rules might shift the focus on neglected areas (e.g. teaching), thereby devaluating the acquired capitals. Hence, heretics are rather at the mercy of power relations. On top of this, the fact of recognizing the possibility of investing 'rationally' is a result not only of ability, let alone of mere effort, but also of the social conditions in which the agent finds himself, both in the past and in the present. This is why Bourdieu conceptualizes 'investment' as the "propensity to act that is born of the relation between a field and a system of dispositions adjusted to the game it proposes, a sense of the game and of its stakes that implies at once an inclination and an ability to play the game, both of which are socially and historically constituted rather than universally given" (Bourdieu & Wacquant, 1992: 118). We now turn to this system of dispositions called habitus, which we find on the meso level of analysis for the study of careers.

CAREER HABITUS: A PRODUCT AND A PRODUCER OF POWER

Originating in the Aristotelian concept of hexis, more elaborately worked out by Thomas Aquinas, and reinvented by Bourdieu (Nickl, 2005), we find habitus as a connection of patterns of thought (and action) on the one hand and social conditions on the other (Mutch, 2003). As such, habitus in general (and career habitus in particular) appears Janus-faced (Lizardo, 2004): On one side, it is a system of dispositions, enabling one to (more or less passively) classify what is right and what is wrong, what should be done and what left out, and what makes a possibility (and what an insurmountable obstacle). On the other side, habitus (more or less actively) structures which things are done and how they are performed, the opinions one has and how they are expressed, or the chances that are realized (and the way in which they are realized—or left out). It represents an embodiment of social structures, unfolding the point where structure meets agency. Wacquant (2013: 6–7) distinguishes three components: (a) cognitive, referring to the classificatory system relating the elements of the social world with each other; (b) conative, meaning the skills incorporated in the body to navigate in this social world effectively; (c) affective, referring to "the vesting of one's life energies into the objects, undertakings, and agents that populate the world under consideration". Hodkinson and Sparkes (2008) conceptualize this as 'horizon for action' left within a field, and Emirbayer and Johnson (2008) speak of a 'space of possibles'.

Career habitus then represents habitus related to a career field, both enabling and restricting career-related strategies and investments. Iellatchitch et al. (2003: 738) use the term as 'fitting' a particular career field and getting potentially "actualized automatically within a career field". However, with this definition every agent entering a field would have a great chance of success, for the structure of the field 'trims' agents to its purposes. While the relation between agent and field is indeed one of conditioning (Bourdieu & Wacquant, 1992: 127), an adaption of agents' dispositions to the structure of the field is only the most probable (and not the only possible) case. Hence, we suggest understanding career habitus rather as (a) the capacity for deriving appropriate strategies and tactics dependent on one's position-taking in the field, (b) the capacity for making profitable investments as realizations of these strategies and tactics, and (c) the capacity of one's physical presence to make relevant agents recognize one's potential for success in one's field.

Career habitus is a multi-level construct in itself, bridging the sociological, the symbolic, and the physical (McNay, 1999: 98).

As far as (a) is concerned, career habitus translates the position-taking on the macro level into 'objective potentialities' (Bourdieu & Wacquant, 1992: 129). Career agency is then far from being intentional with strategic intent, but dependent on the sense of the game derived from the game's score. The higher the capacity for deriving appropriate strategies, the less the individual agent has to be aware of them; much like a duck takes to water, the agent 'knows' what to do (without being necessarily aware of that).

Concerning (b), career habitus has a connection to the micro level of capital as well. Depending on the composition of capital, agents show varying propensities to invest for future returns thereof in the form of prestige and reputation. Here, subjective (career satisfaction) and objective career success (income) collapse as means to the end of power gain. The higher the capacity, the less these investments may appear as strategic/tactical but as (depending on one's world view) gift, talent, or calling. (c) finally refers to the fact that at any given point in time, all three levels interact relationally, and on an unconscious level other agents in the field 'recognize' potentially successful agents. For example, an agent in the field of professional dancing does not have to watch the world champion in Latin American dancing to sense his/her skills. S/he immediately recognizes in the way the champion enters the room and the way s/he walks and stands (in relation to the conventions of the field) that s/he is successful in the field. This identification (or projection, for the appreciation does not always have to be true) is responsible for the games other agents enter (or not). This is behind Bourdieu's principle of isotimy, referring to the necessity of being a player *on a par* for playing the game with others. If agents are not 'equal in honour', they refuse to play right at the beginning, because the chance of losing is just too high.

But more important than what career habitus might be is the question of where it comes from and what purpose it serves. As a product of inculcation it encompasses the past and present (Bourdieu, 1992). It bears both an ontogenetical and phylogenetical heritage. The former points towards the individual experiences stemming from the course of one's lifetime. Genetic dispositions, socioeconomic status, education, and academic achievements fall in this category. The latter refers to anthropology and the history of mankind as a whole. This is why

> the function of the habitus is, precisely, to restore to the agent a generative and unifying power, a constructive and classifying potency, while at the same time reminding us that this capacity to construct social reality, itself socially constructed, is not that of a transcendental subject but that of a socialized body, which engages in practice organizing principles that are socially constructed and acquired in the course of a social experience at once situated and dated.
>
> (Bourdieu, 2000b: 24).

This might serve as an explanation of why children prefer sex role stereotyped toys before even knowing their sex (Bauer, 1993; Fein et al., 1975), or for the effects of the stereotype threat arising from unconscious knowledge about one's alleged position in the social field (Sinclair et al., 2005, 2006). Bourdieu would rephrase the stereotype threat most probably as a reaction to the hysteresis effect (or Don Quichotte effect; see Bourdieu, 1976: 183)—that dispositions do not fit to the position one has (or is assigned to) within a field.

At this point it should have become clear that the career game is not only a game for power, meaning that it is all about capital accumulation and mobilization. It is also a game over power. The former means that the very essence of career is movement within the career field. In the case of career success, this movement equals advancement, which is expressed by an increase in capital, or a return of investment. Consequently, agents who get ahead in the career field possess more power evidenced by their capital portfolio. The latter refers to the fact that this movement (which is an advancement in the best case) apparently changes the structure of the field. As such, careers of individual agents challenge the conversion rates of guises of capital into one another. The more capital of a specific form is prevalent within a field, the less its face value: for example, if institutionalized cultural capital (let's say, an MBA) was necessary to advance within a specific career field, many agents would attend postgraduate education. However, each graduation leads to an inflation of this guise of capital. Hence the careers of individual agents (in particular the careers of the heresy) are of interest for the orthodoxy of the field, for they may challenge their (i.e. the orthodoxy's) position. Consequently, the orthodoxy will try to make sure that their capital portfolio remains precious. And heresy will try not only to acquire as much capital as possible but also to make their existing capital portfolio look much better. Careers are then sites of power, also relevant for the social space in general.

CONCLUSIONS AND DISCUSSION

Contemporary careers research tends to treat career as an individual phenomenon and underemphasizes the relevance of contextual issues and the interplay of the two. Inspired by Bourdieu, we have presented a relational perspective to view careers as results of practices for and with career-related capital within a career field. This allows an analysis on three relationally intertwined conceptual levels: the macro level, focusing on the context of careers—that is, fields; the micro level, emphasizing the content of careers—that is, capital; and the meso level, linking both through habitus. Together these three levels reveal careers as serious games both for power—that is, capital accumulation and mobilization—and over power—that is, sustaining or challenging the social order.

Despite its merits, in relation to careers the Bourdieusian field concept falls short in two major areas. First, the focus is on the individual and individual action (even though the individual him-/herself is a relational, not a psychological construct). While this is fine with an individual career agent, it does not capture the case of collective career agents. They can have a career of their own—that is, banks getting different credit ratings. Even more importantly, collective agents are an essential part of the fields within which individuals' careers take place—for example, by offering career opportunities, providing additional symbolic capital when improving their status as an employer, or acting as gatekeepers for certain career routes. With a few notable exceptions (e.g. Bourdieu, 1996), Bourdieu's work puts collective action and its specific dynamics on the backburner. Second, fields in the Bourdieusian sense are driven by individuals competing for a better position within the field. While conflict and competition are important, cooperation among and between individual and social agents is crucial, too. Forming alliances, supporting each other's professional development, and mentoring are just a few examples of the importance of including more cooperative phenomena. The notion of strategic action fields (Fligstein & McAdam, 2011) with its inclusion of individual and collective actors, viewing collective action as central and including both cooperation and competition, might turn out to be a promising route for further developing Bourdieu's view of fields.

To be sure, power—and, hence, domination—has primacy in Bourdieu's theory both as an end and as a determinant of practice (Friedland, 2009: 888). Translated to the subject 'career' this means that although individual career success may reappear as a gain in power (through an increase in symbolic capital and hence a movement towards the centre of a specific career field), the very concept of career appears as a result of power struggles. In other words, for the individual career agent, 'making a career' means acquiring the distinctive cognitive constructs and the skilled moves as well as developing the proper appetite for the stakes of the corresponding social game. What is referred to as objective career success (e.g. income) or subjective career success (e.g. career satisfaction) appears as means towards the end (the end being an increase in power). From a relational perspective, this does also encompass the capacity of shaping individual bodies and brains in the long run (via career habitus as a result of the interplay between field and capital on the one hand and strategies/investments and their results on the other).

We should not forget that, until the 1850s the term 'career' was used to describe unstable movements (as in the expression "horses careering out of control"; Savage, 1998: 66). It is certainly an interesting study (but beyond the scope of this chapter) to link the discourse of careers research to this perspective. It allegedly implies that the contemporary meaning might stand for the carrot of societal progress provided by the field's orthodoxy, urging agents to develop a vocational orientation closely aligned with personal progress ('a path with the heart') and individual responsibility for its achievement in order to ensure advancement within a field. Indeed, the promise of career progress as a reward for merit, diligence, and hard work has become a widespread expectation in contemporary times, and there are always individuals who make it to the top through hard work (without being reliable to significant others—at least not visibly—in many cases). But maybe it is only a game to keep people occupied and oriented in a way that is deemed to foster the social order sustainably. In Bourdieu's terminology, it appears likely that many careers operate as paradoxes of doxa, designed to subordinate heresy, yet willy-nilly and without 'objective' need. In that case, career researchers do what 'good' intellectuals always do: they act as the dominated fraction of the dominating class (Bourdieu, 1988).

In other words, on a meta-level it comes as no wonder that the mainstream of careers research overemphasizes the psychological dimension. This fosters the social belief that it is about the individual, who is responsible for his/her career and who faces a plethora of possibilities in an alleged 'boundaryless world'. Much like a hamster in a rat race, perceiving his effort as possibility of eventually getting released, habitus makes sure that the space of possibles is not acknowledged as such. We will conclude that habitus is neither fate nor 'god's will': there are ways of 'doing it' differently, both for researchers of careers and the individuals making them. Knowing that people are neither a puppet of structures nor solely responsible for their behaviour (and, thus, capable of resisting power dynamics) might represent the first step.

REFERENCES

Al Ariss, A., and Syed, J. 2011. 'Capital Mobilization of Skilled Migrants: A Relational Perspective', *British Journal of Management*, 22 (2), 286–304.

Arnold, J., and Cohen, L. 2008. 'The Psychology of Careers in Industrial and Organizational Settings: A Critical but Appreciative Analysis', in G. Hodgkinson and K. Ford (eds.), *The International Review of Industrial and Organizational Psychology*: pp. 1–44. Chichester: Wiley and Sons.

Arthur, M.B. 1994. 'The Boundaryless Career: A New Perspective for Organizational Inquiry', *Journal of Organizational Behavior*, 15 (4), 295–306.

Arthur, M.B., Claman, P.H., and DeFillippi, R.J. 1995. 'Intelligent Enterprise, Intelligent Careers', *Academy of Management Executive*, 9 (4), 7–22.

Bauer, P.A. 1993. 'Memory for Gender-Consistent and Gender-Inconsistent Event Sequences by 25-Months-Old Children', *Child Development*, 64 (1), 285–297.

Becker, G.S. 1962. 'Investment in Human Capital: A Theoretical Analysis', *Journal of Political Economy*, 70 (5), 9–49.

Boogaard, B., and Roggeband, C. 2010. 'Paradoxes of Intersectionality: Theorizing Inequality in the Dutch Police Force through Structure and Agency', *Organization*, 17 (1), 53–75.

Bourdieu, P. 1976. *Entwurf einer Theorie der Praxis auf der ethnologischen Grundlage der kabylischen Gesellschaft*. Frankfurt: Suhrkamp.

Bourdieu, P. 1977. *Outline of a Theory of Practice*. Cambridge: Cambridge University Press.

Bourdieu, P. 1984. *Distinction: A Social Critique of the Judgement of Taste*. London: Routledge and Kegan Paul.

Bourdieu, P. 1986. 'The Forms of Capital', in J. Richardson (ed.), *Handbook of Theory and Research for the Sociology of Education*: pp. 241–258. Westport, CT: Greenwood.
Bourdieu, P. 1988. *Homo academicus*. Frankfurt: Suhrkamp.
Bourdieu, P. 1990. *In Other Words: Essays towards a Reflexive Sociology*. Stanford, CA: Stanford University Press.
Bourdieu, P. 1992. *Rede und Antwort*. Frankfurt: Suhrkamp.
Bourdieu, P. 1996. *The State Nobility: Elite Schools in the Field of Power*. Oxford: Polity Press.
Bourdieu, P. 2000a. *Distinction: A Social Critique of the Judgement of Taste*. London: Routledge.
Bourdieu, P. 2000b. *Pascalian Meditations*. Cambridge: Polity Press.
Bourdieu, P. 2001. *Masculine Domination*. Stanford, CA: Stanford University Press.
Bourdieu, P., and De Saint Martin, M. 1987. 'Agrègation et sègrègation. Le champ des grandes ècoles et le champ du pouvoir', *Actes de la recherche en sciences sociales*, **69**, 2–50.
Bourdieu, P., and Wacquant, L.J.D. 1992. *An Invitation to Reflexive Sociology*. Chicago: University of Chicago Press.
Boxall, P., Purcell, J., and Wright, P. (eds.). 2007. *The Oxford Handbook of Human Resource Management*. Oxford: Oxford University Press.
Bradbury, H., and Bergmann Lichtenstein, B.M. 2000. 'Relationality in Organizational Research: Exploring the Space Between', *Organization Science*, **11** (5), 551–564.
Collin, A. 2006. 'Career', in J.H. Greenhaus and G.A. Callanan (eds.), *Encyclopedia of Career Development*: pp. 60–36. Thousand Oaks, CA: SAGE.
Dickmann, M., and Doherty, N. 2008. 'Exploring the Career Capital Impact of International Assignments within Distinct Organizational Contexts', *British Journal of Management*, **19** (2), 145–161.
Duberley, J., and Cohen, L. 2010. 'Gendering Career Capital: An Investigation of Scientific Careers', *Journal of Vocational Behavior*, **76** (2), 187–197.
Duberley, J., Mallon, M., and Cohen, L. 2006. 'Exploring Career Transitions: Accounting for Structure and Agency', *Personnel Review*, **35** (3), 281–296.
Eby, L., Butts, M., and Lockwood, A. 2003. 'Predictors of Success in the Era of the Boundaryless Career', *Journal of Organizational Behaviour*, **24** (6), 689–708.
El-Sawad, A. 2005. 'Becoming a Lifer: Unlocking Career through Metaphor', *Journal of Occupational and Organizational Psychology*, **78**, 23–41.
Emirbayer, M. 1997. 'Manifesto for a Relational Sociology', *American Journal of Sociology*, **103** (2), 281–317.
Emirbayer, M., and Johnson, V. 2008. 'Bourdieu and Organizational Analysis', *Theory and Society*, **37** (1), 1–44.
Erel, U. 2010. 'Migrating Cultural Capital: Bourdieu in Migration Studies', *Sociology*, **44** (4), 642–660.
Fein, G., Johnson, D., Kosson, N., Stork, L., and Wasserman, L. 1975. 'Sex Stereotypes and Preferences in the Toy Choice of 20-Month-Old Boys and Girls', *Developmental Psychology*, **11** (4), 527–528.
Fligstein, N. 2008. 'Fields, Power and Social Skill: A Critical Analysis of the New Institutionalisms', *International Public Management Review*, **9** (1), 227–253.
Fligstein, N., and McAdam, D. 2011. *A Theory of Fields*. Oxford: Oxford University Press.
Forrier, A., Sels, L., and Stynen, D. 200). 'Career Mobility at the Intersection between Agent and Structure: A Conceptual Model', *Journal of Occupational and Organizational Psychology*, **82** (4), 739–759.
Foucault, M. 1982. 'The Subject and Power', *Critical Inquiry*, **8** (4), 777–795.
Foucault, M. 1983. *Sexualität und Wahrheit. Erster Band. Der Wille zum Wissen*. Frankfurt: Suhrkamp.

Fournier, V. 1998. 'Stories of Development and Exploitation: Militant Voices in an Enterprise Culture', *Organization*, 5 (1), 55–80.
French, J.R.P., and Raven, B.H. 1959. 'The Bases of Social Power', in D. Cartwright (ed.), *Studies in Social Power*: pp. 150–167. Ann Arbor: University of Michigan.
Friedland, R. 2009. 'The Endless Fields of Pierre Bourdieu', *Organization*, 16 (6), 887–917.
Golsorkhi, D., Leca, B., Lounsbury, M., and Ramirez, C. 2009. 'Analysing, Accounting for and Unmasking Domination: On Our Role as Scholars of Practice, Practitioners of Social Science and Public Intellectuals', *Organization*, 16, 779–797.
Grandjean, B.D. 1981. 'History and Career in a Bureaucratic Labor Market', *American Journal of Sociology*, 86 (5), 1057–1092.
Gunz, H.P., and Mayrhofer, W. 2011. 'Re-conceptualizing Career Success: A Contextual Approach', *Journal for Labour Market Research*, 43 (3), 251–260.
Hall, D.T. 1996. 'Protean Careers of the 21st Century', *Academy of Management Executive*, 10 (4), 8–16.
Hall, D.T. 2004. 'The Protean Career: A Quarter-Century Journey', *Journal of Vocational Behavior*, 65 (1), 1–13.
Hartmann, M. 2000. 'Class-Specific Habitus and the Social Reproduction of the Business Elite in Germany and France', *Sociological Review*, 48 (2), 262–282.
Hellriegel, D., and Slocum, J.W. 1978. *Management: Contingency Approaches*. Reading: Addison-Wesley.
Herkner, W. (ed.). 1980. *Attribution: Psychologie der Kausalität*. Bern: Huber.
Hodkinson, P. 2008. 'Understanding Career Decision-Making and Progression: Careership Revisited'. John Killeen Memorial Lecture. Woburn House, London.
Huppatz, K. 2009. 'Reworking Bourdieu's "Capital": Feminine and Female Capitals in the Field of Paid Caring Work', *Sociology*, 43 (1), 45–66.
Huppatz, K., and Goodwin, S. 2013. 'Masculinised Jobs, Feminised Jobs and Men's "Gender Capital" Experiences: Understanding Occupational Segregation in Australia', *Journal of Sociology*, 49 (2–3), 291–308.
Iellatchitch, A., Mayrhofer, W., and Meyer, M. 2003. 'Career Fields: A Small Step towards a Grand Career Theory?', *International Journal of Human Resource Management*, 14 (5), 728–750.
Inkson, K., and Arthur, M.B. 2001. 'How to Be a Successful Career Capitalist', *Organizational Dynamics*, 30 (1), 48–61.
Inkson, K., Gunz, H.P., Ganesh, S., and Roper, J. 2012. 'Boundaryless Careers: Bringing Back Boundaries', *Organization Studies*, 33 (3), 323–340.
Kelley, H.H. 1967. 'Attribution Theory in Social Psychology', *Nebraska Symposium on Motivation*, 15, 192–238.
König, A., and Berli, O. 2012. 'Das Paradox der Doxa—Macht und Herrschaft als Leitmotiv der Soziologie Pierre Bourdieus', in P. Imbusch (ed.), *Macht und Herrschaft. Sozialwissenschaftliche Theorien und Konzepte*: pp. 303–334. Wiesbaden: Springer.
Lahire, B. 2003. 'From the Habitus to an Individual Heritage of Dispositions: Towards a Sociology at the Level of the Individual', *Poetics*, 31, 329–355.
Latzke, M., Mayrhofer, W., Pernkopf-Konhäusner, K., Rohr, C., and Schneidhofer, T. 2013. 'Career Capital in Transitions Crossing Career Fields', paper presented at EGOS, Montreal, Canada, 4–6 July.
Latzke, M., Schneidhofer, T.M., Pernkopf-Konhäusner, K., Rohr, C., and Mayrhofer, W. Forthcoming. 'Relational Career Capital: Towards a Sustainable Perspective', in A. De Vos and B. Van der Heijden (eds.), *Handbook of Research on Sustainable Careers*. Cheltenham, UK: Edward Elgar.
Lizardo, O. 2004. 'The Cognitive Origins of Bourdieu's Habitus', *Journal for the Theory of Social Behaviour*, 34 (4), 375–401.

Lounsbury, M. 2002. 'Institutional Transformation and Status Mobility: The Professionalization of the Field of Finance', *Academy of Management Journal,* **45** (1), 255–266.
Lounsbury, M., and Kaghan, W.N. 2001. 'Organizations, Occupations and the Structuration of Work', *Research in the Sociology of Work,* **10**, 25–50.
Lounsbury, M., and Ventresca, M. 2003. 'The New Structuralism in Organizational Theory', *Organization,* **10** (3), 457–480.
Lovell, T. 2000. 'Thinking Feminism with and against Bourdieu', *Feminist Theory,* **1** (1), 11–32.
Lukes, S. 2005. *Power: A Radical View* (2nd ed.). London: Macmillan.
Martin, J.L. 2003. 'What Is Field Theory?', *American Journal of Sociology,* **109** (1), 1–50.
Mayrhofer, W., and Schneidhofer, T.M. 2009. 'The Lay of the Land. European Career Research and Its Future', *Journal of Occupational and Organizational Psychology,* **82** (4), 721–737.
Mayrhofer, W., Steyrer, J., and Meyer, M. 2007. 'Contextual Issues in the Study of Careers', in H.P. Gunz and M. Peiperl (eds.), *Handbook of Career Studies*: pp. 215–240. Los Angeles: SAGE.
Mayrhofer, W., Strunk, G., Schiffinger, M., Iellatchitch, A., Steyrer, J., and Meyer, M. 2002. 'Career Habitus—Theoretical and Empirical Contributions to Make a Black Box Gray', paper presented at Academy of Management Annual Conference, Denver, Colorado, 9–14 August.
McCall, L. 1992. 'Does Gender Fit? Bourdieu, Feminism, and Conceptions of Social Order', *Theory & Society,* **21** (6), 837–867.
McNay, L. 1999. 'Gender, Habitus and the Field: Pierre Bourdieu and the Limits of Reflexivity', *Theory, Culture & Society,* **16** (1), 95–117.
Moore, C., Gunz, H.P., and Hall, D.T. 2007. 'Tracing the Historical Roots of Carer Theory in Management and Organization Studies', in H.P. Gunz and M. Peiperl (eds.), *Handbook of Career Studies*: pp. 13–38. Thousand Oaks: SAGE.
Mutch, A. 2003. 'Communities of Practice and Habitus: A Critique', *Organization Studies,* **24** (3), 383–401.
Nickl, P. 2005. *Ordnung der Gefühle: Studien zum Begriff des Habitus* (2nd ed.). Hamburg: Felix Meiner Verlag.
Ortner, S.B. 2006. *Anthropology and Social Theory: Culture, Power, and the Acting Subject.* Durham: Duke University Press.
Orton, J.D., and Weick, K.E. 1990. 'Loosely Coupled Systems: A Reconceptualisation', *Academy of Management Review,* **15**, 203–223.
Özbilgin, M.F., and Tatli, A. 2005. 'Understanding Bourdieu's Contribution to Organization and Management Studies', *Academy of Management Review,* **30** (4), 855–869.
Parker, P., Khapova, S.N., and Arthur, M.B. 2009. 'The Intelligent Career Framework as a Basis for Interdisciplinary Inquiry', *Journal of Vocational Behavior,* **75** (3), 291–302.
Perrow, C. 1984. *Normal Accidents.* New York: Basic Books.
Pfeffer, J. 2010. *Power: Why Some People Have It—And Others Don't.* New York: Harper Business.
Raghuram, P., Henry, L., and Bornat, J. 2010. 'Difference and Distinction?: Nonmigrant and Migrant Networks', *Sociology,* **44** (4), 623–641.
Ross-Smith, A., and Huppatz, K. 2010. 'Management, Women and Gender Capital', *Gender, Work and Organization,* **17** (5), 547–566.
Savage, M. 1998. 'Constructing the Modern Organization. Discipline, Surveillance and the "Career": Employment on the Great Western Railway 1833–1914', in A. McKinley and K. Starkey (eds.), *Foucault, Management and Organization Theory: From Panopticon to Technologies of the Self*: pp. 65–92. London: SAGE.

Savage, M., Warde, A., and Devine, F. 2005. 'Capitals, Assets, and Resources: Some Critical Issues', *British Journal of Sociology*, 56 (1), 31–47.

Schein, E.H. 1978. *Career Dynamics: Matching Individual and Organizational Needs*. Reading, MA: Addison-Wesley.

Schein, E.H. 2007. 'Afterword: Career Research—Some Issues and Dilemmas', in H.P. Gunz and M.A. Peiperl (eds.), *Handbook of Career Studies*: pp. 573–576. Los Angeles: SAGE.

Schneidhofer, T.M. 2013. 'Bridging (at least?) Sociology and Psychology? A Relational View on Career Boundaries at the Nexus of Structure and Agency', paper presented at 29th EGOS Conference, Montreal, Canada, 4–7 July.

Schneidhofer, T.M., Latzke, M., and Mayrhofer, W. Forthcoming. 'Karrieren von Diversitätsmanager_innen: Im Spannungsfeld sozialer Arenen', *Diversitas: Zeitschrift für Managing Diversity und Diversity Studies*.

Sinclair, S., Hardin, C.D., and Lowery, B.S. 2006. 'Self-Stereotyping in the Context of Multiple Social Identities', *Journal of Personality and Social Psychology*, 90 (4), 529–542.

Sinclair, S., Huntsinger, J., Skorkinko, J., and Hardin, C.D. 2005. 'Social Tuning of the Self: Consequences for the Self-Evaluations of Stereotype Targets', *Journal of Personality and Social Psychology*, 89 (2), 160–175.

Skeggs, B. 2004. 'Context and Background: Pierre Bourdieu's Analysis of Class, Gender and Sexuality', in L. Adkins and B. Skeggs (eds.), *Feminism after Bourdieu*: pp. 19–34. Oxford: Blackwell.

Sturges, J., Simpson, R., and Altman, Y. 2003. 'Capitalising on Learning: An Exploration of the MBA as a Vehicle for Developing Career Competencies', *International Journal of Training and Development*, 7 (1), 53–66.

Suutari, V., and Mäkelä, K. 2007. 'The Career Capital of Managers with Global Careers', *Journal of Managerial Psychology*, 22 (7), 628.

Tams, S., and Arthur, M.B. 2010. 'New Directions for Boundaryless Careers: Agency and Interdependence in a Changing World', *Journal of Organizational Behavior*, 31 (5), 629–646.

Tatli, A. 2010. 'Towards an Integrated Relational Theory of Diversity Management', paper presented at Annual meeting of Academy of Management, Montreal, Canada, 3–10 August.

Tatli, A. 2011. 'A Multi-layered Exploration of the Diversity Management Field: Diversity Discourses, Practices, and Practitioners in the UK', *British Journal of Management*, 22, 238–253.

Wacquant, L. 2013. 'Homines in Extremis: What Fighting Scholars Teach Us about Habitus', *Body & Society*, 20 (2), 3–17.

2 Change and Inertia in (re)Formation and Commodification of Migrant Workers' Subjectivities
An Intersectional Analysis across Spatial and Temporal Dimensions

Barbara Samaluk

INTRODUCTION

This chapter offers a theoretical and methodological toolkit for exploring change and inertia in (re)formation and commodification of migrant workers' subjectivities across spatial and temporal dimensions. The focus on the (re)making of subjectivities can uncover which dimensions intersect and who are legitimate actors in the process of commodification of migrant labour. Research demonstrates that diverse groups of migrants are differently received, assigned particular racialized class positions that consequently determine the types of jobs they end up with (Anderson, 2010; McDowell, 2009; McDowell et al., 2007; Samaluk, 2014b; Wills et al., 2010). This opens up the question of how and why particular groups of migrant workers are defined, commodified, and utilized as such. This research question further opens up theoretical and methodological concerns how we go about exploring these multidimensional and complex structural and agentic mechanisms, economic and cultural practices, and discursive and material elements. To address these concerns this chapter proposes the adoption and operationalization of a Bourdieusian conceptual framework.

Rather than starting with fixed categories, an adopted Bourdieusian conceptual framework explores how and by whom identities are discursively constructed and how they are transformed and performed across spatial and temporal dimensions. Such a framework can on one hand expose changes, various mobilities, and translations of categories, and on the other it can demonstrate that what appears as mobile and changing can sustain deep-seated power relations. By transcending objectivist and subjectivist oppositions and theoretical boundaries, the chapter accounts for agentic and structural mechanisms, discursive and material practices, and cultural and economic elements that generate change or sustain the status quo within and across (trans)national labour markets. The chapter offers a theoretical and methodological framework for conducting a complex intersectional analysis across spatial and temporal dimensions, which goes beyond established categorical approaches and paradigms by focusing on processes of group formation and their effects. As such it brings new insights into already established intersectional and Bourdieusian scholarship exploring class, race, gender relations, and the way these dimensions intersect also with other elements and across spatial and temporal dimensions (Adkins and Skeggs, 2004; Brah and Phoenix, 2004; Haylett, 2001; Healy, 2009; McCall, 2005; McDowell, 2008; Puwar, 2004; Samaluk, 2014a; Tatli and Özbilgin, 2012). Particularly this chapter provides a guideline to researchers empirically exploring transnational cultural political economy and accompanying migration processes. The chapter starts by presenting the need for complex intersectional analysis that can expose commodification of migrant labour across spatial and temporal dimensions; it then argues for the usefulness of an adopted Bourdieusian conceptual framework. The chapter then turns to methodology and elaborates research design and operationalization of adopted theoretical concepts. Finally, the conclusion summarizes the usefulness of this approach and its possible applications.

INTERSECTIONAL COMMODIFICATION OF MIGRANT WORKERS ACROSS SPATIAL AND TEMPORAL DIMENSIONS

Within contemporary capitalism characterized by changed and transnationalized production and consumption patterns guided by price-based competition, the embodied and cultural dispositions of (migrant) workers become increasingly commodified and as such assigned a specific exchange value (Collins, 2006; Greer and Doellgast, 2013; McDowell et al., 2007; Samaluk, 2014a). For instance, cultural and embodied markers of central and eastern European (CEE) migrant workers are being appropriated and assigned a racialized 'price tag' by employment agencies as they market and supply them to the UK labour market (Samaluk, 2014a). Through symbolic inscription, migrant workers get specifically categorized and attached a particular value, social positions, and performative roles. To continue with the foregoing example, CEE migrant workers are in the UK most commonly categorized as 'Eastern Europeans', embodied through their shaded whiteness, constructed through the narratives of hard work and their willingness to labour without complaint, and as such utilized by client employers and consumed by customers for particular types of jobs at the lower ends of the economy (Anderson et al., 2006; MacKenzie and Forde, 2009; McDowell et al., 2007; Samaluk, 2014a, 2014b; Wills et al., 2010). Here one has to take into account that not every foreigner is presented and imagined as a migrant (Anderson, 2009). Those categorized as 'migrants' are most often of lower-class and/or postcolonial origin, while those of upper-class origin are mainly categorized as 'expats' and unlike the former often non-problematized within the receiving societies (Wacquant, 2014).

This indicates that in order to understand the workings of unequal economic geographies we should first understand how and why diverse groups of migrants are differently received, categorized, commodified, and then utilized in line with these symbolic markers. In this regard Wills argues that "making class a political project would demand a focus on identity-making rather than the excavation and mobilization of identities that already exist" (2008, p. 308). This, according to Wacquant (2014), further demands that different scholarly disciplines, which are often exclusionary, work together in order to explain the complexities of rising and interlinked ethnic, racial, and class inequalities (re)produced by the globalized political economy characterized by neoliberalism. Moreover, in transnational labour migration processes race, ethnicity, and class importantly intersect with gender, age, migration status, and other economic, political, and/or cultural elements (McDowell, 2008; Samaluk, 2014a, 2014b). All this indicates that it is necessary to engage with a complex and transdisciplinary intersectional analysis across spatial and temporal dimensions.

Intersectionality was first born out of black feminist struggles that challenged the universal conceptions of the category 'woman' (hooks, 1981). These struggles were recognized when intersectionality experienced academic and political legitimization in the 1990s, the term having been coined by Kimberly Crenshaw (1991). According to Brah and Phoenix, intersectionality means "the complex, irreducible, varied, and variable effects which ensue when multiple axes of differentiation—economic, political, cultural, psychic, subjective and experiential—intersect in historically specific context" (2004, p. 76). This definition is useful because it points to the complexity of contextual and temporal socio-economic, political, and cultural dimensions that influence how multiple axes of differentiation intersect within a specific time and place and the way they affect individuals and groups on the micro-subjective and experiential level.

In order to take into account the foregoing intersectional complexity some scholars call for the transcending of disciplinary boundaries or even for a theoretical promiscuity (Brah and Phoenix, 2004; Healy, 2009; McCall, 2005; McDowell, 2008; Metcalfe and Woodhams, 2012; Samaluk, 2014a; Tatli and Özbilgin, 2012). Similarly I argue that there is a need to maintain complexity that can, on one hand, grasp the power and politics of established categories and, on the other, not lose sight of the ongoing processes that constantly (re)define and (re)produce them. Therefore at the same time as we take into account rapid changes, various mobilities, and translations of categories, we must not forget that "what appears as mobile and changing can *hold its shape*" (Ahmed, 2012, p. 186). Exploring the commodification of migrant labour and its effects thus entails an analysis that is able to grasp how migrants are constructed and perceive this construction differently in different places and times that are part of their migratory trajectory. In this regard McDowell (2008) argues that intersectional analysis should incorporate spatial and temporal dimensions. Such a framework can expose the structural conditions that produce unequal economic geographies and define how migrants are perceived in receiving societies and also how they imagine their prospects there and experience their newly imposed positioning. Although many scholars mentioned in this section offer methods for how to approach complex intersectional analysis, there are still many unanswered questions about how such a complex intersectional analysis can be achieved conceptually, methodologically, and empirically. The fundamental question is thus how we should study intersectional complexity and what exactly it is that we should be studying at an intersectional analysis of transnational labour migration. Rather than focusing on one or the other categorical approach that has caused lots of confusion within intersectional analysis, as is well presented by McCall (2005) and McDowell (2008), I argue that an intersectional analysis should transcend the binary oppositions of structuralist and post-structuralist knowledge production by focusing on the processes of group formation and their effects. This chapter aims to provide a theoretical and methodological approach for such an intersectional analysis by adopting and operationalizing a Bourdieusian conceptual framework.

SYMBOLIC POWER AND GROUP FORMATION

Rather than starting with fixed categories, a Bourdieusian framework provides theoretical and methodological tools for uncovering social class formation and its effects. The Bourdieusian conception of social class is inherently relational in a sense that it overcomes both objectivist and subjectivist stances. It does that by locating social agents within objective positions they are assigned within a social space and by taking into account their individual perception, appreciation, or rejection of these objective positions as they struggle and compete for resources:

> What exists is not 'social classes' as understood in the realist, substantialist and empiricist mode of thinking adopted by both opponents and proponents of the existence of class, but rather a social space ... a multi-dimensional space that can be constructed empirically ... by discovering the powers or forms of capital which are or can become efficient ... in the struggle (or competition) for the appropriation of scarce goods of which this universe is the site.
>
> (Bourdieu, 1987, p. 3)

Rather than presupposing class identity and action, Bourdieu is concerned with how social class is constructed, how it comes to be through relational, spatial, and temporal dimensions. This conception of social class importantly sets Bourdieu apart from both Marxist and Weberian approaches to class (Wacquant, 2013). Instead of *"imposing a vision of division"*, a Bourdieusian framework allows us to uncover how divisions are constructed through symbolic power and what its effects are (Bourdieu, 1989, p. 19). This has important cultural, economic, and political implications, because it can expose the cultural construction of class and its economic and political effects. It allows the exploration of how workplace identities are being formed within a broader socio-economic and historical context, which can explain why diverse groups of (migrant) workers occupy diverse social positions within labour markets and organizations in a particular place and time. By moving beyond workplaces to explore class formation, a Bourdieusian framework can uncover symbolic power—for example, the power to make groups or the power that *"aims at imposing the vision of legitimate division"* (Bourdieu, 1989, p. 22). In other words, he recognizes the importance of knowledge and linguistic production in group making. According to Bourdieu, groups begin to exist only through knowledge and recognition:

> A group, a class, a gender, a region, or a nation begins to exist as such, for those who belong to it as well as for the others, only when it is distinguished, according to one principle or another, from other groups, that is, through knowledge and recognition.
> (Bourdieu, 1989, p. 23)

He argues that social space functions as symbolic space that is organized according to the logic of difference and acts "as distinctive signs and as signs of distinction" (Bourdieu, 1989, p. 20). Bourdieu thus realizes the importance of signs and their meanings—for example, of semiosis in group making. This realization comes as a critique of Saussurean approaches to semiosis that tend to focus only on the internal constitution of text and ignore the socio-historical conditions of its production and reception (Thompson, cf. Bourdieu, 1991, p. 4). Taking into account power dynamics in the language exchange, which is hidden in the history of group making, a Bourdieusian framework also enables the uncovering of the postcolonial condition (Loyal, 2009; Puwar, 2004, 2009; Samaluk, 2014b). Or as Bourdieu puts it, in order to

> escape the effects of the labour of *naturalization* which every group tends to produce in order to legitimize itself and fully justify its existence, one must reconstruct the *historical labour* which has produced social divisions and the social vision of these divisions.
> (Bourdieu, 1991, p. 248)

In other words, he argues that groups are products of historical knowledge production and are constantly being transformed by ongoing and emerging history.

Exposing the commodification of migrant workers' subjectivities and its effects demands engagement with postcolonial history that characterizes migrants' places of origins and their destination countries. Locating the exploration of intersectional commodification of migrant labour within (post)colonial history uncovers inertness not only of former colonial power relations but also of ongoing and emerging colonial processes, which includes places that are often not researched and thought of as such (Samaluk, 2014a, 2014b). The focus on the ongoing history of group making enables us to see that the symbolic power to make groups further rests on the condition that those who are imposing a specific vision need to be recognized as legitimate actors. In this regard, Bourdieu argues that "a 'class', be it social, sexual, ethnic, or otherwise, exists when there are agents capable of imposing themselves, as authorized to speak and to act officially in its place and in its name" (Bourdieu, 1987, p. 15). Agents thus need to be recognized and granted symbolic power to make groups.

For instance, ongoing colonial processes are in Europe maintained by the soft power of Western ideologies and paradigms that rarely recognize knowledge production coming from its post-socialist East or explore this region and its subjectivities on their own terms (Böröcz, 2001; Inotai, 2002; Kideckel, 1996; Kürti, 2008; Samaluk, 2014a, 2014b; Slovova, 2006). Due to this dominant knowledge production CEE workers are assigned a specific class position, which entails a cultural inferiority that is visible not only in discourses but also in material racist practices directed towards this group of workers (Anderson, 2000; Currie, 2007; Downey, 2008; Samaluk, 2014b; Stevenson, 2007; Wills et al., 2010). Linguistic exchange, which has the power to create groups and inscribe value to them, is thus also an economic exchange that acts as a "*sign of authority*", which legitimizes unequal economy and makes it possible (Bourdieu, 1991, p. 66; Skeggs, 2004). This indicates that discourse plays an important part in social reality; therefore, a historical exploration of group formation can greatly benefit by incorporating both discursive and material elements into the analysis. This is crucial not only for critical exploration of how a particular *vision of division* came to be, but also to understand how it affects migrants and how migrants themselves reinvest in symbolic struggles.

Workplace identities are often multiple and contradictory and encompass compliance as well as resistance (McDowell et al., 2007). It is thus necessary to take into account the fact that workers' symbolic strategies can consist of "the manipulation of the most reliable symbols of social position, those which sociologists are fond of using as indicators, such as occupation and social origin" (Bourdieu, 1987, p. 12). This last instance is very important because it points to how workers themselves can strategically use these symbols in order to engage within the symbolic struggles of the field. A Bourdieusian framework is thus able to transcend the problematic division between structural and agentic position, economic and cultural practices, and discursive and material elements. Nevertheless, there are still many unanswered questions as to how this complex analysis can be achieved conceptually and methodologically. In the following section, I present how a Bourdieusian general theory of field, habitus, and capitals can be adopted and operationalized in order to explore intersectional commodification of migrant workers and its effects across spatial and temporal dimensions.

METHODOLOGICAL APPROACH TO A COMPLEX INTERSECTIONAL ANALYSIS ACROSS SPATIAL AND TEMPORAL DIMENSIONS

The methodology for a complex intersectional analysis across spatial and temporal dimensions has been devised by adopting and operationalizing a Bourdieusian conceptual framework in accordance with ontological, epistemological, and methodological approaches from critical realist and feminist scholars that have emphasized the importance of semiosis and of complex intersectional analysis that goes beyond structure and agency divide (Adkins and Skeggs, 2004; Chouliaraki and Fairclough, 1999; Healy, 2009; Jessop, 2004; Joseph and Roberts, 2004; Layder, 1997; Lovell, 2007; McCall, 1992; Sayer, 2000; Skeggs, 2004). This methodology thus offers an explanatory critique that focuses on the symbolic power of group making and enables the analysis of causation in a non-positivistic way. Since critical realism is inclined towards methodological pluralism, it is compatible with a relatively wide range of research methods. However, a common aspect of critical realist research is that the priority is given to theoretical abstractions and conceptions which are used to define the object of the study. In this regard the adopted Bourdieusian conceptual trinity of field, habitus, and different forms of capital represents the orienting concepts that define the object of the study and are used to develop methodology (Layder, 1998; Sayer, 2000). To further provide a clear research design, I also utilize Layder's (1993) research map, which explicitly separates out macro, meso, and micro levels of research for pragmatic analytical purposes (see Table 2.1). This is explored ahead through the operationalization and adoption of Bourdieusian theoretical concepts.

Table 2.1 Research Map (adapted from Bourdieu, 2005; Bourdieu and Wacquant, 1992; Fairclough, 2003; and Layder, 1993)

Research Element	Research Focus and Objectives	Field and Genres/Texts
Setting (Nation state)	Focus: Governance Research objective: To examine how a particular (migrant) group is objectified and homogenized with the receiving nation state	Field: Receiving meta-field Genre: National and government statistics and official reports on particular migrant group accompanied by literature review
Context (Relationship among [trans]national fields)	Focus: (Meta)governance Research objective: To challenge methodological nationalism and examine the construction of a particular migrant group within wider historical and socio-economic context	Field: (Global) economic field, political and media field Genres: Political reports, policy and other documents, public statements, and newspaper articles accompanied by literature review

(Continued)

Table 2.1 (Continued)

Research Element	Research Focus and Objectives	Field and Genres/Texts
Situated activity (activity of actor(s) within [global] economic field)	**Focus:** Utilization of (meta) governance by important actor(s) for specific economic purposes **Research objective:** To examine how a particular migrant group has been discursively commodified within a particular setting	**Field:** (Global) economic field **Genre:** Depending on the choice of actor(s) operating within transnationalized labour relations
Self (migrant workers)	**Focus:** Experiences, perceptions, and strategies of migrant workers **Research objective:** To explore how previously explored (meta)governance and commodification affect a particular group of migrant workers	**Field:** (Global) economic field and sending and receiving meta-field **Texts:** Emerging from any qualitative method used to gather data from migrant workers

DISCURSIVE GROUP FORMATION ACROSS TRANSNATIONAL FIELDS

In order to achieve conceptual and methodological clarity for exploring intersectional commodification in discursive practices and its material effects across spatial and temporal dimensions, a Bourdieusian conceptual framework can be integrated with critical discourse analysis (Chouliaraki and Fairclough, 1999; Samaluk, 2014a). This integration offers a very useful conceptualization for uncovering the order of discourse that represents a semiotic form of (meta)governance that constitutes individual fields and relationships among them (Fairclough, 2005, 2009). For Bourdieu to think in terms of fields, it is to think relationally, and the concept of the field is "designed to be put to work empirically in systemic fashion" (Bourdieu and Wacquant, 1992, p. 96). Bourdieu often explains the concept of the field through the metaphor of a game that consists of rules, stakes, and various actors who compete in this game through acquisition and appropriation of legitimized forms of capital that determine their value in the game (Bourdieu and Wacquant, 1992). In order to explore intersectional commodification of migrant workers across spatial and temporal dimensions, it is important to first identify the fields that determine the game.

Bourdieu has recognized through his empirical work that the state represents a sort of meta-field, which is particularly important in the context of migration. Nation states not only produce specific migration policies and differentiate nationals from non-nationals, but also have the monopoly over legitimate physical and symbolic violence (Bourdieu and Wacquant, 1992). Through its order of discourse the state produces official classifications that perform diagnostics of individuals and groups and assign them specific identities, determine their rights and obligations, and monitor their actions through normative and seemingly 'universal' state taxonomies (Bourdieu, 1990b, p. 136). These three functions of the state thus impose a right, correct, and dominant vision that legitimizes social divisions and inequalities that become a living reality for individuals and groups.

Using this perspective the macro level of research should first start with the setting to critically assess the state taxonomies in order to explore how particular groups of migrants are constructed within their frame (see Table 2.1). Although Layder (1993) advocates that research should start with the context and be followed by the setting, the exploration of class formation demands that this is inverted. Rather than taking the 'naturalized' categories and discourses that define migrant groups within state taxonomies for granted, these should be challenged and thus become the initial object of analysis. Challenging "methodological nationalism" (Wimmer and Schiller, 2002, p. 304) that takes national discourses, agendas, and histories for granted represents the necessary first step in uncovering the making of a particular group. This enables critical evaluation and the questioning of the frame that constructs specific migrant groups and produces their value (Bourdieu, 1990a, 1998; Loyal, 2009; Sayad, 2004; Skeggs, 2004). A good place to start such an exploration is by questioning the indicators used and data presented in migration statistics' reports and governmental policies. The most problematized migrant groups are usually especially well monitored, often statistically separated from other groups and under consideration in group-specific reports. In case of CEE country nationals in the UK, these were, for instance, accession monitoring reports (Home Office 2009). By doing that one can expose the problematic knowledge production that objectifies migrant workers' subjectivities within its narrow frame of reference and helps identify research questions and objectives that challenge methodological nationalism. As Sayad argues, "any study of migratory phenomena that overlooks the emigrant's conditions of origin is bound only to give a view that is at once *partial* and *ethnocentric*" (2004, p. 29). Reflexive sociology of migration thus takes seriously historical and socio-economic realities of both the sending and receiving nation states and other fields that influence them.

Although nation states are crucial in exploring migratory processes, it is also important to take into account that the state not only influences but also is itself influenced by other fields as well as the global economic field (Bourdieu, 1998, 2005; Jessop and Oosterlynck, 2008). The global economic field is characterized by (meta)governance that encompass a whole set of political and legal measures that impose the rule of free exchange on the global market. This is particularly visible in the EU, whose (meta)governance is based upon the freedom of movement, which in practice implies the free movement of capital, goods, and services, while the free movement of labour has been restricted by transitional measures for persons from the new member states and those outside EU/EEA countries (Samaluk, 2014b). With growing penalization of the global poor, visible in expanding policing of national borders and the 'war on crime', the powerful actors assert their authority through "bureaucratic theatre geared to staging the 'sovereignty' of the state at the very moment when this sovereignty is being breached by the unbridled mobility of capital and by juridical-economic integration into supranational political ensembles" (Wacquant, 2014, p. 1701). Migration being the actual cause of other types of mobilities should thus be explored across "transnational social fields" (Levitt and Schiller, 2004, p. 1003) that are characterized by (meta)governance, which affects and assigns value to particular regions and groups arising from them and fuels migration.

After exposing the problematic national setting, the exploration of formation of particular migrant groups should turn to historical and socioeconomic contexts across spatial and temporal dimensions to discover how this setting came to be (see Table 2.1). In order to do that one must establish who legitimate actors are and what kinds of networks are formed across transnational fields. The macro context thus needs to be situated within the global economic field that is characterized by the (meta)governance that forms part of wider global political economy and is influenced by various actors. In the case of Europe, (meta)governance is apart from the EU itself, imposed to a large degree by multinational corporations, the most powerful states, and international institutions, such as the World Bank, International Monetary Fund, and World Trade Organization, which those states control (Bourdieu, 2005, p. 230). As such these international institutions along with other actors operating across transnational fields, such as employment agencies and various experts, journalists, and lobbyists, also have the authority to act as intermediaries, whose role is also "the *translation and evaluation* of other cultures" (Skeggs, 2004, p. 148). For instance, labour migration from post-socialist CEE to the West and CEE workers' position in the West were greatly affected by transition and Europeanization processes imposed through (meta)governance directed by these international actors and domestic elites (Samaluk, 2014b; Stenning et al., 2010).

(Meta)governance is semiotically formed through the order of discourse and is actualized through networks of genres within and among diverse fields that act as 'filtering devices', selectively including or excluding discourses that figure in the ways of representing the material world (Fairclough, 2005, p. 65). Genres can be understood as ways of acting or (inter)acting discursively and can be a particularly useful analytical category for exploring the regimes of (meta)governance (Fairclough, 2005). Genres can come in the form of reports, policies, newspaper articles, websites, and so forth. In other words, different fields are characterized by different governing genres. The examples of governing genres in relation to CEE countries could be European Commission Progress reports towards accession that served as colonial monitoring and assessment mechanisms that legitimized EU policies with regard to accession countries and their nationals. These reports provided a necessary foreground for political and legal measures that enabled seemingly free yet unequal exchange between newly joining and old member states of the enlarged EU. For instance, pre-accession debates resulted in the Nice Treaty, which allowed old member states to postpone the opening of their labour markets to workers from these countries and finally resulted in four different regimes being put in place in the 15 EU member states (Bohle, 2006; Samaluk, 2014b; Tutti, 2010).

Policies on the EU level thus directly impact governmental policies and strategies within specific member states. For operationalization purposes researchers thus need to explore the network of governing genres among the global economic field and the meta-field that together produce a specific order of discourse on particular regions, countries, and workers arising from them. These in turn both significantly influence and are influenced by the economic and media fields that importantly co-determine the (re)formation of migrant workers' subjectivities within a particular national context. Through a network of genres that forms the relationship across transnational fields, one can identify key texts for analysis, which can uncover the structural order of discourse that assigns particular racialized class positions to a specific migrant group. As Fairclough argues, "texts semiotically construe identities and simultaneously seek to make these construals persuasive" (2009, p. 180). For instance, discourses found in EU reports form a genre network with particular national government reports, policy papers, press releases, and political campaigns. Moreover, these discourses resonate in newspaper articles in the popular press and the documents, statements, and press releases of employers' organizations. The selection of specific texts for analysis thus needs to be well defined according to specific research questions and might due to research constraints be limited to key political, economic, and social change within a particular context, setting, and situated activity arising from them. Moreover, changes in (meta)governance also bring changes in the set of genres that govern (Skeggs, 2004). For instance, websites of various organizations or service providers, such as employment agencies (Samaluk, 2014b), can nowadays act as important governing genres.

After exposing the macro context and setting, the focus of research on the meso level should turn upon the situated activity. As elaborated in the examples provided, one can explore the situated activity of transnational employment agencies that are important actors on the global economic field and thus have the power to create a specific value of migrant workers, who are marketed and supplied to the West (Samaluk, 2014b). Situated activity can also be explored, for example, within a specific sector or an organizational context, depending, of course, on specific research questions. The provided research design on the macro and meso levels thus envisages analysis of the structural order of discourse that assigns migrant workers a specific value, affects the way they are treated, and also informs workers' choices and strategies. This is explored further ahead.

THE STYLE OF WORKER—ASSIGNED AND PERFORMED HABITUS

The order of discourse also participates in the invention of specific class habitus by producing a certain style through the conversion of capitals. The concept of habitus functions as a bridge between structure and agency and is "both a system of schemes of production of practices and a system of perception and appreciation of practices . . . habitus implies a 'sense of one's place' but also a 'sense of place of others'" (Bourdieu, 1989, p. 19). Style, on the other hand, represents an aspect of the order of discourse that functions "as socially constructed identity, as a marker of identification and behavioural guideline" (Samaluk, 2014b, p. 158). Also Bourdieu (1990b) argues that discourse contains an 'objective intention' that offers a stimuli to a modus operandi of which it is the product. By appropriating and combining Bourdieu's (1990b) and Fairclough's (2003) concepts, I argue that *style should on the one hand be perceived as discursively objectified and racialized class habitus*. Since the style names the character and the profile, it discursively brands the class habitus, which is determined by the translation, appropriation, and accumulation of different forms of capital (Bourdieu, 1990b; Fairclough, 2003). A Bourdieusian concept of different forms of capital offers an emic approach to intersectionality and thus also an alternative approach to both the ethnicity and the black-and-white paradigm that can expose how different cultural and embodied markers and their intersections get appropriated across spatial and temporal dimensions in order to assign migrant workers a specific class habitus (Samaluk, 2014b; Tatli and Özbilgin, 2012).

Nevertheless, this construction is not simply imposed but rather objectified also through performative practices of individuals. *Style should thus on the other hand be perceived also as an individual habitus, as a distinctive way in which individuals assume social roles and perform, transform, or resist objectified social identities.* Although each individual performs his or her personal style, this style is always in part influenced by a common style or discursively objectified class habitus. This is not to say that habitus is a mechanical reaction to the field's structural conditions, but it is rather "an 'intelligent' response to an actively selected aspect of the real" that links individuals' past trajectory with the current forces of the field (Bourdieu, 2005, p. 212). In other words, discourse constructs a specific social identity and value that shape the way people are perceived by others and themselves and therefore the way they perform and transform their identities in order to create value for themselves. The micro level of research should thus focus on the 'self' (Layder, 1993), the experiences, perceptions, and strategies of migrant workers across spatial and temporal dimensions (see Table 2.1).

The concept of habitus allows us to comprehend that migrants inhabit social orders of the places that are part of their migratory trajectory, which influence the filtering of new experiences and also their (self)positioning within the new field and in relation to others. As Bourdieu argues, "habitus changes constantly in response to new experience. Dispositions are subject to a kind of permanent revision, but one which is never radical, because it works on the basis of the premises established in the previous state" (2000, p. 161). Habitus can thus seem perfectly adjusted to the field, or there may be tensions between the field and the habitus, depending on the accumulation of capitals that give the proper 'feel for the game'. This is very well explained by the Bourdieusian metaphor of a fish in a tank. "When habitus encounters a social world of which it is the product, it is like a 'fish in water': it does not feel the weight of the water and it takes the world about itself for granted" (Bourdieu and Wacquant, 1992, p. 127).

Since workers' identities are culturally defined, migrant workers often have difficulty in reading newly assigned performative roles (McDowell, 2009, p. 54). This makes newly arrived migrant workers particularly vulnerable for exploitation. As migrant workers can 'feel like a fish in the water' within their places of origin, they might not feel that way when they start swimming the waters within a new country. Within these new waters they are assigned a new social position, new class habitus which they can read only through their embodied history, which might uncomfortably clash with the newly assigned history they encounter in a new place. Bourdieu argues that habitus functions as an "embodied history, internalized as a second nature that is conveniently forgotten as history" (Bourdieu, 1990b, p. 56). Migrants thus carry with them a certain history that is often simply forgotten or rewritten in the receiving society. This forgotten history, which is unfortunately also too often forgotten in research, among other things disables the uncovering of various internal divisions among simplistically homogenized groups.

For instance, central and eastern European (CEE) migrant workers are from a Western perspective most commonly constructed as the same, despite the fact that they embody different histories and localized orientalizing and racist practices which define how diverse CEE workers position to one another and other groups within a new context (Bakić-Hayden, 1995; Buchowski, 2006; Kuus, 2004; Samaluk, 2014b). Nevertheless, habitus also changes with new experience and in accordance with racialized practices that migrant workers encounter within a new context, which can hybridize their (self)identities (Bhabha, 1995) and inform their performative strategies. For instance, Perrons et al.'s (2010) research on male migrant domestic services in the UK shows that, due to popular stereotypes, public discourse, and the branding of Polish handymen as high-quality, other CEE workers often use the Polish label to market their services.

The concept of habitus thus enables us to critically explore agency. This also means that agency need not necessarily result in effective change but can also reinforce dominant and emerging power structures (Lovell, 2003; Puwar, 2004). For instance, research on CEE migrant workers also exposes transnational working of whiteness that demonstrates how whiteness travels with CEE migrants as an embodied history of European colonialism grounded in Enlightenment ideas of nationalism and racism (Samaluk, 2014b). Due to that, also Roma migrants to the UK often have very different reasons for migration than other CEE groups, related to high levels of racial discrimination in their places of origin (Cook et al., 2010; Poole, 2010). As CEE migrant workers appropriate their cultural capital to claim their superior Europeaness and whiteness, so do the established black minority ethnic groups by using their national cultural capital to claim their deservingness in the rat race for scarce resources (Samaluk, 2014b). All in all, the concept of habitus and its discursive styles enable us to uncover how, on the one hand, power structures travel with migrants as an inert embodied history. On the other hand, it can be used to explain how power structures reshape through cultural-economic practices across transnational fields and ultimately how both inform the (self)positioning of diverse groups within a particular field.

CONCLUSION

By adopting and operationalizing a Bourdieusian conceptual framework this chapter offers a theoretical and methodological toolkit for a complex intersectional analysis, uncovering change and inertia in (re)formation and commodification of migrant workers' subjectivities across spatial and temporal dimensions. Although this framework can be utilized and tailored for any intersectional analysis exploring group formation and its effects across spatial and temporal dimensions, it can be particularly useful for empirical exploration of the transnational cultural political economy and accompanying migration processes. As argued within the chapter the usefulness of a Bourdieusian framework lies in his conception of social class as a multidimensional social space that is inherently relational, encompassing cultural, economic, and political elements and able to overcome both objectivist and subjectivist stances. This enables critical exploration of both structural and agentic mechanisms and symbolic and material practices that operate in the racialized class formation across spatial and temporal dimensions.

Through transdisciplinary adoption and operationalization of Bourdieusian concepts this chapter offers clear theoretical and methodological tools for an intersectional analysis across spatial and temporal dimensions, which goes beyond established categorical approaches (McCall, 2005; McDowell, 2008) by focusing on processes of group formation and their effects. It demonstrates that a transdisciplinary adoption of a Bourdieusian framework contributes by offering a very useful conceptualization and operationalization for uncovering a discursive form of (meta)governance that constitutes (trans)national fields and assigns value to particular regions and groups of workers arising from them. It offers an exploration of the formation of a particular style of (migrant) worker that should be perceived, on the one hand, as discursively objectified and racialized class habitus and, on the other, as an individual habitus, visible in the way in which individuals assume social roles and perform, transform, or resist objectified social identities. On one hand this enables us to expose the objectified position assigned to a particular group of migrant workers, and on the other it can uncover how this objective position is performed, transformed, and resisted by individuals or groups as they struggle and compete for resources or capitals. This enables us to critically explore workers agency and hybridity and how workers themselves reproduce, change, or maintain unequal power structures.

Moreover, a Bourdieusian focus on class/group formation allows the centring of analysis upon the knowledge production that is hidden in the history of group making. This enables the uncovering of postcolonial conditions and ongoing colonial processes that maintain old and make new colonial subjects. Empirical research done in this way can explain why some colonial power structures stay inert and alive although the imperial world has seemingly long perished. By not presupposing a given class/group position, it is further able to uncover constant shifts within a global cultural political economy that is characterized by ongoing and emerging colonial processes that importantly define specific regions and countries, enforce new migration patterns, and re-valuate migrants' subjectivities within historical yet also constantly shifting racialized class logic. As such it can expose persistent and inert power structures, as well as uncover changes that shape with new and emerging colonial struggles among diverse actors and groups and also within places that are often not researched and thought of as such. Methodologically this framework contributes by challenging methodological nationalism and by refusing to take established class, ethnic, or racial paradigms for granted. As such it offers a novel approach to a complex intersectional analysis that can uncover multiple and misrecognized power relations associated with embodied, cultural, and other markers, spatial and temporal dimensions, and varying modalities of knowledge. This approach thus also opens possibilities for alternative knowledge production and counter mapping of established scholarly paradigms and their research areas. As such it also carries a political potential for exposing an often taken-for-granted symbolic economy that drives capital accumulation and exchange within inert yet constantly shifting (post)colonial workings of contemporary capitalism.

REFERENCES

Adkins, L., and Skeggs, B. (2004) *Feminism after Bourdieu*. Oxford: Blackwell/Sociological Review.

Ahmed, S. (2012) *On being included: Racism and diversity in institutional life*. Durham: Duke University Press.

Anderson, B. (2000) *Doing the dirty work? The global politics of domestic labour*. London: Zed Books.

Anderson, B. (2009) Recession and demand for (migrant) labour. Paper presented at the conference *The impact of migrant workers on the functioning of labour markets and industrial relations*. Keele University, Keele, United Kingdom, 11 November.

Anderson, B. (2010) Migration, immigration controls and the fashioning of precarious workers. *Work, Employment & Society*. 24 (2). pp. 300–317.
Anderson, B., et al. (2006) *Fair enough? Central and East European migrants in low wage employment in the UK*. Oxford: COMPAS.
Bakić-Hayden, M. (1995) Nesting orientalism: The case of former Yugoslavia. *Slavic Review*. 54 (4). pp. 917–931.
Bhabha, H. (1995) Cultural diversity and cultural difference. In Ashcroft, B., Griffiths, G., and Tiffin, H. (eds.), *The post-colonial studies reader*. New York: Routledge.
Bohle, D. (2006) Neoliberal hegemony, transnational capital and the terms of the EU's eastward expansion. *Capital & Class*. 30 (Spring). pp. 57–86.
Böröcz, J. (2001) Introduction: Empire and coloniality in the 'eastern enlargement' of the European Union. In Böröcz, J., and Kovasc, M. (eds.), *Empire's new clothes: Unveiling EU enlargement*. Telford: Central Europe Review.
Bourdieu, P. (1987) What makes a social class? On the theoretical and practical existence of groups. *Berkeley Journal of Sociology*. 32 (1). pp. 1–17.
Bourdieu, P. (1989) Social space and symbolic power. *Sociological Theory*. 7 (1). pp. 14–25.
Bourdieu, P. (1990a) *In other words*. Stanford, CA: Stanford University Press.
Bourdieu, P. (1990b) *The logic of practice*. Cambridge: Polity.
Bourdieu, P. (1991) *Language and symbolic power*. Cambridge: Polity Press.
Bourdieu, P. (1998) *Practical reason—On the theory of action*. Cambridge: Polity Press.
Bourdieu, P. (2000) *Pascalian meditations*. Cambridge: Polity Press.
Bourdieu, P. (2005) *The social structures of the economy*. Cambridge: Polity Press.
Bourdieu, P., and Wacquant, L. (1992) *An invitation to reflexive sociology*. Cambridge: Polity Press.
Brah, A., and Phoenix, A. (2004) Ain't I a woman? Revisiting intersectionality. *Journal of International Women's Studies*. 5 (3). pp. 75–86.
Buchowski, M. (2006) The specter of orientalism in Europe: From exotic other to stigmatized brother. *Anthropological Quarterly*. 79 (3). pp. 463–482.
Chouliaraki, L., and Fairclough, N. (1999) *Discourse in late modernity: Rethinking critical discourse analysis*. Edinburgh: Edinburgh University Press.
Collins, P. H. (2006) New commodities, new consumers—Selling blackness in a global marketplace. *Ethnicities*. 6 (3). pp. 297–317.
Cook, J., et al. (2010) The experiences of Accession 8 migrants in England: Motivations, work and agency. *International Migration*. 49 (2). pp. 54–79.
Crenshaw, K. (1991) Mapping the margins: Intersectionality, identity politics, and violence against women of color. *Stanford Law Review*. 43 (6). pp. 1241–1299.
Currie, S. (2007) De-skilled and devalued: The labour market experience of Polish migrants in the UK following EU enlargement. *International Journal of Comparative Labour Law and Industrial Relations*. 23 (1). pp. 83–116.
Downey, L. (2008) *Racialization of central and east European migrants in Herefordshire*. Exeter: Exeter University.
Fairclough, N. (2003) *Analyzing discourse: Textual analysis for social research*. London: Routledge.
Fairclough, N. (2005) Critical discourse analysis in transdisciplinary research. In Wodak, R., and Chilton, P. (eds.), *A new agenda in (critical) discourse analysis: Theory, methodology and interdisciplinarity*. Philadelphia: John Benjamins.
Fairclough, N. (2009) A dialectical-relational approach to critical discourse Analysis in social research. In Wodak, R., and Meyer Wodak, M. (eds.), *Methods of critical discourse analysis*. London: SAGE.
Greer, I., and Doellgast, V. (2013) Marketization, inequality and institutional change (working paper). Available from: http://gala.gre.ac.uk/10294/1/WERU5_Greer_Doellgast_working_paper.PDF [Accessed: 14 March 2014].

Haylett, C. (2001) Illegitimate subjects?: Abject whites, neoliberal modernisation, and middle-class multiculturalism. *Environment and Planning D: Society and Space.* 19 (3). pp. 351–370.
Healy, G. (2009) Reflections on researching inequalities and intersectionality. In Özbilgin, M. (ed.), *Equality, diversity and inclusion at work: A research companion.* Cheltenham: Edward Elgar.
Home Office. (2009) *Accession monitoring report (May 2004—March 2009).* London: Home Office/UK Border Agency.
hooks, b. (1981) *Ain't I a woman: Black women and feminism.* Boston: South End Press.
Inotai, A. (2002) Special challenges and tasks of 'eastern' enlargement. *Intereconomics.* 37 (4). pp. 180–183.
Jessop, B. (2004) Critical semiotic analysis and cultural political economy. *Critical Discourse Studies.* 1 (1). pp. 1–16.
Jessop, B. and Oosterlynck, S. (2008) Cultural Political Economy: on Making the Cultural Turn without Falling into Soft Economic Sociology. *Geoforum.* May (3). pp. 1155–1169.
Joseph, J., and Roberts, J. M. (2004) Introduction: Realism, discourse and deconstruction. In Joseph, J., and Roberts, J. M. (eds.), *Realism, discourse, and deconstruction.* London: Routledge.
Kideckel, D. A. (1996) What's in a name: The persistence of East Europe as conceptual category. *Replika.* Special Issue: *Colonization or Partnership. Eastern Europe and Western Social Sciences.* 21 (1). pp. 16–37.
Kürti, L. (2008) East and West: The scholarly divide in anthropology. *Anthropological Notebooks.* 14 (3). pp. 25–38.
Kuus, M. (2004) Europe's eastern expansion and the reinscription of otherness in East-Central Europe. *Progress in Human Geography.* 28 (4). pp. 472–489.
Layder, D. (1993) *New strategies in social research: An introduction and guide.* Cambridge: Polity.
Layder, D. (1997) *Modern social theory: Key debates and new directions.* London: UCL Press.
Layder, D. (1998) *Sociological practice: Linking theory and social research.* London: SAGE.
Levitt, P., and Schiller, N. G. (2004) Conceptualizing simultaneity: A transnational social field perspective on society. *International Migration Review.* 38 (3). pp. 1002–1039.
Lovell, T. (2003) Resisting with authority: Historical specificity, agency and the performative self. *Theory, Culture and Society.* 20 (1). pp. 1–17.
Lovell, T. (2007) Introduction. In Lovell, T. (eds.), *(Mis)recognition, social inequality and social justice: Nancy Fraser and Pierre Bourdieu.* London: Routledge.
Loyal, S. (2009) The French in Algeria, Algerians in French: Bourdieu, colonialism and migration. *Sociological Review.* 57 (3). pp. 406–427.
MacKenzie, R., and Forde, C. (2009) The rhetoric of the 'good worker' versus the realities of employers' use and the experiences of migrant workers. *Work, Employment and Society.* 23 (1). pp. 142–159.
McCall, L. (1992) Does gender fit? Bourdieu, feminism, and conceptions of social order. *Theory and Society.* 21 (6). pp. 837–867.
McCall, L. (2005) The complexity of intersectionality. *Signs: Journal of Women in Culture and Society.* 30 (3). pp. 1771–1800.
McDowell, L. (2008) Thinking through work: Complex inequalities, constructions of difference and trans-national migrants. *Progress in Human Geography.* 32 (4). 491–507.
McDowell, L. (2009) *Working bodies: Interactive service employment and workplace identities.* Oxford: Wiley-Blackwell.

McDowell, L., Batnitzky, A., and Dyer, S. (2007) Division, segmentation, and interpellation: The embodied labors of migrant workers in a greater London hotel. *Economic Geography*. 1 (25). pp. 1–25.

Metcalfe, B. D., and Woodhams, C. (2012) Introduction: New directions in gender, diversity and organization theorizing: Re-imagining feminist post-colonialism, transnationalism and geographies of power. *International Journal of Management Reviews*. 14 (2). pp. 123–140.

Perrons, D., Plomien, A., and Kilkey, M. (2010) Migration and uneven development within an enlarged European Union: Fathering, gender divisions and male migrant domestic services. *European Urban and Regional Studies*. 17 (2). pp. 197–215.

Poole, L. (2010) National action plans for social inclusion and A8 migrants: The case of the Roma in Scotland. *Critical Social Policy*. 30 (2). pp. 245–265.

Puwar, N. (2004) *Space invaders: Race, gender and bodies out of place*. Oxford: Berg.

Puwar, N. (2009) Sensing a post-colonial Bourdieu: An introduction. *Sociological Review*. 57 (3). pp. 371–384.

Samaluk, B. (2014a) Racialised 'price-tag': Commodification of migrant workers on transnational employment agencies' websites. In Pajnik, M. and Anthias, F. (eds.), *Work and the challenges of belonging: Migrants in globalizing economies*. Newcastle upon Tyne: Cambridge Scholars.

Samaluk, B. (2014b) Whiteness, ethnic privilege and migration: A Bourdieusian framework. *Journal of Managerial Psychology*. 29 (4). pp. 370–388.

Sayad, A. (2004) *The suffering of the immigrant*. Cambridge: Polity Press.

Sayer, R. A. (2000) *Realism and social science*. London: SAGE.

Skeggs, B. (2004) *Class, self, culture*. London: Routledge.

Slovova, K. (2006) Looking at western feminisms through the double lens of Eastern Europe and the Third World. In Lukić, J., Regulska, J., and Zaviršek, D. (eds.), *Women and citizenship in Central and Eastern Europe*. Aldershot: Ashgate.

Stenning, A., et al. (2010) *Domesticating neo-liberalism: Spaces of economic practice and social reproduction in post-socialist cities*. Oxford: Wiley-Blackwell.

Stevenson, B. (2007) *A8 nationals in Glasgow*. Glasgow: City Council.

Tatli, A., and Özbilgin, M. F. (2012) An emic approach to intersectional study of diversity at work: A Bourdieuan framing. *International Journal of Management Reviews*. 14 (2). pp. 180–200.

Tutti, P. (2010) Narratives of origins and the emergence of the European Union. In Lessard, H., Johnson, R., and Webber, J. (eds.), *Storied communities: Narratives of contact and arrival in constituting political community*. Vancouver: UBC Press.

Wacquant, L. (2013) Symbolic power and group-making: On Pierre Bourdieu's reframing of class. *Journal of Classical Sociology*. 13 (2). pp. 274–291.

Wacquant, L. (2014) Marginality, ethnicity and penalty in the neoliberal city: An analytic cartography. *Ethnic and Racial Studies*. 37 (10). pp. 1687–1711.

Wills, J. (2008) Making class politics possible: Organizing contract cleaners in London. *International Journal of Urban and Regional Research*. 32 (2). pp. 305–323.

Wills, J., et al. (2010) *Global cities at work: New migrant divisions of labour*. London: Pluto Press.

Wimmer, A., and Schiller, N. G. (2002) Methodological nationalism and beyond: Nation-state building, migration and the social sciences. *Global Networks*. 2 (4). pp. 301–334.

3 Bourdieu's 'Carnal Theorising' in Organisations and Management

Bridging Disembodiment and Other Old Dichotomies

Kanellos-Panagiotis Nikolopoulos and Katerina Nicolopoulou

INTRODUCTION

The purpose of this chapter is to contribute to this edited volume on Bourdieu by expanding on the concept of 'carnal theorising' and the ways in which this has been applied in the field of organisation and management. The present work can contribute to making a shift from a fragmented perception of knowledge in organisation and management research to a unified one. Such a perspective could enable 'the relationship with the other'—that is, the embodied or disembodied self—thus stressing, in turn, the benefits of a relational approach to social phenomena in relevant research. In order to do so, the chapter will move from conceptualising 'carnal theorising' via the lens of sociology into the field of organisations; we aim to create a contribution to the edited volume by, further, relating 'carnal theorising' to a number of relevant constructs in the field of management—that is, *habitus* and its relation to the structure/agency or micro/macro dichotomy, as well as the ways in which these contribute to our understanding and relevance of this topic in organisational life and practice.

Engagement with the 'body', as Buchholz (2006) explains, has evolved into the perspective of 'embodiment', by shedding light on the dynamics of the *corporal* formation of the 'social agent'. The embodied and embedded capacity of 'history' made into 'body' is traced in Bourdieu and Wacquant's *An Invitation to Reflexive Sociology* (1992) to the concept of habitus. Habitus in Bourdieu's words (1977: 72, 95) is "the strategy-generating principle enabling agents to cope with unforeseen and ever-changing dispositions . . . a system of lasting and transposable dispositions which, integrating past experiences functions at every moment as a matrix of perceptions, appreciations and actions make possible the achievement of infinitely diversified tasks." In other words, as Chell (2007) argues, habitus is the holistic structuration of one's circumstances and surroundings.

Habitus is linked to temporality, as time is socially constructed; social agents have followed a trajectory and occupy a location in social space in a resilient distribution of resources independent of their will and consciousness (Wacquant, 2014). While the habitus is sufficiently open to allow for human agency, it is nevertheless the product of social conditioning. The dispositions that dictate cultural consumption are learned in the family, as well as other social settings and formations, and are thus a map of the material conditions and social conditionings that one experiences as the result of one's location in "*capital space*" (Allen and Andersen, 1994: 72).

Prior research (Levy et al., 2013; Woodward et al., 2008) has identified similarities between the cosmopolitan 'elite' disposition and Bourdieusian habitus; our chapter will also highlight those, and will bring, thus, to the fore, a more rounded perspective in relation to conceptual dichotomies (such as 'self'-'other'; 'body'-'mind'; 'embodied'—'social' self) that can be bridged through revising the lens of 'carnal theorising' within organisations and management. Bourdieu's theory of social reproduction focuses on the notion of the body as an object of distinction and a carrier of status, thus suggesting that the body can influence social positioning (Aroni, 2008).

The present book chapter is structured in three main parts: (a) The sociological roots of carnal theorizing, (b) habitus and capitals as central constructs in defining and problematizing embodied culture in organisations (c) a 'gendered' perspective in carnal theorizing and the embodiment of the self in organisations, and (d) conclusions, implications and recommendations for research and practice.

CARNAL THEORIZING AND SOCIOLOGY

We can trace the origins of the long tradition of carnal theorizing in the anthropocentric philosophy of Socrates and Plato, according to whom, body and mind are considered uneven- the body being the prison (*eirkti*) of the soul. Classical sociology adopted a *disembodied* approach towards its subject; this is largely due to a philosophical tradition influenced by Cartesian thought, which affirmed the mind/body dichotomy and focused on the mind as that which primarily defines humans as social beings. Still, according to Turner (1991), one of the main reasons for adopting this approach was to be found in the epistemological and methodological roots of classical approaches to sociology. This perspective impacted organisational studies by disconnecting, in ontological, as well as epistemological terms, ways of thinking from ways of being in organisations. The proliferation of theories and metaphors that are based on psychological or cognitive insights (for example computational metaphors or knowledge-based theories) has been disproportionate to the number of theories that focus on an 'embodied' way of being in the field of organisations and management.

Shilling (2013), in his highly influential work *The Body and Social Theory*, gives a detailed account of the evolution of sociological thinking about the *body*. Shilling's work highlights that the methodological approaches used by the discipline of sociology placed great emphasis on "abstract cognitive enquiry" (p. 27), although the fact that the "founding fathers (of sociology)" (p. 27) were conceptualised and embodied as *men* implies an endogenous connection between knowledge and embodiment.

Additionally, as Shilling (2013) argues in his work, the continuing eagerness of the discipline of sociology to maintain itself as separate from other social sciences resulted in locating the mind/body dichotomy within the philosophical realm, rather than that of other social sciences. It was the current of pragmatism, as Shilling (2013) identifies, and the form in which it was espoused as a social philosophy (Dewey, Mead, James, and Peirce) that identified embodiment as the cultural mediator of the external and internal environments of human action. Crucially, it is the embodied subject that *mediates* these environments through its sensory, intentional, and situated action (Shilling, 2013: 30–31).

Shilling (2013) further explains that sociology focused on other conceptual dichotomies central to its studies, such as the structure/agency and subject/object dilemma. For students and scholars of the social sciences and organisational studies, such dichotomies lie within the paradigms perspective taken within the roots of the discipline (e.g. as those are addressed by Burrell and Morgan, 1979). Consequently, while structuralist and interpretivist sociologies (Shilling, 2013: 30) were concerned with ideologies and questions of language meaning and understanding, they remained uninterested in explaining the significance of bodily features which are explicable in terms of the biological sciences; instead, they focused on social aspects—that is, language (associated with structure) and consciousness (associated with agency). In this way, Shilling (2013) concludes that the body came to be seen as a subject that could throw new light on several of those problems which were traditionally seen to preoccupy sociologists alongside the structure/agency micro/macro divisions.

Such divisions, however, also influence ways in which the individual is conceived in terms of both modernism and postmodernism. The 'modern man', for example, features relevant qualities, such as countable features that constitute his or her personality; for Gergen (1991), nonetheless, the 'postmodern man' does not deal with the body. Within the framework of postmodernism, individuals are under a constant process of construction and reconstruction, a state of constant change and flux. The body, from this point of view, is seen as 'a mirror of the self', exactly in the same ways as in the past individuality has been seen as 'a mirror of the soul' (Turner, 1991). Turner (1991) further highlights this, through the example of *diet*; originally used as a mechanism of discipline for religiously defined salvation of the soul, the diet has currently turned its focus on the physical body. We have established that when seen from a postmodern point of view, the body becomes a basic constituent of identity and self. Falk (1994) further identifies this within the trajectory of sociocultural processes; the speed and the width of social changes affect the image of the stable subject, thus making the sense of identity of self fluid, volatile, and fragmented. The body, on the other hand, becomes both the first matter to be processed and the immediate receptor of this processing (Falk, 1994).

At this stage, we agree with Makrinioti (2004), who identifies both epistemological and methodological implications from such considerations regarding carnal theorising. Social constructionism, phenomenology, and several feminist theories confirmed the destabilisation of the Cartesian world view, by adopting a critical stance towards the undisputed nature of empirical (biological or physical) data (Aroni, 2008). Makrinioti (2004), however, argues that the element of relativity plays a crucial role in examining those from within the framework of social and political circumstances of a certain period, as well as within the particular matrix of power relations and the reasons for their maintenance and legalisation. From this perspective, factors such as gender, social class, tribe, and ethnicity can subvert a more 'oecumenical nature' of social reality and cause inequalities, divisions, and clashes (Makrinioti, 2004) in terms of that 'perfect' Cartesian universe which is fragmented. Such a conceptualisation of fragmentation actively prohibits a realisation, deeper understanding, and interpretation of the in-between social phenomena for organisations and management. Studying habitus and capitals in depth within the proposed framework can, in turn, help us acquire a more elaborate understanding of related phenomena, such as the ensuing power relations and resultant divisions and inequalities in societies. In the following sections, we will further the application of the foregoing theoretical analysis to the fields of organisation and management studies.

CULTURE, HABITUS, AND CAPITALS IN RELATION TO THE BODY

People find expression through the creation of civilisations and differentiate themselves through culture. Society and organisations consist of individuals and the embodiment of their 'being' ('the body'), which can be seen as a carrier of information relating to culture. This is one of the main reasons why the study of *culture* is central to *carnal theorising* with regards to the study of society and institutions. Wacquant (2014) highlights a move from a sociology *of* the body as socially constructed object to a sociology *from* the body as socially construc*ting* vector of knowledge, power, and practice. Buchholz (2006) explains that the rising concern with the 'body' during the last two decades has shifted to an analytic perspective of 'embodiment' which aims to shed light on the corporal formation of social agents. What is at stake in such an approach is not the study of particular corporeal domains but a larger understanding of the material basis of subjectivity, interaction, and practice. As described by Turner (1991) the shift of focus on 'embodiment' and therefore the function of the body implies a process of *becoming a body* in social space.

Buchholz (2006) refers to Turner's (1991) *The Body and Society*, where three traditions are distinguished regarding carnal *theorising*: (1)

Conceptualising the body as a 'system of signs', which provides a frame for scrutinising bodily symbolism in ceremonies, religious rituals, or metaphors of social life; (2) following the tradition of writings of Michel Foucault (1982), whereby the body is perceived as a system of signs which stand for and express relations of power; and (3) identifying the concept of the body as 'a set of social practices'. Buchholz (2006) traces this third tradition back to Marcel Mauss , 1973), who argues that cultures have 'techniques of the body' that simultaneously provide their members with identity and govern the different ages in the life of men; the agglomeration of these concepts can find its most elaborate expression in Bourdieu's notion of habitus.

Jenkins (2002) in his discussion on Bourdieu and culture explains that for Bourdieu culture is encoded *in* or *on* the body. What he refers to as habitus and *hexis* are, in effect, different dimensions of this embodiment. Bourdieu's original contribution to carnal *theorising* is that some of the power of habituation derives from the role of the body as a *mnemonic device in cultural coding* (Jenkins, 2002: 179). This potentially creates a bridge between the 'microsociology' of bodily expression and the wider sociology concerned with the relationship between culture, (and by extension) social structure, and agency in an interactive dialectical fashion. According to Karatas-Ozkan (2006), and with reference to Bourdieu's (1998) distinction between 'culture' and habitus, culture focuses on the 'collective', whereas habitus transcends the dichotomy between 'collective' and 'individual'. This is done by allowing the interplay of individual behaviours with collective ones; thus, individuals possess some autonomy of action in the way of agency, even though following conventionally laid down paths shaped by habitus (Karatas-Ozkan, 2006).

Özbilgin and Tatli (2005) argue that one of the most crucial implications of the adoption of the concept of habitus by organisational researchers is found in the *historical dimension* of habitus. For organisational research, the necessity of the inclusion of the embodiment of a temporal dimension in habitus—as expressed in *Outline of a Theory of Practice* (Bourdieu, 1977), where the concept is defined and also linked to the micro level of agency—focuses on the production and reproduction of and change in organisational culture in a way that requires a historical treatment of the organisation (Özbilgin and Tatli, 2005: 864). In an organisational context, habitus is the site of tension and negotiation among different organisational members, which reproductively transforms organisational culture (Özbilgin and Tatli, 2005).

As explained by Wacquant (2014) habitus can be individual, and it can consist of a singular social trajectory and set of life experiences that form the combination of shared constituents. These individual experiences are defined by membership in *collectives* and *institutions, in which* social vision and division are relevant for strategies of group formation. Therefore, habitus can also be defined by gender, class habitus, class fraction, and ethnicity (local, regional, national, etc.) (Wacquant, 2014: 3). Thus conceived, the body for Bourdieu is seen as an imperfect entity which develops together and in connection with various social forces, and constitutes an integral element of the maintenance of social inequalities (Aroni, 2008).

In turn, Buchholz (2006) points to the fact that with respect to research of *embodiment*, Bourdieu's notion of habitus in relation to social practices offers a rare insight into a non-idealistic perspective. This links the constitution of the embodied social agent to its sensual immersion in specific environments, and takes place because the habitus operates only in relation to a social field; additionally, the same habitus can produce very different practices according to what is going on in the field (Jenkins, 2002). Rather than leading to crude materialism or even 'sociologised biology' (Alexander, 1994: 144), its endeavour is to think of the material, the ideal, and ultimately the body and the mind in ways which are intricate and complex (Buchholz, 2006).

This description of how habitus becomes the bridge between agency and structure is concluded in *An Invitation to Reflexive Sociology* (1992), where Bourdieu and Wacquant connect the concept of habitus to the macro level of structures. According to Özbilgin and Tatli (2005), the meso level of analysis in Bourdieu's work brings together the micro and macro levels, thus allowing for a reading of their interplay, as Bourdieu has also examined the (micro) individual and (macro) structural considerations independent of their meso-level interdependence (Özbilgin and Tatli, 2005).

The benefit of such an approach and the potential of the insights it can offer can be read in new considerations about culture. Earley (2006), for example, has criticised values-based large-scale surveys like Hofstede's (1984) and those of the GLOBE Research Program (2004). Instead, Earley (2006) proposed a theory that can help identify the linkages between culture and organisational phenomena, and at the same time, he provided a list of such studies. Archer (2000, as found in Ritzer and Goodman, 2004) argues that it is useful for social scientists to understand structure and agency as *independent*, because this makes it possible for them to analyse the interrelations between the two sides. To the foregoing, Bourdieu provides habitus as a middle ground for the interaction between structure and agency.

Bourdieu analysed social inequalities in terms of four different types of capital and the ensuing struggles for their possession mediated by the enabling and constraining facets of habitus. According to Bourdieu and Wacquant (1992) possession of capital is a precondition for the participation of the agent in the field; Bourdieu (1998) stresses symbolic capital as both the amalgam and the situated value, of all other forms of capital that individuals draw on. Three forms of capital (i.e. economic, cultural, and social) become socially effective as resources, and their ownership is legitimised through the mediation of symbolic capital (e.g. power, status, or authority). In terms of Bourdieu's carnal theorising, the notion of cultural capital refers not merely to a culturally specific 'competence' but also to a resource or a power in a particular social setting (Weininger, 2005). In highly differentiated societies, 'inculcating' cultural capital takes place via the family and the school, and needs an investment in time (Weininger, 2005).

A related, final distinction by Bourdieu (1986) crucial for carnal theorising is found in separating cultural capital into *embodied, objectified*, and *institutionalised*. The specific form of cultural capital which is conceptualised by Bourdieu (1986) as "embodied capital" (p. 4) refers to external wealth converted into an integral part of the person, as well as a habitus, which cannot be transmitted instantaneously (unlike money, assets, or titles). Embodied capital is knowledge associated with one's education and upbringing. The primary responsibility for embodied capital lies with the family. The objectified form of capital concerns material objects and media, such as writings, works of art, monuments, and artefacts, which are produced or consumed via several forms of embodied cultural capital (Bourdieu, 1986). Finally, capital may occur in an institutionalised form—that is, in the form of an embodied competence which has been certified by an official agency possessing the authority to legally 'warrant' its existence (e.g. educational credentials) (Bourdieu, 1986).

As Bourdieu (1986) explains, the most important feature of cultural capital lies in its mode of transmission, which is hereditary; thus it contributes significantly to the inter-generational reproduction of class divisions. The social conditions of its transmission and acquisition are, somehow, more disguised than those of economic capital. Additionally, a class element is significant to consider as legitimisation of cultural capital is questionable for 'autodidacts' rather than members of middle/elite classes. Finally, the latter, according to Bourdieu (1986), exhibit an element of autonomy in terms of the capacity to attain the final conversion into economic capital. In the following section, carnal theorising will be considered from the point of view of gender, which has been one of the key dimensions of conceiving the body within organisations.

EMBODIMENT, DISEMBODIMENT, MASCULINITY, FEMININITY: THE GENDER DIMENSION OF CARNAL THEORISING

Scholars have also problematised the body from within a gender-based perspective, by attributing meaning to a theorisation which is based on the distinction between characteristics which can be considered as predominantly 'masculine' or 'feminine'. In gender-based feminist writing, the body becomes the instrument through which experience flows. Additionally, it can also become a terrain of battle or oppression regarding ways in which embodiment takes place from within a 'critical feminist' perspective; this 'battle' or 'oppression' can be reproduced within organisational realities, even via ways in which knowledge and information are often embodied within organisational structures (Calas and Smircich, 1992; Calas et al., 2009). More often than not, such organisational 'embodied' realities are perceived as masculine, rather than feminine. Haraway (1998), for example, identifies that science is masculinised, and not really allowed to have a body (at least not a feminine one).

The distinction between 'masculinity' and 'femininity' is yet another turn in the embodiment/disembodiment debate. Entrepreneurial discourses, for example, in the process of enterprise creation (traditionally a capitalist, wealth creation–oriented activity) are typically 'masculinised' (Diaz Garcia and Welter, 2011). From the perspective of Diaz Garcia and Welter (2011), there are two ways in which masculinity and femininity are embodied in entrepreneurial activity and identity construction; the first is the enactment of the identity of 'the other' (i.e. the female), urged to accommodate herself within a universe of masculine-constructed norms and behaviours; the second is identity construction between two opposing constructs ('feminine' and 'entrepreneur') which results in women re-enacting ('doing' and 'redoing' gender) in the process of identity formation.

Organisational perceptions of female embodiment are also interesting for their normative application of measures of discipline; those are commonly applied in order to accept the female embodiment in a predominantly male setting. Tretheway (1999) summarises aspects of the normative embodiment in a manner that highlights fitness and discipline to the female body. Such a body is typically perceived as 'overflowing', as it is seen in the way of a mechanism of emission of sexual signals; thus, the female body is seen as exceedingly sexual.

Where does Bourdieu stand in terms of such tensions and divisions? Skeggs (2004) provides an overview of those works in which Bourdieu focused on gender, sex, and the body (*Distinction*; *Masculine Domination*; *Outline of a Theory of Practice*). Within the array of relevant topics, Bourdieu situates gender as a construct anchored in socially created traditions; those are bounded by different forms of symbolic violence which are perpetuated through the existence of institutions and established modes of social life (as found in *Distinction*, 1984). 'Cultural capital' according to Ross-Smith and Huppatz (2010) is a conceptual combination of power and gender in the ways in which they are depicted upon the body. Adkins and Skeggs (2005), on the other hand, highlight that engagement with Bourdieu could reignite interest in the embodied self, thus revisiting ways of talking about phenomena (which has been termed 'the linguistic turn'), a trend which typically dominated the field of feminist studies. For Bourdieu, according to Skeggs (2004), embodiment is primarily the embodiment of capital, and the capacity to fit between the habitus and the field. This makes Bourdieu consider the embodiment as 'going beyond' the carnal, into 'space'. In this dimension, it is a "social embodiment" (Skeggs, 2004: 22). This is particularly the case in terms of the middle and elite classes, about which Bourdieu exhibits richer insights (Skeggs, 2004). These insights will be explored in the section ahead.

CLASSES AND CULTURAL CONSUMPTION: ELITE AESTHETICS AND THE BODY

Another way to conceptualising embodiment and carnal theorising is through *consumption*, and in the particular case of Bourdieu, consumption has mostly been connected to *cultural consumption*. Bourdieu (1984) identifies three classes (or class fractions) on the basis of the distribution of economic and cultural capital: *bourgeoisie* or the dominant class, *petite bourgeoisie*, and *les classes populaires* (the working class). Weininger (2005) explains that this class model can be understood as a space defined by different co-located axes. The first axis differentiates locations in the occupational system according to the total *volume* of capital (economic and cultural) possessed by incumbents. The second axis differentiates positions within class locations (the Marxian term is 'class fractions'). For Bourdieu (1984), classes are divided internally according to the *composition* of the capital possessed by incumbents. In that second axis, the dominant class is differentiated between the industrialists and commercial employers, who possess economic capital but possibly little cultural capital, and professors and artists, for whom the exact opposite applies. Similarly, petty bourgeoisie is differentiated between the small business owners and primary school teachers.

The different positionings alongside these axes highlight *trajectories* that trace change of stability experienced over time in composition of capital. As Weininger (2005) notes, such mobility can be traced alongside vertical or horizontal movements—highlighting variations in terms of the class location of an individual and his or her fraction location, over time. Such movements play a role in the transformation or 'conversion' of capitals. Weininger (2005) additionally highlights consumption as one aspect of embodiment, which also relates to class. For example, professionals (senior executives) do not indulge in the overt luxury of employers; at the same time, they avoid the 'asceticism' of intellectuals but, rather, adopt a lifestyle which exhibits traits of modernism, dynamism, and cosmopolitanism (Weininger, 2005: 94). These, according to Weininger (2005: 94–95), can include openness to new technologies and foreign cultures, as well as a comfortable and liberated approach to life.

Allen and Anderson (1994: 72) elaborated upon Bourdieu's theory and the links with consumer behaviour; Bourdieu has regarded the consumption field as a site of struggle over the definitions of *legitimate*, *middlebrow*, and *popular* culture. From that point of view, the socially and economically dominant in any society seek to maintain a strict hierarchy of cultural forms so that all judgements in the consumption sphere are subject to the hegemony of 'legitimate' (i.e. dominant) cultural tastes (Allen and Anderson, 1994). Bourdieu's sociology of culture is a sociology of cultural consumption, its definitions, and its subsequent uses (Jenkins, 2002); therefore, cultural consumption is emphasised as a terrain of struggles for social recognition or status. Turner (1988: 66) explains that for Bourdieu status is in fact *lifestyles, the sum of cultural practices such as dress, speech, outlook, and bodily dispositions.* Struggles and competitions over status have to do with recognition (cultural distinction). Jenkins (2002) argues that behind this lies a specific logic about accumulation of symbolic capital; this makes *the body*, for Bourdieu, a *vehicle for capital storage and transformation.*

Differences in lifestyle (Weininger, 2005) are, for Bourdieu, implicated in conflicts over the location of individuals in social space as well as its structure and thus have a strong symbolic component. For Bourdieu, struggles about the meaning of things and specifically the meaning of the social world are also an aspect of class struggle (Jenkins, 2002). In this respect, this definition stems from the same argument that Bourdieu made in *Reproduction in Education, Society and Culture* (Bourdieu and Passeron, 1977), that is, the social reproduction of the established order is largely secured by symbolic violence, a process of cultural reproduction, which imposes systems of symbolism and meaning (i.e. culture) upon groups or classes in such a way that they are experienced as legitimate (Jenkins, 2002). As described by Bourdieu (1984: 26),

> The educational institution succeeds in imposing cultural practices that it does not teach and does not even explicitly demand, but which belong to the attributes attached by status to the position it assigns, the qualifications it awards, and the social positions to which the latter gives access.

Allen and Anderson (1994) stress that in Bourdieu's theory of consumer taste formation, as described in *Distinction* (1984), although the traditional notion of 'tastes' (i.e. consumer preferences) is rejected, tastes are still are identified as the result of innate, individualistic choices of the human intellect. Bourdieu (1984: 5) argues that this "Kantian aesthetic" fails to recognise that tastes are socially conditioned and that their related symbolic hierarchy is maintained by the socially dominant so as to enforce their distance and distinction from other classes of society. Lacking the lived experience that produce the elite habitus, the petite bourgeoisie, for example, misrecognise what are essentially arbitrary aesthetic selections for special knowledge of what is acceptable or 'legitimate' in the social sphere. The petite bourgeoisie operate as autodidacts that have not acquired culture in the legitimate order established by the educational system, and mistakenly identify culture with knowledge, therefore not knowing "how to play the game of culture as a game" (Bourdieu, 1984: 330). This becomes more prominent when viewing culture as embodied capital. It is thus Bourdieu's fundamental thesis that, precisely because individuals perceive one another primarily through the symbolic 'status', different conceptualisations of the economic and cultural capital moderate the different forms of habitus and enable their realisation. When differences of economic and cultural capital are misperceived as differences of honour (i.e. prestige) they can also function as symbolic capital (Weininger, 2005: 101).

There is another related aspect which plays a role in conceptualising the embodiment of habitus. Nielsen (2003), Kakabadse and Kakabadse (2012), and Nicolopoulou, Kakabadse, Sakellariou, and Alcaraz (2014) highlight different categories of elites—namely, 'transnational leisure elites', 'power elites', and 'transnational entrepreneurial elites'. While all three categories can transcend national boundaries, constituting a single social group, the first two groups operate from a base of glamour, wealth, and power, while the latter operates from a base of opportunity, innovation, and curiosity (Nielsen, 2003; Kakabadse and Kakabadse, 2012; Nicolopoulou et al., 2014). Based on such considerations, we can then argue for two coexisting realities: when examined from a Bourdieusian perspective, elites both consume and create, as a manifestation of the 'embodiment' of their habitus; this also takes place through capitals which are mobilised and transformed in order to do so. While glamour and power can dispose towards the manifestation of embodied cultural capital, innovation and opportunity can dispose towards the creation of such.

Ostrower (1998) highlights that such cultural capital serves as the differentiating boundary between the classes; while this is presented as endogenous to the class system of a country like France ("arts are valued by the elites and do not facilitate class cohesion"; p. 44), still a more general appreciation of art and aesthetics is viewed positively. In another country (like the US), Ostrower (1998) argues that this takes place in a more institutionally supported manner. Nonetheless, related aspects of the embodiment/disembodiment debate are relevant for such conceptualisations, as typically, artistic endeavours can be seen as belonging to a disembodied, intangible sphere, with questionable intrinsic value. For that reason, aesthetic capital (Nicolopoulou, 2014) is also considered important, for its legitimation and also transformation capacity into other forms of capital; Ostrower (1998) firmly connects the aesthetic disposition to an elite disposition.

This argument could be extended for the value of other 'disembodied' or intangible forms of art, such as perfumery. The sense of smell, for example, is more connected to the neurochemical composition of the brain and hormones, rather than the 'carnal body', its conceptualisation of fleshy and tangible form. In that sense, we can draw an understanding that relates the elite disposition with the appreciation of the intangible and therefore disembodied forms of art: that resembles the role of 'spirit' as imprinted upon intangible artistic imprints. Indeed, various forms of art have been safeguarded, for several centuries, for the exclusive benefit of the elites.

CONCLUSIONS

The present chapter aimed to outline and enhance the understanding of Bourdieu's approach and contribution to carnal theorising and to create a bridge between such insights and the world of organisations and management studies. Its main thrust has been the conceptualisation of the body as a 'social construct' which is mediated by the role of habitus; the latter is defined as an embodiment of social, cultural, and gender-related aspects.

The main contribution of the chapter has been twofold: first, a summary understanding of carnal theorising from within the main tenets of Bourdieu's theories; second, an application of related key learnings on the field of organisations and management, with specific relevance to international management as well as marketing and consumer behaviour. According to Buchholz (2006), the focus on the incarnate agent and embodiment has implications for subjectivity, interaction, and practice. Social science could benefit from further engagement with psychology in order to recover the 'carnality of action' that conventional accounts of social life eradicate (Wacquant, 2014: 1).

In Bourdieu's view (1984) the socially and economically dominant in any society seek to maintain a strict hierarchy of cultural forms so that all judgements in the sphere of consumption are subject to the hegemony of 'legitimate' (i.e. dominant) cultural tastes. This is accomplished without direction or coercion, because a class habitus presents its individual with a pre-existing set of 'natural' classifications that constitute his or her 'unreflective recognition' of reality (Allen and Andersen, 1994: 72). Hosking and Hjorth (2004) argue that interactions *co-construct* people and worlds. This means that both self *and* other (people, material objects, events, and social structures) exist—as social realities—only as relational dualities and not as separate entities. Conceptualisation of organisational culture as habitus (Özbilgin and Tatli, 2005) helps us to appreciate further the interactions between organisational habitus and the other forms of habitus of individual incarnate agents through study of their dispositions.

One related implication of this line of thinking lies in the field of international management. Companies operate in a transnational, globalised environment, which can be conceptualised as a complex matrix of cross-national fields in interaction with social actors' habitus, *consisting* of dual cultural, institutional, and structural features, schemas, and resources. This is the terrain through which entrepreneurs, as world creators and wealth creators, can formulate their strategies of action (Drori et al., 2006). Related implications from considering Bourdieu's carnal theorising might impact aspects of global knowledge work and workers, for whom cultural diversity is considered an asset (Nicolopoulou and Karatas-Ozkan, 2007; Nikolopoulos, 2011). Further research along such lines would require an interdisciplinary approach which combines the fields of cosmopolitanism, international entrepreneurship, culture, and diversity management. Darchen and Tremblay (2010) argued that global knowledge workers (as representatives of the creative classes) transfer not only know-how but also cultural capital, and by so doing, they help shape a new global reality (Nicolopoulou, 2011; Nicolopoulou et al., 2014). 'Place' for this class is not a single conceptualisation of location of activity, but it rather includes 'human capital, creative clusters, cultural diversity, lifestyle, proximity to an environment that would entail green and natural features' but also, proximity to communities of practice as well as mechanisms for support and career development (Nicolopoulou, 2011: 526; Nicolopoulou et al., 2014).

The foregoing can also have direct relevance for marketing and consumer behaviour. Allen and Anderson (1994: 73–74), following Bourdieu (1984), argue that consumer preferences and aesthetic dispositions have deep roots in a class-based hierarchy that is imposed on society by those who are culturally dominant; if the conditions that allow the hierarchy to change are to be altered, "the conditions of access to what the present offers us that is most universal" (Bourdieu and Wacquant, 1992: 84) need to be universalised. Those potential implications for management, entrepreneurship, marketing, and consumer behaviour merit further research, as they can help management and marketing scholars further conceptualise what is globally acceptable in terms of market-driven tastes and how it can influence consumer behaviours.

We would like to close this exploratory chapter with a philosophical reference which is different from those which have been used in the opening of the chapter (i.e. Plato and Socrates, in their conceptualisation of the relation between the body and mind). Prior to knowledge-based (epistemological) as well as ontological dichotomies, such as those outlined in the beginning of this chapter, philosophical thinking recognised extensively the unification of knowledge in both its theoretical and practical dimensions. Neoplatonic philosophy exemplified such holism, as this is captured in the 'as above, so below' principle which underlies the organisation of the universe and human systems (Karatas-Ozkan et al., forthcoming). From this perspective and within a more expanded point of view which captures business and organisational life, a relational epistemology becomes important to adopt, in terms of relating with the 'other' (i.e. the embodied or disembodied self). We, therefore, propose a final strand of theorising for future research endeavours, which will focus on the effects of the reconsideration of capital transformations whereby agency will be located on the relational 'network' (network of relations) rather than the 'individual agent'. In this sense, as organisations would be more widely viewed as networks of relations, embodiment and disembodiment could become mutually coexistent positions of a dialectical nature.

REFERENCES

Adkins, L., & Skeggs, B. (Eds.) (2005). *Feminism after Bourdieu*. Oxford: Blackwell.
Allen, D. E., & Anderson, P. F. (1994). 'Consumption and Social Stratification: Bourdieu's Distinction', *Advances in Consumer Research*, vol. 21, pp. 70–74.
Archer, M. S. (2000). *Being Human: The Problem of Agency*. Cambridge, UK: Cambridge University Press.
Aroni, A. (2008). *Koinonikes Anaparastaseis, praktikes kai chriseis tou somatos*. Athina: Panteion Panepistimio Koinonikon Kai Politikon Epistimon. Tmima Psychologias.

Bourdieu, P. (1977). *Outline of a Theory of Practice.* Cambridge, UK: Cambridge University Press.
Bourdieu, P. (1984). *Distinction: A Social Critique of the Judgement of Taste.* Cambridge, MA: Harvard University Press.
Bourdieu, P. (1986). 'The Forms of Capital', in J. G. Richardson (ed.), *Handbook of Theory and Research for the Sociology of Education* (pp. 241–258). New York: Greenwood Press.
Bourdieu, P. (1998). *Practical Reason: On the Theory of Action.* Cambridge: Polity Press.
Bourdieu, P., & Passeron, J. C. (1977). *Reproduction in Education, Society and Culture.* London: SAGE.
Bourdieu, P., & Wacquant, L. (1992). *An Invitation to Reflexive Sociology.* Cambridge: Polity Press.
Buchholz, L. (2006). 'Bringing the Body Back into Theory *and* Methodology'. *Theoretical Sociology,* vol. 35, pp. 481–490.
Burrell, G., & Morgan, G. (1979). *Sociological Paradigms and Organizational Analysis.* London: Heinemann.
Calas, M., & Smircich, L. (1992). 'Using the 'F' Word: Feminist Theories and Social Consequences of Organizational Research', in A. J. Mills & P. Tancred (eds.), *Gendering Organizational Analysis* (pp. 222–234). London: SAGE.
Calas, M. B., Smircich, L., & Bourne, K. A. (2009). 'Extending the Boundaries: Reframing "Entrepreneurship as Social Change" through Feminist Perspectives'. *Academy of Management Review,* vol. 34, no. 3, pp. 552–569.
Chell, E. (2007). 'Social Enterprise and Entrepreneurship: Towards a Convergent Theory of the Entrepreneurial Process', *International Journal of Small Business,* vol. 25, no. 5, pp. 5–24.
Darchen, S and Tremblay, D (2010) 'What attracts and retains knowledge workers/students: the quality of place or career opportunities? The cases of Montreal and Ottawa', *Cities,* vol. 27, pp. 225–233.
Diaz-Garcia, M., & Welter, F. (2011). 'Gender Identities and Practices: Interpreting Women Entrepreneurs' Narratives'. *International Small Business Journal,* vol. 31, no. 4, pp. 384–404.
Drori, I., Honig, B., & Ginsberg, A. (2006). 'Transnational Entrepreneurship: Toward a Unifying Theoretical Framework'. *Academy of Management Best Paper Proceedings,* 1: Q1–Q6.
Earley, C. P. (2006). 'Leading Cultural Research in the Future: A Matter of Paradigm and Taste'. *Journal of International Business Studies,* vol. 37, pp. 922–931.
Falk, P. (1994). *The Consuming Body.* London: SAGE.
Foucault, M. (1982). 'The Subject and Power'. *Critical Inquiry,* vol. 8, no. 4, pp. 777–795.
Gergen, K. J. (1991). *The Saturated Self: Dilemmas of Identity in Contemporary Life.* New York: Basic Books.
Global Leadership and Organizational Behavior Effectiveness (GLOBE) Research Program. (2004). 'Culture, Leadership, and Organizations: The GLOBE Study of 62 Societies'. Wharton School of Business, University of Pennsylvania.
Haraway, D. (1988). 'Situated Knowledges: The Science Question in Feminism and the Privilege of Partial Perspective'. *Feminist Studies,* vol. 14, no. 3, pp. 575–599.
Hofstede, G. (1984). *Culture's Consequences: International Differences in Work-Related Values.* Beverly Hills, CA: SAGE.
Jenkins, R. (2002). *Pierre Bourdieu.* Rev. ed. London: Routledge.
Kakabadse, A., & Kakabadse, N. (Eds.) (2012). *Global Elites: The Opaque Nature of Transnational Policy Determination.* London: Palgrave.
Karatas-Ozkan, M. (2006). *Nascent Entrepreneurship.* Doctorate thesis, Southampton University School of Management.

Karatas-Ozkan, M., Karatas, E., & Nicolopoulou, K. (Forthcoming). 'Mystical Writings, Spirituality and Relationality: Implications for 21st Century Organisations', in M. Ozbilgin (ed.), *Spirituality in Organisations*. Cheltenham, UK: E. Elgar.
Levy, O., Peiperl, M., & Jonsen, K. (2013). *Cosmopolitanism in a Globalised World: A Multidisciplinary Approach*. Academy of International Business: Istanbul.
Makrinioti, D. (2004). *Ta oria tou somatos: Diepistimonikes prosengiseis*. Athina: Ekdoseis nisos-P. KAPOLA: Athina
Mauss, M. (1973). 'Techniques of the Body', *Economy and Society*, vol. 2, pp. 70–88.
Nicolopoulou, K. (2011). 'Towards a Theoretical Framework for Knowledge Transfer in the Field of CSR and Sustainability'. *Equality, Diversity and Inclusion: An International Journal*, vol. 30, no. 6, pp. 524–538.
Nicolopoulou, K., Kakabadse, N., Sakellariou, K., & Alcaraz, J. (2014). 'Cosmopolitanism and the Elite Disposition as Diversity Factors in Entrepreneurship'. British Academy of Management conference, Belfast, September.
Nicolopoulou, K., & Karatas-Ozkan, M. (2007). 'Practicing Knowledge Workers: Perspectives of an Artist and Economist'. *Equal Opportunities International*, vol. 26, no. 8, pp. 872–878.
Nielsen, K. (2003). 'Toward a Liberal Socialist Cosmopolitan Nationalism'. *International Journal of Philosophical Studies*, vol. 11, no. 4, pp. 437–463.
Nikolopoulos, K. P. (2011). 'Creation of Social Capital for Innovation through the Mobility of Knowledge Workers in European Union ICT SMEs'. Working paper presented at the International Small Business Entrepreneurship Conference, Sheffield.
Ostrower, F. (1998). 'The Art as Cultural Capital among Elites: Bourdieu's Theory Reconsidered'. *Poetics*, vol. 26, pp. 43–53.
Özbilgin, M., & Tatli, A. (2005). Book review essay: 'Understanding Bourdieu's Contribution to Organization and Management Studies'. *Academy of Management Review*, vol. 30, no. 4, pp. 855–877.
Ritzer, G., & Goodman, D. J. (2004). *Sociological Theory*. New York: McGraw-Hill Higher Education.
Ross-Smith, A., & Huppatz, K. (2010). 'Management, Women and Gender Capital'. *Work and Organization*, vol. 17, no. 5, pp. 547–566.
Shilling C. (2013). *The Body and Social Theory*. SAGE: London
Skeggs, B. (2004). 'Context and Background: Pierre Bourdieu's Analysis of Class, Gender and Sexuality'. *Sociological Review*, vol. 52, no. 2, pp. 19–33.
Tretheway, A. (1999). Disciplined Bodies: Women's Embodied Identities at Work. *Organization Studies*, vol. 20, no. 3, pp. 423–450.
Turner, B. S. (1988). *Status*. Milton Keynes: Open University Press.
Turner, B. S. (1991). *The Body and Society: Explorations in Social Theory*. Oxford: Blackwell.
Wacquant, L. (2014). 'Putting Habitus in Its Place: Rejoinder to the Symposium'. *Body and Society*, vol. 20, no. 2, pp. 118–139.
Weininger, E. B. (2005). 'Foundations of Pierre Bourdieu's Class Analysis', in E. O. Wright (ed.), *Approaches to Class Analysis* (pp. 82–118). Cambridge: Cambridge University Press.
Woodward, I., Skribs, Z., & Bean, C. (2008). Attitudes towards Globalisation and Cosmopolitanism: Cultural Diversity, Personal Consumption and the National Economy. *British Journal of Sociology*, vol. 59, no. 2., pp 207–226.

4 "Turning the Lens on Ourselves"
Bourdieu's Reflexivity in Practice[1]

Boris H.J.M. Brummans

> Strange, that the ordinary, worn-out ways of everyday encompass the imagined and endless universe woven by reflections.
>
> (Borges 1999: 107)

Most management and organisation scholars would probably agree that reflecting on our academic practices is important (see Alvesson and Deetz 2000; Alvesson and Sköldberg 2000; Hardy and Clegg 1997; Hardy, Phillips, and Clegg 2001; Weick 1999, 2002). We don't reflect much, however, on the way our practices constitute, and are constituted by, the fields and subfields of which we are a part. As scholars, we usually study *other* people's organising while ignoring how our own practices constitute the socio-material spaces that legitimise our work and define who we are—spaces that can be seen as organisations in and of themselves. By disregarding the constitutive relationship between what we do and the spaces we enact, we, in turn, create academic universes in which it is difficult to battle "the bewitchment of our intelligence" (Wittgenstein 1953/2001: 40)—that is, to reflect on how we create relationships of "ontological complicity" (Bourdieu and Wacquant 1992: 20) with academic fields through our work.

Practicing this reflexivity is at the centre of Bourdieu's work (see esp. Bourdieu 1988, 2000b; Bourdieu and Wacquant 1992), yet few, including Bourdieusian experts like Evens (1999), Everett (2002), King (2000), Sweetman (2003), and Wacquant (1989), have demonstrated its practical value. To show the usefulness of Bourdieu's reflexivity, this chapter examines how 12 senior scholars constitute relationships of ontological complicity with the field of organisational communication studies by focusing on their 'textwork' (Van Maanen 1996), because an academic field is co-created, first and foremost, through the production of texts. As I will show, these prominent scholars constitute their complicities by engaging in 'textwork-games', games through which they identify themselves and legitimise their expressive interests within organisational communication studies and other fields. Thus, this chapter provides valuable theoretical and empirical insights into the practice of academic reflexivity as Bourdieu envisioned it. In the next section, I will outline my inquiry by presenting its conceptual framework, which is grounded in Bourdieu's writings. I will subsequently describe the methods I used to conduct my empirical research and present its results. To conclude, I will discuss the implications of my findings.

THE ONTOLOGICAL COMPLICITY BETWEEN SCHOLAR AND FIELD

Many scholars have written about academic research as a social practice (see Gilbert and Mulkay 1984; Gross 1990; Latour and Woolgar 1979), but relatively few empirical studies have looked at the way scholars constitute relationships of ontological complicity with academic fields. Hence, we are left to wonder how researchers experience and make sense of their work, as well as how they integrate themselves into a given socio-material space's fabric through their day-to-day practices. Sociologists of knowledge, for example, may study how biologists construct facts, yet they may discount how their own relationship to the field of sociology (and the subfield of the sociology of knowledge) yields a specific practical sense for studying the world, involving a particular set of presuppositions and dispositions developed through training and experience.

Some scholars have investigated this complicity more closely. Centring on the interconnections between language practices, knowledge, and power, Michel Foucault's (1970/1994, 1972/1989) studies are exemplary in this respect. Foucault's work demonstrates that academic fields are discursive spaces—historical artefacts, institutionalised, and sustained through language (Dreyfus and Rabinow 1983). As his analyses demonstrate, it is impossible to separate the human sciences as a generic field from the conditions that gave rise to these sciences, and his work questions whether it is possible to conceive of an objective human science, autonomous from socio-historical processes.

A second scholar who has focused on the relationship between scholars and fields is Pierre Bourdieu (1988, 1990a, 1990b, 1991a, 1991b, 2000b). Bourdieu argues that the struggle for forms of capital drives the operations of scholars who co-produce fields through their actions and who identify with fields through the positions they enact within them. Academics and fields thus mutually constitute each other: Scholars enact a field by researching a subject (physics, philosophy, mathematics, etc.); textualising this research in the form of academic texts; using these texts to educate students; and talking about texts at conferences. A field, in turn, evaluates scholars' actions, especially by assessing the texts they produce. Based on these evaluations, scholars gain capital and constitute more or less identifiable positions (academic identities) in a given social space. In this context, 'capital' refers to the value of socially scarce goods and values that scholars accumulate (or lose) through their operations in a field. Bourdieu classifies these accumulations into different forms: economic capital (monetary and material resources);

cultural capital (educational credentials, skills, expertise, 'taste', and the ability to use language appropriately—a special kind of cultural capital referred to as 'linguistic capital'); social capital (access to and membership in professional or academic networks); and symbolic capital (credibility, recognition, status, prestige, and personal authority). Through their activities in a field, scholars' identities thus become linked to the field's operational and interactional/communicative dynamics.

While Foucault's macro-historical analyses of how fields hierarchically structure perceptions regarding objects of knowledge, such as madness, the body, and the self, through discursive practices are compelling, his work has been critiqued for failing to explain how agents constitute discursive spaces. Bourdieu addresses this issue by focusing on the historical games for legitimacy of fields and studying how the practices of academic agents constitute fields around antinomies—contradictions or oppositions between positions that cause controversies because scholars consider these oppositions to be irresolvable. These positions are enacted in everyday communication—for instance, in debates about relationships between concepts (mind-body, subject-object, action-structure), the focal differences between and within fields of study (psychology-communication, organisational communication-management and organisation), or the incommensurability between "isms" (functionalism-interpretivism, structuralism-post-structuralism). A field's *raison d'être* therefore revolves around the presupposition that its operations are *necessary* to inform or resolve debates like these. Bourdieu's work aptly points out that everyday challenges in the practice of research result from the fact that scholars engage in these historical games and, in so doing, create bonds between their positions and the spaces that allow these positions to be identifiable. Bourdieu thus counters the social determinism that haunts Foucault's work by suggesting that scholars constitute, and are constituted by, fields through relationships of ontological complicity.

Bourdieu's Conception of Ontological Complicity

A Field's Features

According to Bourdieu, scholars act in relation to each other and thereby co-enact a relatively structured configuration of positions or field of inquiry. Besides these academic fields (communication, physics, philosophy) and subfields (organisational communication, nuclear physics, analytical philosophy), universities, colleges, and departments constitute fields, too. Obviously, social life is made up of non-academic fields as well, such as the political field, the artistic field, or professional fields (medicine, law, architecture). Although fields differ from each other in more or less distinct ways, they share four common features.

First, a field is relatively objective in that it constitutes an existence beyond the immediate consciousness and will of the agents who enact it.

This 'objectivity' is created through the distribution of capital, "resources and means of appropriation of socially scarce goods and values" (Bourdieu and Wacquant 1992: 7). For example, a university's existence depends, among other things, on its number of notable professors, the quality of its infrastructure (libraries, computing and information services, etc.), and its reputation vis-à-vis other universities.

Second, a field is a space of contest in which agents struggle to acquire economic, cultural, social, and symbolic capital. These forms of capital are highly correlated. Having a doctorate from the University of Cambridge (cultural capital), for instance, may be highly correlated with getting a well-paid position in a reputable research institute (economic capital). Moreover, the first three forms of capital (economic, cultural, and social) each become symbolic capital when agents in a field recognise them as legitimate forms. The value of capital depends on the collective construction of value and meaning, implying that someone's capital may be valued differently in different fields (a doctorate in English literature from the University of Cambridge may be invaluable in the academic field of English literature, yet relatively worthless in the professional field of medicine).

Third, because a field encloses and intersects with other fields, its borders are imprecise—even though people may experience them as real. What happens in one field may therefore affect other social spaces. Fields vary in their autonomy, however, leading to a relative degree of distinction between fields. Perhaps the best examples of relatively autonomous social universes are academic fields, since they act more or less independently from the political, artistic, or professional field (Bourdieu 2000b). Furthermore, due to the imbricated nature and permeability of fields, scholars generally constitute positions in different social spaces at the same time. So Karl Weick simultaneously enacts a position in management and organisation studies, organisational psychology, and organisational communication, as well as in the institution that employs him, the University of Michigan.

Fourth, to explain the complicity between fields and agents, Bourdieu argues that a field is characterised by a 'habitus', a historically developed system of dispositions that defines a practical sense for how to operate (feel, judge, think, move) in a given social space. A habitus functions as a system of classification that enables agents to make sense of the world from the point of view of a field. This system develops over time, based on a particular 'doxa', a set of central (and often unquestioned) presuppositions that define what a field considers valuable (innovative, productive, insightful, legitimate, ethical, etc.). By incorporating a habitus during their education and socialisation, scholars learn to embody this doxa and develop a sense for seeing, appreciating, and doing their work. In time, a field's 'common sense' becomes an individual sense, creating a relationship of ontological complicity between scholar and social space. Because a habitus is embodied over a period of time, it becomes second nature for agents to act according to the field in which they operate. Consequences produced within a field are therefore "neither the purely additive sum of anarchical actions, nor the integrated outcome of a concerted plan" (Bourdieu and Wacquant 1992: 17); rather, by participating in the enactment of a habitus, agents develop a sense for how to operate in a field without necessarily acting in a conscious way, which means that they act *as a field*, transcending the sum of their individual actions.

At first sight, the notion of habitus seems to rob agents of their individuality and agency, leading to the same kind of determinism that troubles Foucault's work. Bourdieu claims, though, that agents constitute their uniqueness by giving relatively distinct expressions to a habitus and enacting their position in a field in ways that make them more or less distinguishable. For this reason, it is possible to speak of 'someone's habitus'. Bourdieu argues that agents operate most effectively when there is a relative affinity between their habitus and the position they enact within a given social space (Sweetman 2003). There generally is a relative homology, likeness in structure, or 'fit' between the historical space of positions (field) and an agent's system of dispositions (habitus). If this homology is strong, experienced scholars who have gained considerable amounts of capital in a field may act as 'fish in water' by writing elegantly and speaking eloquently about their research subject. At times, however, they may be 'out on a limb' due to a discordance between their habitus and the fields in which they are acting. This may occur when reading new literatures, using new analytical techniques, or trying to publish in fields whose practices and stakes are unfamiliar. The 'unpreparedness', mismatch, or 'misfiring' of someone's habitus thus becomes most obvious in encounters with uncertain, untried situations (Bourdieu 2000b).

Countering the critique that the habitus functions as a deterministic schema, Bourdieu emphasises, moreover, that the habitus is a system of *dispositions* (i.e. propensities, virtualities, potentialities, and eventualities), which only "reveals itself in reference to a definite situation", and it is "*in relation to* certain structures that habitus produces . . . discourses and practices" (Bourdieu and Wacquant 1992: 135, emphasis in original). A habitus, in other words, does not act like a straitjacket that predicts and constrains every thought and move; instead, it gives rise to improvisation and invention and, in so doing, creates a dynamic between an individual and a collective. Bourdieu's perspective therefore centres on practice in context without assuming that agents act as wilfully or rationally as Habermas (1984) suggests, or as self-reflexively as Giddens (1991) claims.

Constituting Complicities through Language-Games

Language is essential to the way complicities between scholars and fields are constituted. According to Bourdieu (1991a), a field's 'linguistic habitus', which forms one aspect of its overall system of dispositions, enables scholars to express themselves. This linguistic habitus affects agents' "propensity to speak and to say determinate things", as well as their "capacity to speak, which involves both the linguistic capacity to generate an infinite number of grammatically correct discourses, and the social capacity to use this competence adequately in a determinate situation" (p. 37). Agents learn this linguistic habitus when entering a field. During their graduate studies, students learn the language of management and organisation studies, which allows them to produce texts this field values. Likewise, scholars entering the field of psychology after having been trained and socialised in sociology need to adjust their language to be heard and respected. By changing their language practices, scholars can thus acquire or reacquire linguistic capital—a special type of cultural capital referring to "the ability to demonstrate competence in the use of magisterial, scholarly, or bourgeois language, in one's ability to decipher and manipulate the complex structures of that language" (Everett 2002: 63).

An important merit of Bourdieu's work lies in its demonstration of how a field's socio-material conditions give scholars the experience of being involved in a serious game. Scholars become invested in this game because by gaining capital, their sense of self-worth becomes increasingly associated with the arena in which they act and interact. They become 'caught up' in a field's dynamics, as it were—vested in the continuation of the field because the position they enact in it is valued in economic, cultural, social, and symbolic ways (Bourdieu 1988, 1990a, 1990b, 2000b). Sustaining oneself therefore becomes a matter of sustaining the field (and vice versa). Scholars do not engage in this game because they are honouring a signed contract; rather, while playing, they become increasingly convinced that their participation is "worth the candle" (Bourdieu and Wacquant 1992: 98). The competitive interactions caused by this complicity constitute the field as a dynamic configuration of interdependent positions.

Bourdieu (1991a, 2000b) derived his idea of games from Wittgenstein's (1953/2001) notion of language-games. Like Wittgenstein, Bourdieu argues that a field works according to rules that can be experienced only by partaking in its games. Like the mastery of a language, mastering these games depends on the habitus that scholars learn to incorporate. Bourdieu extends Wittgenstein's work by suggesting that a field's linguistic habitus, as a system of classification, disposes scholars to privilege certain positions over others, which creates hierarchical relations in the distribution of capital. Hence, power is not simply enforced or reasoned, nor is it possible to locate power in one source; rather, exercising power is inherent in a field's competitive workings. Power finds its expression in language but also censors expression. A field's habitus, in turn, controls how scholars make sense of the world by reinforcing a classificatory system that privileges particular presuppositions, practices, ideas, and people, while marginalising others.

Because scholars are educated and socialised ('dispositioned' or 'naturalised') to invest in the language-games of a field and to believe in its legitimate existence through the acceptance of a particular doxa, they are not inclined to pause and reflect on these games. That is, due to their "feel for the game" (Bourdieu 1990b: 66) and commitment to its continuation, they do not only take these games for granted but also prevent their questioning and alteration to reinforce their established position within an established order. A field therefore "tends to produce . . . the naturalisation of its own arbitrariness" (Bourdieu 1977: 164) to prevent its games from being "given away" (Bourdieu 2000b: 5).

While Bourdieu's writings offer a useful starting point for conceptualising the constitution of ontological complicities between scholars and fields, more conceptual work is needed to detail how these complicities are constituted and reconstituted through scholars' everyday communicative practices. I will address this question by extending Bourdieu's ideas in the next section and then empirically examining this question in the context of an actual academic field.

Extending Bourdieu's Work

The Centrality of Positioning in Constituting Complicities

Bourdieu (2000a) sees a position as a symbolic location in a particular socio-material space. For example, someone may simultaneously constitute a position in psychology, organisational psychology, and the University of Michigan. These positions are more or less homologous with the systems of dispositions that characterise each of these fields. If a scholar's position has become an identifiable part of a field's dynamics, this person has a relatively good sense of how to act according to this position and how to acquire capital through this enactment.

Bourdieu's work insufficiently explicates and investigates how scholars in a field engage in, experience, and reflect on this positioning. For this reason, I conceptualise scholars' positioning practices as the communicative activities through which scholars become more or less distinguishable in a field. Scholars' positions are thus constituted through a field's interpretation and evaluation of their communicative actions. For example, Weick's actions in management and organisation studies, organisational psychology, and organisational communication studies have become relatively recognisable and distinctive from the ways in which other scholars position themselves in these fields. Weick's communicative activities constitute positions that are more or less distinguishable, not only due to the topics he chooses to study, how he studies them, and the way he writes up his research, but also due to the amount of cultural (especially linguistic), social, and symbolic capital he has acquired within these spaces.

The academic game of distinction, I argue, is reinforced by a field's linguistic habitus that shapes the language-games in which scholars position themselves vis-à-vis others. Academia comprises different fields and subfields, as Bourdieu (2000b: 99) notes, each being "the institutionalization of a point of view in things and in habitus". These fields are engaged in contests to legitimate their existence in relation to other fields. Depending on the length and intensity of these competitions, each field develops relatively autonomous ways of educating and socialising scholars to alter their dispositions towards the world and accept a particular set of fundamental presuppositions (doxa). A field's language-games constitute these presuppositions as antinomies or irresolvable conflicts and contradictions between positions. These opposing positions, in turn, characterise a field's habitus, generating debates about the relationship between particular concepts, the focal differences within and between fields, and the incommensurability of 'isms'. In other words, these antinomic language-games define the spirit of a field, invoking and legitimating the game of scholarship by giving it its game-like character and sustaining the momentum of a field's dynamics. Opposition is functional, because it makes scholars believe in the game's merit. It helps them distinguish themselves from others within the field as well as from 'outsiders', and it helps them build social support for a particular position by using antinomies as pedagogical anchor points for explaining the field's workings to newcomers (Bourdieu and Wacquant 1992). This explains why questioning the doxa in which one has been educated and socialised is relatively unnatural ("para-doxical"), since it implies questioning one's own identity in a field, dispositions, and reasons for participation and investment.

Practicing Bourdieu's Reflexivity by Investigating the Constitution of Complicities through Textwork-Games

To show how useful it is to practice Bourdieu's idea of reflexivity, it is important to reflect critically on the way scholars constitute complicities with an actual academic field. I suggest that this can be accomplished by investigating how scholars position themselves in a field through their 'textwork'—that is, textualisation practices such as "note taking; reading; outlining; corresponding; engaging in shop talk with colleagues; making formal and informal presentations of work planned, in-progress, and accomplished; drafting (and, alas, redrafting) articles as research proposals, reviews, commentary, journal articles, chapters and books; and so on" (Van Maanen 1996: 377).

Textwork is often portrayed as an individual, solitary affair, ignoring the social influences of the field in which textwork is practiced (see Deetz 1996; Putnam 1996; Van Maanen 1996). However, I regard these dispositional activities as central to the academic endeavour, because they enable scholars to identify their position in a field by communicating their work to others. Textwork refers to the practice of transforming the unwritten into the written and enables scholars to 'objectify' and publicise their thoughts—that is, to expresses them so they can be interpreted beyond direct experience and consciousness in the form of a text, a set of "definite forms of words, numbers or images that exist in materially replicable form" (Smith 2001: 164).

Yet, as Bourdieu (1990a) suggests, publication also entails, quite literally, making oneself public and 'officialising', ratifying, and legitimising oneself in a field. Publishing allows scholars to make a name that is authenticated and recognised; it ensures that they 'exist officially'. Besides constituting a position through their speech in talks and presentations, then, scholars constitute their positions through the production of written texts imbued with particular perspectives, styles, and subject matters.

I will refer to the dispositional, and often unconscious, practice of making a text more or less identifiable as 'voicing a text'. Following Bourdieu's work (1991a), I suggest that this voicing occurs in accordance with a field's doxa, which defines a set of historically formed presuppositions concerning what a proper academic text should include, how it should be written, and so forth. Depending on the autonomy of a field, a doxa defines the more or less distinctive rules of the language-games through which a field accomplishes textualisation, which I will call 'textwork-games'. Textwork-games define the 'linguistic market' (Bourdieu 1991a) on which texts are traded and priced as products to gain capital. This implies that scholars, regardless of their position in a field's hierarchical organisation, compete for limited textual space in journals or books with varying reputations, and scholars gain symbolic capital by competing successfully. An increase in symbolic capital is, in turn, correlated with an increase in social capital because membership to collegial networks depends on a scholar's reputation and recognition. And an increase in these forms of capital may correlate with scholars' linguistic capital—their "capacity to produce expressions *à propos, for* a particular market" (Bourdieu 1991a: 18, emphasis in original)—because they are better able to influence the market through improved reputation and connectivity.

Bourdieu's market analogy is informative, though also somewhat misleading, since it suggests that scholars simply act in ratio-economical ways, consciously calculating the maximisation of their gains and the minimisation of their losses (see Bourdieu and Wacquant 1992). This is only partly true. In line with Wittgenstein's ideas, players are not fully conscious of the rules of a field's textwork-games and operate based on their dispositional sense or habitus. They act based on a 'feel for the game' that makes sense to those who believe investing in these games is 'worth the candle', meaning that their actions are less ratio-economic than the market analogy would suggest.

Thus, my main argument in this chapter is that the ontological complicities between scholars and fields are communicatively constituted through their textwork. By learning to embody a field's linguistic habitus, scholars learn to monitor their own communicative practices and balance their own expressive interests against the doxa of the field, which censors these expressions. The field may exert this censorship by monitoring content (e.g. devaluing fictional data or failure to cite canons), style (e.g. devaluing a poetic or a very personal style), and structure (e.g. devaluing a non-standard arrangement of sections). Hence, a field is co-enacted through a continuous give and take in which scholars sense if the position they constitute through their expressions is within the boundaries of the social universe in which they operate, or if these expressions place them in left field.

To investigate these ideas empirically and demonstrate the value of practicing Bourdieu's reflexivity, I examined the main characteristics of the textwork-games through which scholars constitute a relationship of ontological complicity with the field of organisational communication studies and how the contest for capital fuels these textwork-games. I will describe the methods I used to conduct this study in the next section (for a more detailed description, see Brummans 2004).

METHODS

I had several reasons for conducting this inquiry in the field with which I myself have developed a relationship of ontological complicity. Due to my positioning in this space, I am familiar with its doxa, practices, and canons, and I have access to its key players. Because I have a vested interest in its continued existence, I also have a stake in contributing to this space through my own textwork. Put differently, I conducted this study presuming that investigating my own subfield's modes of operating would be 'worth the candle'. Obviously, studying one's own playground also has its drawbacks. My ontological complicity may have blinded me to my subfield's peculiarities, for example. In addition, I risk *losing* capital, because peers may not appreciate my textwork, resulting in the devaluation of my position.

Data Collection and Analysis

To examine the aforementioned questions, I interviewed 12 senior organisational communication scholars about their textwork. Organisational communication studies originated as a subfield of communication studies in the 1940s (see Putnam and Mumby 2014). Although scholars across the globe study organisational communication, I focused on US and Canadian scholars who played an integral role in founding this field. Hence, I asked scholars to participate in this study if they received their doctorate in the mid- to late 1970s or the 1980s (during these years, the field underwent significant changes and increasingly embraced a plurality of metatheoretical perspectives and methodological approaches); were employed by a US or Canadian research university; were actively involved in organisational communication research; and had acquired a considerable amount of capital in the subfield, the larger field of communication studies, and, in most cases, other fields of inquiry. I sampled purposively to ensure diversity in subject areas (ranging from organisational leadership to networks), metatheoretical perspectives, and methodological approaches. I also tried to include a proportionate number of men and women (four women and eight men participated).

I conducted two interviews with each participant—considering interviewing to be a performance in which both the interviewer and interviewee co-produce a situated account (see Alvesson 2003). For each interview, I developed a script, and I conducted pilot interviews with two faculty members from my own department to test the questions. In the first interview, I asked participants to reflect on their academic trajectories by discussing their reasons for choosing an academic career and for choosing organisational communication as a field of study, as well as the metatheoretical perspective and methodological approach they preferred. In the second part of the interview, I asked participants general questions about their research practices and textwork. Here, we would speak, for example, about mental practices that enable someone to conceptualise and design a study, practices that enable someone to implement a study, writing and reading practices, and decision points for publishing work. At the end of this first conversation, I asked participants to select two publications (journal articles, book chapters, or complete books) for the second interview, one representing their early-career work and one recent one. In the follow-up interview, the participants reflected on how they had produced the two texts—for example, by conceptualising, designing, and implementing an empirical study. After this, I asked the participants to think about how the publications reflected what they were trying to accomplish in organisational communication studies, the larger field of communication studies, and possibly other fields. I also asked them to reflect on their practice of voicing the texts—for example, by asking them how they kept a specific audience in mind when they were writing. We spoke about selecting a publication outlet, writing according to a particular format, and the influence of writing genres, too. By comparing the early with the recent publication, I tried to gain insight into the development of participants' habituses through changes in their textwork. Prior to the interviews, I informed participants that I could not guarantee their anonymity, since we would discuss their published materials. While writing this chapter, I decided, however, to protect participants' privacy by using pseudonyms and not directly quoting or citing their publications.

All interviews were transcribed, generating about 20 pages of single-spaced text per conversation. I then conducted an inductive thematic analysis (see Ryan and Bernard 2003) to investigate the key characteristics of the textwork-games through which scholars constitute their ontological complicity with organisational communication studies and how the contest for capital fuels these games. Based on this analysis, I will show in the next section how scholars legitimise their expressive interests within organisational communication by engaging in these games, as well as their expressive interests within other fields, such as management and organisation studies and organisational psychology.

ORGANISATIONAL COMMUNICATION SCHOLARS' CONSTITUTION OF ONTOLOGICAL COMPLICITIES

Legitimising Expressive Interests within Organisational Communication Studies

The scholars who participated in this study, my analysis suggests, constitute relationships of ontological complicity with organisational communication studies through textwork-games, because these games enable them to legitimise their expressive interests by ratifying their position in this sociomaterial space. This ratification is the product of the continuous interaction between the interests someone tries to realise through textwork and the field's censorship, as Margaret's account illustrates:

> [My textwork] depends on where I want to be. Like I still want to publish in [*Communication*] *Monographs* [the flagship journal of communication studies], right? And that means that I might not have the freedom [to exactly express myself as I would like] . . . I think I will always write [by respecting the standards of a given journal] to a certain degree . . . [But] I'll always try to fool around with it in a way that I can kind of push those boundaries out a little bit further and, then, if someone already respects my work . . . they'll say: "Well, I should look at this. This is Margaret. I know her work but see what she's doing now", you know? And maybe accept it because of the foundation that I've established.
> (Margaret is Professor of Organisational Communication at a southwestern US research university)

The following excerpt illustrates in further detail how Margaret practices textwork vis-à-vis the field's censorship, turning her textualisation into a rhetorical instrument for gaining capital:

> All editors say: "We publish anything", but we know—everyone knows—that your chances of getting certain types of work published under the editorship of certain people is just not gonna happen. So I'll look and see who's out there. I'll know their work . . . and I'll know whether or not they might work to help me get something . . . [unconventional] published . . . And if I can't find it through the publication outlet or the editor, then I either don't write it, or I might seek out an opportunity to put it into an edited book . . . where there's a little bit more flexibility and people are willing to explore . . . I think it's inevitable [that this censorship occurs] . . . I do think that we've been working to change that . . . [To affect such change, you have] to build a cadre [of scholars] and get people in editorial positions . . . So you have to work the system to change it within.

Margaret's account shows how she seeks to market her textwork by balancing her expressive interests against the field's censorship. She compromises her expressive interests to gain voice (linguistic capital), access to networks of influential scholars (social capital), and overall status (symbolic capital) on the linguistic market. Through the acquisition of these forms of capital, Margaret seeks to strengthen her position not only in organisational communication but also in the larger field of communication studies. Gaining capital, she suggests, increases her freedom to produce texts that align with her expressive interests and to change the direction in which the field is going. This excerpt thus shows how the ontological complicity between scholar and field is a function of textwork-games, because the successful pursuit of individual interests is intimately tied to the field's valuation of a scholar's expressions. However, some scholars may perceive considerable difficulties in influencing the tide of these textwork-games, as Michael's account shows:

> In this discipline [referring to organisational communication studies], yeah, I suppose I'm something of an oddity—yeah, that's the way I would put it. First of all, I'm interested in science. Science isn't very popular in this discipline right now. There are still some people who do it, but fewer and fewer all the time, it seems, and they come under a lot of criticism . . . [be]cause of the politics of social research, basically . . . I mean . . . since [the introduction of interpretivism and critical theory into organisational communication], I think it's become—I don't know—maybe not so inclusive, or it seems to exclude perspectives that I'm interested in . . . and [some people] deny them, and even . . . call them 'evil' and 'corrupt'.
> (Michael is Professor of Organisational Communication at a southwestern US research university)

Michael continued:

> [Interpretivism] was not taught to me as some sort of an opposing position. You know, it was . . . another sort of useful way of looking at things. [Now] it seems to have sort of turned into a group that seems intent on battling the people who, you know, favour science . . . and so, yeah . . . the whole thing is sort of distressing, I think.

Michael's reflections indicate that a scholar's position—here especially defined in the form of an antinomy between post-positivism and critical theory as well as interpretivism—can become obsolete in light of a field's historical developments. Changes in organisational communication's habitus, occurring vis-à-vis changes in other fields, such as management and organisation studies or organisational sociology, thus may place an agent 'offside'. Michael reflects on this field-effect by noting that his linguistic capital has decreased. He experiences difficulties maintaining or increasing his symbolic capital. The fact that scholars have been promoted to professor—based on their acquisition of a relatively high amount of cultural (especially linguistic), social, and symbolic capital—does not mean that legitimising their position becomes less important. Because the field's textwork-games are ongoing (and uncompromising), enacting a position means more than 'playing it safe'— that is, textwork is a matter of continuously making a difference by textualising knowledge, based on a position that is valued in the eyes of others who operate in the same social universe. The field's move towards complementing a post-positivist approach with interpretive and critical approaches, Michael believes, increasingly defines the 'name of the game' and decentralises his position. He, in turn, construes these changes as *political* moves, driven by the competition of interests between what Margaret called 'cadres' of scholars.

The scholars in this study frequently indicated that they rely on their network of colleagues (social capital) to gain access to, and power in, the field. In fact, all participants acknowledged that textwork is a collaborative affair and that a text is an 'intertext' (Cheney and Tompkins 1988: 460)—a co-authored, co-referential product. Some interviewees nonetheless expressed their discontentment about the influence of social capital on the linguistic market. As Michael noted, for example,

> [M]erely getting [texts] out there, that's gratifying, I suppose, because it's sort of a professional affirmation that you've been allocated a scarce resource to put your ideas out there. But that's not the same as having them, practically speaking, extend beyond you very much. Sad, it seems to me—and the older I get, the more it seems this way—that that's more of a matter . . . personal relationship to people.

Michael's account corroborates the idea that textwork enables scholars to constitute a relationship of complicity with the field by implicating themselves in a network of colleagues. The field does not take scholars' dependence on social capital into account when evaluating their individual performance and accrediting them symbolic capital, however. Several of the scholars I interviewed argued that this misevaluation is "part of the game". "That's the way of the world", as Owen said. "If Schumacher [the renowned Formula 1 racer] wins a race, all the people who made it possible for Schumacher to win the race don't get any professional credit" (Owen is Emeritus Professor of Organisational Communication at a Canadian research university). While the textualisation of knowledge is an inherently collaborative affair, the field thus promotes a sense of 'capitalism' that encourages individualism through social opportunism. In these textwork-games, the knowledge scholars develop is important, yet it is also how they play the game by gaining influence through alliances with others.

So the scholars' accounts demonstrate that they legitimise their expressive interests through textwork. However, their accounts also indicate that the stakes of a field's textwork-games might change along the course of their academic career. Instead of concentrating on becoming a legitimate player in the game of "requisite numbers", Helen has, for example, become increasingly concerned with leaving a legacy and influencing the field's direction as her career progresses:

> I'm more concerned now about contribution and legacy than I was early on. Early on, I was happy if I got published [laughing] . . . You were just . . . happy if you did the requisite numbers and quality, you know? And so, as you evolve in your career, then it's not so much: How much have I published? Or even: Where have I published? But: What have I published and how much of a contribution does that leave?
> (Helen is Professor of Organisational Communication at a midwestern US research university)

The colloquial phrase "I got published" is particularly interesting here, because it exemplifies the *ontological* relationship between scholar and field: by publishing, scholars identify themselves in a field, yet the field's existence also depends on individuals' constitution of their academic identity through publication. Field and a scholar's identity are thus mutually constitutive. Through textwork, a scholar's positioning becomes interweaved with the field's constitution, meaning that self-promotion increasingly goes hand in hand with promoting the field, as is illustrated by Helen's concern about leaving a legacy.

The organisational communication scholars' accounts illustrate that this dual promotion occurs by engaging in textwork conversations with oneself and others. In the practice of textwork, the conceptual division between author and reader "blurs together", as Liam said (Liam is Professor of Organisational Communication at a southwestern US research university). Like all authors, scholars create textual relationships with others (audiences) and themselves in writing and reading. As flesh-and-blood 'empirical authors', they engage in imaginary conversations with 'model readers'. And they act as 'empirical readers' by conversing with the 'model authors' they imagine when reading the texts of others—or even their own (see Eco 1992). In textwork conversations like these, the 'other' is thus a conflation of a literal other and "oneself as another" (Ricoeur 1992). To what degree these conversations are imagined is questionable, though, especially in a field where authors envision dialogues with peers they know well. Besides, particularly in an academic field, textwork conversations take place through face-to-face talks, e-mail correspondence, and so on. Empirical-model author-reader distinctions therefore tend to become foggy in the practice of academic textwork.

The scholars I interviewed corroborated the idea that textwork conversations play an important role in the constitution of complicities and the legitimisation of their expressive interests. In these conversations, scholars shift almost undetectably from empirical to model author and from author to empirical and model reader. By perfecting this shifting ability during the course of their academic career, they have learned to write for others *as if* they are writing for themselves (and vice versa). Thomas's account illustrates how author and audience become increasingly conflated as the constitution of a scholar's position becomes entangled with the field's constitution:

> [T]he older I get and the more mature I get as a writer, the more I'm writing for myself, because I don't feel like I have to necessarily please an audience in a way. They're a model audience for me in the sense that I really want to write something that is going to be exciting to them. Not so much in the sense that I want to be sure to meet their expectations in some way . . . It's not a judgemental kind of thing or an anticipation of judgement . . . I feel like this community—this is a funny thing to say—depends on me to play a kind of role [laughing] and I want to come through with that. I don't want to let them down. I don't want to put out something that's gonna be mediocre or uninspiring.
> (Thomas is Professor of Organisational Communication at a southeastern US research university)

This excerpt exemplifies that a scholar writes for a market. In time, Thomas's model reader has become part of his linguistic habitus and, thus, forms an integral part of the way he practices textwork. Thomas's textualised position has simultaneously become implicated in the field's workings and contributes to its constitution. Accordingly, Thomas's writing for himself more or less equals his writing for others (and vice versa). Textwork conversations therefore create relationships of complicity between scholar and field by enabling the persuasion of self *and* others, which corroborates Gross's (1990: 3) observation that "[r]hetorically, the creation of knowledge is a task beginning with self-persuasion and ending with the persuasion of others". In contrast to what Gross's statement intimates, however, it seems that this persuasion has no clear starting or ending point and that the distinction between self and other blurs in practice. That is, textwork involves the constant and almost imperceptible alteration between self and other through which scholar and field become married.

Legitimising Expressive Interests within Other Academic Fields

In line with the idea that scholars' individual fates are linked to the fate of the social space in which they operate, several interviewees were concerned about bolstering the position of organisational communication vis-à-vis other fields, such as management and organisation studies and organisational psychology. These scholars use their textwork to differentiate the field from these other social spaces, and, in turn, they often construe a greater difference between their authorial selves and the model readers in these fields than when dialoguing with model readers in their own field—suggesting that their self is less constructed as another in these 'foreign' spaces. Helen, for example, has been working to change the underdog status of organisational communication scholars in management and organisation studies. As she stated,

> It's just that their orientations are so different. The languages are different and so—I don't know how to put it exactly but—it's very much . . . simple, clear baby-steps that you have to take with these people and overexplain every damn thing, okay? Because . . . they think communication is soft and squishy and something they don't wanna deal with. So you have to make that palatable . . . I will also get mad and choose not to publish [in their field] . . . because a part of me just gets mad at them and gets mad at their parochialism . . . I know and trust [organisational communication colleagues when they review my work] . . . They're not gonna let me get away with anything. They're gonna tell it to me straight . . . When they tell me something . . . I know where they're coming from . . . I know their background . . . I know who they are. It makes a difference, you know? It has more weight with me than somebody from a management discipline . . . [where] certain individuals . . . have their own axe to grind.

Helen's use of the word 'palatable' intimates that textwork is evaluated based on a field's habitus. This system of dispositions yields a 'taste' that is particular to the market in which scholars present their work. If their habitus differs significantly from the habitus of a more or less foreign field, scholars face standards for evaluating the quality of textualised knowledge that do not match their 'natural' sense of judgement. Consequently, it might be difficult to communicate in a way that the field deems appropriate (cultural capital, especially its linguistic kind), gain entry into this field's networks (social capital), and gain credibility and status (symbolic capital).

Part of scholarly practice thus consists of trying to find out how to market one's work in these foreign markets. Helen's account illustrates that this marketing entails having textwork conversations in which she constructs her model readers as obstinate pupils, instead of peers. She perceives these others as adversaries to the cause of organisational communication, because they are focused on protecting their own turf. Hence, Helen does not trust that these others will help her guard herself 'against' herself, as it were, for they might let her "get away" with work that is lacking in quality—or taste. Also John's account illustrates this 'other-ing' of scholars in fields outside of organisational communication:

> I think strategically about when I'm gonna put work in another discipline . . . what voice I wanna have . . . and how much I have to accommodate to their language . . . to their structures . . . and how much I wanna

bring communication . . . And sometimes I'm very strategic in the kinds of references I make in the bibliography . . . [I put in] things that I might not otherwise put in if I was writing only for communication . . . because I almost feel the need to introduce them to those references if they wanna follow up . . . [S]o I will often pad, if you will, the references.
(John is Professor of Organisational Communication at a southwestern US research university)

By thoughtfully referencing texts produced within organisational communication, John aims to strengthen the position of the field with which he feels ontologically complicit, which shows how an academic field builds and legitimises itself through the internal and external reinforcement of its intertextuality. This shows how scholars are rewarded for corroborating the field by citing its canons. As Owen noted, scholars are also censored, however, for failing to do so:

I was inspired by literatures that are not generally part of the canon [of organisational communication] . . . [This has] been . . . a disadvantage, because it meant I felt isolated from the field for a very long time. But I think it turns out . . . to be an advantage, because it means . . . not just following on in the same track . . . a track that's always been well worked out . . . There are very strong constraints on [trying to change the field by introducing new literatures], because when you submit an article, the first thing they wanna know is . . . [whether] you've done the correct literature referencing and you won't get published unless you do that. My work is constantly being criticised, because I don't refer to the right people . . . and that's a . . . very powerful structuring device that the field has, which does limit creativity.

Owen's account illustrates that a field's corpus can weigh heavily on those who are trying to look beyond the field. Upon entering, scholars are trained to recognise this corpus and incorporate it into their sense of practice. Through this canonisation, certain perspectives, theories, concepts, or methodologies may become 'trademarked' by a given field. In turn, as John's next account indicates, a field's literature may become a beacon through which authors can navigate their textwork and a standard through which a field constitutes and controls its frontiers:

Psychologists beat me up regularly for ['misusing' a particular construct, first developed in psychology] . . . I think their construct signifies something that had a very different meaning [from the way I was using it] . . . And so I think, if anything, that point . . . early in my career . . . taught me to stay faithful to the language use of whatever community I had entered . . . because those things had real meaning . . . I'd really got beat up pretty good as an assistant professor . . . Getting reviews sent back: "What the hell were you thinking using this construct? Yeah, this is already in use" ... This is almost like it has a trademark on it ... And they were probably right, you know? ... I may have taken it too far.

Noteworthy here is that John *agrees* with the censorship that was imposed on him by psychology scholars, showing how this field socialised him to censor his own expressive interests. Early censorship experiences like the ones mentioned earlier trained John to stay faithful to a field's linguistic habitus—that is, to alter his textwork to gain linguistic and symbolic capital. When comparing scholars' accounts about their textwork in fields other than organisational communication, it becomes clear, though, that scholars vary in their perception of other fields' foreignness. In addition, scholars vary in the degree to which their textwork centres on legitimising organisational communication vis-à-vis other fields. Ethan's account provides an interesting contrast in this regard. He remarked,

> I think some, and occasionally worry, about the role of communication as a discipline. I worry about it, or at least think about it, because I didn't come from communication. A lot of what I do is also done very well by folks in other disciplines: information science, management, social psychology, psychology in general, sociology, in some cases, economics ... In some cases, there's a lot of overlap between what we do in our field and what they do. In some cases, maybe the overlap between what I do and what my friends in ... management ... or psychology [do] ... is higher than the overlap between what I do and [what] some of my friends in communication ... [do], which doesn't bother me.
> (Ethan is Professor of Organisational Communication at a midwestern US research university)

The picture that emerges from comparing different accounts is thus that scholars vary in their perception of a field's foreignness, since they vary in their capacity and willingness to express themselves in different languages. My Bourdieusian analysis indicates that the experience of foreignness depends mainly on the homology between the positions scholars constitute through their textwork and the habitus of the spaces in which this constitution occurs. This homology tends to be the strongest in the field with which scholars have developed a strong relation of ontological complicity. Ethan's account illustrates, however, that scholars' habitus may also be homologous with multiple fields. In this case, scholars are disposed to acquire linguistic, social, and symbolic capital in these other spaces without having to change their sense of practice in substantial ways. Those whose positions are homologous with several fields' systems of dispositions thus constitute multiple ontological complicities that are relatively strong. And because these scholars' fates do not depend on the fate of one social collectivity, they may be less intent on defending one field against another.

To conclude, unsurprisingly perhaps, only a few of the scholars I interviewed seemed aware of how their 'academic subjectivity' is tied to the organisational communication field, and how this complicity affects their research practice. Several scholars suggested that there is little need to reflect on this complicity, because their goal is to understand *other* people's communicative behaviour. As Elizabeth stated,

> I suspect that I would be more self-reflexive ... if I had chosen philosophy as a topic, but I'm a field researcher primarily ... and I'm very much about trying to understand other people's lives [laughing] ... You know, I live in my life; I don't need to spend huge amounts of time trying to understand it.
> (Elizabeth is Professor of Organisational Communication at a southwestern US research university)

In turn, several interviewees were convinced that their interpretation of other people's practical logic was accurate or self-evident. As Susan said, for example, referring to her analysis of data for a particular study,

> I think anybody ... if somebody read the data, they'd see all these different stories and things like that ... and they might pick up on some of these pieces immediately, because it was pretty easy to pick up on some of it.
> (Susan is Professor of Organisational Communication at a midwestern US research university)

By making the practice of reflecting on a field's habitus *part of* its habitus (Brubaker 1993), a field may develop a form of reflexivity that resists this kind of "scholastic epistemocentrism" (Bourdieu 2000b: 50) and guard itself against itself, as it were. Through this reflexivity, in other words, scholars may become more aware of their blindfolds, investments in contests for capital, and attachments to positions whose constitution takes considerable time and effort. Practicing this reflexivity as a field requires that a field rewards scholars for questioning the consequences of their actions in the world, so this kind of criticality becomes part of the mutual constitution of scholars and field. This is no easy feat, as Paul indicated: "If you ... try and situate [what you do as a scholar] in a context of broader societal issues, it might almost sort of drive you crazy and ... make you think: [What] ... kind of difference is this gonna make?" (Paul is Professor of Organisational Communication at a southeastern US research university). Paul remarked, though, that the peril of madness notwithstanding, "turning the lens on ourselves" *as a field* is very important and useful:

> [O]ne of the most important things we do as researchers ... is to study the taken-for-granted, right? [To] study the common sense practices that

people generally aren't reflectively engaged in. And . . . the idea of sort of turning the lens on ourselves and looking at . . . scholarly practice as a . . . largely . . . taken-for-granted process, I think is really useful . . . I think [there is] a general kind of perhaps lack of reflexivity that all of us have . . . We all come out of particular . . . scholarly communities and we all, in a fairly early point in our training, try to internalise the principles of our academic community, and I think . . . you forget how . . . revelatory that stuff was initially . . . It just sort of becomes a way of feeling . . . talking . . . thinking . . . experiencing and practicing.

DISCUSSION AND CONCLUSIONS

In this chapter, I have demonstrated the importance of putting Bourdieu's reflexivity into practice by reflecting on the relationship between scholars' textwork and the "form of life" (Wittgenstein 1953/2001: 10) these practices constitute. My study shows that through textwork, scholars identify and legitimise themselves as individuals and as a field. My research also reveals that scholars reflect on their reasons for studying a subject, taking a metatheoretical perspective, and adopting a methodological approach, but they are less aware of their ontological complicities with academic fields, let alone of the consequences of these complicities for their academic practices and the world they study.

Because scholars' sense of practice acts as the main arbiter of their own practices and is intimately linked to the historically developed habitus of their field, it is imperative for a field to reflect systematically on its modes of operating in order to prevent itself from getting caught up in its own dynamics. This kind of reflexivity may destabilise a field's constitution, yet it does not trivialise, deny, or delegitimise its operations. To the contrary, this reflexivity is necessary for understanding how certain modes of operating inhibit or derail the field's production of knowledge. Even more importantly, it helps scholars understand how to act *ethically* as a field (Evens 1999). Critically reflecting on the values that drive a field's enactment is therefore not accomplished by "turning . . . subjectivities upon themselves" (Bourdieu 2000b: 119), but by cultivating awareness of "the creative and paradoxically natural conduct whereby humans together inform themselves and their world, both wittingly and not, with second-nature or value" (Evens 1999: 7).

My study shows that examining a field's textwork-games provides a good starting point for generating this kind of reflexivity. By making reflection on the ways a field constructs a subject and investigates it through textwork-games part of its habitus, a field can become more aware of itself as a social collectivity (see also Brummans 2006). In line with Bourdieu's ideas, my research demonstrates that the complicity between scholars and field depends on the homology between their positioning in a social space and this space's system of dispositions. While practicing textwork, this homology reveals itself as a *sens pratique* that gives scholars a feeling of dexterity. Yet when being asked to reflect on their 'sense for the game', scholars often tend to be conflicted, because it confronts them with the games through which they are constituted, as well as with the social space that makes this constitution possible. In such instances, a scholar's habitus is 'caught in its own act', so to speak; it 'misfires', being insufficiently capable or prepared to cope with the contradictions it produces. Reflexive moments like these present a window for considering how and why scholarly practices constitute a view on a reality from a position in an academic field with a historically developed set of presuppositions, dispositions, and stakes. By not reflecting on this complicity, scholars risk projecting their system of dispositions onto research participants who mostly operate in non-academic fields like the political, professional, or artistic field, each with their own "logic of practice" (Bourdieu 1990b). The danger of this scholastic epistemocentrism is that it can result in the construction of knowledge that is overly academic—developed based on the habitus of an academic universe.

My inquiry raises several questions that invite further investigation. First of all, my research suggests that some scholars constitute complicities with multiple academic fields, but they may also constitute complicities with non-academic fields, such as the political field (in which they act as party members) or the professional field (in which they act as consultants). Especially in his later publications, Bourdieu (1998a, 1998b, 2001) addressed the interaction between fields (academic and non-academic) and their imbricated nature, though these works do not treat this subject in great empirical detail, and future research should take a closer look at the way this interaction affects scholars' operations.

Besides the interaction between fields, Bourdieu's work does not specify how scholars learn to incorporate a habitus through education, socialisation, and the experience of operating in a field. Through subtle (and not-so-subtle) communicative processes, newcomers learn to embody a field's doxa, which seems quite foreign at first. As this study illustrates, a doxa can become quite natural, logical, and incontrovertible over time. No wonder that Latour and Woolgar (1979) viewed academic communities as exotic tribes. These tribes employ various initiation and indoctrination rituals to secure their continued existence. Examining these persuasion practices more carefully is important, because such research will shed more light on the way agents become scholars vis-à-vis agents who do not constitute complicities with academic fields.

Furthermore, in view of Bourdieu's emphasis on social life as embodied praxis, it is important to discuss this study's focus on textwork. Although textwork plays an integral part in the practice of research, academic work consists of many other practices, such as teaching, mentoring students, attending faculty meetings, and so on. In addition, many other types of activities influence scholars' research practice, such as giving workshops or presentations to non-academicians, talking with their children, playing music, or reading non-academic literature. Hence, this study was limited in that it asked scholars to zoom in on a particular stream of activities, and it would be useful to shadow scholars to gain insight into the confluence of different streams of activities that form their lives (Dick and Ziering Kofman's 2002 documentary, *Derrida*, illustrates how eye-opening it can be to shadow a scholar during his or her everyday life).

To conclude, it is important to ask how the inferences drawn from this study may pertain to other scholars. For example, how do graduate students, assistant professors, or associate professors constitute relationships of complicity with organisational communication studies by participating in the field's textwork-games? My inquiry was based on conversations with, and works of, a distinct set of scholars whose careers more or less parallel the trajectory of this field and who actively pursue research. Talking with scholars in different career stages, as well as scholars who do not concentrate on research as much as the scholars who participated in this study do, would probably produce different insights. It is also not clear to what extent this study's results are field- and subfield-specific. Are complicities constituted in similar ways in other subfields of communication studies (health communication, intercultural communication, interpersonal communication), other social science and humanities fields (management and organisation, psychology, sociology, philosophy), or natural science fields (physics, chemistry, biology)? Exploring these questions of transferability (Lincoln and Guba 1985) will be important, yet I hope this text has convincingly shown how practicing Bourdieu's reflexivity can improve our production of socially significant, ethical knowledge, regardless of the spaces with which we align ourselves.

NOTE

1. Thank you kindly, François Cooren, Linda Putnam, and James Taylor, for providing helpful comments on an earlier version of this chapter, which was presented at the 2005 International Critical Management Studies Conference in Cambridge, UK. Texas A&M University's Melbern G. Glasscock Center for Humanities Research generously supported the dissertation research that formed the basis for this text. This chapter is dedicated to the late James Arnt Aune, who introduced me to Bourdieu and helped me understand his logic of practice.

REFERENCES

Alvesson, M. (2003) 'Beyond Neopositivists, Romantics, and Localists: A Reflexive Approach to Interviews in Organizational Research', *Academy of Management Review*, 28(1): 13–33.
Alvesson, M., and Deetz, D. (2000) *Doing Critical Management Research*, London: SAGE.

Alvesson, M., and Sköldberg, K. (2000) *Reflexive Methodology: New Vistas for Qualitative Research*, London: SAGE.
Borges, J. L. (1999) 'Mirrors', in *Selected Poems*, trans. A. Hurley, New York: Penguin, 105–107.
Bourdieu, P. (1977) *Outline of a Theory of Practice*, trans. R. Nice, Cambridge, UK: Cambridge University Press.
Bourdieu, P. (1988) *Homo Academicus*, trans. P. Collier, Stanford, CA: Stanford University Press.
Bourdieu, P. (1990a) *In Other Words: Essays towards a Reflexive Sociology*, trans. M. Adamson, Stanford, CA: Stanford University Press.
Bourdieu, P. (1990b) *The Logic of Practice*, trans. R. Nice, Stanford, CA: Stanford University Press.
Bourdieu, P. (1991a) *Language & Symbolic Power*, ed. J. B. Thompson, trans. G. Raymond and M. Adamson, Cambridge, MA: Harvard University Press.
Bourdieu, P. (1991b) *The Political Ontology of Martin Heidegger*, trans. P. Collier, Stanford, CA: Stanford University Press.
Bourdieu, P. (1998a) *Acts of Resistance: Against the Tyranny of the Market*, trans. R. Nice, New York: New Press.
Bourdieu, P. (1998b) *Practical Reason: On the Theory of Action*, Stanford, CA: Stanford University Press.
Bourdieu, P. (2000a) 'The Biographical Illusion', in P. du Gay, J. Evans, and P. Redman (eds.), *Identity: A Reader*, London: SAGE, 297–303.
Bourdieu, P. (2000b) *Pascalian Meditations*, trans. R. Nice, Stanford, CA: Stanford University Press.
Bourdieu, P. (2001) *Firing Back: Against the Tyranny of the Market 2*, trans. L. Wacquant, New York: New Press.
Bourdieu, P., and Wacquant, L.J.D. (1992) *An Invitation to Reflexive Sociology*, Chicago: University of Chicago Press.
Brubaker, R. (1993) 'Social Theory as Habitus' in C. Calhoun, E. LiPuma, and M. Postone (eds.), *Bourdieu: Critical Perspectives*, Chicago: The University of Chicago Press, 212–234.
Brummans, B.H.J.M. (2004) 'Dispositional Reflections', unpublished doctoral dissertation, Texas A&M University, College Station, TX.
Brummans, B.H.J.M. (2006) 'The Montréal School and the Question of Agency' in F. Cooren, J. R. Taylor, and E. J. Van Every (eds.), *Communication as organizing: Empirical and theoretical explorations in the dynamic of text and conversation*, Mahwah, NJ: Lawrence-Erlbaum, 197–211.
Cheney, G., and Tompkins, P. K. (1988) 'On the Facts of the Text as the Basis of Human Communication Research' in J. A. Anderson (ed.), *Communication Yearbook 11*, Newbury Park, CA: SAGE, 455–481.
Deetz, S. (1996) 'Commentary: The Positioning of the Researcher in Studies of Organizations: De-Hatching Literary Theory', *Journal of Management Inquiry*, 5(4): 387–391.
Dick, K. (Director), and Ziering Kofman, A. (Director and Producer) (2002) *Derrida* [Documentary], New York: Zeitgeist Films.
Dreyfus, H. L., and Rabinow, P. (1983) *Michel Foucault: Beyond Structuralism and Hermeneutics*, 2nd ed., Chicago: The University of Chicago Press.
Eco, U. (1992) *Interpretation and Overinterpretation*, ed. S. Collini, Cambridge, UK: Cambridge University Press.
Evens, T.M.S. (1999) 'Bourdieu and the Logic of Practice: Is All Giving Indian-Giving or Is "Generalized Materialism" Not Enough?', *Sociological Theory*, 17(1): 3–31.
Everett, J. (2002) 'Organizational Research and the Praxeology of Pierre Bourdieu', *Organizational Research Methods*, 5(1): 56–80.

Foucault, M. (1970/1994) *The Order of Things: An Archaeology of the Human Sciences*, New York: Vintage Books.
Foucault, M. (1972/1989) *The Archaeology of Knowledge*, trans. A. M. Sheridan Smith, New York: Routledge.
Giddens, A. (1991), *Modernity and Self-Identity: Self and Society in the Late Modern Age*, Stanford, CA: Stanford University Press.
Gilbert, G. N., and Mulkay, M. (1984) *Opening Pandora's Box: A Sociological Analysis of Scientists' Discourse*, Cambridge, UK: Cambridge University Press.
Gross, A. G. (1990) *The Rhetoric of Science*, Cambridge, MA: Harvard University Press.
Habermas, J. (1984) *The Theory of Communicative Action*, vol. 1, trans. T. McCarthy, Boston, MA: Beacon Press.
Hardy, C., and Clegg, S. (1997) 'Relativity without Relativism: Reflexivity in Post-Paradigm Organization Studies', *British Journal of Management*, 8(1): 5–17.
Hardy, C., Phillips, N., and Clegg, S. (2001) 'Reflexivity in Organization and Management Theory: A Study of the Production of the Research "Subject"', *Human Relations*, 54(5): 531–560.
King, A. (2000) 'Thinking with Bourdieu against Bourdieu: A "Practical" Critique of the Habitus', *Sociological Theory*, 18(4): 417–433.
Latour, B., and Woolgar, S. (1979) *Laboratory Life: The Social Construction of Scientific Facts*, Beverly Hills, CA: SAGE.
Lincoln, Y. S., and Guba, E. G. (1985) *Naturalistic Inquiry*, Newbury Park, CA: SAGE.
Putnam, L. L. (1996) 'Commentary: Situating the Author and Text', *Journal of Management Inquiry*, 5(4): 382–386.
Putnam, L. L., and Mumby, D. K. (2014) 'Introduction: Advancing Theory and Research in Organizational Communication', in L. L. Putnam and D. K. Mumby (eds.), *The SAGE Handbook of Organizational Communication*, Thousand Oaks, CA: SAGE, 1–18.
Ricoeur, P. (1992) *Oneself as Another*, trans. K. Blamey, Chicago: University of Chicago Press.
Ryan, G. W., and Bernard, H. R. (2003) 'Techniques to Identify Themes', *Field Methods*, 15(1): 85–109.
Smith, D. E. (2001) 'Texts and the Ontology of Organizations and Institutions', *Studies in Cultures, Organizations and Societies*, 7(2): 159–198.
Sweetman, P. (2003) 'Twenty-First Century Dis-ease? Habitual Reflexivity or the Reflexive Habitus', *Sociological Review*, 51(4): 528–549.
Van Maanen, J. (1996) 'Commentary: On the Matter of Voice', *Journal of Management Inquiry*, 5(4): 375–381.
Wacquant, L. (1989) 'Towards a Reflexive Sociology: A Workshop with Pierre Bourdieu', *Sociological Theory*, 7(1): 26–63.
Weick, K. E. (1999) 'Theory Construction as Disciplined Reflexivity: Tradeoffs in the 90s', *Academy of Management Review*, 24(4): 797–806.
Weick, K. E. (2002) 'Real-Time Reflexivity: Prods to Reflection', *Organization Studies*, 23(6): 893–898.
Wittgenstein, L. (1953/2001) *Philosophical Investigations*, 3rd ed., trans. G.E.M. Anscombe, Oxford, UK: Blackwell.

Part II
Empirical Insights

5 Reintroducing Power and Struggles within Organisational Fields
A Return to Bourdieu's Framework

Karim Hamadache

INTRODUCTION

The influence of Bourdieu's oeuvre on organisational analysis is mostly manifest in the widespread use—even unequally and often separately—of the three concepts that form the cornerstones of his sociology—namely, 'field', 'habitus', and 'capital'. Among these constructs, that of field is probably the most mobilised since its introduction by DiMaggio and Powell in their highly influential 1983 article. The concept of 'organisational field', inspired in large part by the Bourdieusian one of field, represents one of the two signposts, along with that of 'institutional isomorphism', which paved the way of the new institutionalism in organisational analysis. However, if it is undeniable that this concept, as it was conceptually framed and empirically explored in new-institutional theory, had improved our comprehension of "how, why, and which organizations respond in particular ways to institutional expectations" (Greenwood and Meyer, 2008: 261), power relations and permanent struggles between agents within organisational fields, which were outlined by DiMaggio and Powell in their seminal article, were largely overlooked (Emirbayer and Johnson, 2008; Greenwood and Meyer, 2008).

The difficulty of the new institutionalism to deal with power relations and struggles is partly inherent to the dominant conception developed within this research trend regarding organisational field construction/structuration. As emphasised by Hoffman (1999), most researchers had in fact adopted the idea that an organisational field structures itself around a specific market and/or technology. For instance, in their work, Leblebici et al. (1991) focused on the American radio industry field, while Powell (1999) chose to investigate the US biotechnology field. Accordingly, organisational field is seen as an objective reality imposing itself upon disparate organisations, pushing them to become more similar to one another.

Within Bourdieu's framework, field construction is conceived as a political process involving different agents in a permanent struggle to define the issue (*enjeu*) of the field (Bourdieu and Wacquant, 1992: 98). "Field—even the scientific field—defines itself (among other things) defining specific stakes (*enjeux*) and interests which are irreducible to the stakes and interests specific to other fields (. . .) and which are not perceived by someone who has not been shaped to enter that field" (Bourdieu, 1993: 72). This approach of field construction was reintroduced by Hoffman, who suggested that an "organizational field is formed around the issues that become important to the interests and objectives of a specific collective of organizations" (1999: 352). However, although Hoffman's approach constitutes an important step in the way of reintroducing power relations and struggles in new-institutional theory, it still fails to fully exploit the theoretical and empirical possibilities provided by Bourdieu's framework by not tackling directly the question of how and why a particular issue became at the centre of field construction.

This chapter focuses on field construction process considered as a political and strategic activity. Through a return to Bourdieu's framework, the chapter offers three main contributions. First, it sheds light on power relations and the role of agents in the process of field construction. Second, it illustrates this topic through a case study of the construction of the orphan drug field in the US. Third, the chapter relates the Bourdieusian concepts of field, habitus, and capital to the recent research in new institutionalism in organisational analysis.

To illustrate the theoretical framework elaborated in this chapter, I chose to study the construction process of the orphan drug (OD) field in the US from the mid-1970s to the late 1990s, relying on a wide variety of publicly available sources (hearings before Congress, official reports, legal texts, newspaper and medical journal articles, proceedings of conferences, books, etc.). ODs are products intended for the treatment of rare diseases (RDs)—that is, diseases with low prevalence in the general population. Because the cost of developing and bringing to the market such drugs would not be recovered by their expected sales, pharmaceutical companies are unwilling to develop ODs under normal market conditions. Giving this situation, several patient organisations have undertaken since the early 1980s a persistent lobbying of Congress to enact legislation aiming to create a favourable environment for the development and the commercialisation of ODs. This movement led to the formation of diverse inter-organisational relations (collaboration, confrontation, manipulation, etc.) between the agents engaged in the construction of the OD field (pharmaceutical industry, public authority, health professional, and RD patient groups), each of them working to shape the construction process to its advantage. To fully understand this process, two main research questions must be answered: (1) How and why did RDs become at the centre of the construction of a new organisational field? (2) What is the influence of the positions of agents, their capitals, and their habitus on the actions they undertook to shape the construction of the OD field?

This chapter is divided into three sections. In the first one, I provide a critical examination of the concept of organisational field as it was developed in the new institutionalism in organisational analysis. From the background of this examination, I elaborate a theoretical framework, based on a return to Bourdieu's oeuvre, which integrates power relations and the role of agents in the process of field construction. In the second section, I outline the methodology developed to study the construction of the OD field in the US. The final section presents the results of the case study, showing the process of social construction of the notion of orphan drugs as an object of debate and struggle between different agents, and examining the actions undertaken by these agents to shape the construction of the field in relation to their positions, capitals, and habitus.

THE CONCEPT OF FIELDS IN ORGANISATIONAL ANALYSIS

Introducing 'Organisational Field' in the New Institutionalism

The relationship between organisations and their environment constitutes one of the most important and enduring debates in organisational analysis. The new institutionalism,[1] whose conceptual foundations were established in large part in the works of Meyer and Rowan (1977) and DiMaggio and Powell (1983), has made an important contribution to this debate by considering that institutional environment, defined as "widespread social conceptions of appropriate organizational form and behavior" (Tolbert, 1985: 2), mediates and shapes social choices (Hoffman, 1999). Within institutional environment, one can see the emergence and structuration of 'organisational fields', which, in DiMaggio and Powell's words, represent "those organizations that, in the aggregate, constitute a recognized area of institutional life: key suppliers, resource and product consumers, regulatory agencies, and other organizations that produce similar services or products" (1983: 148). As the authors pointed out, "[t]he virtue of this unit of analysis is that it directs our attention not simply to competing firms, as does the population approach of Hannan and Freeman (1977), or to networks of organizations that actually interact, as does the interorganizational network approach of Laumann et al. (1978), but to the totality of relevant actors" (1983: 148).

Although Bourdieu was not explicitly cited by DiMaggio and Powell in their 1983 article, he was clearly a core inspiration behind the concept of organisational field. In a book chapter published the same year, DiMaggio proposed that organisational field be thought of "in the dual sense in which Bourdieu (1975) uses 'champ', to signify both common purpose and an arena of strategy and conflict" (1983: 149). But this second element of the definition was the missing piece in the DiMaggio and Powell article which did not sufficiently emphasise the political and conflicting dimensions of organisational fields—a conceptual weakness that led to the rejection of the article by *The American Journal of Sociology* (Greenwood and Meyer, 2008: 260). The conception of field as an arena of permanent struggle between agents occupying different subject positions, a central element in Bourdieu's definition, was largely overlooked by organisational analysts who focused their attention on the process of homogenisation—that is, the "constraining process that forces one unit in a population to resemble other units that face the same set of environmental conditions" (DiMaggio and Powell, 1983: 149).

One of the elements allowing building a political view of organisational fields lies in the systematic analysis of the structuration process underlying the emergence and evolution of organisational fields. Such analysis, for which DiMaggio and Powell (1983) had called, has not been undertaken in sufficient depth, as many neo-institutional scholars came to recognise (e.g. DiMaggio, 1991; Lawrence and Phillips, 2004). In fact, most researchers have considered that organisational fields are structured around companies with a common technology and/or market (Hoffman, 1999). This had led to a conception of field structuration as a constraining process which determines the agents that take part and the patterns of relations between them (cooperation, confrontation, etc.). The diversity of agents' interests, as well as the asymmetric distribution of resources, and therefore the unequal capacity of agents to influence this process were poorly captured by the dominant conception of field structuration.

Returning to Bourdieu's Framework

A return to Bourdieu's conception of fields can open up new possibilities for theory and practice in organisational analysis, and provide more coherence to ideas and insights that have already been explored by neo-institutional scholars (Emirbayer and Johnson, 2008). However, reaching such an ambitious objective requires not isolating the concept of field from the whole sociological perspective developed by Bourdieu. In particular, this concept must be articulated with those of habitus and capital, which form the theoretical triad underlying Bourdieu's oeuvre.

As stressed by Bourdieu, "[t]o think in terms of fields is to *think relationally*" (Bourdieu and Wacquant, 1992: 96). Fields can be defined as systems of objective relations between differentiated and socially constructed positions which can be analysed independently of the characteristics of their occupants (Bourdieu, 1993; Bourdieu and Wacquant, 1992). The structure of the field at a given moment reflects the temporary state of power relations among the agents engaged in the struggle for the monopoly of legitimate violence which is characteristic of the field in question (Bourdieu, 1993). These agents exert variable effects depending on the volume and structure of different species of capital they possess (economic, cultural, social, and symbolic capital), and whose value can be determined only in relation with the field and even with the successive states of the same field (Bourdieu, 2005).

What makes the construction of a field possible is the existence and the legitimation by agents of specific stakes or issues (*enjeux*). "In order for a field to function, there have to be stakes and people prepared to play the game, endowed with the habitus that implies knowledge and recognition of the immanent law of the field, the stakes and so on" (Bourdieu, 1993: 72). The idea that a field forms around a specific issue, rather than a central technology or market, was reintroduced by Hoffman (1999) in a study of the construction of the field centred around corporate environmentalism in the US. This theoretical renewal in new institutionalism enables thinking of organisational fields as "centers of debates in which competing interests negotiate over issue interpretation" (Hoffman, 1999: 351). The construction and evolution of an organisational field can present several issues for a given organisation. Thus, when a new issue emerges, some agents will try to disregard it while others will try to crystallise the field construction around it. For example, as shown by Levy and Egan (2003), major transnational automobile and oil companies have denied for years the correlation between human activities—especially those based on fossil energies utilisation—and global climate warming, even though the majority of scientists provided strong evidence of this relationship and warned against the dangers of climate change.

However, the question of how and why a specific issue is chosen among competing issues at a given moment to become the centre of field construction remains unaddressed. Following Bourdieu, I suggest that the field issue does not impose itself automatically upon field constituents, but it is *constructed* and then *legitimated* through the struggle between agents possessing different capitals (in terms of volume and structure) and endowed with different habitus. These agents are constantly trying to delimitate a perimeter—that is, field boundaries—where their capitals could take greater value relative to other possible perimeters, and therefore could occupy a dominant position in the field (Hamadache and Brabet, 2014).

A return to Bourdieu's conception of fields as arenas of power relations within which struggles take place over issue definition can give the current research on organisational analysis more theoretical underpinnings and methodological tools to explain field construction and the strategic role of agents in this process. To provide an empirical illustration of the virtues of this renewed approach, I chose to investigate the construction of the OD field in the US. I will expose, in the remaining sections of this chapter, the methodology and the main results of this study.

METHODOLOGY

Research Context: Understanding the Origins of the Orphan Drugs

On the fringe of the 'therapeutic revolution', starting with the rise of the modern pharmaceutical industry in the early 1920s, which brought to market lifesaving medicines for a variety of common diseases, patients suffering from RDs (e.g. Tourette's syndrome, Huntington disease, Fabry disease) continued to face their illnesses and the isolation accompanying them with little hope for progress. The financial logic guiding the pharmaceutical industry had in fact pushed private companies to focus on the development of drugs for common diseases in rich countries (e.g. diabetes, arterial hypertension, etc.) and thereby to ignore diseases which affect small numbers of individuals. In the early 1960s, only a few dozen RDs benefited from effective treatments, most of them stemming from traditional medicine and public research (Asbury, 1985). This situation was exacerbated in 1962 after the passage of Kefauver-Harris amendments to the Federal Food, Drug, and Cosmetic Act of 1938, which, by imposing new and significantly higher standards for gaining marketing approval of a new drug, have dramatically increased costs and delays of developing new drugs (OTA, 1993). Consequently, the development of many promising drugs intended for RDs was interrupted by the pharmaceutical industry. Because they have no industrial 'parent' to pursue their development, these drugs were commonly referred to as 'orphan drugs'.

Although the Kefauver-Harris amendments did not mark the origin of the problem of drugs for RDs, they did exacerbate it, "creating particularly acute problems" (Asbury, 1985: 21). Awareness arising from this situation motivated different stakeholders to engage in inter-organisational relations (collaboration, confrontation, manipulation, etc.) to elaborate and promote new solutions. As a result, a new field, centred around the issue of drugs for RDs, has emerged.

Data Collection and Analysis

To explore the construction process of the OD field in the US, I relied on a wide variety of publicly available sources: hearings before Congress, official reports, legal texts, newspaper and medical journal articles, proceedings of conferences, books, and so forth. In particular, the hearings before Congress, held to investigate the issues of ODs, constituted important material because they express the public statements of the different agents involved in the field construction process.

Data analysis involved two main stages. In the first one, I analysed the issues that ODs present for a set of agents (public authority, rare disease patients, pharmaceutical industry, and health professionals) by examining the different terms used to label them. Indeed, several terms have been used simultaneously or consecutively to qualify a set of heterogeneous products that present specific issues for given groups of organisations. During the construction of the organisational field, each agent promoted the use of a term that most reflected his own issues. As a result of these struggles, the term 'orphan drug' was adopted in the regulatory and medical terminologies as well as in the layman's language.

In the second stage, I analysed the actions undertaken by the different agents involved in the construction process of the OD field in the US from the mid-1970s to the late 1990s. To explain these actions, I examined the positions of agents in the field, the different species of capital mobilised to influence this process, and the habitus that structure issue interpretation and actions of each agent. This approach to data collection and analysis follows Bourdieu's call to consider the "field of positions as methodologically inseparable from the field of stances or position-takings (*prises de position*), i.e., the structured system of practices and expressions of agents" (Bourdieu and Wacquant, 1992: 105).

THE CONSTRUCTION OF THE ORPHAN DRUG FIELD IN THE US

Orphan Drug Issues

The category of ODs is a social construct, resulting from the actions undertaken by different agents, each of them dealing with specific issues in connection with a heterogeneous set of medicinal products. To understand the construction process of this autonomous category, it is necessary to analyse those medicinal products and the specific issues they present for the different agents enlisted in the construction process of the OD field in the US.

Issues for the Pharmaceutical Industry

Despite the financial pressure exerted on the pharmaceutical industry, some firms have been, in certain cases, developing non-profitable drugs which were distributed for affordable prices in hospitals in developed countries or through humanitarian aid programs in poor countries. To label this specific category of products, pharmaceutical industry representatives used the term 'public service drugs' (Goldstein, 1988; Macarthur, 1987). This term was chosen to emphasise the industry's commitment to work towards the public interest and not only to serve private profit. As the president of the Pharmaceutical Manufacturers Association (PMA)[2] testified before Congress, 39 public service drugs were developed by 30 different pharmaceutical companies in the US during the 1970s (U.S. Congress, 1981: Testimony of Lewis Engman). These drugs include the following (Spilker, 1986; Macarthur, 1987):

- Drugs intended for the treatment of RDs;
- Drugs initially withdrawn from the market because of serious undesirable side effects but subsequently revealed to be effective and safe in other indications;
- Drugs discontinued by their manufacturers, either because of falling sales or because regulatory review requires expenditure on new studies that the potential commercial returns cannot justify;
- Drugs that cannot be protected by legal or ownership rights (unpatentable drugs);
- Drugs intended for infectious diseases that cause high mortality among poor people in developing countries (e.g. malaria, African trypanosomiasis). These diseases are commonly referred to as 'neglected diseases'.

For the pharmaceutical industry, the heterogeneous set of products included in the category of public service drugs presents a unique issue: the lack of profitability. From a technological point of view, public service drugs have no specificity; their development involves the same basic knowledge, techniques, and research protocols that are necessary to the development of other drugs.

Issues for the Public Authority

Since the early 1960s, different agencies from the Department of Health, Education and Welfare (DHEW) have dealt with the problem of shortage of many drugs known to be useful but not industrially manufactured mainly because research, development, and production are deemed too expensive relative to expected economic return (FDA, 1975, 1979). One of the first organised attempts in this field was the voluntarily initiated DHEW Interagency Committee on Drugs of Limited Commercial Value established in 1974 and coordinated by the Food and Drug Administration (FDA). The Committee in its 'Interim Report' of 1975 described the problems associated with these drugs, principally those concerned with hazy definition, the availability of governmental and industry support, and legal and insurance issues, and recommended further study by the FDA to fully define the problem and develop potential solutions (FDA, 1975). In 1978, the FDA convened the Interagency Task Force on Significant Drugs of Limited Commercial Value to continue the work of the 1974 committee. In its final report, the Task Force defined 'Drugs of Limited Commercial Value' as drugs not commercially available because of one or more of the following circumstances (FDA, 1979: 19–20):

- Where the drug is intended for the treatment of a RD;
- Where there is absence of dependable sources of manufacture or assurance of high quality at all times (e.g. where product has a short shelf life);
- Where the efficacy and/or security of the drug must be further established, but the firm cannot meet the conditions for achieving scientific acceptance, because of complex methodology, scarcity, or unavailability to it of the target population, or perceived difficulty of regulatory compliance;
- Where the drug cannot be protected by legal or ownership rights (unpatentable drugs);
- Where the drug creates potential liability which cannot be justified on humanitarian or profitability grounds.

From the US public authorities' point of view, the existence of the category of drugs of limited commercial value is mainly a result of a 'market failure' (Englander, 1991: 139; Waxman, 1986: 135). The private pharmaceutical system which has provided breakthrough drugs for many common illnesses has no financial incentives to produce drugs intended for the treatment of small numbers of individuals. This situation calls the public authority to assume its responsibility for providing help to those categories of citizens suffering from the "natural law of the industrial and agricultural markets and of society", as Representative Henry Waxman put it (1986: 135). The need for public intervention was pointed out by the DHEW Task Force, which explicitly identified the issue of drugs of limited commercial value as a public policy issue:

> Fundamentally, the production of drugs of substantial therapeutic potential which are deemed to be of limited economic value presents a public policy issue in the largest sense. Research, development, distribution and other efforts toward ultimate availability of such drugs require supra-market incentives. Normal competitive motivations must be supplemented by some stimulus or direct advantage beyond that generally expected in the free enterprise arena of pharmaceuticals.
>
> (FDA, 1979: 24)

For US public authorities, the public policy in the field of drugs of limited commercial value has to focus primarily on the needs of populations living in the territory of the US. Consequently, such policy is unable to deal with the problem of drugs for neglected diseases which requires an international joint action combining humanitarian and economic components.

Issues for Health Professionals

Health professionals have faced the problem of RDs since the turn of the 20th century. In the absence of approved drugs for these diseases, physicians relied on non-conventional therapies. First, they used substances which have not been approved as drugs but whose properties would, in the light of available scientific knowledge, provide a therapeutic benefit to the patient. Second, they administered a drug approved for other indications but not for the RD in question, which constitutes an 'off-label' use of the drug. Both methods are generally legal unless they violate specific ethical guidelines or safety regulations, but they do carry health risks and expose the physician to legal liability.

The most widely used term within the scientific community to designate these products was 'drugs for rare diseases' (Lyle, 1974; Walshe, 1975; 1988; Asbury, 1985). Dr Walshe, a pioneer physician in the field of RDs, summarises the health professionals' vision of drugs for RDs as follows.

> Personally, I am involved in this issue since the mid-1950s, but once I was using instead the term 'drugs for rare diseases' (. . .) Originally, the term 'orphan drug' meant exactly what I called 'drugs for rare diseases':

> it was the production of a chemical designed to be administered to human beings when it could not offer him an effective conventional therapy (hence the term orphan patient); but the disease in question should be so rare that the cost of drug development would not be recovered by its expected sales.
>
> (Walshe, 1988: 25)

The word 'orphan' was first used in medicine in connection with the use of drugs in infants and children. In a 1968 *Journal of Pediatrics* editorial entitled 'Therapeutic Orphans', Dr Shirkey pointed out that the majority of drugs approved since 1962 in the US could not be administered to children and infants because they had not been tested on this population owing to ethical and regulatory issues.

> (. . .) many of the drugs released since 1962 carry an 'orphaning' clause, e.g. Not to be used in children . . . is not recommended for use in infants and young children since few studies have been carried out in this age group . . . clinical studies have been insufficient to establish any recommendations for use in infants and children . . . should not be given to children.
>
> (Shirkey, 1968: 119)

The same year, Dr Provost, in an article entitled 'Homeless or Orphan Drugs', proposed the term 'homeless drugs' to describe substances, such as shelf chemicals, intended for chemical laboratory or manufacturing purposes and not approved for human use. Many of these chemicals were used in clinical practice, however, and were demonstrated to be effective. Because of their small target populations or inability to be patented, as well as the costs of meeting FDA requirements, these substances did not appear profitable enough to warrant commercial interest (Provost, 1968). While the introduction of the term 'orphan drug' in medical terminology was "certainly a stroke of genius" (Walshe, 1988: 25), its dissemination among the scientific community has been relatively low. One can reasonably think that its religious connotation made it less 'scientific' from an academic point of view. Similarly, the term 'homeless drug' has not benefited from a widespread use. The term 'drug for RDs' was considered more objective by health professionals and was widely adopted.

Issues for Rare Disease Patient Organisations

During the 1970s, several patient organisations representing individual RDs (e.g. National Myoclonus Foundation, Tourette Syndrome Association, Wilson's Disease Association) were active in providing support to families and raising money for research on their disease. Some patient organisations actually financed research on new treatments that were successful. "But the academic investigators could not find pharmaceutical manufacturers that would make the drugs commercially available. Companies felt that the target population for each drug was too small, and thus would not be profitable enough" (Meyers, 2000: 1). Nevertheless, patient organisations' action did not take the form of a protest movement either against the pharmaceutical industry or against the public authority. For many years, the lack of interest by the pharmaceutical industry in RDs was considered as a fatality resulting from the 'natural laws' of the market and the society (Waxman, 1986).

Beyond the clinical diversity of RDs, patients and their relatives were confronted with the same wide range of difficulties arising directly from the rarity of these pathologies. "Specific issues are equally raised regarding access to quality health care, overall social and medical support, effective liaison between hospitals and general practices, as well as professional and social integration and independence" (Orphanet, 2014). But during the 1970s, patients suffering from RDs had not developed a collective representation of these specific and cross-cutting issues. No single term encompassing all these issues had been shaped and used by RD patient organisations. Subsequently, no organised collective action had been undertaken. Furthermore, patients' management in different units and by different health professionals maintaining little contact between them made the meeting of patients and the sharing of stories, necessary conditions for the development of a collective representation, unlikely to happen. Table 5.1 summarises the issues presented by multiple categories of products for the agents involved in the construction of the OD field in the US and the terms used to label them.

Table 5.1 The Issues of Orphan Drugs

Agents	Used term	Products	Main issue
Pharmaceutical industry	Public service drugs	Drugs for rare diseases Drugs withdrawn due to safety issues Drugs discontinued due to economic issues Unpatentable drugs Drugs for neglected diseases	Lack of profitability
Public authority	Drugs of limited commercial value	Drugs for rare diseases Drugs not available due to manufacturing issues Drugs not available due to the incapacity to establish their efficacy and/or security Unpatentable drugs Drugs not available due to liability issues	Market failure (need for public policy)

(*Continued*)

Table 5.1 (Continued)

Agents	Used term	Products	Main issue
Health professionals	Drugs for rare diseases	Drugs for rare diseases Substances not approved for human use Drugs used off-label Drugs for paediatric use	Lack of conventional therapies (legal liability)
Rare disease patients	None	Drugs for rare diseases (considered individually)	Lack of access to quality health care

Power and Struggles within the Orphan Drug Field in the US

During the late 1970s, several individual voluntary rare disease groups, acting on their own, tried to draw public opinion and congressional attention to the specific problems they were facing. But despite their attempts, these groups failed to achieve the desired outcomes mainly because of the multiplication of individual initiatives and the lack of resources (particularly economic and political capitals). Instead, these attempts gave rise to the cynical Congress expression "disease-of-the-month" (Macarthur, 1987: 11).

Nevertheless, some patients and their relatives were made aware that the problems facing them are common to all persons suffering from RDs, and that to give these problems a public dimension they have to federate all those who are concerned about the notion of rarity. Abbey Meyers, mother of three children suffering from Tourette's syndrome, a rare disease associated with troublesome tics, was one of the first persons to work towards this objective. Her commitment to the fight against RDs started in 1980 when McNeil Pharmaceuticals decided to discontinue the production and distribution of pimozide, an experimental treatment for schizophrenia, after discovering serious side effects associated with the use of this drug at a high dose. McNeil Pharmaceuticals also stopped the supply of pimozide as a public service drug in the treatment of Tourette's syndrome, even though the dosage used for Tourette's patients did not show the same side effects. Consequently, Tourette's suffers were left without treatment. Given this situation, Abbey Meyers decided to investigate the existence of similar cases.

> I knew that it was unlikely that firms or governments' bureaucrats change their policy just for a child with Tourette's syndrome. So I started to write letters to patient organizations dedicated to single rare diseases to know whether they had been similarly affected by the problem of orphan drugs. I learned about the existence of penicillamine for the treatment of Wilson's disease, sodium valproate for some rare forms of epilepsy, L-5HTP for myoclonus, as well as other orphan drugs.
> (Meyers, 1988: 50)

The patient organisations that knew effective therapies for their disease were available but not industrially developed begun mobilising other RD patient organisations that did not yet have potential treatments for their diseases by convincing them that this problem would eventually affect them too (Meyers, 2000). As a result, the National Coalition for Rare Diseases (NCRD) was created in 1982, federating over 50 patient organisations, physicians, researchers, lawyers, journalists, and artists concerned about RDs[3] (MacArthur, 1987). NCRD's objective was to focus the attention of public opinion, government, health professionals, and the pharmaceutical industry on the general problem of treatment development for RDs.

Under the pressure of patients' repeated demands and following the recommendations of the FDA Task Force, some members of Congress decided to take action in order to tackle the problem of drugs for RDs. Acting on this aim, Representative Elizabeth Holtzman introduced a bill (H.R. 7089; 17/4/1980) to establish the Office of Drugs of Limited Commercial Value, which would have been responsible, among other things, for providing direct financial assistance to the sponsors of such drugs, which in turn would agree to reimburse the Office if the drug turned out to be particularly profitable. The bill defined a Drug of Limited Commercial Value as a drug for an RD that is commercially unavailable because the estimated revenue from the sale of such drug is not sufficient for its development by private companies, and/or exclusive rights for the drug cannot be obtained.

Thereafter, the Holtzman bill was referred to the Subcommittee on Health and the Environment of the House Committee on Interstate and Foreign Commerce. Representative Henry Waxman, the chairman of the Subcommittee, held a hearing on June 1980 in which several physicians, government officials, and representatives of patient associations, including Abbey Meyers, brought poignant testimonies on the specific difficulties faced by patients suffering from RDs (U.S. Congress, 1980). These testimonies brought the abstract RD issue "vividly to life with searing human examples of who it affects and why Congress must act on it" (Waxman, 2009: 55). Unfortunately, the hearing attracted poor media coverage. The issue of RDs was so obscure that only a single newspaper, the *Los Angeles Times*, sent a reporter to the hearing (Green, 2012). But the *Times* article caught the eye of Maurice Klugman, Hollywood writer and producer of the hit television drama *Quincy*, which starred his brother, the actor Jack Klugman, as a crusading medical examiner. Maurice Klugman, who himself suffered from a rare cancer, was moved by what he read and decided to devote an episode of the show to the problem of RDs. "In the weeks and months after the show aired, thousands of letters poured into the *Quincy* production studio from viewers eager to help raise public awareness" (Waxman, 2009: 57).

To capitalise on the publicity provided by the *Quincy* episode, Waxman invited Jack Klugman to testify before the Subcommittee along with pharmaceutical industry representatives, government officials, and RDs patient organisations at a second hearing held in March 1981 on the Holtzman bill, which had been reintroduced by Representative Ted Weiss (H.R. 1663; 2/4/1981). Klugman's appearance before Congress generated very wide press and television coverage that focused national attention on the problem of drugs for RDs. The pharmaceutical industry, represented by the PMA, opposed patient associations' and Congress's efforts to deal with the problem of drugs for RDs. Indeed, the PMA declined the Subcommittee invitation to attend the first hearing, as they refused earlier to participate to the FDA Task Force. They claimed that drug companies had no problem developing treatments for RDs and there was no need for legislation in this domain (Waxman, 2009). As surprising and "unbelievable" (Meyers, 2000: 2) this position could appear, it is actually coherent with the common norms and values of PMA members, who are top executives of most important pharmaceutical companies operating in the US. In fact, the PMA opposed the bill because they perceived that it would impose an important political cost (Englander, 1991: 138). Supporting the Holtzman-Weiss propositions would be for the PMA an admission of the limits of economic liberalism and an important ideological defeat for its partisans (a defeat whose implications would overtake the field of the pharmaceutical industry). Accordingly, the PMA had to deny the existence of specific problems related to drugs for RDs and appear confident about the capacity of private firms to respond effectively to the needs of the whole American population, as its president stated before the Congress.

> (. . .) let me stress our belief that the private sector can work effectively to meet the challenge posed by rare diseases. The pharmaceutical industry is prepared to work with interested private and public groups to define the issues more clearly, improve mutual understanding, and remove impediments on the development of more public service drugs.
> (U.S. Congress, 1981: Testimony of Lewis Engman)

The PMA and their allies in Congress used the hearings before the Subcommittee to denounce what they referred to as "FDA's regulatory overkill" (U.S. Congress, 1981: Comments of Representative James Scheuer), which "created a drug review process which is complex, time consuming and costly" (U.S. Congress, 1982: Testimony of Peter Hutt, PMA). In fact, the major political objective of the pharmaceutical industry in the early 1980s was to deregulate the entire drug approval process (Englander, 1991). So, the PMA feared that approving legislation which would ease the drug approval requirements for RDs would reduce the momentum for their overall deregulatory effort, as noted in the following exchange between the PMA's attorney Peter Hutt and Representative Bob Whittaker:

MR. WHITTAKER: Do you believe part of your reservation to support our legislative solution could be based in part, on a belief that if we provide relief from FDA regulation in the area of orphan drugs, it might detract from your industry's over-

	all effort to obtain relief from the FDA regulations for all new drugs?
MR. HUTT:	That could be a bad byproduct of it, but it does not get to the heart of the problem (. . .) the best way to look for drugs for rare diseases is to look at all drugs for all diseases (. . .) when you look at drugs for common diseases you will find drugs for rare diseases. Anything that will stimulate new drug development is going to help the discovery of drugs for rare disease (U.S. Congress, 1982).

Thanks to its enormous financial and political resources, the PMA succeeded in blocking the Holtzman-Weiss bill. But Representative Henry Waxman did not stop his effort, and introduced a new bill (H.R. 5238; 15/12/1981) which was the first legislative text to use the term 'orphan drug' instead of 'drug of limited commercial value'. As Waxman noted, "the naming of drugs of rare diseases as 'orphan drugs' was not done frivolously. They are very much like children who have no parents, and they require special effort" (quoted in Weck, 1988: 14). Because it carries a high emotional charge, this term transcended the economic realm to which terms used before had confined these drugs, and focused attention on social issues related to them by questioning fundamental values of society such as solidarity and assistance for the most vulnerable groups of people.

The Waxman bill defined an OD as a drug for "rare disease or condition"; this term "means any disease or condition which occurs so infrequently in the U.S. that there is no reasonable expectation that the cost of developing and making available in the U.S. a drug for such disease or condition will be recovered from sales in the U.S. of such drug". Regarding previous bills, H.R. 5238 included several new propositions. First, to accelerate and simplify the OD approval process, it provided for the reduction of the number of required clinical trials and the standard of proof of efficacy. In return, post-approval surveillance would be strengthened to catch any safety or efficacy problems that did not surface prior to the approval. To deal with the problem of unpatentable drugs, the bill would prohibit the FDA from approving another version of the same OD for the same indication during a period of seven years (a provision referred to as 'marketing exclusivity'). The bill also included a section requiring the FDA to provide the sponsor of an OD, upon request, written protocol assistance during development to guide the study of the product towards approval. Finally, the Waxman bill switched the method of providing the federal government's financial support from direct financial assistance to an income tax credit equal to 100 percent of the qualified clinical trial expenses.

But despite the incentives included in the Waxman bill, the pharmaceutical industry continued to deny the existence of a specific problem related to ODs and to oppose all legislative attempts. During the third hearing before the House Subcommittee on Health and the Environment held in March 1982, Peter Hutt testified that the drug industry was "proud of the contributions it has made toward developing therapies for rare diseases" and recommended that the administrative application of the existing law be implemented in a more flexible manner (U.S. Congress, 1982). To block the bill in the Senate, the PMA benefited from the support of Senator Orin Hatch, chairman of the Senate Labor and Human Resources Committee, which had jurisdiction over drug legislation.

Regarding the PMA's inflexible position, RD patient organisations, better structured and resourced—particularly because of the growing support of public opinion—decided to intensify their media campaign against the pharmaceutical industry. Once again, Jack and Maurice Klugman dedicated an episode of *Quincy* to the problem of ODs (shot in September and aired in October 1982). "This time the story line revolved around an orphan drug bill that was being held up by a heartless senator. In the show's pivotal scene, the senator dismisses the need for orphan drugs, telling Klugman, 'Nobody cares about this bill'. A righteous Klugman fires back, 'Look outside'. Peering down from his office window, the senator sees a large crowd chanting and holding signs that read: We Want the Orphan Drug Act" (Waxman, 2009: 67).

The *Quincy* episode brought a new wave of public pressure on the PMA and their allies in Congress. Consequently, they decided to negotiate with FDA officials, Henry Waxman, and patient organisation representatives to elaborate a solution "that is acceptable to all parties" (Waxman, 2009: 62). So, the provision reducing standards of proof of efficacy was suppressed at the request of the FDA. In order to protect its control over financial incentives, the Senate Finance Committee wanted to replace the 100 percent tax credit with an annual $50 million grant program (indeed, a tax credit takes effect immediately, whereas a grant requires not only an authorisation but also an appropriation—that is Congress had to not only authorise the grant but also hand it over). But the pharmaceutical industry considered the tax credit an important incentive. Finally, a compromise was reached, with the reduction of the tax credit to 50 percent of the qualified clinical trial expenses and the creation of an annual $4 million grant program. This constituted a good stimulator for both small firms seeking governmental grants to cover the costs of clinical trials and major companies which wanted tax credits to reduce their investment in clinical research (Meyers, 2000). The seven years of marketing exclusivity for unpatentable ODs and the written protocol assistance given from the FDA were maintained. The updated Waxman-Hatch bill passed the House on 14 December and the Senate two days later. On 4 January 1983, President Ronald Reagan signed the Orphan Drug Act (ODA), which became a law (P.L. 97–414).

In the first years following the enactment of the ODA, several small firms, especially biotechnology-based start-ups, succeeded in developing and marketing many ODs, some of them proving highly profitable. Regarding this success, the pharmaceutical industry worked to extend the scope of incentives given to the sponsors of ODs. So, in 1984, Congress amended the ODA

(P.L. 98–551) to clarify the definition of ODs, which was problematic for both the FDA and pharmaceutical companies. Under the new definition, a rare disease or condition was defined as a disease or condition affecting fewer than 200,000 people in the US. In 1985, a new amendment (P.L. 99–91) extended marketing exclusivity to patentable as well as unpatentable drugs. It also extended the definition of an OD to antibiotics. In 1988, this extension concerned vaccines, health foods, and medical devices through a new amendment (P.L. 100–290), which also increased the amounts of the grant program to $10 million for 1988, $12 million for 1989, and $14 million for 1990. Finally, the 1997 amendment (P.L. 105–115) exempted ODs from the payment of registration fees—which were equal to $896,200.

About 30 years after its enactment, the ODA led to the development of an increasing number of lifesaving drugs for RDs (e.g. IOM, 2010). However, the Act also "created issues which, in some cases, have led to commercial and ethical abuses" (Wellman-Labadie and Zhou, 2010: 216) as some ODs proved to be particularly costly and profitable (e.g. EvaluatePharma, 2013). This situation maintains the struggle over field domination as the pharmaceutical industry continues to work actively to preserve—or even to extend—the incentives given to the sponsors of ODs, and critics, mainly from public authorities and private and state-funded insurance, try to restore the Act's spirit by preventing the exploitation of its loopholes by the profit motive of some companies.

DISCUSSION

In this chapter, I relied on a renewed approach to Bourdieu's framework to analyse the construction process of the OD field in the US, showing how this approach can improve our understanding of field construction and the role of agents in this process. By so doing, I highlighted the struggles that took place between agents to construct the issue which structures the construction of the field. Indeed, the *terminological work* undertaken by agents to legitimate and de-legitimate alternative issues (i.e. the creation, promotion, diffusion, contestation, and so forth of different terms), far from being neutral and passive, has proven to be strategic, defining field boundaries and the 'actants' (individuals, organisations, objects, concepts, etc.) that constitute the field (Callon, 1986). The use of the term 'orphan drug' has been instrumental in shaping the meaning of the issue related to these products as a public health policy issue rather than a simple economic or technical problem that the pharmaceutical industry can address by itself. The semantic framework elaborated around the notion of 'orphanage', with its connotations of loss of parent, need for special care, and so forth, has designated a specific class of population (i.e. patients with RDs) as the victims of a social choice—the commoditisation of health care. This process of victimisation (Hunt, Benford, and Snow, 1994) appealed for and legitimated public authority intervention on behalf of the principle of social solidarity and assistance to vulnerable populations by allocating public funds to provide incentives for the development of drugs intended to address their suffering. The adoption, no pun intended, by the PMA of the term OD in the last stages also allowed it to appear as "a genuine adoption agency whose babies are projects of orphan drugs, and pharmaceutical companies the prospective adoptive parents" (Goldstein, 1988: 59).

The struggles over field domination did not take place only in the semantic arena. The different agents involved in the construction of the OD field in the US mobilised several species of capital in order to influence this process. While significant economic and political resources of the pharmaceutical industry allowed it to resist the critics from patients' organisations in the early stages of contestation, the media resources mobilised by the latter created an equilibrium of forces which has obliged the pharmaceutical industry to negotiate with other agents. This shows that the relative value of capitals within a given field can change over time (Bourdieu, 2005). Thereby, there is permanent competition between agents not only to control the different species of capital available at a given moment but also "to leverage their particular forms of capital to (...) shape the field in ways that privilege their own skills and resources" (Maguire, Hardy, and Lawrence, 2004: 676). The new distribution of capitals gives rise to a new configuration of positions which changes agents' capacity of action as well as the repartition of benefits resulting from the functioning of the field. But the configuration of agents' positions and the relations between them remains in a permanent evolution as the control of capitals and their relative value evolve constantly.

This study also shows that the habitus of different agents can evolve through interactions between them. For instance, executives of pharmaceutical companies have been conditioned to think, particularly through business school programs, that drugs for small numbers of individuals cannot be profitable. Nevertheless, the repeated interactions between agents during the process of field construction have led to the elaboration of new interpretations of existing issues which enable pharmaceutical companies' executives to perceive the opportunity for industrials to generate profits through the development of drugs for RDs. The evolution of agents' habitus determines the evolution of their actions, especially the way they conceive and shape their relations with other fields' agents. For example, the early stages' confrontation between RD patient groups and the pharmaceutical industry turned thereafter into cooperation because both parties understood the existence of common interests in the development and the commercialisation of drugs for RDs.

CONCLUSION

This research offers several contributions to the study of organisational field construction by: (a) highlighting power relations and the role of agents in the process of field construction; (b) illustrating this topic through the case of the OD field in the US; and (c) relating Bourdieusian concepts of field, habitus, and capital to the current research in new institutionalism in organisational analysis. Following Hoffman's (1999) conception of fields as centred around issues rather than technologies or markets, I addressed directly the question of how and why a specific issue is chosen among competing ones at a given moment to become at the centre of field construction. By so doing, I showed that issue construction is a political and strategic activity which involves agents, possessing different capitals (in terms of volume and structure) and endowed with different habitus, in a struggle for the legitimation and de-legitimation of alternative issues. This struggle takes place in the semantic arena where agents are working to shape the meaning of the issue by creating, promoting, diffusing, and contesting different terms, as well as in the material arenas (legislative chambers, justice courts, medias, etc.) as agents mobilise different forms of capital to influence issue construction.

Another major contribution of this chapter concerns the debate revolving around field boundaries and constituents (e.g. Wooten and Hoffman, 2008). By focusing on the struggles that take place between disparate agents to construct a field issue, I showed how these struggles largely influence the manner in which problems are presented, solutions retained, and the agents included or excluded from the field (Hamadache and Brabet, 2014). Agents who are able to mobilise sufficient and relevant capitals to interpret complex social problems in a way that highlights their own issues are more likely to elaborate and impose solutions that are favourable for them. By so doing, these agents delimit a perimeter (i.e. field boundaries) from which other agents who could engage in the field are excluded. But as the dominant conception of the field issue is constantly challenged by those agents who were excluded and those who occupy less favourable positions, field boundaries and constituents remain in a permanent evolution.

I tried in this chapter to provide some insights into how Bourdieu's sociology can consolidate the theoretical foundations of the new institutionalism in organisational analysis. As I mentioned earlier, this ambitious project cannot be accomplished without a careful articulation of the concepts of field, habitus, and capital. From this perspective, one future research direction can be the study of the temporal dynamics of field, habitus, and capitals to understand the influence of each element on the others. Another question outlined in this chapter and which calls for further examination is that of the influence of the interactions between agents during the process of field construction on the evolution of their habitus. Tackling this important question could permit us to understand how a habitus, formed to enable action in a given field, can generate new patterns of actions in completely different situations created by the engagement of agents in a new field and new relations.

NOTES

1. For a presentation of the new institutionalism, see, for instance, DiMaggio and Powell (1991), and Greenwood and Meyer (2008).

2. The PMA is a trade union representing leading innovative pharmaceutical companies operating in the US. Formed in 1958 and headquartered in Washington, DC, it advocates in the US and around the world on public issues critical to the discovery and development of innovative medicines. It was renamed the Pharmaceutical Research and Manufacturers of America (PhRMA) in 1994.
3. NCRD was renamed the National Organization for Rare Disorders (NORD) in 1983. Abbey Meyers was its president for 25 years.

REFERENCES

Asbury, C. H. (1985) *Orphan Drugs, Medical versus Market Value*. Lexington: Lexington Books.
Bourdieu, P. (1975) The Specificity of the Scientific Field and the Social Conditions of the Progress of Reason. *Social Science Information* 14(6): 19–47.
Bourdieu, P. (1993) *Sociology in Question*. London: SAGE.
Bourdieu, P. (2005) *The Social Structures of the Economy*. Cambridge: Polity Press.
Bourdieu, P., and Wacquant, L. (1992) *An Invitation to Reflexive Sociology*. Cambridge: Polity Press.
Callon, M. (1986) Some Elements of a Sociology of Translation: Domestication of the Scallops and the Fishermen. In: Law, J. (ed.) *Power, Action and Belief: A New Sociology of Knowledge*. London: Routledge & Kegan, 196–230.
DiMaggio, P. J. (1983) State Expansion and Organizational Fields. In: Hall, R. H., and Quinn, R. (eds.), *Organizational Theory and Public Policy*. Beverly Hills: SAGE, 147–161.
DiMaggio, P. J. (1991) Constructing an Organizational Field as a Professional Project: U.S. Art Museums, 1920–1940. In: Powell, W. W., and DiMaggio, P. J. (eds.), *The New Institutionalism in Organizational Analysis*. Chicago: University of Chicago Press, 267–292.
DiMaggio, P. J., and Powell, W. W. (1983) The Iron Cage Revisited: Institutional Isomorphism and Collective Rationality in Organizational Fields. *American Sociological Review* 48(2): 147–160.
Emirbayer, M., and Johnson, V. (2008) Bourdieu and Organizational Analysis. *Theory and Society* 37(1): 1–44.
Englander, E. J. (1991) The Political Economy of Biotechnology: Innovation and Politics in an Emerging Industry. *Business and Economic History* 20: 136–141.
EvaluatePharma. (2013) *Orphan Drug Report 2013*. London: EvaluatePharma.
FDA: Food and Drug Administration. (1975) *Interim Report of the Committee on Drugs of Limited Commercial Value*. Rockville: FDA.
FDA. (1979) *Significant Drugs of Limited Commercial Value: Report of the Interagency Task Force to the Secretary of Health, Education, and Welfare*. Rockville: FDA.
Goldstein, G. (1988) The PMA Commission on Drugs for Rare Diseases. *Prospective et Santé* 45(S): 57–62.
Green, J. (2012) Jack Klugman's Secret, Lifesaving Legacy. *Washington Post*, 25 December.
Greenwood, R., and Meyer, R. E. (2008) Influencing Ideas: A Celebration of DiMaggio and Powell (1983). *Journal of Management Inquiry* 17(4): 258–264.
Hamadache, K., and Brabet, J. (2014) Rethinking Institutional Entrepreneurship: The Case of the Construction of the Orphan Drug Field in Europe. *Society and Business Review* 9(2): 139–152.
Hannan, M. T., and Freeman, J. H. (1977) The Population Ecology of Organizations. *American Journal of Sociology* 82(5): 929–964.

Hoffman, A. J. (1999) Institutional Evolution and Change: Environmentalism and the U.S. Chemical Industry. *Academy of Management Journal* 42(4): 351–371.

Hunt, S. A., Benford, R. D., and Snow, D. A. (1994) Identity Fields: Framing Processes and the Social Construction of Movement Identities. In: E. Laraña, E., Johnston, H., and Gusfield, J. R. (eds.), *New Social Movements: From Ideology to Identity*. Philadelphia: Temple University Press, 185–208.

IOM: Institute of Medicine. (2010) *Rare Diseases and Orphan Products: Accelerating Research and Development*. Washington: National Academies Press.

Laumann, E. O., Galaskiewicz, J., and Marsden, P. (1978) Community Structure as Interorganizational Linkage. *Annual Review of Sociology* 4: 455–484.

Lawrence, T. B., and Phillips, N. (2004) From Moby Dick to Free Willy: Macro-Cultural Discourse and Institutional Entrepreneurship in Emerging Institutional Fields. *Organization* 11(5): 689–711.

Leblebici, H., Salancik G., Copay, A., and King, T. (1991) Institutional Change and the Transformation of Interorganizational Fields: An Organizational History of the U.S. Radio Broadcasting Industry. *Administrative Science Quarterly* 36(3): 333–363.

Levy, D. L., and Egan, D. (2003) A Neo-Gramscian Approach to Corporate Political Strategy: Conflict and Accommodation in the Climate Change Negotiations. *Journal of Management Studies* 40(4): 803–829.

Lyle, W. H. (1974) Drugs for Rare Diseases. *Postgraduate Medical Journal* 50(580): 107–108.

Macarthur, D. (1987) *Orphan Drugs: Public Service . . . and Private Profit?* Richmond: PJB.

Maguire, S., Hardy, C., and Lawrence, T. (2004) Institutional Entrepreneurship in Emerging Fields: HIV/AIDS Treatment Advocacy in Canada. *Academy of Management Journal* 47(5): 657–679.

Meyer, J. W., and Rowan, B. (1977) Institutionalized Organizations: Formal Structure as Myth and Ceremony. *American Journal of Sociology* 83(2): 340–363.

Meyers, A. S. (1988) The Evolution of the Orphan Drug Act: A Consumer's View. *Prospective et Santé* 45(S): 49–56.

Meyers, A. S. (2000) *Understanding the History of the Orphan Drug Act*. Speech at the International Conference of Rare Diseases and Orphan Drugs, Spain, 18 February. www.rarediseases.org/docs/policy/OrphanDrugDevelopmentConference.pdf (Accessed on February 2014).

Orphanet. (2014) About Rare Diseases. www.orpha.net/consor/cgi-bin/Education_AboutRareDiseases.php?lng=EN (Accessed on February 2014).

OTA: Office of Technology Assessment. (1993) *Pharmaceutical R&D: Costs, Risks, and Rewards*. Washington: U.S. Government Printing Office.

Powell, W. W. (1999) The Social Construction of an Organisational Field: The Case of Biotechnology. *International Journal of Biotechnology* 1(1): 42–66.

Provost, G. P. (1968) Homeless or Orphan Drugs. *American Journal of Hospital Pharmacy* 25: 609.

Shirkey, H. C. (1968) Therapeutic Orphans. *Journal of Pediatrics* 72(1): 119–120.

Spilker, B. (1986) The Development of Orphan Drugs: An Industry Perspective. In: Sheinberg, I. H., and Walshe, J. M. (eds.), *Orphan Diseases and Orphan Drugs*. Manchester: Manchester University Press, 119–134.

Tolbert, P. S. (1985) Institutional Environments and Resource Dependence: Sources of Administrative Structure in Institutions of Higher Education. *Administrative Science Quarterly* 30(1): 1–13.

U.S. Congress. (1980) *Drug Regulation Reform-Oversight, Orphan Drugs: Hearings before the Subcommittee on Health and the Environment of the House Commission on Interstate and Foreign Commerce. 96th Congress, 2nd Session.* Washington: U.S. Government Printing Office.

U.S. Congress. (1981) *Orphan Drugs: Hearings on H. R. 1663 before the Subcommittee on Health and the Environment of the House Commission on Energy and Commerce. 97th Congress, 1st Session.* Washington: U.S. Government Printing Office.

U.S. Congress. (1982) *Orphan Drug Act: Hearings before the Subcommittee on Health and the Environment of the House Commission on Energy and Commerce, 97th Congress, 2nd Session.* Washington: U.S. Government Printing Office.

Walshe, J. M. (1975) Drug for Rare Diseases. *British Medical Journal* 3(5985): 701–702.

Walshe, J. M. (1988) Academia: Problems of Basic Research. *Prospective et Santé* 45(S): 25–29.

Waxman, H. A. (1986) The History and Development of the Orphan Drug Act. In: Sheinberg, I. H., and Walshe, J. M. (eds.), *Orphan Diseases and Orphan Drugs*. Manchester: Manchester University Press, 135–145.

Waxman, H. A. (2009) *The Waxman Report: How Congress Really Works*. New York: Twelve.

Weck, E. (1988) Medicine's 'Orphans': Drugs for Rare Diseases. *FDA Consumer* 22(1): 12–21.

Wellman-Labadie, O., and Zhou, Y. (201019) The U.S. Orphan Drug Act: Rare Disease Research Stimulator or Commercial Opportunity? *Health Policy* 95(2–3): 216–228.

Wooten, M., and Hoffman, A. J. (2008) Organizational Fields: Past, Present and Future. In: Greenwood, R., Oliver, C. Sahlin, K., and Suddaby, R. (eds.), *The SAGE Handbook of Organizational Institutionalism*. London: SAGE, 130–147.

6 Bourdieu, Representational Legitimacy, and Pension Boardrooms
A Contested Space?

Susan Sayce

INTRODUCTION

The aim of this chapter is to extend the debates about concepts of legitimacy and representation in UK pension schemes boardrooms through utilizing Bourdieu's social theory. The intent is to use the conceptual tools of habitus, capital, illusio, and doxa provided by Pierre Bourdieu to empirically investigate the legitimacy that more diverse pension board members bring to the field of the boardroom and how this fits with the dominant norms, expectations, and attitudes of the boardroom and ultimately its relevance for patterns of inclusion and exclusion.

Research into board management indicates that boards have their own norms and behaviours where actions and manners are reproduced (Pye and Pettigrew 2005). However, for pension boards in the UK the regulatory need for representational legitimacy has helped increase the diversity of pension board composition by bringing trade union representatives or members who choose to stand for election into the mix of employer/sponsor representation and employee representation. This research builds upon previous empirical studies that have utilized Bourdieu's work to explain the stability of boardrooms norms and behaviours (Maclean et al. 2010; Harvey and Maclean 2008). These investigations demonstrate how dynamic power relations in corporate boardrooms push the constituents to reproduce the field of relations through different generations of incumbents (Calhoun 1993: 72; Sayce and Ozbilgin 2014). However, the increase of representation on pension boards of more diverse candidates has the potential to challenge this situation. Here empirical research that focuses on citizenship and democratic participation using Bourdieu's concept of habitus, democratic doxa, and different social backgrounds and resources indicates that this difference can lead to patterns of exclusion (Harrits 2013), and this theme of inclusion and exclusion is returned to in the discussion of legitimacy in entrepreneurship (De Clercq and Voronov 2009).

The chapter's empirical focus will develop further our understanding of how Bourdieu's theorizing as discussed in earlier chapters can explain stability in the basic field of relations while incumbents and actions change. In this chapter we explicitly address how changes in the field, such as new regulation, offer the potential for change while also acknowledging that existing patterns of social life at board level continue, which can constrain the behaviour of legitimate agents within the field. Thus the research question for this chapter is how does representational legitimacy impact on pension boards' dominant customs and behaviours?

The discussion about legitimacy and the move towards greater representational legitimacy on UK pension boards drawing on a Bourdieu analysis is structured as follows: First we discuss Bourdieu's theory of habitus and the regenerative nature of boards and the implication for pension boards in the interplay of capital and power relations and legitimacy. The contextual nature of organizations' pension boards as well as the methods to collect data is outlined next. The empirical section analysis focuses on incumbents' interpretation of habitus and how doxa and illusio are used to unconsciously generate existing values and behaviour to new outsiders. The analysis then shifts towards analysing new entrants' experiences of adapting or challenging these strongly embedded boardroom norms. Then the discussion returns to the research question about representational legitimacy and how this can sometimes be informally challenged through the differing interplay of boardroom members' levels of capital, before concluding on continuity and change with respect to increasing diversity on pension boards through legitimate representation.

BOURDIEU'S THEORETICAL FRAMEWORK, BOARDS, AND PENSION BOARDS

In order to answer the question of how representational legitimacy impacts on pension boards' dominant customs and behaviours, a theoretical framework was needed that could examine boardroom customs and norms. Here the literature on Bourdieu and corporate boards was informative of the regenerative nature of boardroom customs and practices. How people change their behaviours and attitudes in order to fit in is linked to their dispositional habitus (Maclean et al. 2010). Habitus is the embodiment of one's history of past experiences in relation to work experiences and social experiences. Habitus is defined here as an ensemble of schemata of perception—thinking, feeling, evaluating, speaking, and acting—that perforates all the expressive verbal, practical manifestations and utterances of an actor (Bourdieu 1985; Krais 2006; Sayce 2006). Through habitus boardroom attitudes and behaviour can establish patterns over time, which are neither fully the product of external structures of the organizations nor fully the product of mere subjective intentions; thus habitus is constantly in motion. Or as Bourdieu words it, "social agents put into action the incorporated principles of a generative habitus" (1990: 9).

For a boardroom context it is the notion of a generative habitus that is key to a Bourdieu perspective. Maclean et al. (2010) claim that it is the generational reproduction of corporate boardroom membership and behaviour that leads to continuity in how people act when entering the boardroom, although they come from different generations and may have different backgrounds. This suggests that the boardroom's dominant masculine, managerialist attitudes and behaviours, which come to dominate boardroom behaviour, pervade the presuppositions of the field and the rules of the boardroom and what individuals consider is possible in this context (doxa), to the point that these rules are accepted as natural and right (Bourdieu 2001: 8). In this social world these dominant rules reproduce themselves within the cognitive and structural basis of the boardroom, where individuals are caught up by how these silent rules and regulations work but also have a stake in the maintenance of these rules (Bourdieu 1990: 66).

Habitus are continually developed and refined through social interactions and learning throughout a person's lifetime, including the world of work, where boardrooms sit at the apex of corporate decision making (Scott 2008). Corsun and Costen (2001: 18) explain Bourdieu's idea of dispositional habitus by mirroring Bourdieu's game analogy, and this analogy is used to help explain what happens in the field, the pension boardroom:

> Using games as a metaphor, the field of play is not one on which boundaries are indelibly painted. Rather, as the players in the field constantly renegotiate them, it is more appropriate to think of the lines as imaginary vectors connecting the positions of the most peripheral players. As players move about, enter or exit the field, the boundaries may change.

Action is guided by *"the feel for the game"* (Bourdieu 1990: 11); consequently action may appear to an outsider as rational, but as Bourdieu outlines that action may not be based on reason. This situation occurs because in practice often time is limited on boards, information may be restricted, challenges may be discarded rather than explored, and the continuance of personal relationships may be more influential. This suggests that the outward appearance of rationality in connection to board actions may be more about maintaining 'illusio' by supporting existing norms and behaviours in order to thrive in this environment, illusio being defined here as *"investment in the game"* (Bourdieu and Wacquant 1992: 98).

The players renegotiate—sometimes subtly, sometimes explicitly—the rules of the game as they play, making the requirements for entry (the various types of capital) dynamic. The dominant in a field seeks to manipulate the boundaries, the human and other capital required for entry, rules of play, definitions of success and value, and the rewards attendant to the fields in which they play (Bourdieu and Wacquant 1992). In highly regulated and scrutinized pension boardrooms the fiduciary responsibilities demand that all participants' primary intent must be to act in the interests of all the pension plan's members. In order to comply with these responsibilities the board requires compromises from both employee and employer/sponsor representatives and a more consensual approach to decision making.

The need to employ a more consensual approach can place in tension the legitimacy of different players, whose cognitive reasoning may challenge the long-standing structure and culture of the board as labour representatives, blue-collar workers, or even older managers, who may all struggle to adapt their style of management, activism, or communication to a more consensual approach. Nevertheless the more powerful in board participation can be seen to be active and dominant in several of these interrelated fields, while the less powerful, such as blue-collar workers or new female entrants, may find themselves on the periphery of the game as they learn and adapt to the specific rules and norms of their pension board. In time they may become complicit in their domination, integrating their habitus into a symbolic order that fits with the existing order's ways of communicating and acting, thus reproducing the dominant boardroom culture (Bourdieu 1991: 51).

PUTTING PENSION TRUSTEESHIP INTO CONTEXT

The dominant boardroom culture in the UK was shaken up in 2004 when it became mandatory in the 2004 Pension Act for one third of the seats on private sector pension committees' boards to be held by member-elected representatives, which have to include active and retired member-elected employee representatives. These representatives then participate alongside employer, labour, finance specialist, independent, and other stakeholder representatives on occupational pension committees and their boards. Thus pension boards have become political institutions that seek to combine the functions of representation with pension governance and functional competence in relation to trustees' fiduciary responsibilities (Clark 2007; Clark and Urwin 2008). This dynamic includes balancing the political interests of the many stakeholders in pension schemes, including the more recent elected representatives on occupational pension plan boards (Weststar and Verma 2007). However, the high level of social power of boards continued and even increased as the financial and social impact of pension funds makes the pension board an important institutional 'rule maker' in society (Streeck and Thelen 2005), in terms of both global financial markets and global corporate investment policy (Gribben and Gitsham 2006). This is linked to how in 2011 UK pension trustee boards were reported to have overseen the management of financial assets in the region of £1.5 trillion (Towers Watson 2012).

The Labour government's move towards greater representative legitimacy in the Pension Act of 2004 is linked to wider trends to improve governance by increasing levels of transparency and accountability (Wheeler 2010)—in this case to the membership. This is related to how sponsors/employers have a significant equity interest in their pension schemes, which in monetary terms can sometimes exceed or match the value of the sponsor's business. Prior to 2004 sponsors/employer representatives dominated trustee decision making, particularly when schemes were in profit. Sponsors' representatives have traditionally utilized their capital to be the pension board's dominant power holders within the "world of grey men" (Hymans Robertson 2007). This dominance means that pension boards can mirror the norms and attitudes of industry's corporate boards, including their pattern of social life and stability, reproducing the habitus of corporate boardrooms (Maclean et al. 2010; Calhoun 1993). So the increasing importance of representation on boards, which may encapsulate the demographic diversity of board members (e.g. gender, ethnicity, occupation, experience) and/or diversity in the stakeholder groups they represent, raises questions with respect to legitimacy, which can threaten the stability of the boardroom's field of relations. Maintaining this stability could include challenging new members' legitimacy around their capability to contribute to this high-level decision-making process as new agents in the game.

Institutionally labour organizations helped establish many of the occupational pension schemes in union-recognized contexts. Labour bodies continue to view occupational pension administration as an important issue for their membership. The labour movement through the Trade Union Congress's (TUC) trustee network (www.tuc.org.uk/economic-issues/pensions-and-retirement/member-trustees) and its trade unions is active in supporting new elected employee trustees and also appointed labour trustees. However, for trustees who come from this background their differing political context can mean that they see themselves as 'outsiders' in relation to the boardroom content and its unspoken presuppositions of how to act and behave in this context, as well as on the behalf of the membership (Sayce et al. 2014; Sayce 2012), thus leading to a pattern of exclusion.

The composition of pension boards and their trustees is becoming increasingly diverse (Rafferty et al. 2008). New trustees can often come from different political or social groups and are not necessarily affiliated to labour groupings. Nevertheless, they are less likely to come from traditional occupational backgrounds that dominate boardrooms, such as management, finance, and HR, and may perceive themselves as 'outsiders' within a boardroom context (Sayce and Ozbilgin 2014). Thus there are concerns that labour or elected member trustees may hamper board function because they may enter their role with limited exposure to pension issues, the finance industry, or investment concepts (Clark 2007; Treasury Report 2004; Woods and Urwin 2010). This perspective is sometimes challenged by employee representatives' higher level of commitment and motivation to the role (Ambachtsheer 2007). This is linked to how appointed trustees can find it more challenging to combine their managerial role with their associated role as the employer's representative, as well as continue with the continuous learning needed to expand their skills with respect to pension activity (Sayce 2012). Indeed, a heterogeneous board may also increase conflict or hinder board functioning as they get to grips with challenging pension issues. However, greater diversity and representation are associated with good governance practice as they permit a greater questioning of the decision-making process in line with trustees' fiduciary responsibilities (Higgs 2003; Tyson Report 2003).

METHODS

A qualitative interpretative approach was chosen to ensure that a diverse range of views were considered when investigating the trustees' perceptions of their role and their participation within their boardroom's decision-making process to ensure the nuances of their experience were fully captured (Neuman 2003). However, pension trustees are a difficult-to-reach population for fine-grained research because of their geographical spread. Also because of the executive nature of the role they have busy agendas and have limited time for interviews, so a snowballing technique was used, mobilizing contacts in the pension industry and labour bodies to reach a cross section of geographically spread pension trustees to explore issues around the increased diversity of pension boards. The key concepts identified for sampling were experience of regulatory changes, public/private sector, and gender, including a cross section of elected, appointed, and independent trustees. The semi-structured interview agenda focused on how they deal with the responsibility and ongoing challenges of the role, how they interpret diversity, and how this influences decision-making dynamics. Interviews lasted on average 90 minutes, and all interviews were audio-recorded and transcribed verbatim. A thematic analysis was used with the research data, and the themes were: diversity and participation, work and pension experience and capability, engagement in board activities, and the challenge of entering into and maintaining board-level discussions.

The research profile of the 17 interviewees was representative of the diversity of pension boards relative to age and occupational background. Elected representatives came from a broader range of occupations, such as data processing, engineering, and science, than the more economist/legal and managerial background of appointed trustees (Kakabadse and Kakabadse, 2005), which may reflect the impact of elections on pension board composition (see Table 6.1).

Table 6.1 Pension Trustee Profile

Trustees' Age	M/F	Pension Role	Fund Type	Occupational B/ground
1 Trustee 60+	F	Elected	Public DB	Pension fund mgr and secretary trade union rep
2 Trustee 50+	F	Elected	Private DB	Data processing
3 Trustee 50+	F	Appointed	Private DB	HR director
4 Trustee 50+	F	Independent (chair)	Public DB	Manager and NED
5 Trustee 50+	M	Pens. Advisory Committee	Private DB and DC	Trust company lawyer
6 Trustee 50+	M	Appointed	Private DB	Lawyer and company secretary

(Continued)

Table 6.1 (Continued)

Trustees' Age	M/F	Pension Role	Fund Type	Occupational B/ground
7 Trustee retired 60+	M	Appointed	Private DB	HR director
8 Trustee 50+	M	Independent	Private DB and DC	Actuary, director corporate trustee companies
9 Tstee Retired 60+	M	Appointed	Private DB	Education Director
10 Trustee 60+	M	Appointed	Private and DC	Former CEO and non-exec director
11 Trustee 50+	M	Elected	Private DB and DC	Scientist
12 Trustee 50+	M	Appointed	Public and private DC	Financial director
13 Trustee 50+	M	Elected (union rep)	Private DB	Engineer
14 Trustee 50+	M	Elected	Private DB	Technician
15 Trustee 60+	M	Professional	Private DB	Consultant actuary director; advisor to trustee schemes
16 Trustee 40+	F	Independent	Public DB	Management consultant
17 Trustee 60+	M	Co-chair appointed	Private DB	Executive manager

Note: DB Defined Benefit; DC Defined Contribution Scheme; NED Non-executive director

BOURDIEU, CAPITAL, AND PENSION BOARDS

The fields reflect the nature of capital which is essential for pension trustees to possess so that they become fully included participants. It is in this area that legitimate representatives may face conflict. High-status managerial roles can help managers accrue sizeable economic capital, but this lack can be addressed by one's differing access to social capital gained over a lifetime of work.

Social capital is the social interaction and relationship development and dynamics that are evolved through social connections in a group or class membership. At a board level social capital is an important feature (Vinnicombe et al. 2008). A feature of corporate boardrooms is the degree of interconnectedness between directors, where members may not be directly linked to other directors but do have links to people they both know, thus forming institutionalized relationships of mutual acquaintance and recognition (Scott 2008). When members of a group or class move through a life path they tend to move as a whole. Thus they manage to permeate each other's social capital so that all members of the group are taken on the same route or pathway (Bourdieu 1986), thereby establishing a critical mass that allows them to be influential in the field, in different formats, such as in the boardroom, the 'city', or senior roles in public life.

The foregoing situation also has cultural overtones as many people at this level may share similar educational backgrounds, gained titles through their services to industry or pensions (as had one of our interviewees while another sat with a 'Sir' on the board), or inherited these levels of social dispositions. One of the visible outcomes of those who have high levels of cultural capital, whether gained over a lifetime or inherited, is the ease and naturalness with which they view the boardroom habitus compared to those with much lower levels of capital. However, the introduction of political representation of employee representatives on pension boards means that new entrants may have other aspects of social capital, such as trade union or professional organizations' social networks and membership, which they can use to help them to challenge or even adjust boardroom activities and behaviours.

Corporate boardrooms are closely associated with organizational hierarchy. However, pension boards are different because, unlike corporate managerial boards, the "ecology of decision-making contains aspects of collegiality and fiduciary duty, representativeness and collective commitment" (Clark and Urwin 2008: 38). Consequently, the composition of pension boards is much more heterogeneous than other boards. Nevertheless, this chapter argues that the culture of behaviour and attitudes, or 'demeanour', as one labour pension trustee coined it (Sayce 2009), does share some similarities with managerial boards with respect to the high level analytical thinking that is required and the degree of influence that these decisions have for the sponsoring organization in the private sector, as well as the status of the role.

For pension boards, higher levels of social and economic capital can help influence any deficiency of cultural value judgement, particularly at a boardroom level, where people entering come with varied backgrounds of work and life experiences. So while pension trusteeship is dominated by white, ageing men, there has been an increase in the diversity of occupations from whence they come (Sayce 2012). Nevertheless people's positions within the boardroom are connected to their present experience in pension experience, such as their seniority in the sponsoring organization and their familiarity with high-level financial decision making. They may have specific knowledge that supports good governance in managing pension funds or a familiarity with dealing with complex and ethical benefits decisions made with respect to individual members and their pension claims, which will fundamentally impact on members' life in retirement. Consequently, all of these knowledges are collectively important to the smooth running of pension boards in the fulfilment of their fiduciary responsibilities, which supports the legitimacy of a more diverse pension board.

Using Bourdieu's social concepts, the analysis of the data is structured as follows: firstly it begins with an examination of habitus and representational legitimacy, which brings in people with differing levels of political perspectives, experience, and capital, such as trade union representatives and member-nominated representatives, who are all subject to the same fiduciary responsibilities. However, a focus on trade union representatives and member-nominated representatives as outsiders to boardroom activities also indicates how those who have been involved in trusteeship a long time can help reinforce existing power relations of board-level representatives and the establishment of a dispositional habitus around incumbents' behaviours and knowledge. How existing boardroom incumbents' values and the ability to constrain actions can occur for new entrants is clearly indicated when Bourdieu's concept of illusio and doxa is used to show how new entrants' board experiences can result in compliance as they encounter the dominant pension board culture and either adapt to the culture or attempt to change it.

Pension Boards Habitus and Outsiders

The foregoing has outlined how Bourdieu's framework of habitus can help us explore how representational legitimacy impacts on a pension board's dominant customs and behaviours and how, using Bourdieu, we can begin to identify 'breaks' that distinguish social arrangements and cultures when different issues arise Calhoun (1993: 67). Here the key breaks are adaption of diverse members into a consensus about boardroom values and behaviours. The first break being examined is how experienced trustees indicate how labour representative behaviours and customs that may be fit for purpose in union negotiations are not suitable in the boardroom. Another break is when the organizational context for board behaviour changes and suddenly trustees who took a more paternalistic stance can find themselves out of step with a less 'the company knows best' approach. These two 'breaks' are analysed, helping us to understand how experienced pension trustees perceive new entrants to the boardroom, acknowledging that they may have made a strong investment into boardroom rules and have a greater feel for how regulations proceed and communicate specific pension boards' norms and attitudes to legitimate outsiders. This grouping can thus include union representatives and member-nominated representatives.

Many of the trustees' organizations (Pension Trustees 13, 5, 11, 4, and 1, 17) have a long history of labour representatives participating in pension board discussions, often through appointment as employee representatives, such as in the Universities Superannuation Scheme. In principle the trustees who had a union presence were supportive of labour representatives. There were a couple of concerns about this, the first being that the representative had to recognize that being a trustee representative was different from being a union representative, and that trusteeship was not about favouring one group over another. However, the trustees suggested that most union representatives could distinguish between their union role and their trustee role. An important adjunct to this is that one could argue that organizationally directors also faced the same conflict of interest, as they too should not place the sponsoring organization's priorities first.

> I represent all the members, not just the pensioners. I don't feel that I stand to represent any particular group like a shop steward, while the relationship with the company has changed it had been very . . . cosy is not quite the word, historically it had been paternalistic; that has been diluted but there was still some commonality, and it was only recently that conflicts of interests (between the company and the employee perspectives) has raised its head.
>
> (Pension Trustee 7)

The changing economic and regulatory climate for boards in general has challenged the previous, more collaborative (Kakabadse et al. 2003), or, in the foregoing case, paternalistic, approach to business. What this has meant for board behaviour is also indicated by Pension Trustee 11, who commented that he too had seen older appointed representatives in his paternalistic company struggle with the changes both in trusteeship representation and in the approach to decision making on his pension board.

What this means is described in the following quotation as well as what demeanour is required at board level—for instance, the inappropriateness of a more aggressive stance to pension trusteeship, as outlined by Pension Trustee 6, whose union representative when 'doing his job' had a more aggressive style. The aim in pension boardrooms is to persuade the employer/sponsor to gradually move forward in a different direction, creating a more consensual approach to decision making than the more adversarial 'them and us' approach:

> Trade unions do have a role to play because they can bring in professional advisors and scrutinise the detail and the proposals and present alternative approaches; so they do have a valuable role to play. It is just this sort of black and white approach which you can sometimes get (the them and us) which is totally unhelpful. We had one individual who was a shop steward, and he never changed his style and approach; anything that was presented by the company he had to define the position of the members. That is a bit difficult but that is life.
>
> (Pension Trustee 11)

The foregoing point seems to justify the addition of trade union representatives to the pension boardroom—if one of the key responsibilities of trustees is to question the decision-making process and the assumptions on which decision are taken to benefit the membership and not just union members. So while the legitimacy of trade unions and their representatives appears accepted by trustees, the attitudes and behaviour that they bring to the board can be questioned because of the consensual nature of pension board decision making. Another trustee, who acts as an independent trustee with experience on 13 pension boards, comments that there can be problems with representation but that this is often linked to a lack of trust between the employees and the employer/sponsor:

> I have seen trustee boards where there is a tension (over representation), but I think that is a reflection of industrial relations in the organization generally. Even now there are organizations where shop floor does not sit comfortably down with management; and that is as true in the trustee meetings as anywhere else. I don't think the union element changes it very much. I think sometimes companies get the industrial relations they deserve, and sometimes they are very good and sometimes they are not. I think there are loads of very good member-elected trustees, some of whom are union representatives and some who are not.
> (Pension Trustee 8)

What seems to be important to note here is that the dispositional habitus of the boardroom is reflective of the industrial relationship itself, a major concern for Bourdieu and the historical and situational nature of habitus (Bourdieu 1985). This is linked to how present dispositions are shaped by past experiences; thus poor treatment with respect to employees may in part influence attitudes in the future. So having experienced a tradition of hostility or even a more paternalistic approach within the sponsor's workplace can influence the board's dispositional habitus. This is an important point to consider when you recognize that elected representatives have to be members of the pension plan. Thus this was also an issue for those trustees who, as Pension Trustees 11 and 7 pointed out, had come from a paternalistic orientation.

Key to being accepted as legitimate is gaining cultural and social capital to develop a dispositional habitus that fits in with the boardroom structures, not forgetting that many union representatives may themselves be familiar with an existing organizational masculine habitus from their union activities (Healy and Kirton 2000). But what is also indicated is that for blue-collar workers adapting to change is more of a challenge as they enter the boardroom and learn the rules of the game, or, in the case of older executives, learn the new rules of how the game is played. However, the difference between the groupings is that senior executives can use their illusio, their investment in the game with colleagues, to help them shape changes in norms and attitudes into managerial ones they feel they can be more comfortable with. The next quotation subtly indicates the importance of capital in being appointed as an employee representative, as well as how the 'doxa' of the boardroom and its unspoken presuppositions of how to act and behave in this context on the behalf of the membership can be set:

> What we tend to find is that there are four company members. One of them is a group finance director who has very limited time. The other is the group head of HR who also has very limited time and then we

have a vacancy for 12 months simply because the company wasn't able to persuade someone of appropriate seniority to do it. I am another company-appointed trustees, so as a legal executive I am probably doing more than my fair share. I enjoy doing this role. It is all convenient to my office in London so I don't have to travel round the country. The meetings are at a convenient time in the afternoon. The fellow trustees are without exception generally people that I have worked with for many years and know very well.

(Pension Trustee 12)

The foregoing seems to be suggesting that the dispositional habitus is very much led by the employer representatives and their command of the game, which makes it convenient and easy for them to function as board members, time pressures permitting. However, pension boards can be structured differently to corporate boards, which can influence the dispositional habitus. For example, one private sector fund pension board interviewee, an executive of the sponsoring company, outlined how he has a joint co-chair, a senior official of one of the six trade unions who represent the organization's members. In this case it is the union who conducts the process to be a member-nominated trustee, although candidates do not have to come from a union background. In this case the two chairs do sometimes disagree about how issues should be handled, however:

We do have different views on things and sometimes it can get quite heated. I mean it rarely gets personal but it can get quite forceful. But generally, it is not something that means we haven't been able to go for dinner or a drink and sort it.

(Pension Trustee 17)

These two chairs have worked together for a long time, and there is clearly an element of trust between them, but there also appears to be an element of trust within the industrial relations context. This more pluralistic approach is also supported by the organizational owner, who progressed from the shop floor and developed the company into an international presence. In this organization it could be argued that this background has helped to create a different dispositional habitus, which has enhanced the legitimacy of employee/employer representatives, as each has a chair to champion their viewpoint. It also helps to avoid the possibility of a 'them and us' position emerging, which is unwelcome at this level of decision making.

This section has demonstrated the importance of recognizing how the industrial relations context and the approach a company takes to managing its employee relations are influential in the dispositional habitus that trustees bring to a pension board (Sayce 2006). But in order to fully understand the differing doxa that appointed and elected representatives bring it is useful to see how 'outsiders' to pension boards perceive their experience of entering the boardroom.

Entering the Boardroom and Acknowledging the Rules of the Game and the Role of Doxa and Illusio

A secondary area of analysis may be in examining the doxa and illusio that new entrants bring to the field of the pension boardroom, as this may also help to explain the regenerative qualities of boardrooms and how using Bourdieu's analogy of the game the rules and expectations of board behaviours and values are transferred to new members, who may be unfamiliar with board contexts. Here the viewpoint of people who may consider themselves to be 'outsiders' on pension boards, such as women, blue-collar workers, and labour representatives, may offer useful insight into doxa and illusio. In pension trusteeship there is a need to challenge assumptions within the decision-making process. However, at the same time decisions also need to be consensual as all trustees have a responsibility to act in the primary interests of the members. Usually boards are united in the direction that the board is going, but often there can be disagreements about the way to get there. It is this aspect where legitimacy is important in influencing which decisions are taken. However, entering the boardroom can be a challenge to those not initiated in how to act and behave. This point is made in the following quotation from a public sector pension board member who was recruited through advertising because she offered a fresh and independent viewpoint. But as an outsider to the public sector and pension boards she comments that at times this rhetoric seems at odds with what the board does:

> How did you become a pension trustee? It is usually down with the club (old boys club) in this particular public sector. All pension funds that have lay members are looking for independence. They either go directly to a consultancy that they know that provides them with an independent trustee or they know someone and they approach them directly. One year an advertisement was sent out, and four applied, but then it came out a lot later that the three had been made offers, but they didn't apply. They were asked to join, and a lot later I found out that the guy from the fund manager had actually worked with one of our senior executives. So how fair and honest is the process of actually getting these guys on the board? It was a kind of job for the boys and they were actually all boys (men) this time.
>
> (Pension Trustee 16)

The UK pension regulators' guidelines for new entrants do indicate the importance of challenging and questioning the decision-making process; however, the scope of the role is itself very intimidating. New entrants, even if they may have been senior executives, still find the process intimidating (Sayce and Ozbilgin 2014). One elected female data processor trustee comments that she was 'dumbstruck' when she first entered, while another employer-appointed representative outlined how as a HR director she felt that they considered she had more knowledge than she actually had: "I think they were more or less speaking a foreign language when I first started. I think they assumed that I knew more than I did" (Pension Trustee 3). One of the very experienced independent trustees acknowledge that for new entrants picking up on what was happening in the board meeting was difficult. While The Pension Regulator demands that trustees should be up to speed in six months. He thought that was very challenging. His advice to new entrants was: "I think it is appropriate for newer trustees not to defer to more experienced trustees but to listen to what more experienced trustees have said" (Pension Trustee 8). This point is important because when people feel insecure they can take their cues on how to behave from their more experienced colleagues, which can be influential in the generational reproduction of board attitudes and behaviour. The chairs of pension boards who were interviewed (4, 15, 11, 17) recognized the challenge facing all new entrants to the boardroom. However, one business consultant and new entrant adjusting to the public sector doxa said that questioning, which is part of their role, takes a lot of confidence as an outsider to the group:

> When I ask questions about things I ask them for a reason; it's not, you know, petty. It truly is to understand, so sometimes I think it is inappropriate for the more experienced of the forum to get antsy with my questions.
>
> (Pension Trustee 16)

The danger for new entrants is that more powerful others can dissuade people from fully participating in challenging the decision-making process if the existing board members react negatively to being questioned, or show dislike of the manner in which they are being questioned. As the independent trustee (8) correctly points out, it is a delicate balancing act between supporting new entrants and perhaps intimidating new entrants, which can unintentionally place trustees at odds with their interpretation of their fiduciary responsibility. Thus the legitimacy of new entrants and in particular entrants not familiar with the knowledge of the language, the jargon used in discussion as highlighted by two new female outsiders (2, 3) contributes to them feeling like outsiders within this level of decision-making, especially if they are not familiar with the ways in which boardroom discussion are conducted (16, 11). For instance, if one appears to be trying too hard to act in a manner one does not usually adopt or makes mistakes in using jargon or communicating, the more experienced participants could use this lack of knowledge to help limit the legitimate contribution of these representatives until they learn the rules of the game that is played on their specific pension board. At its most extreme, unscrupulous employer/sponsor pension boards could use this situation to exclude greater input or challenges to the decision-making process, as discussed in Sayce and Gold's (2011) research into Canadian pension boards in Quebec, which also has elected representation on its pension committees.

Linguistic differences too can affect the board's valuation of outsiders' contributions, which could include women, as indicated earlier (2, 3, 16), but also men who come from the shop floor. Here gender interpretations of ways of speaking may lead to them being categorized as too assertive, like Pension Trustee 16, which could explain the negative response to her questioning (Tannen 2004). Or, as in the case of union trustees, being too aggressive in communicating may label them as outsiders as they are not used to the jargon or the board's linguistic norms. Here the dominant group's intimation of what is perceived as correct behaviour influences the dispositional habitus of the boardroom and ultimately what individuals perceive as possible in this context, and this influences new entrants to comply with existing norms and values. However, what is troubling for pension trusteeship is that this could ultimately impact on decision making, with some people's contribution being less valued than others because it does not fit in with professional male managers' patterns of speech and thus is unconsciously rejected.

DISCUSSION: LEGITIMACY AND POLITICAL REPRESENTATION

Pension board members' fiduciary responsibilities mean acting in the interests of members; however, stakeholders, plan sponsors/employers, employee unions, retirees, and the community can also have a legitimate claim for views to be heard in the board's decision-making process. Underpinning this representation is the notion of representative democracy. This makes pension boards more heterogeneous than other managerial boards, which means that pension boards may have different perspectives about key principles in decision making, such as risk, time, and value of information (Clark et al. 2007). However, the major academic debate in pension trusteeships and their pension boards is over competence and the potential conflict "between claims made for stakeholder representation and claims made for board-level expertise that is consistent with the capacity of institutions to meet their obligations" (Clark 2007: 2). While representation should confer legitimacy, that can be challenged by other stakeholders, such as the pension community and investment experts, as in the consistency of decision making and the competency of pension trustees (Ambachsteer 2007). The Bourdieusian analysis has shown how habitus can generate the adoption of its dominant managerialist values and attitudes and extend these to constituents who do not necessarily share a managerialist background, such as trade unionists and elected members from different occupational backgrounds, in helping to maintain the existing rules of the game.

Clark et al. (2007) and Clark and Urwin (2008), for example, critique the consistency of pension trustees' decision making, citing an experiment between Oxford graduates and pension trustees. However, the rationality of this claim can be challenged by Bourdieu's macro and micro focus, as the experimental nature of the research assumes that in all contexts all the information is given; it ignores the personal interaction, the differing time constraints under which decisions are made, and the differing priorities that may be placed on that decision by the board, which is also a feature of boardroom decision making (Pye and Pettigrew 2005; Pettigrew and McNulty 1998). In other words, the historical, cultural, and situational nature of organizations and their boards within Bourdieu's analytical approach to habitus is lost, and as the analysis shows this has important explanatory power for continuity within pension board behaviours and values over time. How habitus is improvised is linked to environmental changes, such as new regulation about board composition and governance, but the improvisation also expresses the subjective intentions of players in the game who operate within structural boundaries and use tools such as doxa and illusio unconsciously to maintain their position within power relations. Nevertheless, the foregoing debate emphasizing financial and analytical decision making has implications for legitimacy, the differing level and type of capital that pension board members bring to the boardroom, and expectation for boardroom behaviours, where people acquire legitimacy with other pre-existing field incumbents and influence the board's power relations. The closer that board members are to each other in the social space [e.g. Pensions Trustee 12's comment, "all people I know very well"] the closer they are to belonging to a similar theoretical class according to Bourdieu (1989: 17). Thus there can be an intricate interplay between newcomers' intentions and the focus of power and the dominant cultural norms at work in the boardroom context.

All entrants to the boardroom receive legitimacy through representation of the employer or the employee. Bourdieu (1987: 3) himself argues that forms of capital are powers in their own right and, using his preferred game analogy, act as aces do in a card game. However, as Maclean et al.'s (2010) research shows, the field of the boardroom has its own norms and behavioural expectations and attitudes that may reshape this legitimacy into its own image in accord with the overall volume of capital and how different aspects of capital in the social space are constituted and used.

De Clercq and Voronov (2009: 8010) claim that legitimacy is a reciprocal process whereby new entrants comply with field-imposed expectations and current power arrangements where incumbents may be complicit in its continuation. Illusio and doxa can be used as tools to strengthen links between social and symbolic capital (Bourdieu 1987), and what individuals perceive to be possible and legitimate in a boardroom context. Disruption of the field, as discussed in Sayce and Ozbilgin (2014), by newcomers is a challenging enterprise, despite increasing diversity on pension boards and of board affiliation, and collegiately and fiduciary duty. How this is done may vary according to trustees' collective commitment (Clark and Urwin 2008). Thus while democracy and governance reasoning argue that greater representation will make boards more accountable and transparent, leading to 'good' governance, there is a danger that without clear leadership by board chairs or co-board chairs the legitimacy of newcomers to challenge long-standing assumptions will be disputed or undermined by existing attitudes and behaviours. Thus new entrants have to find a way to challenge that fits in with prevailing cultural norms or otherwise continue to defer to their more long-standing colleagues. Challenging long-standing boardroom assumptions is possible but requires a critical mass of new entrants with similar views (discussed in Sayce and Ozbilgin 2014).

CONCLUSION

The purpose of the book is to give insight into Bourdieu's conceptualization of social theory. The empirical chapters develop this by indicating how a Bourdieusian analysis can help to explain compliance rather than change within different settings. Bourdieu's theory of habitus can explain generational reproduction across different decades, and this underpins the analysis of representation and legitimacy on pension boards, where trustees participate in the highest level of organizational decision making. Understanding the inherent tensions in challenging the composition of these boards and existing power relations through regulation indicates how other Bourdieusian concepts like doxa and illusio can be used as tools to explain compliance with dominant norms despite major change. In this chapter they explain how legitimacy can be informally challenged by the beliefs and actions of existing incumbents.

Pension boards do have some similarities with corporate boardrooms in how to act, how to speak, and how to behave, but they also have some important differences. For example, Clark and Urwin (2008: 40) argue that the ecology of decision making on pension boards is different because of the collegiality of boards, where members are individually and collectively legally liable for their decisions with respect to the membership and for the representational ethics and collective nature of the decision making, and because of how board members understand proper behaviour, which demands a more consensual approach to decision making than corporate boardrooms. The danger with this from a Bourdieusian perspective is that decisions need to be consensual rather than complicit, which a well-functioning, more heterogeneous board should help ensure, thus underpinning the importance of representation and legitimacy. Nevertheless, the level of influence and the degree of decision making have important economic and social consequences to the many stakeholders in pension occupational plans, including employers/sponsors, active and retired employees, government, and labour bodies, which demands a greater understanding of the decision-making process and the integration of these different legitimate perspectives within it as boards strive to balance sponsor/employer representation with employee representation.

The chapter's exploration of how representational legitimacy does impact on pension boards' dominant customs and behaviours indicates that in different contexts boards' structure can take different forms to enhance the legitimacy of opposing stakeholders—for example the pension board which has the employer and employee union representative as co-chairs. However, what is also clear is the embedded nature of board customs and practices around communication and behaviour and the potential for complicity of dominated and dominant board members in unconsciously perpetuating these.

New member-nominated trustees may not experience overt challenges to their legitimacy when they enter the boardroom. But what we can see is that entering pension boardrooms can be a challenging and intimidating experience for all, and more so for those trustees who perceive themselves as outsiders because of a different social disposition and habitus. This indicates that there is a research gap in the area of socialization and pension boards that needs to be filled, to establish more clearly what is going on heterogeneous pension boards with respect to establishing a board's organizational norms and customs and how this may or may not map onto the sponsor's own boardroom values and beliefs. Otherwise it is possible for people with higher levels of investment in the game to perpetuate the reproduction of these customs and norms in many contexts, leading to new entrants having to, in the main, adapt to the predominant style of communication and the existing norms of their boardrooms or remain an outsider.

REFERENCES

Ambachtsheer, K. (2007) 'The Three Grades of Pension Fund Governance Quality: Bad, Better, and Best', Working Paper, 1–12 July, Rotman Management School, University of Toronto.

Bourdieu, P. (1985) 'The Genesis of the Concepts of Habitus and Field'. *Sociocriticism* 2: 11–24.

Bourdieu, P. (1986) 'The Forms of Capital' in Richardson, J. G. (ed.), *Handbook of Theory and Research for the Sociology of Education*. Greenwood, New York, 241–258.

Bourdieu, P. (1987) 'What Makes a Social Class? On the Theoretical and Practical Existence of Groups'. *Berkeley Journal of Sociology* 32: 1–18.

Bourdieu, P. (1989) 'Social Space and Symbolic Power'. *Sociological Theory* 7(1): 14–25.

Bourdieu, P. (1990) *In Other Words*. Polity Press, Cambridge.

Bourdieu, P. (1991) *Language and Symbolic Power*. Polity Press, Cambridge.

Bourdieu, P. (2001) *Masculine Domination*. Polity Press, Cambridge.

Bourdieu, P., & Wacquant, L. (1992) *An Invitation to Reflexive Sociology*. Polity Press, Cambridge.

Calhoun, C. (1993) 'Habitus, Field and Capital: The Question of Historical Specificity', in Calhoun, C., LiPuma, E., & Postone, M. (eds.), *Critical Perspectives*. Polity Press, Cambridge, 61–88.

Clark, G. L. (2007) *Governing Finance: Reconciling Functional Imperatives with Stakeholder Representation in Financial Institutions*. Governing Finance Conference, Beijing, June.

Clark G., & Urwin, R. (2008) 'Making Pension Boards Work: The Critical Role of Leadership Rotman'. *International Journal of Pension Management* 1(1): 38–64.

Clark, G. L., Caerlewy-Smith, E., & Marshall, J. C. (2007) 'The Consistency of UK Pension Fund Trustee Decision-Making'. *PEF* 6(1): 67–86.

Corsun, D. L., & Costen, W. M. (2001) 'Is the Glass Ceiling Unbreakable? Habitus, Fields and the Stalling of Women and Minorities in Management'. *Journal of Management Inquiry* 10(1): 16–25.

De Clercq, D., & Voronov, M. (2009) 'The Role of Domination in Newcomers Legitimation as Entrepreneurs'. *Organization* 16: 799–827.

Gribben, C., & Gitsham, M. (2006) 'Will UK Pension Funds Become More Responsible? A Survey of Trustees' (UK Social Investment Forum, London).

Harrits, G. S. (2013) 'Class, Culture and Politics: On the Relevance of a Bourdieusian Concept of Class in Political Sociology'. *Sociological Review* 61: 172–202.

Harvey, C., & Maclean, M. (2008) 'Capital Theory and the Dynamics of Elite Business Networks in Britain and France'. *Sociological Review* 56: 103–120.

Healy, G., & Kirton, J. (2000) 'Women, Power and Trade Union Government in the UK'. *British Journal of Industrial Relations* 38(3): 343–360.

Higgs, D. (2003) Review of the Role and Effectiveness of Non-executive Directors. London: Department Trade and Industry.

Hymans Robertson. (2007) 'Trustees: Increasingly Powerful'. Retrieved 2 February 2015, from www.engagedinvestor.co.uk/Journals/Newsquest2/Engaged_Investor/July/August_2007/attachments/EI_JA07_p35_38.pdf.

Kakabadse, N., & Kakabadse, A. (2005) 'Prudence vs. Professionalism: Exploratory Examination of Pension Trustee Capability'. *Personnel Review* 34(5): 567–587.

Kakabadse, N., Kakabadse, A., & Kouzmin, A. (2003) 'Pension Fund Trustees: Role and Contribution'. *European Management Journal* 21(3): 376–386.

Krais, B. (2006) 'Gender, Sociological Theory and Bourdieu's Sociology of Practice'. *Theory, Culture Society* 23: 119–134.

Maclean, M., Harvey, C., & Chia, R. (2010) 'Dominate Corporate Agents and the Power Elite in France and Britain'. *Organization Studies* 31: 327–348.

Neuman, W. L. (2003) *Social Research Methods*. Boston: Allyn and Bacon.

Pettigrew, A., & McNulty, T. (1998) 'Sources and Uses of Power in the Boardroom'. *European Journal of Work and Organizational Psychology* 7(2): 197–214.

Pye, A., & Pettigrew, A. (2005) 'Studying Board Context, Process and Dynamics'. *British Journal of Management* 16: 27–38.

Rafferty, M., Ham, R., & Bryan, D. (2008) *Governance and Performance in Superannuation Fund Management—An Issues and Research Design Article*. Report to the Australian Institute of Superannuation Trustees.

Sayce, S. (2006) 'Gender Change? Locked into Industrial Relations and Bourdieu'. *Employee Relations* 28(5): 468–482.

Sayce, S. (2009) 'Motivation and Pension Trusteeship Survey Report'. Centre of Diversity and Equality of Careers and Employment. University of East Anglia, June.

Sayce, S. (2012) 'Being a Female Pension Trustee'. *Equality, Diversity and Inclusion* 31(3): 1–16.

Sayce, S., & Gold, M. (2011) 'Revisiting Industrial Democracy and Pension Trusteeship: The Case of Canada'. *Economy and Industrial Democracy* 32(3): 477–498.

Sayce, S., & Ozbilgin, M. (2014) 'Pension Trusteeship and Diversity in the UK: A New Boardroom Recipe for Change or Continuity?' *Economic and Industrial Democracy* 35: 1.

Sayce, S., Weststar, J., & Verma, A. (2014) 'The Recruitment and Selection of Pension Trustees: A Model of Integration?'. *HRM Journal* 24(3): 307–322.

Scott, J. (2008) 'Modes of Power and the Re-conceptualisation of Elites'. *Sociological Review* 56: 25–43.

Streeck, W., & Thelen, K. (2005) 'Introduction: Institutional Change in Advanced Political Economies', in Streeck, W. & Thelen, K. (eds.), *Beyond Continuity: Institutional Change in Advanced Political Economies*. OUP, Oxford, 1–39.

Tannen, D. (2004) 'Cultural Patterning in Language and Women's place', in Lakoff, R. T. (ed.), *Language and Woman's Place: Text and Commentaries*. Oxford University Press, Oxford, 158–164.

Towers Watson. (2012) 'Global Pension Assets Study'. Retrieved 20 May 2012, from www.towerswatson.com.

Treasury Report. (2004) 'Myners Principles for Institutional Investment Decision-Making: Review of Progress', December, HM Treasury.

Tyson, L. D. (2003) Report on the Recruitment and Development of Non-executive Directors Department of Trade and Industry, London June.

Vinnicombe, S., Singh, V., Burke, R., Bilmoria, D., & Huse, M. (2008) *Women on Corporate Boards of Directors: International Research and Practice*. Edward Elgar, Cheltenham.

Weststar, J., & Verma, A. (2007) 'What Makes for Effective Labor Representation on Pension Boards?' *Labour Studies Journal* 32(4): 382–410.

Wheeler, S. (2010) 'Board Composition and Female Non-executive Directors', in MacNeil, I. & O'Brien, J. (eds.), *The Future of Financial Regulation*. Bloomsbury, London, 271–287.

Woods, C., & Urwin, R. (2010) 'Putting Sustainable Investing into Practice: A Governance Framework for Pension Funds'. *Journal of Business Ethics* 92: 1–19.

7 Of Trump Cards and Game Moves
Positioning Gender Equality as an Element of Power Struggles in Universities

Johanna Hofbauer, Angelika Striedinger, Katharina Kreissl, and Birgit Sauer

INTRODUCTION

In this chapter we discuss the role of gender equality policies as elements of field-specific power struggles in Austrian universities. A first glance at legal requirements and at universities' self-portrayal raises high expectations for the endorsement of gender equality among academic staff: it is the legal duty of universities to contribute to equality between women and men (Flicker et al. 2010), and commitments to this aim are an important feature of the self-representation of many Austrian universities. And indeed, gender asymmetries among academic staff have—slowly, but steadily—decreased in the past two decades.

We argue, however, that it would be naïve to interpret the implementation of gender equality measures solely as a translation of a societal consensus for equality into the organizational structures of universities. More generally, our aim is to argue against a simplistic account of change that relies on describing modifications of formal procedures (for a more general critique of managerialism in higher education along these lines, see Taksa and Kalfa, this volume). Instead, we apply Bourdieu's theoretical lens and embed our observations of universities' gender equality policies and structures in a wider analysis of how players aim to strengthen their relative positions of power within the field. Bourdieu's *relational* view on power seems of particular value (see also Emirbayer 1997) to highlight the complex conditions for change. While research on organization informed by Bourdieu accounts for power relations, it tends to neglect wider implications of relational methodology. For example, the concept of capital is frequently deployed in rather substantialist ways, understanding capital, such as scientific expertise or network ties, as properties that exist independently of the social context in which they are constituted and reproduced (Emirbayer and Johnson 2008: 2f.).

Furthermore, the notion of the organizational field, even though inspired by Bourdieu's field-theory, is mostly used in research on clusters of organizations, while leaving relations to macro-level contexts aside. Emirbayer and Johnson (ibid.) mention "the economy" or "the political sphere" to stress this point—we suggest adding academia or 'the scientific community' to the list. Apart from the missing interlinkage between organization and macro-level contexts, the absence of single organizations in field-theoretical terms is noted (ibid.). We take up the call for a more "unified field-based framework" (ibid.) and attempt to show that an analysis of the implementation of equality policies in the course of the managerialization of Austrian universities benefits from (a) a focus on power struggles within single organizations in field-theoretical terms, and (b) cross-referencing between field levels. This approach highlights that multiple sources of power and legitimation of decision making exist within single organizations, and that different organizations establish characteristic modes of contestation of power sources.

Bourdieu's notion of the *field of social forces* provides an important way of advancing existing criticism of public sector reforms within organization research. For example, Nils Brunsson (2006: 11) convincingly argues that managerial reforms nourish "the dream of rational organization" (ibid.), despite innumerable failures of reforms. Bourdieu enables us to understand this "dream of rational organization" as part of the deep structures of persistent systems of belief (a field's *doxa*), and to consider the relation to an organization's structure of power and domination. Bourdieu connects structures of meaning with relations of power and domination. This enables a comprehensive understanding of the seemingly paradoxical phenomenon that the belief in rationality seems induced, rather than diluted, by governance reform projects that fail to challenge relations of power inherited from the past. Inherent to Bourdieu's notion of the field is the metaphor of social life as a game, which allows us to connect our empirical findings to the theoretical concepts: the metaphor of players pursuing moves and playing trump cards in their struggle over the definition of the rules of the game and the distribution of stakes.

Equipped with these theoretical tools and concepts, we aim to discuss the role and function of gender equality in the power struggles that emerge or intensify around the implementation of a new career model in Austrian academia: the tenure track model. The process of implementing this career model promises particularly good insight into the power games in universities, because the stakes are high. The allocation of these new positions not only decides the career perspectives of junior academics but also is connected to the university-internal distribution of significant amounts of resources, with strategic planning and research foci, as well as with the constellations of persons and tasks in the university's faculties and institutes. In this situation, internal struggles intensify, and otherwise invisible structures of meaning and power become the subject of debates.

We ask how the implementation of gender equality policies influences and is influenced by the power structures in universities and the boundaries of the field, as well as which moves and manoeuvres players apply to strengthen their relative positions of power. We expect that this analysis will help to systematically account for differences between universities in terms of the extent and character of their gender equality activities, and we aim to draw conclusions concerning opportunities and pitfalls for gender equality in the context of university reform.

The following section will sketch Bourdieu's field theory and outline the higher education reform in a field-theoretical context. For the sake of our argument, we shall refer mostly to the bureaucratic and the scientific fields. Both fields are significant contexts for the evolution of the university as a field-within-fields—a field of social forces itself. The third section provides information on the research design and data collection of our empirical study, while the fourth section describes the framework of legal change concerning the academic career model. The fifth section presents the evidence from our study.[1] The last section aims to summarize the argument and to draw conclusions for the opportunities and pitfalls of the implementation of tenure track positions with respect to equal opportunity.

CONCEPTUALIZING THE FORCES OF FIELDS: THE CASE OF UNIVERSITIES

Field and Capital

Bourdieu's understanding of the social universe is a world made of *fields of social forces*, by which he means relations of power and domination (Bourdieu and Wacquant 1992: 94ff.). In order to explain the inherent dynamics of fields and to account for their reproduction, Bourdieu frequently uses the analogy of a game: "We can indeed, with caution, compare a field to a game (*jeu*) although, unlike the latter, a field is not the product of a deliberate act of creation, and it follows rules or, better, regularities, that are not explicit and codified. Thus we have *stakes* (*enjeux*) which are for the most part the product of the competition between players" (ibid.: 98). Bourdieu argues that agents in a field are *driven* by the power struggles or power games in the field; their engagement relates to an "*investment in the game, illusio* (from *ludus*, the game): players are taken in by the game, they oppose one another, sometimes with ferocity, only to the extent that they concur in their belief (*doxa*) in the game and its stakes; they grant these a recognition that escapes questioning" (ibid.).

Similar to the struggle for stakes in a game, a social field is characterized by struggles for means of power which Bourdieu conceives as *forms of capital*: "a species of capital is what is efficacious in a given field, both as a weapon and as a stake of struggle, that which allows its possessors to wield a power, an influence, and thus to *exist*, in the field under consideration, instead of being considered a negligible quantity" (ibid.). Active players in the game use their relative power to enforce what is regarded as a valuable stake, conceived as *symbolic capital* in a given field (Bourdieu 1986). The notions of field and capital are tightly connected; the value of a species of capital "hinges on the existence of a game, of a field in which this competency can be employed" (Bourdieu and Wacquant 1992: 101). Accordingly, the relative value of a certain species of capital varies across various fields. The chances of potential players or newcomers to gain acknowledgement of a stake accumulated in another field (or previous game) depend on the prevalent definition of symbolic capital, which may operate as a kind of shortcut to the existing relations of force among the active players.

Bourdieu explains women's disadvantages of access to a field's symbolic capital in terms of an adverse "conversion rate of capital" (Bourdieu and Wacquant 1992: 17). He argues that gender affects the value of capital like a "symbolic coefficient" (Bourdieu 1998: 100).[2] Metaphorically speaking, then, gender may be addressed as a *negative* or *positive symbolic capital* in a field (McCall 1992; Moi 1991: 1036), depending on the relations of force established during past struggles over the classification of symbolic capital. For example, the scientific field is gendered to the extent that women were excluded from the field in the past. Women's scientific achievements have long been misrecognized and still tend to be underestimated, as made visible by the gap between the cultural capital women achieve in higher education and the difficulties they face in converting university degrees and titles into academic posts and careers. Equality officers and commissioners in universities are in charge of controlling for the devaluation of women's cultural capital. One way to exert this form of control is to engage in decision making of managerial authorities, who dispose of the allocation of resources—for example, tenure positions.

The conception of a field requires the depiction of its boundaries or conditions of access: "People are at once founded and legitimized to enter the field by their possessing a definite configuration of properties" (Bourdieu and Wacquant 1992: 107f.). Bourdieu and Wacquant mention the metaphorical notion of "'admission fee' that each field imposes and which defines eligibility for participation, thereby selecting certain agents over others" (ibid.: 107). For example, in order to exert an influence on decision making concerning the university's personnel policy, equality officers need to enter the inner circles of power of the university (see the section on *university-as-field* ahead). In order to partake in the games played within this field, they need to establish informal contacts within the field—that is, acquire the necessary amount of social capital. Social capital, defined as more or less institutionalized relationships or network ties (Bourdieu 1986: 51), helps to establish relations of trust and symbolic exchange (confidential information, shared norms and values—e.g. concerning political causes) which enables players to overcome the access barriers to the inner circles of decision making in universities.

As a matter of fact, Bourdieu considers barriers to access or conditions of participation in a field an important mechanism of a field's reproduction. At the same time, he concedes that the boundaries of fields are dynamic borders (ibid.: 104): "Those who dominate in a given field are in a position to make it function to their advantage but they must always contend with the resistance, the claims, the contention, 'political' or otherwise, of the dominated" (ibid.: 102).

Borders are not only a key to the conception of access barriers (cf. "definition of eligibility for participation" or "social selectivity of fields" mentioned earlier). The notion of borders also refers to the analysis of relationships *between* fields or to the relationship of a field and its environment. Generally speaking, social fields are relatively *autonomous* entities that translate environmental influence according to their own conditions. Bourdieu draws on the notion of a *prism* that refracts external forces according to the internal structure of the field (Bourdieu and Wacquant 1992: 17). External forces may challenge established relations of power and domination (games and rules), depending on the degree of autonomy of a given field and on the type or degree of external interference. External interferences may even cause a state of crisis within a field, leading to an intensification of internal struggles up to the point where conditions of power and domination in the field, concealed under normal conditions, are revealed. During these periods, notions of shared belief in the game (*doxa*) are rendered explicit and subject to debates.

In our empirical context, the interplay of three important macro fields seems to have significant effects on universities: firstly, struggles over the definition of dominant governance principles within the political field; secondly, struggles over the modes of implementation of new public management (NPM) and the design of external guidance between the Ministry of Science and the single university within the bureaucratic field;[3] and thirdly, struggles within the scientific field over the classification of scientific performance and reputation. The latter intensified in response to external interferences from the political and bureaucratic field. After all, the implementation of NPM and the introduction of new standards of performance measurement put the autonomy of the scientific field at stake, which resonates in fearful articulations of or attacks against a call for 'marketable science' among high numbers of academics.

Since players within the university are simultaneously engaged as players in the scientific field, the explanation of dispositions towards change (or manoeuvres in the course of games that unfold following the implementation of NPM) is a highly complex matter that calls for thorough empirical analysis. The interesting point is, however, that reluctance to NPM may have a number of causes, which according to Bourdieu can be related to an agent's relative position and corresponding position-taking in another field. Hence, we need to consider that the position-taking of an academic within the university may be fuelled by his or her relative position and future aspirations in the scientific field. This is one explanation as to why some academics oppose the implementation of managerialism in universities, which represents interferences from the political and the bureaucratic field in the scientific field, mediated through NPM at the university.

From the perspective of equality officers, we observe that some elements of managerialism facilitate their work by increasing transparency and creating new points of intervention. The interrelatedness of games via multiple membership in various fields, then, leads to a problematic situation: By opposing new governance modes and new methods of performance assessment, and defending professional norms in the struggle for the autonomy of the scientific field, academics sometimes implicitly hold off changes that are helpful for gender equality work. This situation can lead to alliances between university management and gender equality agents against the professorial body.

University-as-Field

The significance of power games in academia is not obvious. Intellectuals readily agree on the universality of competition for reputation, which also serves as 'boundary work' between disciplines (Gieryn 1995). However, many seem less interested in organizational matters. This could be falsely interpreted as an absence of power interests. Christine Musselin stresses this point, highlighting idiosyncratic outcomes of organizational changes at universities: "Why do academics fight with eagerness against the transformation of formal structures while they always state that their department does not matter much? Because rules and structures nevertheless count! Not in fostering and prescribing cooperation but in defining territories and borders and in protecting insiders [. . .] In universities, [. . .] rules and structure first have a defensive role and create protected territories" (Musselin 2007: 76).

The university reform in Austria put established protected territories at stake: territories were reshaped and confined, giving power to management at the cost of academic self-governance structures. The reform also introduced procedures of decision making which aim to enforce equal opportunity, and improved the formal position of equality officers. The agenda for establishing gender equality among tenured staff, however, remains a complex matter. Bourdieu's notion of field helps us understand the conditions of access to the spheres of power in universities—where decisions over the strategic orientation of the university and over the allocation of tenure positions are taken.

The university has evolved as a relatively autonomous organizational field at the intersection of a number of fields, among which the scientific field (scientific community) and the bureaucratic field (state governance) seem the most important for our research. Apart from those two, the political field is similarly significant—for example, where matters of reform goals are concerned. However, we shall focus on scientific and bureaucratic fields, assuming that the latter translates frames of meaning and legitimation of reform coined in the political field into issues of bargaining between the ministry and the university. Both bureaucratic and scientific fields operate as external forces, exerting considerable influence on a university's daily business.

An entire microcosm of power and domination emerges within the formal boundaries of universities. Dietmar Braun (2001) applies Bourdieu's notion of field to the study of governance reforms and describes the university as a field of power, whose structure derives from entitlement to engagement in various types of decision making (ibid.: 244–260). More generally speaking, the implementation of NPM and the instalment of monocratic decision-making structures accentuate the boundaries between managerial and academic authorities. Research has stated, for example, that observing or influencing decision-making processes of the new monocratic university organs has generally become more difficult (Flicker et al. 2010; Wroblewski 2007: 26ff.), hinting at an increased concentration of power. However, Emirbayer and Johnson (2008: 22f.) argue that, while "official posts do endow their occupants with capital that inheres in the posts themselves", it is important to discern additional sources of power. Beyond an organization's formal hierarchy, spaces of struggle for organizational power emerge. Socio-analysis of organizations needs to search for "an organization's own internal *space of struggle for organizational power*, its internal field of power, where what is at stake is nothing less than the capacity to determine which of the various species of capital extant within the organization will be the most influential in defining its activities and in formulating its policies" (ibid.: 26).

In the following we turn to our empirical study, which focuses on power games around implementation of the tenure track model. These games are relevant in two ways: For junior academics, the outcomes define the conditions for advancing in an academic career, for gaining access to *academic* power. For the actors involved—university leaders, equality officers, and individual professors—these games shape the rules and stakes of the struggle for *organizational* power at universities.

RESEARCH DESIGN AND DATA COLLECTION

In order to investigate the role of gender equality in the context of the implementation of the tenure track model in Austrian universities, we conducted case studies (Yin 1994) of four universities. Our aim was to understand both the formally agreed-upon procedures and the ways in which players apply and refer to these procedures, and what their interests and stakes are. We therefore combined document analysis with in-depth interviews.

The documents analysis focused on university management documents, concretely, on bargaining agreements or guidelines by the rectorate outlining the university-specific rules and procedures for implementing the tenure track model. These documents describe the procedural steps towards creating and filling a tenure track position: who is involved and who is responsible in the decision making, and which criteria these decisions are to be based on. In addition to the implementation procedures, these documents also shed light on the management style and collegial culture within our case study universities: they show, for example, whether these procedures are the outcome of formalized negotiations between the rectorate and the works council or top-down guidelines imposed by the rectorate; the degree of detail in these documents can be used as an indicator for the degree of transparency in the universities' governance procedures.

Documents alone, however, are not sufficient to get an accurate impression of the inner works of an organization. We therefore conducted interviews with relevant players in our case study universities: representatives from the rectorate—mostly the rector and the vice rector in charge of personnel management—the senate, the works council, the equal opportunities working group and the equality office, and the administrative units for personnel issues and quality management. Overall we conducted 30 interviews (5–8 per case study university) in autumn and winter 2013/2014, each lasting between about one and three hours (see Table 7.1).

Table 7.1 Data Collection—Interviews in Four Case Study Universities

	Interviews & interviewees	Gender	Academic position	Duration of the interview	Location of the interview
Rectorate	4 interviews, 6 interviewees	3 women, 3 men	4 full professors, 1 associate professor, 1 non-academic staff	45 minutes–2 hours	Rectors' offices, rectorate meeting rooms
Senate	4 interviews, 4 interviewees	1 woman, 3 men	4 full professors	45 minutes–1 hour, 15 min.	Senate offices
Works council	4 interviews, 4 interviewees	3 women, 1 man	4 associate professors	1–2 hours	Works council offices, academic workspace of interviewee
Equality working group	7 interviews, 7 interviewees	6 women, 1 man	3 associate professors, 2 assistant professors, 2 non-academic staff	1 hour, 30 min.–3 hours	Workspaces (offices) of interviewees, cafés
Equality office	5 interviews, 5 interviewees	5 women	5 non-academic staff	1 hour, 30 min.–2 hours	Equality offices
Administrative units for HR or QM	6 interviews, 6 interviewees	3 women, 3 men	6 non-academic staff	45 minutes–1 hour, 30 min.	Administrative offices, meeting rooms, cafés

In these semi-structured interviews, we aimed at collecting stories that would clarify who really prepares and takes decisions in the implementation of the tenure track model, which rules and criteria are most relevant, and how players pursue their interests. We then related these narratives to our findings from the document analysis—the formally agreed-upon regulations for the tenure track model, as well as our deductions concerning the governance culture in the case study universities. In formulating our conclusions, we focused on the role of gender equality in the implementation of this career model.

FRAMEWORK OF OUR STUDY: THE INTRODUCTION OF THE TENURE TRACK MODEL

The recently introduced tenure track model proves to be a particularly interesting framework for our study because of two reasons: First, the tenure track positions are in high demand—they offer access to secure employment and are a big step on the path towards full professorship—while also being scarce because of hesitant implementation by universities. The distribution of scarce resources opens a more direct line of sight on decision-making patterns and power relations. Second, the tenure track model, with clearly specified performance targets, procedures, and evaluation mechanisms, is a comparatively highly formalized career model. As such, it offers a number of opportunities for equality regulations and interventions, which can be particularly effective due to the important status of these positions.

Before we focus on the details of the tenure model, we shall briefly refer to the notion of the professorial body according to different traditions of academic career systems, such as the Anglo-American tenure model or the 'Habilmodel'.[4] The latter is valid in a number of central European countries, including Austria, Germany, Switzerland, and the Czech Republic (Kreckel 2012). Both models may be described according to three main categories of staff: senior, junior, and assisting staff (ibid.). Among those three categories, senior staff is the most influential group, given the fact that only full professors (equivalent of professors and senior lecturers or readers in the Anglo-American tenure model) dispose of the pivotal means of academic power: a permanent employment contract and full autonomy regarding decisions over research and teaching. The category of junior staff (equivalent of lecturers in the Anglo-American tenure model) entails assistant professors with tenure, who share some privileges with full professors. They have permanent contracts, and thus enjoy a high degree of job security, which allows for considerable discretion in the planning of research strategies and teaching. In addition, they are entitled to claim compensations for travel expenses, or apply for further education programs.

In other words, senior and junior professors have access to resources conditional to the achievement of scientific performance and thus engage in the struggle for the standards of assignment of scientific reputation (classification)—hence, engage in the shaping of the conditions of reproduction of their own status in the field. A few important differences remain, however, concerning access to political and social capital. More important, at this point, is the fact that compared with the fairly large body of senior and junior staff in countries which follow the Anglo-American tenure model, countries with the Habilmodel establish significantly smaller groups of senior and junior staff.[5] While the Austrian model does provide permanent positions for junior researchers, the number of these permanent positions is small, which leads to strong competition around the distribution and allocation of these posts.

The tenure track model was introduced in the course of the establishment of a collective agreement for university staff in 2009. It represents the second fundamental change in the career conditions for university personnel in the space of 10 years. Back in 2001, a reform of the labour law for university employees had abolished the possibility of permanent employment apart from full professorship, and thereby created a radical shift in the working conditions in academia (Pechar 2004: 45f.). The collective agreement reopened the perspective for a permanent position below full professorship, and seemed to bring an end to the period of precariousness and lack of career perspectives for young academic staff. In the tenure model, assistant professors, employed for six years, enter a 'qualification agreement' with the university which details the performance goals to be reached within a certain amount of time. If successful, they are promoted to associate professors, and are offered a permanent employment contract.

However, most Austrian universities have so far been hesitant in implementing these tenure track positions. In our interviews with university leaders and equality agents, we were regularly introduced to the notion of tenure positions as "the most precious good of the university": university leaders are extremely cautious with distributing permanent positions, often highlighting that the pre-2001 personnel structure led to inflexibility for university planning as well as a lack of career perspectives for young academics. According to 2013 personnel data, 915 tenure track positions have been created since 2009, 40 percent of which are already permanently employed, with the others working on completing their qualification targets in order to achieve the conditions necessary to enter permanent employment (www.bmwfw.gv.at). A comparison of the 'old' pre-2001 tenure positions, which are phasing out with respective retirement entry, with the 'new' post-2009 tenure positions shows the university leadership's reservations towards implementing this career model: while the number of old tenure positions decreased by 790 in the past five years, only 350 permanent junior academic positions were created under the new tenure track model.

FINDINGS

In our empirical study we put the focus on power games emerging around the introduction of 'new' tenure positions, and in particular on the role of gender equality in this process: new governance mechanisms create new rules and redistribute some trump cards. Planning and decision-making competences have been moved away from academic self-governance towards centralized management. One element of this managerialization is the establishment of gender equality as a management task. At the same time, equality officers' opportunities for influencing policy and interfering in decision making are widened. In this context we analyse which strategies players pursue and which manoeuvres they perform, which trump cards they play and which forms of capital are relevant. In the following, we provide insight into our case study findings by first defining the university as a field in terms of the relative positions of the players, as well as their respective interests and stakes in relation to the introduction of the tenure track model. In a second step we describe the moves and manoeuvres these players perform in the course of the power struggles specific to this field within fields.

Defining the Field(s)

Changes in the higher education landscape can be observed in university systems across Europe since the 1990s. The unique position of the Austrian situation is, however, that in one fell swoop the formerly stagnant university landscape became a model student for managerialism in Europe. For over a decade now, core concepts of new public management have shaped conditions of knowledge production and academic careers in Austria.

These structural interferences were prepared and enhanced by a fierce struggle *in the political field* over positions, recognition, and resources between political parties and players of universities, labour unions, and industry groups. Fostered by the installation of a conservative, right-wing government in 2000,[6] as well as the establishment of a European higher education area, the political discourse on universities fundamentally changed. Between 1993 and 2009 three shifts in dominant frames of meaning structure the political field, guiding higher education policy discussions (Kreissl et al. 2013). The first frame, 'from local to global', referring to the context of knowledge production, demands competitiveness due to the increasing significance of the international arena. The focus on the international market of knowledge production and education pushes back calls for a socially responsible university that operates for the sake of public benefit and keeps its accountability to tax payers in mind. The second frame, 'from ivory tower to business', concerns the character of the university as an organization. Managerial structures and clear decision-making processes become essential quality markers for a well-functioning and output-oriented university, summarized in catchwords such as 'world class', 'modernity', and 'efficiency'. Finally 'from tenure to excellence', the third frame, refers to the academic subject and is guided by the idea of performance orientation. The state employment and tenuring of academics are regarded as an ideal breeding ground for idleness and poor-quality work. 'Excellence', a strong buzzword in the discourse of the field, should be fostered by encompassing evaluation through 'objective' criteria and achieved through an adequate personnel structure.

These shifts ultimately led to a comprehensive reform. In an attempt to radically transform the old alma mater into a modern organization, the most incisive reform, passed in 2002, moved universities from state control towards increased organizational autonomy, and strengthened administrative and managerial structures. This severely affected the *bureaucratic field*, consisting of the official apparatus, ministries (such as the ministry of science) or committees who are supposed to implement the legislation and derive adequate measures. In the bureaucratic field, negotiations between universities and the state—in form of the ministry of science—over resources, performance, goals and positions take place. In this context, gender equality indicators come into play, as the ministry of science partly links them to budgetary issues. Also, career models and conditions of employment are struggled over as, for example, the number of permanent positions in a university is a matter of bargaining between the universities and the state.

To be sure, scientific capital has traditionally been an important source of power in universities. It still endows inhabitants of managerial universities with power. However, Braun (2001) highlights the tendency of devalorization of scientific capital in the course of implementation of new governance at (German) universities. Among the two traditional forms of academic power distinguished by Bourdieu (1988), administrative[7] and scientific power, the former seems to gain weight over the latter. Hence, with the introduction of NPM, fundamental changes in the *political* and *bureaucratic fields* seem to have affected the professional autonomy and academic rules in the *scientific field*.

University as Field-within-Fields

As outlined earlier, we conceptualize the university as a field-within-fields. The elaborations on the political, bureaucratic, and scientific fields help us understand the parameters within which the power struggles in universities take place. In our attempt to define the university as a field, the first step is to get an overview of the relevant players. Four—partly overlapping—groups of players are central to our analysis of the implementation of the tenure track model: first, the rectorate and other levels or units of university administration; second, academic staff from assistants to full professors; third, the senate; and fourth, equality agents in the university. In the following, we outline their respective roles in the implementation process and describe what is at stake from the perspective of their relative positions in the university as a field of power.

The rectorate has a central role in the implementation of the tenure track model: the university leadership is formally in charge of personnel management, which includes structural planning, allocating positions, and taking recruitment and promotion decisions. However, as both the university documents and our interviews made clear, it would be wrong to conclude that decisions are unilaterally taken by the rectorate, as one senate representative explains:

> Yes, of course, rules do exist. But in the end, well, it's the faculty that has to decide, 'These are the ones we want'. [. . .] The rectorate is so far away, they can't step in and say, 'This is the right area'. That's not possible.
> (Senate chairperson, case study 3, full professor, male)

Rather than taking top-down decisions, the rector or vice rector in charge of personnel management coordinates and negotiates with the deans of faculties and the departments, with individual professors, as well as with other relevant players, which in many cases include equality agents in universities. In this process, the rectorate needs to establish and legitimize its leadership position for personnel management within the university. Representatives from the rectorate argue that the planning and allocation of tenure positions are key steps towards strengthening the university's profile in terms of research priorities and innovation—and that the rectorate, in its role as the developer and guardian of the university's strategic development, needs to guide these decision-making processes. At some universities, this expansion of the rectorate's power leads to conflicts with the deans of faculties, who were previously in charge of this kind of personnel decision and who lose some of "their godly, almighty autonomy", as one equality officer explains with an ironical undertone (equality officer, case study 3, non-academic staff, female).

The senate, a democratically elected board, is tasked with representing the interests of the university as a whole. However, full professors, while only 10 percent of the academic personnel, have an absolute majority in the senate, and therefore an important role in shaping the senate's opinions. In the course of the university reforms, the senate's powers were largely abolished and moved to the rectorate, leaving only the design of curricula and the composition of recruitment commissions for full professorships as its two main formal decision-making competencies. The tenure track model confronts the senate with another loss of power: tenure track positions are very similar to professorships in terms of their strategic importance and their role in research and teaching. The senate, though—contrary to recruitment procedures for full professorships—has no formal role in planning, allocation, and recruitment decisions in the tenure track model. One of our case study universities, in implementing the tenure track model, created a recruitment process which is comparable to that for full professorships, including a selection committee, external assessment, and peer review, as well as hearings. The selection panel, however, is composed by the rectorate, and not by the senate—a distribution of responsibilities which the senate aims to change:

> The tenure track positions are assigned without participation of the senate. Exclusively by the rectorate. [. . .] This is absolutely something we discuss: Whether the senate should be more involved in this process.
> (Senate chairperson, case study 1, full professor, female)

In another one of our case study universities, the members of the personnel development councils, which are the newly created structure in charge of implementing and monitoring the tenure track system, are nominated by the faculty department, and—again—not by the senate. What is at stake with the implementation of the tenure track model for the senate is thus a loss of influence—and initiatives to regain this influence—over core personnel decisions.

Individual academics are also involved in implementation decisions. Their influence is either based on purely academic capital—recognition in their scientific communities to a degree that their voice cannot be overheard when it comes to strategic decisions of the university—or based on *political capital* within the university—through formal membership in decision-making structures, including councils, committees, or advisory boards that have been newly created to govern the implementation of the tenure track model, as well as through informal connections to the university leadership. Different committees or structures are dominated by different personnel groups: as outlined earlier, full professors have a majority in the senate, while the works council and the equal opportunity working group mainly consist of junior academics or assistants. Accordingly, these different bodies tend to be affiliated with the interests of these respective personnel groups, although alliances and negotiations in combination with other issues can be part of the game moves and manoeuvres. We came across diverging stories from different groups of academic staff when it comes to their evaluation of the tenure track model. Pessimistic accounts came from full professors: the new positions can be regarded as "cheap professorships" (senate chairperson, case study 3, full professor, male), and therefore as a devaluation of academic disciplines when positions of full professors are substituted by associate professor posts. Tenure track positions "cannibalize" (ibid.) positions of assistant staff: one tenure track position equals one pre-doc plus one postdoc position. Professors can be tempted to favour the latter, who support and assist the research of the professor, against the former, who will focus on their own research profile and be in a position to compete with, rather than support, the full professor when it comes to resource distribution and influence. From the perspective of junior academic staff, the tenure track model can be understood as a strengthening of this staff group versus full professors, and a way of overcoming the "traditional slavery" (works council chairperson, case study 1, associate professor, male) towards junior academic staff—all the more so if the selection procedure and status are similar to that of full professors, as a works council representative explains:

> When they are associate professors [tenured position], they have to be able to face the others [full professors] and say 'Hold on, our selection procedure was at least as strict as yours! So there's no need to discuss who's better, alright?'. [question: "So this strengthens the non-professorial staff?"] Yes, of course, this is at stake here.
> (Works council chairperson, case study 1, associate professor, male)

Equality agents in universities, concretely the members of the equal opportunity working council, are by law involved in all recruitment decisions that concern publicly advertised posts. This council consists of university staff who, in addition to their actual (academic or non-academic) tasks, monitor personnel procedures, especially the recruitment processes towards full professors. The extent of their involvement in recruitment processes of junior academic staff differs between universities, and is largely dependent on the backing they receive from the university leadership. In the context of the tenure track implementation, their aim is to push for gender equality and gender justice in the distribution of such strategically important posts, and to maintain or increase their influence on personnel processes. Participation in newly created procedures and structures is particularly significant in this context:

> I'm only referring to the formal structure now, but yes, the equality perspective is represented [in the selection panels]. That means, this perspective is part of the panel even if—let's say, worst case—all the other members didn't take it into consideration, there's a person, a member of this body, who can, well, compensate for that.
> (Equality officer, case study 1, non-academic staff, female)

Game Moves and Manoeuvres

Based on this understanding of players' relative positions, interests, and stakes, we now take a look at the role of gender equality in the process of implementing the tenure track model (see Figure 7.1). Informed by Bourdieu's sociology, we understand references to gender equality aims, as well as the introduction of gender equality structures, not simply as applications of a societal consensus for equality but rather as elements of power struggles in universities. Two points of caution need to be highlighted in order not to simplify our analysis: First, it would be misleading to look only at equality officers when analysing how and when the trump card 'gender equality' is played. Although demands for gender equality policies and structures generally work in favour of a disadvantaged group (women), the claim for equality can be of use to the specific strategy of a variety of players in the field.

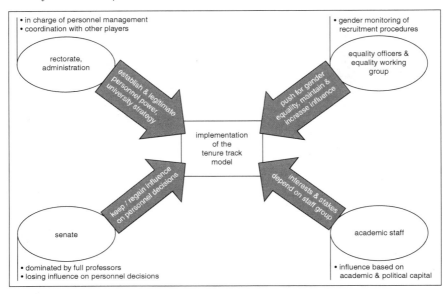

Figure 7.1 Players and Their Stakes in the Tenure Track Implementation

Second, we need to be careful not to confine activities of equality responsibles to the instigation of their official political cause. In fact, it seems much safer to argue that in order to exert an influence upon the ongoing power struggles at university, these players need to be able and willing—or, more precisely, disposed in virtue of the habitus—to engage in the ongoing games with the sort of *libido dominandi* characteristic for dominating players in the field. Following these lines of thought, we group our findings along two themes: first, how players use the gender equality argument with the aim of strengthening their position in the field; and second, which moves and manoeuvres gender equality officers and commissioners use in pursuing their agendas, and which forms of capital they rely on.

As the foregoing overview of the relevant players shows, the tenure track model offers opportunities for the rectorate to widen and deepen its personnel management power. The overall argument as to why it is important that the organizational leadership has a strong voice in this process is that tenure positions are highly relevant when it comes to the strategic development of the university. This concerns the allocation of personnel—permanent positions are established in areas which are defined as research foci of the university—as well as the selection of candidates, and the monitoring of their progress towards fulfilling their performance goals. If the rectorate has a stronger say when it comes to personnel management, this means that faculty deans and individual professors lose some of their power in this area. In this often conflictual situation, the aim of achieving gender equality can be used as an argument to support the extension of the rectorate's power—for example, by pointing out that centralized overview, coordination, and accountability are necessary preconditions for pursuing a gender equality strategy:

> I think that was one of the main problems of the old regulation: That the personnel commission, which was quite big, and where all kinds of political processes were going on, took personnel decisions, which, in the end, no one was responsible for, because they were taken by means of a democratic vote. [. . .] And I'm sure that this is an improvement, that there's someone who has to take responsibility.
> (Rector, case study 2, full professor, male)

Hand in hand with this goes the argument that recruitment procedures that focus on internationalization and excellence are more beneficial for women than in-house career development, which is too often affected by nepotism and male networking. In addition to the selection procedures for new posts, some rectorates create centralized mechanisms that aim at achieving gender equality, which can have the effect of strengthening the newly established hierarchy between the university leadership and deans of faculties. In one case study, we were told about a bonus system, in which faculties are rewarded with additional personnel resources when they recruit women:

> If they put a woman there, they are allowed to create another post. And if they put a woman on that one as well, they get a lecturer post on top of it. And if they don't, they get nothing! [. . .] Yes, in fact, this is like kindergarten for grown-ups!
> (Vice rector, case study 4, associate professor, female)

By handing out rewards and using the metaphor of the kindergarten, this representative of the rectorate presents the relationship between the university leadership and the deans of faculties like a pedagogic relationship between parent and child, with the former educating—or disciplining—the latter towards gender equality.

The university leadership, in expanding its power within the university as a field within fields, can rely on the rules and requirements imposed by the *political* and the *bureaucratic field*. This concerns, on the one hand, the imperative of centralized management as the only valid form of governance, and, on the other hand, the demand to implement gender equality measures: from the perspective of the rectorate, both are beneficial for expanding and consolidating centralized managerial control. This overlap of the agendas of management and equality is also visible in alliances between the rectorate and the equality agents which we observed in some cases—and which are generally directed against professors or the senate. The common ground in these alliances is the aim to decrease the discretionary power of individual professors over the career perspectives of young academics, which can present a barrier to implementing an organizational strategy or equality policies.

> Previously we sometimes found ourselves in a difficult place, where the dean came under pressure from the established professors and then quickly, underhand, created a tenure position. [. . .] And of course, in the overall strategy this is a bit clumsy, right? To suddenly have a huge area full of tenured employees, maybe only men, and in fact what I want is something completely different.
> (Vice rector, case study 4, associate professor, female, 20:20)

Both rectorate and equality agents aim to diminish 'protected territories' of professors and widen avenues for their intervention. Following this thought, Bourdieu's notion of the *prism* which refracts external forces according to the internal structure of the field is to be understood not just in terms of existing power structures within universities but also in terms of the players' intentions: their aims and interests (how they intend to strengthen their own position of power in the field) will influence how external forces are refracted (used as trump cards by the players).

Equality agents follow two core paths of intervention: on the one hand, formalized procedures, particularly through membership in—often newly created—committees and advisory bodies governing the implementation of the tenure track model, and, on the other hand, persistence, vigilance, and proactive participation in informal talks and processes. There are strong differences between the universities in terms of which of these paths of intervention are more relevant. This point can be illustrated and further discussed by comparing two of our case study universities. An analysis of their self-portrayal in core management documents shows that both universities enthusiastically sign up to managerial governance elements, such as the development of a university profile, the coherent application of priorities to activities and resource distribution, and the use of planning and evaluation techniques. However, there is a striking difference in the degree of transparency espoused by the two universities, and in how intensively they make use of official and formalized tools for pushing gender equality goals. An important tool for increasing transparency and formalization in one university is the creation of personnel development councils, which are tasked with the implementation and detailed monitoring of the tenure track model. In addition, there are detailed guidelines for the implementation of the tenure track system—including regulations on how gender equality goals are to be considered in this process. These structures and documents present excellent points of reference and intervention for equality agents:

> As a representative of the [equal opportunity] working council, they are really important to me, because it's easier if I'm asked every six months:

'Are the conditions okay?'—to say at some point: 'No, in fact they're not!'.
(Equality working group chairperson, case study 4, associate professor, female)

By contrast, another one of our case study universities follows a different strategy in the implementation of the tenure track model. This university does not rely on formalized structures and documents, but rather on the decision-making power that the leadership was endowed with in the course of the university reforms, and on the management capability of this leadership. Equality agents in this university adapt to these rules of the game: their core tool is not formalized intervention through councils and committees, but rather personal relationships and talks to the rectorate.

I have a jour fixe with the vice rector for personnel issues. I have a long list of issues which we regularly discuss. [. . .] The only things that fall into oblivion are those that I myself forget.
(Equality working group chairperson, case study 2, assistant professor, female)

While the situation of this equality agent does present a more difficult case than the one described earlier, there are benefits to this situation as well. First, it can make equality work more effective: if interests between gender equality and managerialism align, this less formalized system can make it easier to introduce new regulations, and allow more flexibility in adapting these regulations to concrete situations. Second, from the point of view of equality agents, a personal relationship to the university leadership (*social capital*) also strengthens their relative position in the field of power. By relying on these relationships to push for the equality agenda, they reinforce their power positions in the university.

In both cases—intervention through formalized structures or through personal relations—equality work depends on equality agents' political capital in universities. The difference lies in the specific quality and the precariousness of this capital. In the case of formalized structures, the equality agents' political capital is institutionalized through membership in specific bodies, and therefore relatively stable. In the case of informal intervention, the political capital of equality agents consists largely of social capital; it is dependent on their relationships with the university leadership, and the effectiveness of their intervention greatly hinges on whether the interests of equality and management overlap.

DISCUSSION AND CONCLUSION

With this chapter, we aimed to show how the Bourdieusian notion of *field of social forces* and the metaphor of the social game can contribute to understanding the implementation of government reforms at universities: How does the conceptualization of the university as a *field-within-fields* help us in explaining differences in the implementation of gender equality policies and structures at universities?

Universities are sites of struggle over the distribution of resources. Players engage in games and pursue interests according to their relative position in the field. An analysis of the formal organization alone cannot explain why games differ between universities. Nor are differences an outcome of contingent malfunctions of rational organization. Instead, the notion of power games helps to systematically decrypt social dynamics characteristic for each university, taking into account its history in terms of an outcome of past struggles. As Bourdieu explains, "struggles for the imposition of the principle of legitimate hierarchization do in fact cause the dividing-line between those who belong and those who do not to be constantly discussed and disputed, therefore shifting and fluctuating, at every moment and above all according to the moment" (Bourdieu 1988: 77). Our case studies show how these dividing lines among active players in the game and those not entitled to partake in decision making evolve from the game. An organizational consensus over goals and priorities regarding equal opportunity policy is achieved either in the forefront or behind the scenes, and negotiated among players whose political capital is reproduced depending on this consensus. This mechanism applies not only to hierarchy and belonging but also to interests: according to Bourdieu, interests are not contextually invariant but shaped by moments in the game.

The introduction of the tenure track career model challenges established rules of the game: in this area, traditional forms of allocating positions and developing personnel are suspended, and the strengthened decision-making power of the university leadership limits the power of the professors. This initiates a number of different strategies of players aiming to gain the kind of capital necessary to acquire decision-making power. One strategy is to foster informal connections with the university leadership (social capital) and use these connections to influence decisions—in other words, indirectly accessing the political capital of those formally in charge of taking these decisions. An alternative strategy would be to focus on a specific academic discipline and become indispensable for the university and its strategic development: to strengthen the personal prestige form of academic capital. Our observations show that in the course of managerial reforms, political capital is gaining relevance compared to academic prestige when it comes to decision-making power in the area of personnel management.

This creates the backdrop for new challenges for equality work in universities. One expectation for the governance reforms in universities was that they would increase transparency and diminish the space for decisions based on gender stereotypes, by increasingly formalizing processes and creating avenues of intervention. This has been particularly the case for the highly formalized tenure track career model. What we have observed is that things are more complex indeed: the implementation of the tenure track system, and the extent and shape of equality structures and policies, depends on the strategies of those who are in possession of political capital. This means that equality work is dependent on access to, and a strong position within, the university-specific field of power: on the accumulation of political capital. In universities where influential players are supportive of equality goals, we find conditions which are favourable for equality work. In those universities where equality goals are only weakly institutionalized, the effectiveness of gender equality work hinges on equality agents' personal relationships to the university leadership—that is, on their social capital as a means of accessing political capital. The low degree of institutionalization, however, constitutes a risk in terms of the stability of equality agents' power position.

Further research could draw on the notion of habitus in order to fully capture the dynamic interplay of forces within the power field of a single university. Özbilgin and Tatli (2005) have argued that the introduction of habitus at the organizational level suggests a focus on "the temporal and informal dimension of organizational culture by shedding light on the unwritten and unspoken embedded components of organizational memory" (ibid.: 865), and that "it allows the management and organizational researcher to transcend the level of visible empirical relations in the organization and explore the invisible mechanisms and structures" (ibid.). In our context, the notion of organization habitus could contribute to a better understanding of the difficulties involved with raising awareness for gendered and gendering implications of personnel decisions. Research on organization habitus might start with investigating myths and narratives around the university and the ideal of the scientist. It could encompass a look at the type and level of gender knowledge of decision-makers. Research may furthermore analyse the sources of legitimation of decisions and identify potential collisions with equality policy (as can be the case when it comes to priority-setting and resource distribution following the claim for 'excellence').

The results of our study show how important it is for players to reflectively analyse their own position and critically question the belief in reform and in rational organization. This belief can render responsible authorities and relevant players unable, or unwilling, to analyse the interplay of interests in their field. Our analysis furthermore shows how Bourdieu's theory can contribute to interpreting managerialism at universities. Field theory implies a focus on the struggle for power and for defining field-specific rules. It enables us to understand the difficulties of accessing the university-internal field of power and be included in the relevant power games. Equality officers are dependent on acquiring the symbolic capital of their respective field of power: to accumulate political capital, which includes formal rights to contribute to decisions and intervene in processes, but in fact goes far beyond these formal rights into the sphere of social capital.

With our study, we attempted to come closer to explaining the complex constellations that shape the implementation of gender equality in organizations. We showed that the university as a field—within fields—is a site of struggle for positions of power and for entitlements to decision making. In this context, gender equality is more than a societal goal: it is an element of this power struggle, a stake used by players to advance their relative positions of power.

NOTES

1. The study on Gender in Academia (GENIA), conducted by the authors of this article, explores developments triggered by university reforms in Austria. The project is funded by the Austrian Science Foundation (FWF-I 727-G22), and it is part of an international research program on "Entrepreneurial Universities and GenderChange" (D-A-CH-program): http://genderchange-academia.eu/.
2. "(Q)uelle que soit leur position dans l'espace social, les femmes ont en commun d'être *séparées des hommes par un coefficient symbolique négatif* qui, comme la couleur de la peau pour les Noirs ou tout autre signe d'appartenance à un groupe stigmatisé, affecte négativement tout ce qu'elles sont et ce qu'elles font, et qui est au principe d'un ensemble systématique de différences homologues" (Bourdieu 1998: 100).
3. These struggles unfold according to the fundamental tension between the claim for self-governance by universities, which implies independent goal-setting, and the adherence to state governance and goal-setting according to priorities negotiated in the national political field and beyond (EU-field of higher education policy; cf. Schaller-Steidl 2010).
4. 'Habilmodel' refers to a type of career pattern for employed academic staff. 'Habilitation' means an academic qualifying procedure that is a prerequisite for full teaching authorization in one's academic area (Pechar 2004: 36). Habilitation itself is not a sufficient condition for appointment as professor; candidates need to pass an appointment procedure of the university in order to gain a chair (ibid.). Kreckel (2012) states that the Habilmodel as an academic career structure is generally less open than the Anglo-American tenure model.
5. A study by Kreckel (2012) includes data from the years 2008 and 2009, which show that US-American universities have the largest body of senior staff, consisting of 30 percent full professors and 25 percent associate professors—in total more than half of the university teachers. England's universities employ 18 percent professors and 25 percent senior lecturers and readers—in total 37 percent. Compared to the tenure model, the Habilmodel operates in favour of a smaller group of senior staff. In Austria, senior staff represents only 24 percent of total staff (with 10 percent university professors and 14 percent a.o./assoz. profs.), and in Germany this elite is even smaller, with only 13 percent.
6. Before this major political turn, Austria had been governed by a so-called big coalition of social democrats and conservatives for 13 years.
7. "Administrative power in the university field—that of dean or *recteur* . . . or of commissions and committees of all kinds" (Bourdieu 1988: 97).

REFERENCES

Bourdieu, P. (1986) The Forms of Capital. In Richardson, J. E. (ed.), *Handbook of Theory of Research for the Sociology of Education*. New York: Greenwood Press. 241–258.

Bourdieu, P. (1988) *Homo Academicus*. Cambridge: Polity Press.
Bourdieu, P. (1998) *La domination masculine*. Paris: Seuil.
Bourdieu, P., & Wacquant, L. (1992) *An Invitation to Reflexive Sociology*. Chicago: University of Chicago Press.
Braun, D. (2001) Regulierungsmodelle und Machtstrukturen an Universitäten. In *Die Krise der Universitäten*, Leviathan Sonderheft 20. 242–262.
Brunsson, N. (2006) *Mechanisms of Hope: Maintaining the Dream of the Rational Organization*. Kristianstad: Copenhagen Business School Press/Liber Universitetsforlaget.
Emirbayer, M. (1997) Manifesto for a Relational Sociology. *American Journal of Sociology* 103 (2). 281–317.
Emirbayer, M., & Johnson, V. (2008) Bourdieu and Organizational Analysis. *Theory and Society* 37. 1–44.
Flicker, E., Hofbauer, J., & Sauer, B. (2010) Reforming University, Re-gendering Careers: Informal Barriers to Women Academics in Austria. In Riegraf, B., Aulenbacher, B., Kirsch-Auwärter, E., & Müller, U. (eds.), *Gender Change in Academia: Re-mapping the Fields of Work, Knowledge, and Politics from a Gender Perspective*. Wiesbaden: VS Verlag für Sozialwissenschaften. 123–136.
Gieryn, Th. F. (1995) Boundaries of Science. In Jasanoff, S. (ed.), *Handbook of Science and Technology Studies*. Thousand Oaks: SAGE. 393–443.
Kreckel, R. (2012) Habilitation versus Tenure: Karrieremodelle an Universitäten im internationalen Vergleich. *Forschung & Lehre* 1. 12–14.
Kreissl, K., Striedinger, A., Sauer, B., & Hofbauer, J. (2013) Gleichstellung in der unternehmerischen Hochschule? Diskursive Verschiebungen in der hochschulpolitischen Landschaft Österreichs. In Binner, K., Kubicek, B., Rozwandowicz, A., & Weber, L. (eds.), *Die unternehmerische Hochschule aus der Perspektive der Geschlechterforschung: Zwischen Aufbruch und Beharrung*. Münster: Westfälisches Dampfboot. 20–30.
McCall, L. (1992) Does Gender Fit? Bourdieu, Feminism, and Conceptions of Social Order. *Theory and Society* 21. 837–867.
Moi, T. (1991) Appropriating Bourdieu: Feminist Theory and Pierre Bourdieu's Sociology of Culture. *New Literary History* 22(4). 1017–1049.
Musselin, Ch. (2007) Are Universities Specific Organisations? In Krücken, G., Kosmützky, A., & Torka, M. (eds.), *Towards a Multiversity? Universities between Global Trends and National Traditions*. Bielefeld: Transcript. 63–86.
Özbilgin, M., & Tatli, A. (2005) Understanding Bourdieu's Contribution to Organization and Management Studies. *Academy of Management Review* 30(4). 855–877.
Pechar, H. (2004) The Changing Academic Workplace: From Civil Servants to Private Employees. In Enders, J., & de Weert, E. (eds.), *The International Attractiveness of the Academic Workplace in Europe*. Frankfurt: Gewerkschaft Erziehung und Wissenschaft (GEW). 32–51.
Schaller-Steidl, R. (2010) *Ministerial Equality Policy and Managerial Austrian Universities*. Paper presented at the 6th International Conference 'Gender, Work and Organization', Keele University, Staffordshire, UK.
Wroblewski, A., et al. (2007) *Wirkungsanalyse frauenfördernder Maßnamen im bm:bwk*. Vienna: Bundesministerium für Wissenschaft und Forschung.
Yin, R. K. (1994) *Case Study Research: Design and Methods*. Thousand Oaks: SAGE.

8 Illusio in the Game of Higher Education

An Empirical Exploration of Interconnections between Fields and Academic Habitus

Lucy Taksa and Senia Kalfa

INTRODUCTION

In the late 1990s, increasing numbers of scholars began to engage with the impact of managerialism on higher education institutions. In response to Parker and Jary's (1995) McUniversity thesis, Prichard and Willmott (1997: 292) argued that "the extent to which the New Higher Education or the McUniversity" had "become embedded in the localised practices and discourse of universities" was being overemphasised. Accordingly, they suggested that an analysis informed by the work of Bourdieu would highlight "the continuities in the embedded dispositions of academic life". Although they agreed that the managerialism of higher education (HE) had raised "questions about the durability of the ensemble of schemata of perception or thinking etc embedded in the academic habitus", they concluded that the "extent to which this has reconstructed the associated dispositions of the habitus" was "less clear". Well over a decade later, it is time these competing claims were assessed. Accordingly, we apply a Bourdieusian framework to consider precisely how managerialism of HE has affected the academic habitus in relation to localised HE pedagogical methods to examine an Australian case. This case of managerialism in HE is not unique. Analogous developments have been identified elsewhere in the world. For example, in the mid-1990s Willmott (1995: 994) argued that British universities established before 1992 were "said to be changing from traditional, liberal institutions comparatively unbowed by commercial demands or political ideology into modern, dynamic organizations that are more responsive to their 'customers'". A few years later, Miller (1998: 11) similarly argued that Canadian universities were subjected to pressures for "accountability, efficiency and value for money". Such views have been echoed by the Organisation for Economic Co-operation and Development (OECD), which has stressed for some time that "institutions, systems, and stakeholders must seek to ensure that quality, equity and efficiency characterise all aspects of higher education" (OECD, 2006). As we see it, the imperative for HE institutions to facilitate student acquisition of generic skills that enhance employability because they are valued by employers (Gibbs et al., 1994;

Harvey et al., 1997; Goldfinch et al., 1999; Laybourn et al., 2001) represents one important manifestation of this managerialism in the field of HE and one that can be construed as a game imposed by governments and employers on academics.

Bourdieu's notions of field, doxa, habitus, illusio, and cultural capital are particularly useful for an analysis of the way that academic staff have responded to the imperatives of managerialism. In the first place, these concepts offer "a conceptual framework for a multi-level research agenda" (Özbilgin and Tatli, 2005: 855) and a relational method of social inquiry that is particularly fitting for examining the interconnection between employability, managerialism, and pedagogical practices. Second, Bourdieu's concepts highlight the interdependences between phenomena, allow them to be situated in social and historical contexts (Özbilgin, 2006), and highlight "relations between structures and individuals as dynamic in nature, unfolding, co-generative and ongoing" (Kyriakidou and Özbilgin, 2006: 3). Third, as Hofbauer, Kreissl, Sauer, and Striedinger argue in Chapter 7 of this volume, Bourdieu's theoretical concepts allow organisational researchers to examine how external influences from the bureaucratic and political fields have altered academic practice.

Accordingly, we undertake a multi-level relational analysis of the impact of the employability imperative. We use the concepts of field and doxa to examine developments on the macro/sectoral level of Australian higher education, and examine the impact of such developments on the meso/organisational level of an Australian HE institution through the notions of habitus and illusio. Finally, through the concept of cultural capital we investigate the micro-level individual staff pedagogical practices in a business faculty and how they have been affected by macro- and meso-level changes. The multi-level analysis is supported by data obtained through a case study approach that relies on a range of publicly available HE policy documents and qualitative research methods which draw on 13 interviews undertaken in 2007 with staff members of the business faculty of an Australian university.[1] Unlike many previous studies that have simply drawn on Bourdieu's concepts in a piecemeal fashion (Emirbayer and Johnson, 2008; Golsorkhi et al., 2009), we adopt a more holistic approach. In order to investigate academics' investment in the game of employability, we consider whether this illusio (Bourdieu, 1998) is accompanied by a change in academic habitus, to the extent that academics seek to provide students with not only disciplinary technical knowledge but also transferable generic graduate capabilities, often referred to as 'soft skills'. As we see it, the growing use of group work assignments provides a good example of how HE institutions and academics engage in the game.

Teamwork skills provide a great exemplar of the social competence that is of particular interest for governments and employers. As work in the post-industrial era requires greater cooperation and coordination than ever, both within and between departmental units, scholars (Ilgen and Pulakos, 1999; Humphreys, Greenan, and McIlveen, 1997) as well as employers have emphasised the ability to function effectively in teams as critical to organisational performance. According to King and Behnke (2005), individuals who lack the experience or the skills to work effectively in teams, or who do not value teamwork, will be severely disadvantaged in their professional lives. Based on this rationale, associations of graduate employers have stressed the need for university graduates to be skilled in teamwork (Blowers, 2003). As a result, providing the opportunities for students to work in teams became increasingly widespread not only in Australia but also in the UK during the 1990s (Laybourn et al., 2001). As Laybourn and her colleagues pointed out (2001: 367), "the teaching of transferable skills in UK higher education was set high on the educational agenda by the Dearing Report" produced by the National Committee of Inquiry into Higher Education in 1997. In this context, the inclusion of group work in undergraduate programs gained a prominent role, partly due to its recognition as an important core or generic skill, highly valued by employers (Gibbs et al., 1994; Harvey et al., 1997).

Responding to a similar emphasis on teamwork skills Australian universities also began including them in their lists of graduate attributes, which are said to demonstrate the knowledge, skills, and abilities graduates acquire beyond disciplinary knowledge (Barrie, 2004). Through these lists Australian universities have claimed that they provide opportunities for students to develop generic skills during the course of their studies and have required teaching staff to take responsibility for embedding these graduate attributes in curricula (Barrie, 2006).

We introduce the definitions upon which our analysis is based by beginning with a detailed account of our conceptual framework and methodology. On this basis, we present an outline of the macro-level developments in Australia's HE sector and consider the impact of managerialism on our case study organisation. This approach contextualises Australian universities' engagement in the game of student employability, which promotes practices such as the inclusion of graduate capabilities and learning outcomes in course outlines, and the increased adoption of pedagogical practices that are designed to provide students with opportunities to develop generic skills. We then examine the way staff in the case study organisation approached the adoption of group assignments. Although research on groupwork assignments in HE is abundant, the interests and actual teaching practices of university staff have largely been ignored, as has the impact of the employability game on them. To overcome this gap we review the educational scholarship on groupwork and cooperative learning, and highlight the principles and practices that have been identified as being essential to the learning of generic skills related to working in teams. This enables us to analyse the extent to which cooperative learning principles and practices were incorporated by staff who adopted group assignments in the case study organisation and further to show that such action cannot be taken as evidence of change in academic habitus and of commitment to ensuring student acquisition of transferable skills. By examining academics' interests in the adoption of group assignments as well as their actual approaches, we find evidence of symbolic violence: on the one hand, academics' practices demonstrate attachment to the game of employability, while on the other they show the continuity of academic habitus. Our findings question the extent to which academics in HE institutions have conformed to the "commodifying logic" (Willmott, 1995: 993) of the managerialist agenda and recognise that despite academics' involvement in the game of student employability, their dispositions regarding assessment have not changed to accommodate the priorities set by government and employers. On the contrary, we argue that the approach adopted by staff illustrates the way that increasing managerialism of HE and employability imperatives have given rise to a culture in which compliance and resistance coexist.

CONCEPTUAL FRAMEWORK

The Macro Level

For Bourdieu and Wacquant (1992) the 'field' represents the social context in which interactions happen between people. This context is critical to the effective explanation of social phenomena because it locates the subject of investigation within a specific setting. Agents acting within a field can be individuals, groups, or institutions that are positioned hierarchically according to the levels of power they possess. For our purposes, the notion of 'field' makes it possible to identify the multiple players in business HE and in turn the important role played by university staff in relation to the employability debate.

Each field is characterised by a particular 'doxa', a set of fundamental principles and rules of behaviour which agents in a field view as inherently true (Webb, Schirato, and Danaher, 2002: xi), which they take for granted (Deer, 2008; Thomson, 2008), and therefore internalise and reproduce (Bourdieu, 1998). Bourdieu (1998) claimed that because doxa is the factor that differentiates a field from others and makes it autonomous, challenges arise when one field is increasingly influenced by the doxa of other fields.

According to Hofbauer et al. (this volume) the university as a field has evolved at the intersection of the scientific, the bureaucratic, and the political fields that operate as external forces exerting considerable influence on a university's daily business. The rise of managerialism provides an example of how the doxa of the 'economic field' (Deer 2008: 125) has increasingly encroached on the field of HE. Scholars have represented the rise of managerialism as a paradigm shift associated with "the use of management practices drawn from the private sector" and "a concern for more explicit and measurable standards of performance, and attempts to control according to pre-set output measures" (Chandler, Barry, and Clark, 2002: 1054), which became the guiding principle for public service modernisation (O'Reilly and Reed, 2011; Willmott, 1995). In Australia, higher education is one of the public sector domains that have been significantly affected by managerialism. For proponents of managerialism, increased competition and a focus on cost-efficiency, accountability, and quality audits are appropriate for universities, whose culture of collegial governance has increasingly been represented as outdated (Ylijoki, 2005; Sousa, de Nijs, and Hendriks, 2010). This "managerial assault" (Chandler et al., 2002: 1053) has resulted in what Parker and Jary (1995) have provocatively called the 'McUniversity', where concepts such as 'modernisation', 'rationalisation', 'customers', and 'products' are increasingly deployed (Willmott, 1995; Prichard and Willmott, 1997). Well over a decade ago Prichard and Willmott (1997) maintained that such measures aimed to raise the contribution of academics to national economic performance.

Within this context employers came to expect that universities would prepare graduates for employment by equipping them not only with discipline-specific skills but also with a wide range of generic skills (Hewitt and Clayton, 1999) that can be transferred across multiple contexts (Sullivan, 2001). At the same time, some scholars (Curtis and McKenzie, 2001; Sullivan, 2001) argued that individuals need to constantly adapt by acquiring transferable skills that can be used in different contexts, since qualifications are rendered obsolete more quickly now than any other time in history. This increasing emphasis on student employability provides evidence of the impact of managerialism on academia. For Barnett (1994) the employability imperative represented an unwelcome shift towards utilitarianism from an "academic-led supply model of higher education to an employer-led model" that is closely linked to free-market thinking (Johnston and Watson, 2004: 54). As Gallagher (2001: 19) concluded, the meaning of learning changed so that value was no longer placed upon traditional knowledge and scientific process but on "operational competence through performative learning". For Gallagher (2001: 19) the OECD's assumptions that "experience-based, professionally tacit can-do knowledge" leads to the much needed innovation that will result in economic growth challenges universities to prepare students with professional know-how. More recently, Thanem and Wallenberg (2009: 181) concluded from their case study at Stockholm University that

> while managerialism may be obvious in the more authoritarian and teacher-centred style of conventional teaching practices . . . managerialism also prevails in the more student-centred approaches of contemporary pedagogy which emphasize the freedom and responsibility of individual students to take charge of their own learning and which are being employed to accommodate soaring student numbers, the scarcity of financial resources and increasingly demanding clients (including students, parents, policy makers, and future employers).

The Meso Level

Bourdieu (2005: 43) defines habitus as "a system of dispositions, that is of manners of being, seeing, acting and thinking, or a system of long-lasting (rather than permanent) schemes or schemata or structures of perception, conception and action". For Bourdieu, habitus is the property of social agents (individuals, groups, or institutions); it is structured by one's background and experiences (e.g. upbringing and education) and shapes present and future practices (Maton, 2008). Bourdieu (1990b) particularly stresses the intertwined relationship between a field and its habitus, arguing that they represent "objective and subjective realisations of the same underlying social logic" (Maton, 2008: 56). Habitus determines which of the available choices in a field are discernible and acceptable to individuals (Maton, 2008) and which ones are prohibited (Reay, 2004). The key to understanding practice lies in the relation between field and habitus as one shapes the other (Lareau and Horvat-McNamara, 1999; Maton, 2008).

Bourdieu often uses the analogy of a game to describe a field: a social space where everyone wants to secure the most advantageous position (Grenfell, 2008). While each field has its explicit rules that govern what is permissible and what is not, most social activity is played out according to individuals' *interests*. Initially, Bourdieu described interest as "investment in the game" (Bourdieu, 1990b: 290), although later he depicted such investment as a phenomenon he outlined as *illusio*:

> The fact of being caught up in and by the game, of believing the game is 'worth the candle', or, more simply, that playing is worth the effort. In fact the word interest initially meant very precisely what I include under the notion of *illusio*, that is the fact of attributing importance to a social game, the fact that what happens matters to those who are engaged in it, who are in the game. *Interest* is to 'be there', to participate, to admit the game is worth playing and that the stakes created in and through the fact of playing are worth pursuing; it is to recognise the game and recognise its stakes.
> (Bourdieu, 1998: 76–77; italics in the original)

Illusio is more agentic than the underlying doxa, and according to Colley (2012: 324) it is fundamental to understanding "the socialised subjectivity of habitus and the objective determinations of the field". If agents in a field do not share the illusio, the game will make little sense to them and as a result the agents will cease from engaging in the game (Free and Macintosh, 2009). Equally, any fundamental change in the field is likely to disrupt the illusio and challenge commitment to the game.

How can habitus and illusio enhance our understanding of what guides academic action in the quest for employable graduates? A useful way forward was provided by Maton (2008), who proposed that the practices prevalent in the fields under examination need to be analysed. In order to highlight teachers' dispositions towards groupwork assignments and to establish a firm basis for discussion of the interconnections between employability and managerialism, we focus on the practices that are said to facilitate the development of students' teamwork skills. To uncover illusio we examine the differing interest of multiple agents in the HE field. First, we consider the interests of Australian government agencies in ensuring that universities 'deserve' the public money they receive (Sousa et al., 2010) and of employers in 'work-ready' graduates. Second, on the assumption that there is a difference between "rhetorical expressions of the goals and value-objects of a field" (Colley, 2012: 324) we consider the way that the interests of such dominant agents are represented in a range of sources and also the way that academics represent their interest in and participate in the game of student acquisition of disciplinary knowledge and of generic teamwork skills.

The Micro Level

Cultural capital refers to "widely shared, high status cultural signals (attitudes, preferences, formal knowledge, behaviours, goods and credentials) used for social and cultural exclusion, the former referring to exclusion from jobs and the latter to exclusion from high status groups" (Lamont and Lareau, 1988: 156). Clearly, exclusion is a critical issue. However, since Bourdieu did not deny the possibility of 'lower-class' individuals acquiring dominant cultural signals through education (Lamont and Lareau, 1988), it is important to recognise that social exclusion is not the sole function of cultural capital. As Brown and Scase (1994) point out, the acquisition of cultural capital by students from disadvantaged backgrounds through education can also offer an avenue for social inclusion.

Bourdieu (1986) maintained that cultural capital has three states: objectified, institutionalised, and embodied, the latter two being the most important for the purposes of this chapter. In the institutionalised state, cultural capital takes the form of educational credentials and qualifications. Bourdieu (1996: 118) argued that credentials confer two forms of competence, the first centring on the acquisition of "a certificate of technical competence and technical skills", the second on "social dignity" (Bourdieu 1996: 119) or a level of "social competence" (Lareau and Weininger, 2003: 581), which allows the agent to set themselves apart from others. In our view, these two types of competence form the embodied cultural capital students gain from their participation in HE. This most fundamental state of cultural capital represents "long lasting dispositions of the body and mind" (Bourdieu, 1986: 47). While situated primarily in a specific field (Webb et al., 2002), it is transportable between fields, although its value may differ in each one.

In relation to the field of business HE, embodied cultural capital can be construed as consisting of technical competence or disciplinary knowledge, such as the ability to write a marketing plan or to analyse a company's balance sheet, and social competence, such as teamwork skills that can be transferred from the university context to that of employment. From this perspective, groupwork assignments can be interpreted as one method by which academics attempt to endow students with both technical knowledge and teamwork skills and develop the embodied cultural capital that is valuable in the workplace and as a result will ensure students' inclusion in that field.

Before we proceed to the empirical data, it is important to briefly present the principles that underlie the development of teamwork skills in a classroom environment. These principles, referred to as cooperative learning by educational scholars, highlight how assessment should be structured if teamwork skills are to be developed concurrently with disciplinary knowledge.

COOPERATIVE LEARNING FUNDAMENTALS

Cooperative learning (Johnson and Johnson, 1975) involves "the institutional use of small groups so that students work together to maximise their own and each other's learning" (Johnson, Johnson, and Holubec, 1994: 6). Johnson and Johnson (1975), who popularised the notion, argue that successful cooperative learning depends on five conditions—notably, positive interdependence, promotive interaction, individual accountability, group processing, and social skills. First, under conditions of positive interdependence an individual can attain his or her goal if, and only if, the other participants can attain their goals (Johnson, Johnson, and Maruyama, 1983). Second, face-to-face promotive interaction is achieved when group members assist each other by exchanging learning resources, providing each other with constructive feedback, and engaging in healthy debates. Only by meeting face-to-face can all these activities take place so that members can become personally committed to each other and to their mutual goals. The third characteristic of cooperative learning is individual accountability, which is accomplished by assessing students individually to ensure that each student is responsible for his or her own academic accomplishments. The fourth basic element is group processing, a reflective process during which group members discuss their work and interaction (Johnson, Johnson, and Holubec, 1998). The role of the teacher as a facilitator or informal 'team leader' is critical in ensuring that everything is going according to plan. The fifth and final element involves teaching students social skills, which according to Johnson, Johnson, and Smith (1991) should be undertaken with the same determination as teaching disciplinary skills, because assigning socially unskilled students to a group and asking them to cooperate does not guarantee that they will be able to do so. As we see it, the adoption of these principles and practices signals a commitment to the development of students' teamwork skills, a shift in academic habitus, and investment in the game of employability.

METHODOLOGY

The scholarship dealing with group assessments has relied on quantitative measures, which has left a big gap for in-depth qualitative research that goes beyond descriptive information to a more meaningful exploration of agents' behaviours. For us, qualitative research provides a more helpful avenue. For this purpose a single case study was selected because of its revelatory nature (Yin, 2003). In contrast to statistical methods that omit contextual factors except those selected for measurement, case studies are exceptionally useful in producing a contextualised and holistic description, interpretation, and explanation (Eriksson and Kovalainen, 2010). The ability to generalise is widely acknowledged as a limitation of case study research (Aaltio and Heilmann, 2009). Yet as Yin (2003) pointed out, the logic that case study design should follow is not generalisation, which underpins traditional survey research, but replication, which is the logic followed in experiments. There are two types of replication: literal and theoretical, the former referring to other case studies reaching similar results and the latter to reaching contrasting results but for anticipated reasons. To facilitate replication, researchers are expected to carefully select and implement their case study (Flyvberg, 2004). Given that the managerialisation of HE has been evident in a number of OECD countries for some time, the revelatory nature of our Australian case provides the basis for replication in other national contexts.

The university and more specifically the faculty examined here (hereafter 'the University' and 'the Faculty') are a good case of a large Australian faculty involved in teaching business studies. The University has been consistently recognised for its learning and teaching excellence. The University's Graduate Attributes Policy, initially published in 2003, recognised the importance of teamwork by stating that it aimed to provide a learning environment where students could develop the collaboration skills required in the workplace. In 2006–2007 the Faculty examined was the biggest one at the University, with over 8,000 students enrolled. At the time of data collection it had its own graduate attributes in which groupwork was included, and many academics began to invest in the goals of student employability by including group assignments in their courses in order to comply with the imperatives of this particular graduate attribute. Hence, the size of the University and the business faculty, their status among HE institutions in Australia, and the inclusion of groupwork as a graduate attribute, and hence also as an assessment tool, together make the Faculty a valuable 'instrumental case' (Stake, 1995: 3).

The data collected provides insight into a juncture in the life of the Faculty—that is, "a series of images, impressions and experiences which act to give the appearance of a coherent whole and which influence how (an) organisation is understood" (Mills, 2010: 509). Mills and Mills (2000) argue that to understand a particular time frame in an organisation's history, numerous factors have to be combined in order to fully portray the world view of organisational members at the time. To facilitate such a portrayal, this study engaged in data triangulation by "explicitly searching for as many different data sources as possible, which bear upon the events under analysis" (Denzin, 2009: 301). It is pertinent at this point to highlight that while teamwork practices have been around for many years, the faculty under examination was one of the first to formally seek wider adoption of this practice among staff to enhance student employability.

The primary sources of data included 13 interviews[2] conducted with members of the University's staff, the interviewees' course outlines for the courses they convened in 2007, and a wide range of documentary sources related to learning and teaching (N= 24) produced by the government, the University, and the Faculty. Eleven interviewees were in teaching positions at various academic levels; one was the Faculty's associate dean (hereafter ADE) and one was the University's director of learning and teaching (hereafter Director). Table 8.1 presents the profile of our participants, including their gender, appointment type, level, and discipline. To select relevant staff members and ensure purposeful sampling, an e-mail was sent to all the staff of the Faculty whose publicly available course outlines for 2007 included groupwork assessments. The interviews with staff happened in their offices, lasted between 15 and 40 minutes, and were audio-recorded and transcribed verbatim. The interview data have been subjected to a thematic coding procedure through NVivo, where categories were identified and linked through an iterative process, moving back and forth between

Table 8.1 Participant Profile[3]

	Gender	Appointment Type		Level	Discipline
1	F	FT	CR	A/L	Management
2	M	FT	CN	S/L	Accounting
3	M	FT	CN	S/L	Accounting
4	F	PT	CN	S/L	Management
5	F	FT	CR	A/PROF	Higher education/psychology
6	M	FT	CN	S/L	Information systems
7	M	FT	CN	L	Economics
8	F	FT	CN	A/PROF	Education/international business
9	M	FT	CN	A/PROF	Economics
10	M	FT	CN	L	Information systems
11	M	FT	CN	S/L	Banking & finance
12	F	FT	CN	L	Marketing
13	M	FT	CN	S/L	Marketing

the data, the literature, and emerging empirical categories which emerged through reading and rereading for the empirical evidence (Lok and DeRond, 2013). The key themes that were explored in the interviews included the reasons interviewees utilised group assessments in their courses; the structure of those assessments; the pedagogical benefits and disadvantages of groupwork assignments; common complaints students raised and how interviewees dealt with those; feedback mechanisms; and links between group assessments with learning outcomes and graduate capabilities.

EMPIRICAL DATA: THE CONTEXT

In 1992, the Australian federal government established the Committee for Quality Assurance in Higher Education and through it ran the Australian Graduate Survey (AGS), an annual survey of newly qualified HE graduates, which incorporates the Course Experience Questionnaire (CEQ) and the Graduate Destination Survey (GDS). The CEQ evaluates graduates' generic skills development (Harris and James, 2006), whereas the GDS examines outcomes such as employment status, further study status, job search methods, and broad type of work. In early 2000 the Committee also established the Australian Universities Quality Agency (AUQA), superseded by the Tertiary Education Quality and Standards Agency (TEQSA) in 2011. In April 2012, the federal government established the *myUniversity* website, which uses AGS and other data to rate Australian universities according to the number of graduates they have in full-time employment.

The need for the University to concentrate on generic skills was a topic of contention at the time of data collection as a result of the University's relatively poor performance on the 2004 CEQ (Director, 06/06/07). The poor CEQ results created considerable pressure for the University, and so did the first AUQA audit conducted in 2005. The AUQA report recommended the further development of performance indicators linked to Faculty outcomes. As a result the University put together a list of 'Learning and Teaching (L&T) Performance Indicators', which aimed to document, measure, and assess the mechanisms being implemented at the University that fostered continuous improvement in learning and teaching. Faculties had to provide evidence of both 'input' and 'output' measures, the former involving goals and strategies that improve students' learning and teaching experience, and the latter referring to high student satisfaction rates (Learning and Teaching Performance Fund Discussion Paper, 2005). Financial benefits were promised for the faculties able to report successful performance against these indicators.

Another performance indicator introduced in 2005 was the Course Outline Template, which encouraged staff to align the "overall rationale for assessment components and their relationship with specific student learning outcomes and to establish a link between assessment components and graduate attributes where appropriate" (Course Outline Template, 2005: 5). As the Director (06/06/07) pointed out, staff members were aware that failure to refer to graduate attributes in any given course would have financial repercussions for the Faculty. The course outlines examined for this chapter all included references to specific graduate attributes and learning outcomes. However, only two of these linked group assessments and graduate attributes. When asked about the lack of alignment between assessment, learning outcomes, and graduate attributes, numerous staff members (K, Finance, 23/05/07; B and C, Accounting, 01/06/07; A, Management, 30/05/07) argued that they paid 'lip service' to these policies so that the Faculty would not be financially disadvantaged.

Furthermore, the interview data pointed to the increasing influence of external agents. In addition to their impact through assessment exercises, government agencies also encouraged closer ties between the University and industry. An important example was the recommendation made by AUQA following the 2005 audit for the University to "develop a policy on the systematic external review of programmes and that each Faculty be required to consider the need for external programme advisory committees or other mechanisms to ensure that new programmes and courses are developed and implemented in consultation with relevant stakeholders" (AUQA 2006 audit report, 2006: 6). In this regard, the Director (06/06/07) commented that invited members of a committee established to review the Masters of Commerce included employers, who were also alumni of the University: "the chair of [Company 1] and [Company 2] are members of the student committee and of course the first thing they say is 'well the university should be producing students who can work in teams, who can communicate, etc.'". In the case of the Department of Information Systems (IS), employers were consulted on the design of the curriculum, when in most other schools employer input was informal or advisory. As interviewee F (28/05/07) put it,

> most of what we have done with respect to curriculum and the experiential learning has been derived through a collaboration between us and the industry advisory group we have. These are basically the people that have given the most scholarships and some others that have an affiliation with school for other reasons. And we meet with them probably four or five times a year. And they were involved very heavily in the design of the new curriculum and they actually signed off on it.

An additional source of influence at this time came from accreditation requirements. This provided another means by which employers and industry groups influenced the university and the faculty at the time of data collection. As the ADE (04/07/07) pointed out, besides having to ensure the provision of adequate disciplinary knowledge, business schools "also have to balance requirements for accreditation standards". In addition, the Director

(06/06/07) argued that teamwork was included in the list of the University's graduate attributes because "some people, I think from engineering, brought it up mostly for reasons of accreditation". According to O'Reilly and Reed (2011), this form of collaborating with government and other stakeholders signals a process of mutual regulation.

EMPIRICAL DATA: THE PRACTICE OF GROUPWORK ASSIGNMENTS

In addition to exploring the context in which academics worked, the interviews sought to explore staff members' practices surrounding groupwork assignments. Again the importance of employers' requirements was brought to the fore. For example, C (01/06/07) from the Department of Accounting and A (30/05/07) from the Department of Management both stated that they had begun to adopt teamwork in response to criticisms from the business community regarding graduates' lack of ability to work in groups and collaborate with others. Interviewees expressed the view that groupwork assignments enabled students to develop teamwork or 'soft' skills that could assist them in the workplace. Specifically C (01/06/07) from Accounting commented, "In groupwork students actually prepare for a real job where they will be working in teams. Thus [group assignments] give students the opportunity to practise collaboration, dispute resolution and so on as part of their learning process".

Drawing on her own corporate experience, A (30/05/07) from Management claimed that group assignments "allow students to develop the necessary skills to relate to people, to handle conflict. So group assignments present students the opportunity to learn practical things that are not necessarily in the textbook". Another member of staff pointed out that group assignments provided opportunities not only for collaboration and dispute resolution but also for other practical skills, such as "being responsible to other people for deadlines, time commitments, how to write quality documents" (J, Information Systems, 05/23/07). In that respect, it seems that teachers perceived that group assignments provided learning opportunities for students to improve their skills in managing taskwork and teamwork (Marks, Mathieu, and Zaccaro, 2001).

The interviews with staff members indicate that group assignments in the University were seen to be comparable with the group situations students might face in the workplace and that the teamwork skills developed in the classroom provided an avenue for the development of social competence that could be transferred to the work environment. As M from Marketing (17/05/07) put it, group assignments enabled students

> to interact with one another in some ways that reflect what I believe occurs in the real world. And that is that you have to work with others.

Sometimes you have weak people on groups, strong people on groups. And so I think it simulates very well the workplace, and situations they may face when they go out into the workplace.

It is pertinent at this point to highlight that business schools and/or commerce faculties form a subfield in academia with their own doxa, one arguably more responsive to employer demands for graduate employability than other subfields, and generally one represented as providing a useful training ground for the business world in the sense that what a student learns in a business degree should, in theory, more effectively prepare him or her for professional life and success in the corporate world (Pfeffer and Fong, 2002). Given that this context has enabled employers to criticise business schools for doing a poor job preparing students for the marketplace (Ackoff, 2002; Doria, Rozanski, and Cohen, 2003; Mintzberg and Gosling, 2002), it can be argued that business school academics have come to see it as in their interests to avoid being represented as irrelevant to business by complying with the demands being made of them to help students develop transferable skills (Pfeffer and Fong, 2004).

Yet, despite this rhetoric, social competence was not the primary goal of this pedagogical approach for the majority of interviewees. The most significant aspect of group assignments stressed by interviewees was the opportunity they provided students to explore course content in greater depth. Groupwork assessments allowed students to cover larger problems they would not be able to solve on their own (I, Economics, 23/05/07; J, IS, 23/05/07). The ADE (04/07/07) emphasised repeatedly that the use of groupwork assignments helped students develop "critical, analytical skills because they are asked to evaluate and apply theoretical principles to their group assignment . . . identify what content is relevant, irrelevant, effective, ineffective, usable or not, current or outdated". In short, the traditional emphasis of technical competence remained a priority.

Finally, six interviewees highlighted that one "additional bonus" (I, 23/05/07) of groupwork was the considerable reduction in workload. These interviewees pointed out that increasing class sizes made it necessary for them to select pedagogical tools that allowed them "cut down on some of the marking load" (A, Management, 30/05/07), a point made by Gupta (2004) some years earlier.

As noted in the discussion on cooperative learning, scholars argue that teachers' engagement with and direction of groupwork processes are critical for this tool to be effective. Active participation assumes that teachers will monitor the problems that might arise and evaluate each student separately from the group to ensure individual learning—the principle of individual accountability outlined by Johnson and Johnson (1975). However, all interviewees said that students within a group would receive the same grade for their group project. Another key assumption of cooperative learning is that teachers will actively participate in helping their students to develop the cooperative skills required for successful teamwork (Johnson and Johnson, 1975). Accordingly, interviewees were asked whether they gave their students any guidelines regarding team dynamics before the assessment. Of the 11 participants, only 1 gave students specific written guidelines about group dynamics compiled by the Faculty's educational support unit. Four others reported spending time in class discussing what constitutes appropriate behaviour in a group setting. A (Management, 30/05/07), who devoted a lecture to the theory behind team dynamics, questioned the effectiveness of such tools. For her, students lacked the critical thinking ability to associate the theory on group interaction presented in the lecture with their own personal group experiences and practices. The remaining participants responded that they did not provide any guidelines, as the expectation was that students already possessed ample experience working in groups, thus rendering such guidelines redundant (M, Marketing, 17/05/07).

To further explore whether and how lecturers were involved in the team processes, staff members were asked to identify the most prominent problems they faced with group assignments and how they resolved them. The most commonly mentioned challenge was the phenomenon of social loafing, where one student does not contribute an equal amount or any amount of work to the assignment, a problem well documented by scholars in this field (Ashraf, 2004; Bacon, Stewart, and Silver, 1999; Houldsworth and Matthews, 2000). Three interviewees mentioned that they asked their students to submit a 'team contract' or 'team protocol', which detailed the task allocation within the group and identified deadlines for task completion. The rationale behind the team contract was to discourage social loafing by making students feel accountable to each other for the completion of tasks, and to provide them with written evidence in case things went wrong. Furthermore, 7 out of the 11 interviewees used confidential peer evaluations as per the recommendation of the University's assessment policy. These peer evaluations could alter an individual student's grade if, after consultation with the teacher, there was enough evidence to prove that the student was loafing. Although these practices have obvious merits, we argue that that they do not demonstrate real staff involvement in the group process as cooperative learning literature advocates. In fact we argue the opposite: such practices in essence act to devolve the responsibility for the effective functioning of groupwork from staff to students.

Finally, drawing on the principle of group processing outlined earlier, staff members were asked if they encouraged students to reflect on how they worked together as a group and if that reflection was assessed. Both the Director (06/06/07) and the ADE (04/07/07) recognised the importance of long- and short-term reflection as necessary for allowing students to deeply engage with the benefits of group assignments that might not have otherwise been obvious. The Director (06/06/07) argued that if "students are encouraged to reflect on the group work as a process, thinking about what worked or what didn't, how each individual contributed to a project, then they can develop skills".

Only three interviewees included non-assessable components in their courses to encourage students to reflect on their team experiences. A (Management, 30/05/07) explained that individual student reflections on their group experience formed a compulsory appendix of the group assignment. B (Accounting, 01/06/07) asked his students to hand in a report midway through the semester detailing how "the group was going", and I (23/05/07) from Economics used an anonymous peer evaluation as a tool to gauge team processes. Given the lack of a grade for these components, participants A, B, and I were asked how they motivated their students to submit their reflections. All three responded that they would withhold students' final grades until these additional components were submitted. The remaining interviewees maintained that assessing "how well [students] worked in a group is immensely difficult to judge" (J, IS, 23/05/07). For example, J (23/05/07) from IS, who had once asked students to keep diaries in an attempt to help them reflect on the team process, argued that the diary entries reflected an "immaculate" team process. However, "two days before the assignment is due they would come tell me it's not working". Thus he believed that students were not interested in the team process, a view also shared by A (30/05/07) from Management. Interviewees were also negatively inclined towards assessing the group process, as that would increase their already hectic workloads. Hence, as the interview data fail to demonstrate staff members' engagement with any of the principles of cooperative learning, we are led to the conclusion that staff members who adopted groupwork assignments lacked commitment to the development of teamwork skills, despite claims to the contrary.

DISCUSSION

With this chapter we aimed to show how Bourdieu's concepts of field, doxa, habitus, illusio, and cultural capital can be used to illuminate how managerialism of HE has affected the academic habitus in relation to pedagogical methods in an Australian case study. Bourdieu's framework is particularly useful for an analysis of the way that academic staff have responded to the imperatives of managerialism.

On a macro level, the data presented here illustrate the collapse of boundaries between academia and the 'economic field' (Deer 2008: 125). Bourdieu and Wacquant (1992) contend that while social fields are autonomous they are subject to external forces that may challenge the rules of the game and may even cause periods of crisis in the field, during which the doxa becomes subjected to negotiation. In our empirical context, this research has shown that the employability game involves the encroachment of the economic doxa on the academic field through the influence of external agents. The interview with the Director highlighted the increasing power of government bodies and employers, which resulted in the development of the University's graduate attributes policy and accompanying resources. The abundance of policies guiding course design and assessment towards graduate attribute development can be interpreted as a decline in trust of academics as professionals, which scholars (Dent and Whitehead, 2002; Jary, 2002; Morley, 2003) argue is a characteristic of the risk society, one that legitimates the use of quality audits and accountability measures. This conclusion supports Prichard and Willmott's (1997: 292) claim that academia is being repositioned from a relatively autonomous field "where academics are able to some extent define their own criteria of production, evaluation, organisational identity, purpose, and focus to a field of general production—a market". This is evident in our chapter, as employers' calls for marketable graduates were used by staff members to justify the use of groupwork assignments as an assessment tool that allowed students to develop the embodied cultural capital that employers required, such as cooperation and conflict resolution skills. Employers' influence challenges the traditional boundaries of academic work and the autonomy of the academic field, which gave to the profession coveted exclusivity (Dent and Whitehead, 2002; Hofbauer et al., this volume).

On a meso level, such interferences influence a range of practices in the Faculty under examination in a way that supports the illusio of external agents. For example, measures were adopted by the University following the AUQA audit of 2005 and were in line with its recommendations for the development of "a policy on the systematic external review of programmes", the establishment by each faculty of external program advisory committees or other mechanisms to ensure that new programs and courses would be "developed and implemented in consultation with relevant stakeholders" (AUQA 2006 audit report, 2006: 6). Such measures were imposed to assess universities "against external criteria or targets of performance" and have been designed to ensure that "the student—as consumer, taxpayer, and representative of the state—know[s] what they are getting", through appropriate product labelling and "mechanisms for redress at the level of consumer and state" (Parker 2002: 142). Here we see measures portrayed as "'scientific' and thus accurate and dispassionate, not open to question or doubt as models of truth" (Dent and Whitehead, 2002: 8) and in service to public good. By establishing its own indicators and governing through "bureaucracy wherein goals are set in ever narrowing demands of reporting and where accountability is measured by outputs" (Marshall, 1999: 310), the University conformed to the managerialist illusio. This is demonstrated not only by our Australian case but also in other OECD countries in the context of performance indicators measuring research (e.g. Chandler et al., 2002 [UK]; Ylijoki, 2005 [Finland]; Sousa et al., 2010 [the Netherlands]).

The investment in the employability game has resulted in misrecognition (English, 2012) and symbolic violence, particularly for academic staff

(Bourdieu and Wacquant, 1992: 167) whose adoption of pedagogical practices that are ostensibly designed to ensure student employability challenges the traditional academic habitus, and complies with the doxa of new liberalism (Chopra, 2003) and suits the illusio of governments and employers in the development of 'work-ready' graduates.

At the same time, however, our data shows evidence of resistance to these imperatives, although it is debatable whether this resistance is a conscious choice or the function of a long-standing habitus. On the one hand, interviews with staff demonstrated an obvious engagement of academics with the game of student employability as evidenced by the adoption of group assessments as the appropriate pedagogical tool that allows students to develop the embodied cultural capital that will ensure their inclusion in the field of paid employment. On the other, our findings show that teaching staff were not active participants in the group process, as scholarship on cooperative learning advocates. The interviews showed disengagement with the principles of cooperative learning: staff made limited or no efforts to teach students teamwork skills. In fact, interviewees did not address groupwork-related issues or concepts for a range of reasons, including those elaborated by Schullery and Gibson (2001: 10): notably because they believed that "students already have the skills, may not deem these skills necessary for students, or may find that other curricular demands push group skills beyond the limits of available classroom time". Similarly, staff did not encourage students to engage in group processing. Their primary emphasis on examining disciplinary knowledge ignored the principles of cooperative learning processes, which advocate for the alignment of marking criteria in a way that reflects the emphasis on teamwork skills (Ballantine and McCourt-Larres, 2007; Lewis, Aldridge, and Swamidass, 1998).

That academics continued to evaluate students based on more traditional measures should not come as a surprise. Over a decade ago, scholars acknowledged that while the context in which academics work has changed (Willmott, 1995), because of growing pressures and demands from external agents, these changes in practice were viewed as 'cosmetic' rather than substantive (Prichard and Willmott, 1997: 298). Scholars are almost unanimous in this conclusion. Prichard and Willmott (1997) argued that there was no guarantee that the spirit of performance measures was observed. And Chandler et al. (2002) found that the hold managerialism had on universities was not as strong as was assumed in the literature. More recently these conclusions have been reiterated by Sousa et al. (2010: 1453), who termed such measures "nothing short of meaningless". Similarly, Ylijoki (2005) and O'Reilly and Reed (2011) argued that despite the best efforts of managerialist reforms, academics remain committed to occupational cultures that reject managerialist illusio, as was found by scholars previously. However, the promotion of managerialism at the macro and meso levels has required compromises which have diminished academics' power, authority, and status as public sector employees at the micro level (O'Reilly and Reed, 2011).

As we see it, such compromises are central to the culture evident in this case study organisation, in which compliance and resistance coexist.

The conceptual framework adopted here provides an explanation for this outcome, because it outlines the dynamic relationship between habitus and field. As Maton (2008) explains, even when a field is changing rapidly the habitus does not necessarily follow suit. On the contrary, the habitus can generate practices for some time after the original conditions, which shaped it, are obsolete. Because any change of the habitus is slow and subconscious, the practices of agents in the field can seem "anachronistic, stubbornly resistant or ill-informed" (Maton, 2008: 59). In that sense, while staff purported to engage with the managerialist illusio by valuing and implementing groupwork assignments as a means for students to learn teamwork skills, their practices demonstrated that they were still primarily preoccupied with giving students the opportunity to develop technical competence, in the form of disciplinary knowledge. Thus, the extent to which academic habitus has been affected is less straightforward. Our data indicates that students' engagement with the relevant disciplinary knowledge, a traditional goal of HE, was still more important for staff despite claims of commitment to the development of generic skills. As such, the adoption of group assignments and their association with learning outcomes and graduate attributes in course outlines can best be understood as a simulation of compliance (Willmott, 1995).

LIMITATIONS AND DIRECTIONS FOR FUTURE RESEARCH

Our work is not without limitations. As mentioned earlier in the chapter, we draw on a single case study, which limits the generalisation of our findings. Another limitation of our work is that we drew our data solely from a business faculty, which has its own doxa and illusio. As highlighted earlier, it could be argued that it is in the interest of business academics to develop 'work-ready' graduates to avoid being called 'irrelevant' by critics of business education. However, both these limitations can be utilised as avenues for further research in the sense that other scholars could replicate our design and apply it in different disciplinary contexts, such as the faculties of arts or science. In that way, researchers can examine whether other disciplines are subject to the same pressures as the business discipline is. A third limitation of this chapter is that as the data was collected in 2007, it could be considered outdated and not reflective of the field of business higher education currently. We, however, argue that the pressures of the economic field on the academic field have endured if not intensified since then, at least in Australia. For example, in the 2010–2011 federal budget the Australian government announced a $70 million investment to establish "a regulatory framework which places a renewed emphasis on student outcomes and the quality of student experience" (TEQSA, 2014), including requirements about graduate attributes. Future research could explore how pedagogical practices have been further amended to comply with such legislative and quality assurance requirements.

CONCLUSION

The evidence presented highlights the changing nature of the field of business HE as a result of the increasing emphasis on managerialism and by extension student employability. It has been argued that the imperatives of student employability led the case study business faculty to extend its focus from a sole emphasis on the dissemination of discipline-based knowledge to producing graduates who possess not only theoretical knowledge but also practical skills that make them 'work-ready' for the field of paid employment. This emphasis is a result of the influence that governments and especially employers have been having on business HE. The techniques associated "with medium and large for profit businesses" (Deem, 1998: 49) have been challenging traditional academic habitus for some time (Cowen, 1996). However, as Stilwell (2003: 58) pointed out, a culture in which "academics are treated as employees answerable to employers sits awkwardly in academia". This chapter validates Stilwell's point by drawing attention to group assessments and the rather ignored stakeholder group of university teachers. Interviews showed that students were evaluated only on the theoretical content of their assignments and not on how well they worked together as a team, indicating that disciplinary knowledge continued to be privileged as central to the academic habitus.

Our chapter makes the following contributions. First, the conceptual framework presented here makes it possible to closely examine the nexus between the imperatives of managerialism and employability. Second, it provides a unique insight into pedagogical practices associated with groupwork assignments, thus filling a gap in the literature that has so far neglected both the views of university teachers and their actual practices. Third, it questions the impact that managerialism has had on academic teaching. Fourth, it has enabled us to draw significant inferences about why change efforts in academia may fall short of government and employer expectations. Our conceptual framework and data have allowed us to distinguish between the rhetoric that accompanies the imperatives of managerialism and actual academic practice. Finally, our multi-level approach incorporating the examination of multiple agents' perspectives demonstrates the value of Bourdieu's concepts for the investigation of managerialism in HE. Interest in applying Bourdieu's ideas to enhance organisation analysis has certainly grown over the past 30 years. However, his concepts have tended to be applied in a piecemeal fashion. While field and capital have been most frequently used (Emirbayer and Johnson, 2008), attention to habitus has been limited (Golsorkhi et al., 2009) and doxa and illusio have been neglected. Accordingly, our holistic application of Bourdieu's framework (Emirbayer and Johnson, 2008) is designed to demonstrate the value of a more integrated approach to Bourdieu's ideas, an approach we believe can significantly enrich organisation studies.

NOTES

1. The interviews with 13 members of the University's staff formed part of the data collected for a PhD research project, which encompassed a total of 84 semi-structured interviews conducted over a period of one and a half years. In addition to the 13 interviews reported here, 44 were conducted with undergraduate and postgraduate students, who were enrolled across six schools in the Faculty at the time of data collection. Twenty-seven alumni were also interviewed. The interviews were conducted in confidentiality, and the names of interviewees are withheld by mutual agreement. Citations to organisational documents and reports are also withheld in line with the confidentiality agreement between the researchers and the university.
2. Refer to note 1.
3. Acronyms: FT: full-time; PT: part-time; CN: continuing (similar to tenure); CR: contract (max five-year appointments); A/L: associate lecturer; L: lecturer; S/L: senior lecturer; A/Prof: associate professor.

REFERENCES

Aaltio I, and Heilmann P (2009) Case study as a methodological approach. In A J Mills, G Durepos, and E Wiebe (eds.), *Encyclopaedia of case study research*. London: SAGE, 67–78.

Ackoff R L (2002) Interview by Glenn Detrick. *Academy of Management Learning and Education*, 1(1): 56–63.

Ashraf M (2004). A critical look at the use of group projects as a pedagogical tool. *Journal of Education for Business*, 79(4): 213–216.

Bacon D R, Stewart K A, and Silver W S (1999) Lessons from the best and worst student team experiences: How a teacher can make the difference. *Journal of Management Education* 23(5): 467–488.

Ballantine J, and McCourt-Larres P (2007) Cooperative learning: A pedagogy to improve students' generic skills? *Education + Training* 49(2): 126–137.

Barnett R (1994) *The limits of competence, knowledge, higher education and society*. Society for Research into Higher Education. Berkshire: Open University Press.

Barrie S C (2006) Understanding what we mean by the generic attributes of graduates. *Higher Education* 51(2): 215–241.

Barrie S C (2004) A research-based approach to generic graduate attributes policy. *Higher Education Research and Development* 23(3): 261–275.

Blowers P (2003) Using student skill self-assessments to get balanced groups for group projects. *College Teaching* 51(3): 106–110.

Bourdieu P (2005) *The social structures of economy*. Cambridge: Polity Press.

Bourdieu P (1998) *Practical reason*. Cambridge: Polity Press.

Bourdieu P (1996) *The state nobility: Elite schools in the field of power*. Cambridge: Polity Press.

Bourdieu P (1990a) *In other words: Essays towards a reflexive sociology*. Cambridge: Polity Press.

Bourdieu P (1990b) *The logic of practice*. Cambridge: Polity Press.
Bourdieu P (1986) The forms of capital. In J E Richardson (ed.), *Handbook of theory of research for the sociology of education*. New York: Greenwood Press, 241–258.
Bourdieu P, and Wacquant L J (1992) *An invitation to reflexive sociology*. Chicago: University of Chicago Press.
Brown P, and Scase R (1994) *Higher education and corporate realities: Class, culture, and the decline of graduate careers*. London: UCL Press.
Chandler J, Barry J, and Clark H (2002) Stressing the academe: The wear and tear of the New Public Management. *Human Relations* 55(9): 1051–1069.
Chopra, R (2003) Neoliberalism as Doxa: Bourdieu's theory of the state and the contemporary Indian discourse on globalization and liberalization. *Cultural Studies* 17(3/4): 419–444.
Colley H (2012) Not learning in the workplace: Austerity and the shattering of illusio in public service work. *Journal of Workplace Learning* 24(5): 317–337.
Cowen R (1996) Performativity, post-modernity and the university. *Comparative Education* 32(2): 245–258.
Curtis D, and McKenzie P (2001) 'Employability skills for Australian industry: Literature review and framework development'. Report to Business Council of Australia Australian Chamber of Commerce and Industry and the Australian Council for Educational Research. Canberra, Australia.
Deem R (1998) 'New managerialism' and higher education: The management of performances and cultures in universities in the United Kingdom. *International Studies in Sociology of Education* 8(1): 47–70.
Deer C (2008) Doxa. In M Grenfell (ed.), *Pierre Bourdieu: Key concepts*. Durham: Acumen, 119–130.
Dent M, and Whitehead S (2002). Introduction: Configuring the new professional. In M Dent and S Whitehead (eds.), *Managing professional identities: Knowledge, performativity and the new professional*. London: Routledge Studies in Business Organisations and Networks. Routledge, 1–16.
Denzin N (2009). *The research act: A theoretical introduction to sociological methods*. Piscataway, NJ: Transaction.
Doria J, Rozanski H, and Cohen E (2003) What business needs from business schools. *Strategy + Business* 32: 39–45.
Emirbayer M, and Johnson V (2008) Bourdieu and organizational analysis. *Theory and Society* 37(1): 1–44.
English F W (2012) Bourdieu's misrecognition: Why educational leadership standards will not reform schools or leadership. *Journal of Educational Administration and History* 44(2): 155–170.
Eriksson P, and Kovalainen A (2010). Case study research in business and management. In A J Mills, G Durepos, and E Wiebe (eds.), *Encyclopedia of case study research*. London: SAGE, 93–97.
Flyvberg B (2004) Five misunderstandings about case-study research. In C Seale, G Gobo, J F Gubrium, and D Silverman (eds.), *Qualitative research practice*. London: SAGE, 390–405.
Free C, and Macintosh N B (2009) Bourdieu's logic of practice theory: Possibilities for research on management accounting and control. Unpublished Research Paper no 02–09, Queen's School of Business, Ontario.
Gallagher M (2001) Lifelong learning: Demand and supply issues—Some questions for research. Paper presented at the Business/Higher Education Roundtable Conference on the Critical Importance of Lifelong Learning. Sydney, July.
Gibbs G, Jaques D, Jenkins A, and Rust C (1994) *Developing students' transferable skills*. Oxford: Oxford Centre for Staff Development.
Goldfinch J, Laybourn P, Macleod L., and Stewart S (1999) Improving groupworking skills in undergraduates through employer involvement. *Assessment and Evaluation in Higher Education* 24(1): 41–51.

Golsorkhi D, Leca B, Lounsbury M, and Ramirez C (2009) Analysing, accounting for and unmasking domination: On our role as scholars of practice, practitioners of social science and public intellectuals. *Organization* 16(6): 779–797.

Grenfell M (2008) Interest. In M Grenfell (ed.), *Pierre Bourdieu: Key concepts*. Durham: Acumen, 153–170.

Gupta M L (2004). Enhancing student performance through cooperative learning in physical sciences. *Assessment and Evaluation in Higher Education* 29(1): 63–73.

Harris K L, and James R (2006) *The Course Experience Questionnaire, Graduate Destinations Survey and Learning and Teaching Performance Fund in Australian higher education*. Chapel Hill: Department of Public Policy, University of North Carolina.

Harvey L, Moon S, and Geall V with Bower R (1997) *Graduates' work: Organisational change and students' attributes*. Birmingham: Centre for Research into Quality.

Hewitt F, and Clayton M (1999) Quality and complexity: Lessons from English higher education. *International Journal of Quality and Reliability Management* 16(9): 838–858.

Houldsworth C, and Matthews B P (2000) Group composition, performance and educational attainment. *Education + Training* 42(1): 40–53.

Humphreys P, Greenan K, and McIlveen H (1997) Developing work-based transferable skills in a university environment. *Journal of European Industrial Training* 21(2): 63–69.

Ilgen D R, and Pulakos E (1999) *The changing nature of performance: Implications for staffing, motivation and development*. San Francisco: Jossey-Bass.

Jary D (2002) Aspects of the audit society: Issues arising from the colonization of professional academic identities by a 'portable management tool'. In M Dent and S Whitehead (eds.), *Managing professional identities: Knowledge, performativity and the new professional*. London: Routledge, 38–60.

Johnson D, and Johnson R T (1975) *Learning together and alone: Cooperation, competition and individualisation*. Englewood Cliffs: Prentice Hall.

Johnson D, Johnson R T, and Holubec E J (1998) *Cooperation in the classroom*. Boston: Allyn and Bacon.

Johnson D, Johnson R T, and Holubec E J (1994) *The new circles of learning: Cooperation in the classroom and school*. Alexandria: Association for Supervision and Curriculum Development.

Johnson D, Johnson R T, and Maruyama G (1983) Interdependence and interpersonal attraction among heterogeneous and homogenous individuals: A theoretical formulation and a meta-analysis of the research. *Review of Educational Research* 53(1): 5–54.

Johnson D, Johnson R T, and Smith K A (1991) *Cooperative learning: Increasing college faculty instructional productivity*. Higher Education Report No 4. Washington DC: George Washington University.

Johnston B, and Watson A (2004) Participation, reflection and integration for business and lifelong learning: Pedagogical challenges of the integrative studies programme at the University of Strathclyde Business School. *Journal of Workplace Learning* 16(1–2): 53–62.

King P E, and Behnke R R (2005) Problems associated with evaluating student performance in groups. *College Teaching* 53(2): 57–61.

Kyriakidou O, and Özbilgin M F (2006) Introduction. In O Kyriakidou and M F Özbilgin (eds.), *Relational perspectives in organisational studies: A research companion*. Cheltenham: Edward Elgar, 1–7.

Lamont M, and Lareau A (1988) Cultural capital: Allusions, gaps and glissandos in recent theoretical developments. *Sociological Theory* 6(2): 153–168.

Lareau A, and Horvat-McNamara E (1999) Moments of social inclusion and exclusion: Race, class and cultural capital in family-school relationships. *Sociology of Education* 72(1): 37–53.

Lareau A, and Weininger E B (2003) Cultural capital in educational research: A critical assessment. *Theory and Society* 32(5–6): 567–606.

Laybourn P, Goldfinch J, Graham J, Macleod L, and Stewart S (2001) Measuring changes in groupworking skills in undergraduate students after employer involvement in group skill development. *Assessment and Evaluation in Higher Education* 26(4): 367–380.

Lewis P, Aldridge D, and Swamidass, P (1998) Assessing teaming skills acquisition on undergraduate project teams. *Journal of Engineering Education* 87(2): 149–155.

Lok J, and DeRond M (2013). On the plasticity of institutions: Containing and restoring practice breakdowns at the Cambridge University Boat Club. *Academy of Management Journal* 56(1): 185–207.

Marks M A, Mathieu J E, and Zaccaro S J (2001) A temporally based framework and taxonomy of team processes. *Academy of Management Review* 26(3): 356–376.

Marshall J D (1999) Performativity: Lyotard and Foucault through Searle and Austin. *Studies in Philosophy and Education* 18(5): 309–317.

Maton K (2008) Habitus. In M Grenfell (ed.), *Pierre Bourdieu: Key concepts*. Durham: Acumen, 49–66.

Miller H (1998) Managing academics in Canada and the United Kingdom. *International Studies in Sociology of Education* 8(1): 3–24.

Mills A (2010) Juncture. In A Mills, G Durepos, and E Wiebe (eds.), *Encyclopedia of case study research*. Thousand Oaks, CA: SAGE, 510–514.

Mills J H, and Mills A J (2000). Rules, sensemaking, formative contexts, and discourse in the gendering of organizational culture. In N Ashkanasy, CPM Wilderom, and M F Peterson (eds.), *Handbook of organizational culture and climate*. Thousand Oaks, CA: SAGE, 55–70.

Mintzberg H, and Gosling J (2002) Educating managers beyond borders. *Academy of Management Learning and Education* 1(1): 64–76.

Morley L (2003) *Quality and power in higher education*. Society for Research into Higher Education. Berkshire: Open University Press.

Organisation for Economic Development and Cooperation (OECD) (2006) Higher education: Quality, equity and efficiency. *Institutional Management in Higher Education Info*, July.

O'Reilly D, and Reed M (2011) The grit in the oyster: Professionalism, managerialism and leaderism as discourses of UK public services modernization. *Organization Studies* 32(8): 1079–1101.

Özbilgin M F (2006) Relational methods in organization studies: A review of the field. In O Kyriakidou and M F Özbilgin (eds.), *Relational perspectives in organisational studies: a research companion*. Cheltenham: Edward Elgar, 244–264.

Özbilgin M F, and Tatli A (2005) Book review essay: Understanding Bourdieu's contribution to organisation and management studies. *Academy of Management Review* 30(4): 855–877.

Parker M (2002) The romance of lonely 'dissent': Intellectuals, professionals and the McUniversity. In M Dent and S Whitehead (eds.), *Managing professional identities: Knowledge, performativity and the new professional*. London: Routledge, 138–156.

Parker M, and Jary D (1995) The McUniversity: Organisation, management and academic subjectivity. *Organization* 2(2): 319–338.

Pfeffer J, and Fong C T (2004) The business school 'business': Some lessons from the US experience. *Journal of Management Studies* 41(8): 1501–1520.

Pfeffer J, and Fong C T (2002) The end of business schools? Less success than meets the eye. *Academy of Management Learning & Education* 1(1): 78–95.

Prichard C, and Willmott H (1997) Just how managed is the McUniversity? Craig Prichard, Hugh Willmott. *Organization Studies* 18(2): 287–316.

Reay D (2004) 'It's all becoming habitus': Beyond the habitual use of habitus in educational research. *British Journal of Sociology of Education* 25(4): 431–444.

Schullery N M, and Gibson M K (2001) Working in groups: Identification and treatment of students' perceived weaknesses. *Business Communication Quarterly* 64(2): 9–30.

Sousa, CAA, de Nijs W F, and Hendriks PHJ (2010) Secrets of the beehive: Performance management in university research organisations. *Human Relations* 63(9): 1439–1460.

Stake R E (1995) *The art of case study research*. Thousand Oaks, CA: SAGE.

Stilwell F (2003) Higher education, commercial criteria and economic incentives. *Journal of Higher Education Policy and Management* 25(1): 51–61.

Sullivan A (2001) Cultural capital and educational attainment. *Sociology* 35(4): 893–912.

Tertiary Education Quality and Standards Agency (2014) About TEQSA. Available at: http://www.teqsa.gov.au/about

Thanem T, and Wallenberg L (2009) Paradoxes of academic practice: Managerialist techniques in critical pedagogy. In J Wolfram Cox, T G LeTrent-Jones, M Voronov, and D Weir (eds.), *Critical management studies at work: Negotiating tensions between theory and practice*. Cheltenham, UK: Edward Elgar, 180–195.

Thomson P (2008) Field. In M Grenfell (ed.), *Pierre Bourdieu: Key concepts*. Durham: Acumen, 67–81.

Webb J, Schirato T, and Danaher G (2002) *Understanding Bourdieu*. Thousand Oaks, CA: SAGE.

Willmott H (1995) Managing the academics: Commodification and control in the development of university education in the UK. *Human Relations* 48(9): 993–1027.

Yin R K (2003) *Case study research: Design and methods*. Thousand Oaks, CA: SAGE.

Ylijoki, O-H. (2005). Academic nostalgia. *Human Relations* 58(5): 555–576.

9 Exploring Different Forms of Capitals
Researching Capitals in the Field of Cultural and Creative Industries

Barbara Townley

INTRODUCTION

This chapter explores the concept of capital found in Bourdieu's work and its relationship to his understanding of the production and reproduction of advantage in society and the functioning of power. It explores the variety of forms of capital—economic, cultural, and social—and, illustrating Durkheim's influence in Bourdieu's work, its symbolic dimensions, as well as capital's relationship to Bourdieu's other primary 'thinking tools' of habitus and field. It then considers some of the criticisms that have been levelled at this use—in particular, the contrast with Marx's understanding of capital's role in production and the valorization process. The chapter then amplifies the value of Bourdieu's approach by considering a capitals analysis of a realm more readily associated with the aesthetic and symbolic than dimensions of capital, that of the cultural and creative industries. It suggests that an examination of the interrelationship between capital's various guises offers a means of transcending the culture/commerce dichotomy within which this sector is usually discussed.

WHY CAPITAL?

The significance of the role and importance of capital in Bourdieu's work stems from his understanding of the social world as a 'space' whose dimensions are structured by 'principles of differentiation or distribution'. Within this space agents occupy structured positions according to how much capital they hold: social space is structured by the unequal distribution of capital in both its objective and symbolic forms (Bourdieu 1998). This understanding of the functioning of capital stems from the range of Bourdieu's empirical work and his very broad understanding of the economy and what constitutes economic phenomena. It is discernible in his early works and continues throughout his career (Swedberg 2010; Lebaron 2003). For Lebaron (2003), Bourdieu's early work, during 1958–1966, shows the development of his interest in the concepts of the economy, capital, and interest and their use in social analysis "as generative matrices of new, stimulating observations"

(Lebaron 2003: 552). His early work on Algeria examines the contrast between established and capitalist ways of thinking about the economy, illustrating the functioning of an "economy of honour and good faith" (Swedberg 2010: 3); studies of Béarn illustrate the role of inheritance and reproduction in the expansion of the market economy; studies of deposit banks show the importance of personal capital in the analysis of credit-worthiness; studies of schooling and university give rise to a broader, generalized definition of inheritance from a more restricted economic definition; and studies of photography and museum visits illustrate how aesthetic concepts relate to inheritance and the reproduction of the social order. Through such studies the "notion of capital is stripped of its typical narrow designation as a form of material or financial property" (Lebaron 2003: 562).

Through these studies Bourdieu criticizes economic analyses for their lack of reference to social experience and dispositions, and the importance of cultural and symbolic factors in apparently 'economic' actions: economics ignores symbolic interests (Bourdieu 1977: 177). Bourdieu's analysis of consumption, *Distinction* (1984: 6), demonstrates how "consumption is based on the quest for symbolic difference in a relational social system". In other words, difference is manifest through the quality and use of goods rather than simply their purchase or possession (Lebaron 2003). The recognition that such factors have significance in cultural, leisure, and education practices led to a generalized use of 'capital' in an analysis of cultural practices, their production, and their reproduction (Lebaron 2003: 562).

As Lebaron (2003) notes, through these early studies Bourdieu develops, extends, and transfers the vocabulary and analyses of a more restricted economic foundation (capital, investment, interest, accumulation, profit, and reproduction) to a broader social analysis of fields and objects. In doing so he undermines 'enchanted' concepts of cultural practices and family relations, and develops a market analogy for 'non-profit' practices, despite the espoused view of economic interests being deemed 'impure' or secondary in these fields. The market analogy is not to emphasize that price is present, but that there are choices, competition, winners, and losers within 'non-economic' fields. As Lebaron (2003: 558) notes, Bourdieu "gives economic terms a non-monetary and non-quantified meaning". Monetary and quantitative evaluation is but one historically specific construct giving rise to the economic field, part of a general phenomenon of social evaluation. It is for these reasons that Swedberg (2010: 2) argues that "the richness of his ideas, concepts and observations deserve to be developed in new and surprising directions".

WHAT CAPITAL?

Bourdieu thus sees capital as a social relation, but finds economic capital alone insufficient for his analysis. Possession of material resources through the means of production is insufficient for an appreciation of power and domination in society: "it is impossible to account for the structure and functioning of the social world unless one introduces capital in all its forms and not solely on the one form recognized by economic theory" (Bourdieu 1986: 242). For Bourdieu, social relations in general, and relations of cultural production, are equally as important as economic relations, with the unequal distribution of cultural and social resources critically important to an understanding of society—hence his concern with reproduction and distinction. With the importance of the representation of the social world and symbolic struggles and the refusal to segregate or subordinate the symbolic realm to the economic, Bourdieu suggests that symbolic production and consumption are homologous with the economy, revolving around the accumulation and deployment of different forms of capital.

For Bourdieu (1986: 46) capital is "present in three guises": economic, social, and cultural. Economic capital, immediately convertible into money, takes the form of assets and property rights. Social capital indicates the actual and potential resources linked to the possession of "durable network[s] of more or less institutionalized relationships of mutual acquaintance or recognition" and the social obligations stemming from this, and depends "on the size of the network of connections" an agent can effectively mobilize and on "the volume of capital (economic, cultural or symbolic) possessed in his own right by each of those to whom he is connected" (Bourdieu 1986: 49). Cultural capital exists in several states: an embodied state in the form of long-lasting 'dispositions' (forms of being, behaviour), acquired through socialization of family and peers, or 'work on oneself' ('self-improvement', acquiring 'cultivated' habits and tastes of cultural appreciation and understanding, mastery of knowledge); an objectified state as valued cultural, material objects; and an institutionalized state, as acquired education, knowledge, and qualifications.

Thus capital exists in different forms, objectified through artefacts and embodied in predispositions and propensities. Each of its forms is "capable of conferring strength, power and consequently profit on their holder" (Bourdieu 1987: 4). Bourdieu uses the concept of capital to describe these forms of power because each is the product of an investment strategy, "individual or collective, consciously or unconsciously"; takes time to accumulate; has the potential to produce profits; reproduces itself in identical or expanded form; has a tendency to persist; and, reflecting historical patterns of accumulation, is unequally distributed. An important dimension of Bourdieu's understanding and use of capital is the recognition of the importance of time. Capital is transferred through time in either an objectified—that is, material—or an embodied form. Embodied capital is acquired through immersion in an arena. Time and energy are required to acquire it and to enable individuals to profit from their investment. Investing time and energy and engaging in a field grant legitimacy in themselves.

Although displaying the characteristics of capital, each capital—economic, cultural, and social—remains a distinct and separate form, obeying distinct logics of accumulation and exercise (Brubaker 2004: 39). Access to one, although facilitating access to others, does not automatically entail another. Cultural and social capital may be convertible into economic capital, but only under certain conditions. Despite economic capital being at the root of all other forms of capital, they are "never entirely reducible to that" (Bourdieu 1986: 47). Both cultural capital and social capital are 'transubstantiated' forms of economic capital, derived from, but becoming reconstituted in, the process of conversion. They produce different forms of profit. They also differ according to their transposability across fields and their degree of fungibility—that is, the capacity to transform into a different form—for example, from cultural to economic. The distinctive features of each form of capital, and processes of conversion between the different forms, ensure that each follows distinct logics (Svendsen and Svendsen 2004: 240). Drawing on an analogy of energy, forms of capital or power are potentially inter-convertible forms of power, but mutually irreducible. However, like all forms of capital they need maintenance, and there is a degree of depreciation in their non-use or abuse.

Economic, social, and cultural capital underpins all social functioning. However, distinct and discrete fields (e.g. linguistic, scientific, political, and literary) have their own specific forms of capital (e.g. linguistic, scientific, political, and literary), their symbolic capital. In this sense, forms of capital, like fields, are unlimited. Economic, cultural, and social capital also has the capacity to function as symbolic capital dependent on the field (Bourdieu 2000: 242). Described by Bourdieu (1998: 85) as "capital with a cognitive base" resting on "cognition and recognition", symbolic capital is recognized as "what counts" or what "is at stake" in a field, that which is recognized, acknowledged, and attributed as a field's "currency". "Capital in action is the enactment of the principle of the field" (Moore 2008: 105). Again using the energy analogy, capital is a form of energy driving the development of the field through time. The valorization of symbolic capital depends on the structure of the field—that is, its composition, the relations within it, and its relative position vis-à-vis other fields.

The consciously recognized 'currency' of the field constructs the 'game' of the field. Symbolic power is the power to represent, to define and legitimize what is recognized as prestigious in a field, and, as such, it is "a formidable social power" (Bourdieu 1985: 729). Bourdieu writes, "Knowledge of the social world and, more precisely, the categories that make it possible are the stakes par excellence of political struggle, the inextricably theoretical and practical struggles for the power to conserve or transform the social world by conserving or transforming the categories through which it is perceived" (Bourdieu 1985: 729). As Moore (2008) notes, although proclaiming themselves to be 'disinterested', symbolic fields establish 'hierarchies of discrimination'. The symbolic effects of capital set "the frontier between the sacred and the profane, good and evil, the vulgar and the distinguished" (Bourdieu 1985: 735). The prestige, renown, and honour of a field are 'misrecognized' in that the economic and social conditions of its production remain hidden. There is, however, an ambiguity in the functioning of symbolic forms of capital. They "produce their most specific effects only to the extent that they conceal (not least from their possessors) the fact that economic capital is at their root [and] at the root of their effects" (Bourdieu 1986: 47). An appeal to 'intrinsic worth' is an act of misrecognition: arbitrariness mistaken for legitimate valuation. Thus symbolic capital is intimately linked to power. As Nicolini (2013: 59) notes, it is a form of capital that renders domination and its reproduction invisible, sustaining inequality through what Bourdieu refers to as 'symbolic violence'. It is symbolic violence because disinterest denies the arbitrary character of symbolic capital and the regulation, and consequent distribution, of symbolic capital denies the social and cultural advantage or disadvantage that it brings (Moore 2008). Symbolic capital thus contributes to and reinforces structures of inequality. As Moore (2008: 105) notes, "symbolic capital achieves its effect by virtue of the illusion of autonomy of the field and its intrinsic principle".

Fields are defined by "three fundamental dimensions" of capital: its volume or amount (a "set of actually usable resources and powers"); its structure or composition (i.e. the relative weight of capital); and the change in these two elements over time (Bourdieu 1984: 114). Understood as energy, capital is the medium through which struggles are organized and positions attained, with fields representing arenas for the conservation and transformation of different forms of capital. The efficacy of capital, however, depends on the field in which it operates. Capital is valorized in terms of the structure of a field, be this intellectual, academic, educational, scientific, literary, artistic, linguistic, and so forth. Struggles take place over the relationship among the various forms of capital distinctive to the field: "the relative value of the different species of capital . . . is continually being brought into question, reassessed, through struggles aimed at inflating or deflating the value of one or the other type of capital" (Bourdieu 1987: 10). However, as with social space generally, fields tend to be structured along two hierarchized poles centring around economic and cultural capital, giving rise to the distinctions—for example, between fields of restricted and large-scale cultural production, elitist and populist culture, or 'hard' and 'soft' sciences in academia.

Access to capital, although highly influential, is not, however, deterministic. While capital within one field may also give advantage in others, there is not a 'direct mechanical relationship'. Field positions depend on the agent's trajectory and the position they occupy in the field by virtue of their endowment (volume and structure) of capital; their propensity towards risky or cautious play (willingness to increase or conserve capital); and their propensity towards the preservation or the subversion of the distribution of capital. Drawing the analogy with a game of cards, Bourdieu writes,

> Just as the relative value of cards change with each game, the hierarchy of different species of capital (economic, social, cultural and symbolic)

varies across the various fields . . . there are cards that are valid, efficacious in all fields—these are the fundamental species of capital—but their relative value as trump cards is determined by each field and even by successive states of the same field.

(Bourdieu and Wacquant 1992: 97–8)

The capacity to deal the hand, however, will be deeply influenced by the agent's habitus. In other words, agents have a strong interest in consciously seeking to plan and execute strategies, but coming from individual and collective histories certain strategies are likely to be perceived as being more 'reasonable' than others (Svendsen and Svendsen 2004: 248). The indissolubility between structured space of positions (influenced by the volume and nature of the capital that is ascribed value within it) and 'position-takings', the actual stances that agents adopt, is emphasized by Bourdieu: they are "two translations of the same sentence" (Bourdieu and Wacquant 1992: 105). However, individuals have different 'asset structures', with hierarchies varying according to field they occupy. Agents' strategies, their power to play and influence the 'game', depend on their own capital and the distribution of field-specific capital. To perform effectively a player must have accumulated the appropriate capital; understood the capital configurations of the field; and mastered the ability to use it effectively (mastered the field's habitus). To understand the functioning of capital within a field it is important to understand the structure of the field and the position-takings within it, which are dependent on the volumes and compositions of capital.

Bourdieu identifies a general science of the economy of practice (1977). This involves the importance of grasping capital and profit "in all their forms . . . to establish the laws whereby different types of capital change into one another" (Bourdieu 1986: 243). Although he later expresses doubts as to whether this would be possible (Bourdieu 1998; Swedberg 2010), such a recognition is indicative of, or a pointer to, a possible avenue of application of Bourdieu's capitals framework in an analysis of different fields.

THE VALUE OF CAPITAL

Bourdieu's use of capital has not gone without criticism.[1] This has taken three forms: charges of economism; questioning the appropriateness of his use of the term capital; and whether his understanding of capital constitutes a fully-fledged articulation of a theory of capital, akin to that, for example, of Marx. The use of capital, taken not just as the model for the economy but also as a way of accounting for the structure and development of society, has evoked charges of economism—that is, the reduction of all activity to material self-interest and, through this, the homogenization of fields to the economic (Friedland 2009). Bourdieu (2005) claims such charges come from a 'fast' reading of his work that presupposes that agents are motivated by an 'intellectualist cogito'—that is, the conscious reasoning of rational action theory and neoclassical economics—and, in proposing that the functioning of one field is equally valid for all, denies the specificity of fields. On the contrary, for Bourdieu, although fields may operate in a similar way—that is, there are homologies—a field generates a specific form of interest. Actions are "not necessarily conceived as a calculated pursuit of gain" but have "every likelihood of being experienced in terms of the logic of emotional investment" (Bourdieu 1986: 57). Although interests and investments in different forms of capital are analogous to an economic logic—that is, there is a 'cost' and a 'profit' to all practices—they are not reducible to this logic. Charges of economism stem from every type of capital being reducible to economic capital "in the last instance" (Bourdieu 1993b: 33) and the economic field being a "powerful determinant" (Beasley-Murray 2000: 104). But this ignores the "specific efficacy of other types of capital" and that capital is 'transubstantiated' (Bourdieu 1986), and while the economic field as a dominant field obviously impacts on the efficacy of capital within and outside of the specific field in which it is deployed, it is not deterministic; rather its efficacy depends on the manoeuvrings within the field.

Bourdieu is also critical of the narrow conception of the rationality of practices. The 'rationality' of actors is an empirical question dependent on the state of the field. Equating 'interest' with economic interest stems from our understanding of economic theory. Interest is not to be confused with the trans-historical and universal interest of utilitarian theory. Rather there are as many interests as there are fields. Bourdieu understands interest as 'illusio'. Derived from *ludus*, Latin for game, illusio implies being caught up by, and taking, a game seriously. It is to be 'invested' (both in an economic and psychoanalytic sense) and is opposed to disinterestedness or indifference—that is, "having no interest in, or no preference for, playing; or not being able to differentiate stakes in the game" (Bourdieu and Wacquant 1992: 116). For those with no interest in the particular game, "the obviousness of the illusio [interest] is an illusion" (Bourdieu 1998: 79). It is illusory, having no weight.

From a standard political economy which recognizes the four factors of production—technology, land, physical capital, and human capital—capital is expanded to include non-material as well as material phenomena (Svendsen and Svendsen 2004: 239), with the recognition that capital operates in visible, material forms as well as invisible, non-material forms, both embodied and also inhering in relations. Bourdieu's reformulation of Marx's concept of capital, however, particularly the equivalences drawn between economic capital and its other forms, is contentious, raising criticisms of an "indiscriminate and metaphoric importation of 'economic' concepts into sociological literature" (Baron and Hannan, quoted in Adler and Kwon 2002). Questions stem from the perceived differences between capitals in terms of their degrees of flexibility, fungibility, contextual dependence, and, critically, their alienability (Savage, Warde, and Devine 2005)—that is, the extent to which some capitals are convertible into other forms of capital; their degree of liquidity (with economic capital being the most liquid and most readily convertible); and the extent to which some forms of capital are able to substitute for other forms, and the inability to subject all capitals, unlike economic capital, to quantified measurement (Adler and Kwon 2002). That a broad and heterogeneous family of resources, with their expected flow of benefits, is labelled capitals has led to criticism of there being a plethora of capitals: a criticism addressed by the specificity of fields. More critical are issues as to whether the capitals Bourdieu identifies are appropriable—that is, may be used as a private resource—and thus are alienable. This is particularly a charge against social capital, which raises the particular issue as to whether, given that it is located in a network of relations, it could be conceived as a private good or a form of property, for although exclusive and excludable (i.e. it is possible to exclude others from access), it is non-rivalrous—that is, it may be used by others (Adler and Kwon 2002).

These issues point to a broader question posed by Moore (2008: 116): does Bourdieu present a new lexicon as a new theory? Is Bourdieu using capital metaphorically, analogously, or theoretically? Bourdieu does not see his work as using capital metaphorically (Beasley-Murray 2000). But if used theoretically, is its use as a resource or an asset, rather than a fully articulated concept of the functioning of capital, as, for example, provided by Marx? While Bourdieu's understanding of capital and the functioning of social space differentiates his work from standard readings of Marx and any reduction of "the social field solely to the economic" (Bourdieu 1985: 723), in depicting capital as accumulated labour—that is, it takes time to accumulate and thus has a universal equivalent of labour-time—and as accumulated history, he reproduces certain elements of Marx's theory of capital. The economic definition of capital recognizes it as a resource that facilitates production (Svendsen and Svendsen 2004). Although using certain elements of Marx's understanding of capital, gesturing "towards Marx's labour theory of value", Bourdieu doesn't ground his use and understanding of capital in the cycle of production (Beasley-Murray 2000: 101). Marx's understanding of capital implies surplus and exploitation, and is different from value or wealth, which some see as lying at the foundation of Bourdieu's use of the term. For Bourdieu, value is defined in terms of labour rather than labour power, and as such does not address exploitation and appropriation; it "fails to enable an account of the accumulation of surplus and hence either profit or exploitation" (Beasley-Murray 2000). Rather than capital being produced in the production process as it is for Marx, Bourdieu offers no understanding of the process whereby value is converted into capital, the valorization process. As a consequence, Bourdieu's use of capital has been critiqued for failing to address the relationship between value and capital, valorization in production, and thereby surplus value. Rather, for Guillory (2000: 41 n. 14) Bourdieu's work invokes the paradigm of mercantile capitalism in which surplus capital comes from the process of circulation. For

Beasley-Murray (2000: 102) also, Bourdieu "emphasizes the market at the expense of understanding production". Bourdieu does, however, provide a full account of the reproduction of inequalities in all its guises, and in doing so he "outlines rather a theory of the unequal distribution of capital effected through appropriation" (Beasley-Murray 2000: 105).

For others, Bourdieu's extension of the concept of capitals owes more to Durkheim's work, which sees economic ideas and practices as collective representations (Lebaron 2001, 2003; Svendsen and Svendsen 2004). As Lebaron (2003: 561) notes, "economic theorization and observations are 'corrected' in relation to the symbolic dimensions in which they are embedded". The symbolic dimension thus functions as an 'integrating vector' between economic and social factors, with the studies in Algeria, for example, illustrating how symbolic exchanges are completely integrated with material exchange (Lebaron 2003: 560). For Bourdieu, economic order is symbolic order, there being no ontological heterogeneity between the sphere of representation and economic interests. He criticizes the material and the symbolic distinction and fallacious depictions of base/superstructure. For Bourdieu, the economic/non-economic dichotomy makes it impossible to see the science of 'economic' practices (Bourdieu 1990: 122, quoted in Lebaron 2001: 124). The 'economic' is rather a particular case of illusion and a particular case of a field (Lebaron 2001: 125). It is an example of belief, or illusion, being presented as "pure theory" (Lebaron 2001: 129).

Bourdieu's studies of the symbolic aspects of economic life offer an anthropological critique of dominant economic theory, and a critique of the hegemony and success of rational action theory that has increased the autonomy of the economic field. By disrupting the economic/non-economic dichotomy and identifying market exchange as only one type of economic practice (Svendsen and Svendsen 2004), Bourdieu both avoids a reductionist and enhances an anthropological economics (Svendsen and Svendsen 2004: 242). For Beasley-Murray (2000: 101), he extends the analysis of political economy to a cultural economy, and his concept of cultural capital "reintegrate[s] economics with the study of culture", showing the interrelationship "between economic or material and the cultural or abstract". Whereas the economist makes no distinction about the nature of the goods purchased, cultural capital alerts us to their significance within a space of distinction, with each 'good' being ascribed a value according to the capitals of the field. Another advantage of Bourdieu's analysis for Beasley-Murray (2000) is that it incorporates a concept of time. Rather than just focus on the instance of economic exchange, where the temporality of practice is eliminated by reference to abstract time, Bourdieu illustrates how time is an important dimension in the use and realization of capital, as, for example, seen in his example of the gift, which illustrates how an 'economy of symbolic capital' relies on time. A simple example of its value is provided by the example of reading a book. The act of selecting and reading a book in itself requires cultural capital; however, "the benefits of this investment yield cultural capital that may acquire a new form of exchangeable value at a dinner party or job interview" (Beasley-Murray 2000: 108). An initial economic exchange (the purchase of a book) has the potential to be transformed into a new form of value. This also, for Beasley-Murray (2000), restores 'concrete time' to the exchange process. In recognizing 'concrete time' as opposed to abstract time, it is possible to see more clearly the functioning of the various dimensions of capitals in an economy of practices. It is through the identification and recognition of the salience of time that the economic logic underlying gift exchange can be identified or recognized, even though the exchange is symbolic rather than strictly financial.

By taking concepts from economics—for example, profit, capital, interest, and market—and using these in his sociology in a way "that bears no resemblance to neo-classical economics", Swedberg (2010) sees Bourdieu's work offering a critique of economism. Equally, for Lebaron (2003: 558), studies in which the depiction of "free conscious choice" is contrasted with "ordinary economic agents" and the social reality of empirical markets provide the foundation of the critique of neoclassical economics as a "scholastic fallacy", an "imaginary anthropology". And as Moore (2008: 102) notes, his use of the extended term of capital, employing it "in a wider system of exchanges whereby assets of different kinds are transferred and exchanged within complex networks or circuits within and across different fields takes it away from the narrow instance of mercantile exchange into a wider anthropology of cultural exchanges and valuation of which the economic is only one". The mercantile exchange as just one particular case of exchange strengthens the pluralistic character of interests, resources, accumulation, and profits (Lebaron 2003: 562). It also crosses "anxiously patrolled disciplinary boundaries" (Beasley-Murray 2000: 101), offering a framework for interdisciplinary research (Svendsen and Svendsen 2004: 239). Through the extended use of the term economic and an examination of the conversions that take place between economic and non-economic, it offers the basis for his 'economy of practices'.

CAPITALS IN THE CULTURAL AND CREATIVE INDUSTRIES

So how might this capitals framework aid us in our understanding of the cultural and creative industries (CCI)? The name CCI conjures hotly contested debates reflecting how the cultural and economic have traditionally been understood. Criticisms are raised about allying the 'cultural' with 'industry', the two supposed antithetical provinces of creativity and commerce representing the coupling of the sacred with the profane. Critiques are voiced of an emphasis on the 'economic role' and 'impact' of cultural activities and broader debates on the 'creative economy'. Studies recount how these tensions have been accommodated in the cultural and creative sphere. Using Bourdieu's work, might it possible, however, to transcend such debates and formulate an economy of practices for CCI?

Indeed, Bourdieu's main aim in using the model of the economy to understand society is to transcend the opposition between economic reductionism and cultural idealism (Liénard, Servais, and Bailey 1979). He (1986: 46) writes, "By reducing the universe of exchanges to mercantile exchange, which is objectively and subjectively oriented to the maximization of profit, i.e., economically *self-interested*, it has implicitly defined the other forms of exchange as noneconomic and therefore *disinterested*". For Bourdieu, such conceptualization denies the social conditions, intimately linked to the 'economic', that make the production and consumption of cultural goods possible. Certainly there is a denial of a 'natural' and 'unmediated' appreciation of art. The separation of spheres through the constitution of a separate economic field leaves culture as a "sphere apart in which economic calculation remains hidden" (Beasley-Murray 2000: 116). Although the cultural market bears little resemblance to the free market, there is still an economic logic that underpins it: "cultural appreciation is far from disinterested. Taste conforms to a market system with its own logic and own specific form of capital" (Beasley-Murray 2000: 106). The market of symbolic goods obeys a logic of capital, with symbolic, cultural capital, "disavowed, mis-recognized", acting as a form of economic or political capital, a form of credit which under certain conditions guarantees economic profit (Bourdieu 1980: 262).

Why introduce capital in the CCI field? Acknowledging that "culture is interested and economics is cultural" (Swartz and Zolberg 2004: 6) offers a break with economism and culturalism, recognizing that calculation lies behind economic and symbolic practices (Svendsen and Svendsen 2004: 248). Although cultural fields claim distance from economic fields, and sustain distance through an illusio(n) of autonomy and adherence to intrinsic qualities of truth, beauty, justice, and so forth, for Bourdieu, they are equally implicated in structured inequalities of power. They function to produce and regulate different forms of symbolic capital and police its distribution. Systems of classification structure perceptions of the social world, including objects of aesthetic enjoyment. It is this 'misrecognition' that leads to symbolic violence, the misplaced belief in the arbitrary as being real, reinforcing relationships of hierarchy and domination. Cultural distinctions become the source of symbolic struggles with contestation over that which is valued, reflected in contests between 'higher' and 'lower': "taste classifies and it classifies the classifier" (Bourdieu 1984: 6).

By extending the understanding and use of capital, and illustrating how goods traditionally excluded from economic analysis can be appropriated and constituted as capital, Bourdieu brings into focus processes in which different kinds of assets are transformed and exchanged within complex circuits and networks both within and across fields (Liénard et al. 1979). His 'economy of practices' shows how different capitals operate in practice within a field, and how they may be converted or translated from one form to another through the 'transformational' laws which "govern the transmutation of the different forms of capital into symbolic capital" (Bourdieu 1979: 83), and transubstantiation, "whereby material economic capital presents itself as immaterial cultural or social capital, or vice versa" (Bourdieu 1986: 46). He thus illustrates how "systems of domination persist and reproduce themselves without conscious recognition" (DiMaggio 1979: 1461).

In relation to the cultural and creative industries, Bourdieu's approach offers a useful framework with which to envision this area and its ecology. Given the tension that arises between the creative or artistic and commercial, and their apparent antithetical nature, it is important to frame analysis in a language that does not privilege one particularly over another—that is, does not take as its starting point a 'creative' or a 'commercial' perspective. The concept of capital, although heavily overlain with connotations from the economic sphere, nonetheless has wider purchase given its popular or colloquial use—political capital, for example. Bourdieu's work provides an opportunity for an examination of an economy of practices and the conversions that take place between economic and non-economic through the extended use of the term capital. Indeed, Bourdieu's (1993a) work analyses the relative weight of cultural and economic capital in fields of cultural production and their role in fields of wide-scale and restricted production. However, as with most uses of French sociology in an applied field such as management and organization studies, there is a degree of licence taken with the work, and here is no exception. Although Bourdieu does not specify the importance of acquisition, maintenance, enhancement, and exchange which accompany the use of economic capital, each capital is the product of an investment strategy; each capital must be acquired, maintained, enhanced, and, if possible, exchanged with others to secure resources of various types. This, with his identification of different capitals, permits us to develop a framework within which to analyse the CCIs and their functioning in more detail, both for the individual practitioner and organization and for an analysis at the field level.

Thus we may think of the CCI of being an amalgam of four different but interrelated capitals: intellectual, cultural, social, and economic. Intellectual capital is taken from Bourdieu's (1988) *Homo Academicus*, where it refers to the intellectual work of the academic field (as distinct from academic capital, which indicates position within formal university hierarchies). This use of intellectual capital allows for an analysis of the creation and generation of ideas, their recognition and understanding, protection and dissemination. Social capital, as the actual and potential resources linked to the possession of networks of relationships, is taken to be the access to networks that transmit ideas, employment, project opportunities and sustain activity. Cultural capital as 'dispositions' and acquired education, knowledge, and qualifications—the cultivation of the aesthetic eye—highlights the importance of a knowledgeable audience which has the ability to recognize and deem ideas or creations as being of value. Economic capital is the recognition of the importance of access to finance, be this private or public funding, sponsorship, and so forth. Ahead I elaborate on some of the factors that may be addressed within each form of capital, before considering some of the processes of transformation and transubstantiation their interrelationship entails (see Table 9.1).

Intellectual Capital

While intellectual capital may be used in the management literature as intangible value or human capital, intellectual capital as used here is used as a shorthand term for the 'idea' that lies behind the 'journey' from capital to intellectual property. It may be thought of as 'creativity', a term that Bourdieu does not use, allied as it is with the 'heroic artist' depiction of cultural creation. Its acquisition focuses on the source of new ideas within the creative sphere and its maintenance and enhancement of how ideas become rejuvenated or become more amenable to standardization in production, rather than being dependent on the 'muse', with exchange recognizing the translation of 'ideas' as a form of property through the exploitation of intellectual property rights. The generation of intellectual capital engages with the sources of ideas, whether this is through practice, tradition, or craft or, for example, artists using residencies to generate ideas for new projects; securing 'creativity' in production raises some of the challenges in managing creative talent and strategies that might be adopted for this. The maintenance of intellectual capital highlights issues, for example, of how new games design may become standardized in such a way that the learning process is built into the production process for future games development, strategies through which intellectual capital may become transformed into property through its assimilation within a production process. Through tracing how ideas become recognized as intellectual capital, and strategies for its maintenance and acquisition, the importance of intellectual capital and its recognition as a form of property is highlighted. Intellectual capital and its value might not be immediately obvious to creatives, with an important learning curve being the processes that creatives go through in recognizing the value of their work and their need to protect this and their experiences in securing their rights. The various aspects of intellectual capital underpin this recognition and journey.

Social Capital

Social capital has functioned in the management literature as the development and analysis of social networks with reference to nodes and networks and bridging and bonding capital, a major departure from its use in Bourdieu's work (Townley 2015). The importance of social networks in the cultural and creative industries has long been recognized, given its function in facilitating recruitment and sustaining the latent organizations that typify portfolio employment and project work. The growing impact of digital social networks and social media also highlights its role in the crowdsourcing of ideas, crowd funding of projects, and developing 'word of mouth' support and audiences. Independent film production companies, for example, develop the use of social media as a strategy for building a community and fan base for reaching new audiences as part of their film marketing and distribution campaigns, and as means of maintaining greater control of the film rights to increase their finance. Social media plays a role in trying to understand the nature of audiences, build new social networks to engage them, and achieve wider audience awareness and involvement. More broadly, the infrastructure, both physical and virtual, that can enhance engagement with cultural and creative activities is an important element of building social networks and capital.

Cultural Capital

Following Bourdieu, cultural capital is taken to mean the knowledge of a cultural arena and recognition of its codes. Its acquisition, and participation in cultural forms, is heavily influenced by socio-demographics and income. It underpins distinctions between social groups according to taste and consumption patterns (the participant, the audience, the amateur, the buff, etc.) and 'high-brow' and 'low-brow' art forms, and is seen being played out in attempts to widen a canon or introduce works that might be more widely seen or read. Also important is the role of the cultural intermediary in translating ideas and influencing their perception, as seen, for example, in how museums function in their selection and presentation of material for exhibition, the role and range of digital sites that support cultural intermediation, and in how authority positions and the nature of evaluative discourse become established. The valorization of this capital is reflected in the consecration practices of awards and prizes and the conferring of symbolic capital.

Figure 9.1 illustrates how all these elements of capital may impact on the success or otherwise of a creative organization or a creative field, with each capital requiring strategies and policies to ensure its creation, reproduction, and accumulation. Intellectual capital, reflected in the development of ideas or new creative content, must be acquired, its sources identified either in existing resources or in strategies that allow this to develop. Once acquired, it must be maintained in strategies as diverse as the provision for learning and skills development, providing a creative environment, securing capital through the creation of property rights, and so forth. There also needs to be an ongoing policy to ensure that ideas are continually being added to, either directly or through strategies of co-creation. With these conditions in place there is then the chance for these to be realized in securing a revenue stream. Building social capital aids the process not only of enhancing intellectual capital but also of ensuring an audience or market for this. Again, this reflects the processes of acquisition, through the identification of networks and network building; maintenance, through their

Capitals/Strategies	Intellectual Capital	Social Capital	Cultural Capital	Economic Capital
Acquisition	• Development of new IP content/IP content generation • New product/services development • Identifying creative talent	• Identifying and establishing networks • Network building	• Cultural access • Outreach and education programs • Market analysis	• Accessing financial support • Acquiring business skills for start-ups & business planning • SME policy infrastructure and support
Maintenance	• Managing creative teams • Protecting intellectual property rights	• Collaborative strategies • Managing stakeholder relationships • Managing dispersed production/distribution systems	• Access outreach and education programs • Market planning and promotion	• Business support services • Accessing credit facilities • Developing sustainable businesses • Risk analysis • Securing cash flow
Enhancement	• Client/user-designer co-production • Skills training and development • Managing portfolio careers • Artists' residency/placements	• Network development • Inter-organizational collaboration • Exploiting digitization for network building and enhancing consumer demand • Social media strategies	• Exchange programs and international touring • Engaging cultural intermediaries • Developing brands • Identifying new audiences	• Identifying new business opportunities • Accessing venture capital • Growth strategies, mergers, and acquisitions
Exchange	• Licensing agreements • New product lines/platforms	• Creative cities support • Local and regional infrastructure and digital support	• Leveraging evaluation and impact metrics and assessment • Identifying alternative income streams	• Divestment strategies

Figure 9.1 Researching Capitals in the CCI Field

ongoing management; and enhancement, through increasing collaborations. Social capital is greatly enhanced through digital opportunities; thus strategies that make use of this, as well as broader infrastructure projects that enhance this, are part of the social capital development framework. While the acquisition and development of intellectual and social capital might be something that may be enabled through individual or organizational initiatives, their effectiveness is dependent on the development of cultural capital, which in turn is reflective of structured socio-economic conditions and broader social provision. In an area of good cultural provision in terms of venues, exhibitions, and so forth, or access to digital provision, and an educational environment that encourages and values the cultural and artistic sphere, there is the foundation for the acquisition of cultural capital by both potential practitioner and audience. The richer this environment, the more diverse the opportunities for innovative ideas based on the juxtaposition of seemingly contradictory or antithetical notions or schemas to produce novel outcomes. Cultural capital, however, also operates at a more instrumental level in the branding strategies of corporations, with their identification of stratified user groups to not only differentiate products and services but also develop, some would say manipulate, individuals' understandings of themselves, their social and cultural positions, and the consumption choices that go with this. The acquisition, maintenance, and enhancement of economic capital are equally important for cultural and creative organizations; intellectual, social, and cultural elements of capital must ultimately find purchase in their relationship with economic capital, either directly through income, or indirectly through securing support for maintained public funding. In this way practitioners and organizations can ensure the continued support of their symbolic capital. Again, broader provision through business support services, access to business skills, and so forth in the support for start-up organizations, such as designers or games developers, for example, is an important aspect of the extent to which initial economic capital may be secured; income streams, the maintenance of cash flow, accessing lines of credit with distributors and retail, and so forth sustained, and planning for organization and business development and growth enhanced.

Although those within the CCI field tend to emphasize primarily their symbolic capital—that is, the recognition and prestige that comes from their symbolic cultural capital, their relative standing, and the relative standing of the symbolic cultural capital they profess (albeit while stressing the importance of the cultural sphere as a whole)—it is the functioning of intellectual, social, cultural, and economic capital and their interrelationship that ensures the creation of symbolic capital. Thus, cultural and creative individuals and organizations are continually in the process of trading their capitals, particularly their symbolic capital, for other forms of capital to ensure their survival and flourishing. The application of Bourdieu's framework allows for an examination of how different capitals are negotiated and exchanged both within fields and between dominated and dominant fields, and would illustrate the complexity of the economy in which such individuals and organizations operate. For example, an examination of artists might illustrate how practice and cultural capital become established, from leaving art school, through first exhibitions, representation with galleries, engagement with public and private institutions, and representations at international art shows, the latter greatly enhanced by the social capital that has been built up during an artist's career, but all underpinned by access through some means to economic capital. Through the interplay of these various capitals the recognition and consecration of an artist's symbolic capital can be secured. National cultural agencies try to achieve a balance between the various demands of their constituents, creators, the public, funding bodies, and so forth, in a mission to support production and promote artistic and cultural merit, but they must leverage their symbolic, cultural, and economic capital to augment the political capital necessary for their continued support and survival. For example, national film agencies balance support for individual film producers making films having cultural merit, though not finding broad private financial support, with support for a commercially viable film industry. Thereby, the interplay of cultural and economic is used to raise the symbolic purchase of film as a whole. Theatre needs to demonstrate the value of its cultural capital to gain support across a number of different constituents, often prompting it to engage in a range of different activities (e.g. community theatre, drama therapy, training, and education) outside what is perceived to be its 'core' activity, to illustrate its value to a range of stakeholders (local government, the theatre community, the arts community, national government, the citizens of the local city) to ensure its continuing viability and support. Again economic, social, cultural, and political capitals both reinforce and are reinforced by the symbolic.

Equally, the habitus of those involved is a crucial element of understanding this dynamic. The success of these transformational strategies and the extent to which they achieve their objectives depend on the skills of those involved and the extent to which their habitus is aligned with the habitus of the various fields in which they engage. It is thus common, for example, to see those deeply involved within an artistic arena having neither the understanding nor the appreciation of how to engage in fields demanding different modes of behaviour and presentation. Appeals for initial capital support may be denied, not because of a lack of originality in a creative idea but due to a failure to understand the discipline of a different field and accommodate this. Even where these roles are differentiated to accommodate this, in the separation of artistic director and managing director, for example, tensions may become internal to an organization, as demands, priorities, motivations, and incentives diverge. Figure 9.1 identifies the complexity involved in addressing and negotiating capital in its various guises as part of an ongoing process of 'playing the game'—that is, recognizing the structure and composition of capital of the individual or organization, understanding the field in which the individual or organization is positioned in terms of the structure and composition of its capital, while manoeuvring to ensure that the symbolic standing of the individual or organization is enhanced, to secure a more prominent position within its domain. It is these ongoing enhancements of various forms of capital and the manoeuvrings internal to the field that these engender, as well as changes in broader dominant political and economic fields, that provide the constant change and development of the area to ensure that the criteria used in evaluating worth, be this the recognition of performance art in national art prizes, computer games as part of screen awards, or financial rewards, favour those individuals or organizations 'playing the game'.

CONCLUSIONS

So what are the advantages of a capital-based approach? Conceptually, it identifies the range of factors that have to be addressed in any analysis of a cultural or creative endeavour. Such an 'economy of practices' would focus on how dimensions of capital are understood in a field; how they influence the positions of agents and inform their strategies; the balances that have to be sought and accommodated between various capitals; and how these are played out both in relation to each other and in broader power relations. It provides a necessary understanding for any detailed examination of the securing of symbolic cultural capital depicted in specific case analyses of creators, the habitus of practitioners, and the field in which they operate. Practically, these elements of capital and their interrelationship provide a useful aide-memoire for individual practitioners, small and medium-sized enterprises (SMEs), and cultural organizations, identifying all the factors which contribute to a thriving and successful CCI sector at the field level, while helping those within the creative sphere understand their assets, value, and potential. Politically, it helps address the 'good faith' arguments that are mounted in support of the arts and CCI. In an era when funding for civic cultural activities is coming under increasing strain, public sector–supported cultural provision commonly uses economic impact data to help substantiate its claims about the value of cultural investment. Often this is at the expense of other voices which report on the value of civic cultural provision for their communities, and its role in building social networks and cultural capital. Bourdieu's framework transcends the culture/economic dichotomy that bedevils this debate and frequently leads to impasse. Within this broader framework, there is the potential for an analysis of the 'full picture' (Hines 1988), questioning the neglect of the other dimensions of capital, too often dismissed as externalities. This broader capitals framework thus provides a response to those arguments that rely solely on the economic impact of the arts and cultural industries. Reflecting the crudely quantitative base that this approach often exemplifies, why, within this broader framework, attend to only a quarter of the picture? It is to recognize that the classifications and categories used in debate are a profoundly political exercise. If we live in an environment where capital is valued at the expense of other criteria, then we might at least extend debate to include all forms of capital—that accounted for not only in exchange but also in acquisition, maintenance, and enhancement. A more sophisticated analysis might go further and add depreciation into its assessment: what is lost through, and what is the cost of, not building and maintaining capital in all its dimensions?

NOTE

1. I do not address here more general criticisms of Bourdieu's work—for example, his emphasis on binary oppositions of cultural and economic capital to the neglect of other structured relations, most notably, gender—but rather his depiction of capital.

REFERENCES

Adler P., and Kwon, S. 2002. 'Social capital: Prospects for a new concept'. *Academy of Management Review*, 27(1): 17–40.
Beasley-Murray, J. 2000. 'Value and capital in Bourdieu and Marx'. In N. Brown and I. Szeman (eds.), *Pierre Bourdieu: Fieldwork in culture*. Lanham, MD: Rowman and Littlefield, 100–119.
Bourdieu, P. 1977. *Outline of a theory of practice*. Cambridge: Cambridge University Press.
Bourdieu, P. 1979. 'Symbolic power'. *Critique of Anthropology*, 4: 77–85.
Bourdieu, P. 1980. 'The production of belief'. *Media, Culture and Society*, 2: 261–293.
Bourdieu, P. 1984. *Distinction*. London: Routledge & Kegan Paul.
Bourdieu, P. 1985. 'The social space and the genesis of groups'. *Theory and Society*, 14(6): 723–744.
Bourdieu, P. 1986. 'The forms of capital'. In J. Richardson (ed.), *Handbook of theory and research for the sociology of education*. New York: Greenwood, 241–258.
Bourdieu, P. 1987. 'What makes a social class? On the theoretical and practical existence of groups'. *Berkeley Journal of Sociology*, 32: 1–18.
Bourdieu, P. 1988. *Homo Academicus*. Cambridge: Polity.
Bourdieu, P. 1990. *The logic of practice*. Stanford, CA: Stanford University Press.
Bourdieu, P. 1993a. *The field of cultural production*. New York: Columbia University Press.
Bourdieu, P. 1993b. 'Sociologist in question'. In *Sociology in question*. London: SAGE, 20–35.
Bourdieu, P. 1998. *Practical reason*. Cambridge: Polity Press
Bourdieu, P. 2000. *Pascalian meditations*. Cambridge: Polity Press.
Bourdieu, P. 2005. *The social structures of the economy*. Cambridge: Polity.
Bourdieu, P., and Wacquant, L. 1992. *An invitation to reflexive sociology*. Chicago, IL: University of Chicago Press.
Brubaker, R. 2004. 'Rethinking classical theory'. In D. Swartz and V. Zolberg (eds.), *After Bourdieu*. Dordrecht: Kluwer Academic, 25–64.
DiMaggio, P. 1979. 'On Pierre Bourdieu'. *American Journal of Sociology*, 84(6): 1460–1474.

Friedland, R. 2009. 'The endless fields of Pierre Bourdieu'. *Organization*, 3(4): 209–339.
Guillory, J. 2000. 'Bourdieu's refusal'. In N. Brown and I. Szeman (eds.), *Pierre Bourdieu: Fieldwork in culture*. Lanham, MD: Rowman and Littlefield, 19–43.
Hines, R. 1988. 'Financial accounting: In communicating reality, we construct reality'. *Accounting, Organization and Society*, 13(3): 251–261.
Lebaron, F. 2001. 'Towards a new critique of economic discourse'. *Theory, Culture and Society*, 18(5): 123–129.
Lebaron, F. 2003. 'Pierre Bourdieu: Economic models against economism'. *Theory and Society*, 32: 551–565.
Liénard, G., Servais, E., and Bailey, A. 1979. 'Practical sense'. *Critique of Anthropology*, 4: 209–219.
Moore, R. 2008. 'Capital'. In M. Grenfell (ed.), *Pierre Bourdieu: Key concepts*. Durham: Acumen, 101–117.
Nicolini, D. 2013. *Practice theory, work and organization*. Oxford: Oxford University Press.
Savage, M., Warde, A., and Devine, F. 2005. 'Capitals, assets, and resources: Some critical issues'. *British Journal of Sociology*, 56: 31–47.
Svendsen, G., and Svendsen, G. 2005. 'On the wealth of nations: Bourdieu economics and social capital'. In D. Swartz and V. Zolberg (eds.), *After Bourdieu*. Dordrecht: Kluwer Academic, 239–266.
Swartz, D., and Zolberg, V. 2004. (Eds.) *After Bourdieu*. Dordrecht: Kluwer Academic.
Swedberg, R. 2010. 'The economic sociologies of Pierre Bourdieu'. *Cultural Sociology*, 5(1): 1–18.
Townley, B. 2015. 'Bourdieu and organizational theory: A ghostly apparition?' In P. Adler, P. du Gay, M. Reed, and G. Morgan (eds.), *Oxford handbook of sociology, social theory and organization studies: Contemporary currents*. Oxford: Oxford University Press, 39–63.

10 Strategies of Women Managers in Sport Organisations
A Way of Subversion or Reproduction of the Existing Gendered Field?

Mustafa Şahin Karaçam and Canan Koca

INTRODUCTION

Even though there has been a significant increase in the number of women managers over the past several decades (Powell, 1999), the vast majority of senior management positions have been held by men rather than women throughout the world (Cinar, 2001; Growe and Montgomery, 2000; Stelter, 2002). Studies on under-representation of women in sport organisations have also suggested that there are still far fewer women than men in senior positions in sport organisations in Canada (Hall, Cullen, and Slack, 1990), Germany (Pfister and Radtke, 2009), Scandinavian countries (Ottesen et al., 2010), and the US (Acosta and Carpenter, 2012). For instance, there are low percentages of women managers in sport organisations in Scandinavian countries: 25 percent in Denmark, 26 percent in Sweden, and 31 percent in Norway (Ottesen et al., 2010). This marginalisation is worse for women sport managers in Turkey (5 percent) (Koca, Arslan, and Aşçı, 2011). These studies show that senior management positions in sport are primarily a male preserve, and numerically and culturally the chronic marginalisation of women in management positions in sport organisations is a long-standing and widespread phenomenon in the world.

There has been a plethora of research on the barriers to women's advancement in management positions in sport organisations, yet little is known about the strategies used by women managers who have broken the glass ceiling in sport organisations to acquire a position in a male-dominated field. Therefore, the purpose of this chapter is to examine the experiences of women managers in Turkish sport organisations by the use of Bourdieu's theory and thus to contribute to the explanation of the marginalisation of women in management positions in sport organisations where gender inequality is an institutionalised practice. Firstly, we will analyse the sport organisation as a social field to better understand the women managers' gendered experiences as well as their strategies to accumulate more capital to gain legitimacy within the field. Then, we will discuss thoroughly how their individual strategies locate them within the field and whether their strategies contribute to the reproduction of the existing gendered field. In attempting to achieve the purpose of the study, we did in-depth interviews with nine women sport managers holding middle and senior manager positions at Turkish sport organisations.

In this study, we employed Bourdieu's comprehensive and relational approach to social realities. In this sense, we will argue that Bourdieu's relational approach drawing on his concepts (field, capital, and habitus) provides a multilayered analysis that positions the sport organisation within its wider sociocultural and institutional context, while acknowledging its micro-level realities. This multilayered analysis is useful because "sport organisations are multilevel entities that both shape and are shaped by myriad factors" (Cunningham, 2010, p. 396). In the organisation and management literature, Bourdieu's opus is commonly used for the conceptualisation/investigation of complex phenomena such as gender and racial inequality, diversity, marginalisation, reproduction, and organisational/institutional change. In this chapter we employed Bourdieu's theory to examine the gender inequality, marginalisation of women, and reproduction of inequality within Turkish sport organisations. For doing this, we used succession/subversion strategies deployed by agents to struggle for power and senior position-taking, in order to illustrate the agents' position-taking within Turkish sport organisations, depending on their habitus, capitals accumulated, and field dynamics. A similar approach was applied to universities in Austria in this book (see Hofbauer et al., this volume).

The contribution of this chapter is multi-fold. First, we will contribute to the existing literature on under-representation of women in management by generating insights into a different sociocultural context, which is Turkey as a non-European country. Second, the chapter makes contributions to the empirical investigations based on Bourdieu's theory of action by elucidating how the sport management field is the repercussion of broader social, cultural, and political circumstances. Third, we will contribute to enriching organisation studies and to the understanding of existing gender inequality in terms of the sport management context. Finally, we hope to contribute to the theoretical ground by particularly bringing together Bourdieu's master concepts in a relational and multilayered sense.

This chapter initially begins with an overview of the social and cultural context of Turkey and continues with the contextualisation of sport organisations as a potentially powerful cultural arena for the perpetuation of the ideology of male dominance (Connell, 1987; Cunningham, 2008; Messner, 2002). In the following, we make a brief introduction to some of the theoretical tools of Bourdieu. In the methodology section, we illustrate the study context, interviews, data collection, and data analysis. Finally, we discuss the findings in light of the theoretical framework and summarise the chapter.

SOCIOCULTURAL CONTEXT OF TURKEY

Turkey, like most countries, has an over-representation of men in top management positions (Kabasakal et al., 2011). It can be argued that Turkey, although it maintains a secular state structure, has been steadily turned into a conservative and traditionalist country through the recent state policies and that this fact resulted in the deepening of gender inequality (Acar and Altunok, 2013). The Global Gender Gap Report 2013 of the World Economic Forum states that Turkey ranks 120th out of 136 countries; it compared the percentage of women among legislators, senior officials, and managers in 114 countries, and Turkey ranked 104th, with only 10 percent of these positions being held by women. According to 2012 figures, the labour force participation rate of women is only 29 percent, while that of men is 71 percent (Turkish Statistical Institute, 2013). Unfortunately, the percentage of women both in the labour force and in the upper echelons of organisations has been more or less stable over the years in Turkey.

In her very recent review of the evolution of women's employment in Turkey through the course of nearly 60 years of economic modernisation, Ilkkaracan (2012) has shown that the patriarchal contract has been enhanced through the legal and social security framework as well as the virtual lack of any legal or institutional work-family reconciliation mechanisms. Özbilgin, Tatlı, and Küskü (2005) also argued that Turkish state policies encouraging female employment in professional occupations did not question the traditional family ideology positioning women as the prime domestic workers, and hence left the deeply rooted patriarchal assumptions unchanged. Furthermore, within the changing social structure of Turkey, the daily lives of women are identified with domestic responsibilities, they are expected to have more children, and their lives/bodies are attempted to be controlled by confining them to motherhood, especially through the recent legislative steps (e.g. anti-abortion law proposals in 2013). As a result, the cultural and political atmospheres of Turkey contribute to confine women to culturally and politically accepted domestic labours, as well as shut women off from public spaces, such as sport organisations, as coaches, athletes, and managers in particular.

SPORT (SPORT ORGANISATION) AS A SOCIAL FIELD

Many researchers indicated that sport organisations are often fields that reproduce traditional gender roles and male dominance (Cunningham, 2008; Shaw, 2006). As Cunningham (2008, p. 137) argues, "gender inequality is an institutionalized practice within sport organizations", and the levels of gender inequality, such as the access to middle and upper managerial positions, career appraisal, and progression opportunities in management, are exaggerated within sport and leisure services, in which the legacy of male-dominated provision relative to other service sectors is more pronounced (Aitchison, 2005). Therefore, sport more than any other context provides a unique area that enables systematic reinforcement of the ideology of male superiority and resistance to the inclusion of women. On the other hand, it has profound social consequences outside the sporting arena; thus it seems imperative to understand the factors that affect women's under-representation in sport.

As Bourdieu (1991) argues, any field, first and foremost, is characterised by social activity and discourse. The centrality of the body and physical performance to sporting activity makes sport and sport organisations a particularly powerful cultural setting for the construction and confirmation of gendered discourses. It is well established that dominant discourses about sport valorise masculine qualities, such as mental and physical toughness and competitiveness (Messner, 2002), and that dominant discourses have always been allied with the discourses associated with managerial roles in sport organisations (Knoppers and Anthonissen, 2008). As this institutionalised and deeply embedded masculinity within organisations favours men, it definitely restricts women's access to management positions in sport organisations.

This chapter focuses on women manager's experiences in Turkish sport organisations. Although Turkish women's participation and achievements in sporting activities have increased in recent years in national and international contexts, women are still significantly under-represented in all positions (e.g. athlete, coach, and manager) in the Turkish sport field (Koca and Hacisoftaoglu, 2010). In all Turkish sport organisations, 5 percent of the management positions were occupied by women and 95 percent were occupied by men. This under-representation of women can be explained by several factors, such as masculine domination, described earlier, traditional stereotyped gender role beliefs, pressure regarding their role in their families, less attention from sport-governing bodies to sport for women, and negative attitudes towards women managers in sport organisations, which have all discouraged women in Turkey from participating in the sport field (Koca, Arslan, and Aşçı, 2011; Koca and Hacisoftaoglu, 2010).

In the following section, we will outline the Bourdieu's concepts, particularly with respect to how they help us make sense of strategies used by women managers.

THEORETICAL FRAMEWORK

Bourdieu's sociology has attracted a great deal of scholarly attention in organisational studies recently. In spite of this scholarly attention, criticism of the existing literature of organisational studies using Bourdieusian sociology is centred upon mainly two points: (1) the lack of empirical studies: the strength of any conceptual framework in the social sciences lies in its ability to generate new empirical investigations (Swartz, 2008) and (2) the lack of ensembling of Bourdieu's master concepts in a relational sense (Emirbayer and Johnson, 2008). As these scholars discussed, Bourdieu's sociological approach is used by borrowing piecemeal from his work to investigate the organisational area, but his theory of practice draws its strength from its relational perspective. From this point of view, Bourdieu's concepts of capital at the individual level, habitus at the meso level, and the field at the macro level of analysis (Özbilgin and Tatlı, 2005) will provide us a multilayered and relational analysis while examining experiences of women managers in Turkish sport organisations.

In Bourdieu's framework, fields are semi-autonomous social spaces governed by their own rules and regularities within (Bourdieu and Wacquant, 1992). Each field, functioning according to its own inner logic, is occupied by agents who implicitly acknowledge the rules of the field through the very act of playing the game (Bourdieu and Wacquant, 1992). In doing so, agents can increase the total amount of capitals (Bourdieu, 1987). Capitals function as weapons in the field, and distribution of capitals defines the power relations and the positions of agents in the hierarchy within the field (Bourdieu, 1977). Therefore, agents can be positioned in dominant or subordinated positions in a field based on the types and volumes of capitals. However, not only capitals but also habitus operates the position of agents in the field. Habitus is formed through the past experiences of agents and feeds their present perceptions and actions (Bourdieu, 1977, p. 95). Habitus of each agent within the field, which is formed under specific past conditions, generates a sense of possible position-takings. Agents with habitus least well-suited for the contestations specific to that field are more likely to occupy the subordinated positions in the field, while agents with the most-suited habitus are more likely to occupy the dominant positions.

In the ongoing struggle in a field for any forms of capitals and positions, agents can implement a variety of strategies to change their positions in the field and power relations. Bourdieu (1993a) speaks of three types of field strategies: *conservation, succession,* and *subversion.* Those who hold dominant positions in a field employ conservation strategies to preserve the principle of hierarchisation, the distribution and valuation of species of capitals, that happens to be most favourable to them and to safeguard or even enhance their position within this hierarchy (Bourdieu, 1993a). Those who have less or no seniority may employ succession strategies to access dominant positions or for acceptance and competition for power. Meanwhile those who are the dominated actors adopt subversion strategies to transform the field's system of authority, including its relative valuation of different capitals and, potentially, the very rules of the game according to which it ordinarily functions, to their own benefit (Bourdieu, 1993a). Additionally, while elucidating the cases of reproduction or transformation of a field through the strategies of agents, the concept of doxa should be taken into account. Doxa is "a particular point of view, the point of view of the dominant, which represents and imposes itself as a universal point of view" (Bourdieu, 1998: 57). Therefore, doxa reproduces the unquestioned common sense in the field "which tends to the naturalization of its own arbitrariness" (Bourdieu, 1977: 164). In this sense, agents enacting the 'doxa' may reproduce directly the doxa itself, and indirectly so do the field and habitus whatever agents' position in a field and their strategies.

Relational employment of Bourdieusian analysis would provide us a more dynamic framework to investigate women managers' strategies to take positions in the field as well as to investigate the gender inequalities, subordination of women particularly, and how these inequalities are reproduced. Based on Bourdieu's theory, Turkish sport organisations were addressed as a 'social field' where male domination is traditionally an institutionalised practice and were viewed in the broader cultural and political circumstances of Turkey. In the conservative culture of Turkish sport organisations, practices and capitals of this field were used to discuss the positions and strategies of women sport managers.

METHODOLOGY

Study Context: Turkish Sport Organisations

This chapter focuses on the gendered experiences of Turkish women managers within two Turkish sport organisations (TSOs): Turkish Sport Federations (TSFs) and Turkish Olympic Committee (TOC). However, another organisation, General Directorate of Sport (GDS), was mentioned in the chapter since GDS is the supreme governing body for all sports (mass and elite sport) and holds the authority to make all arrangements and important decisions about sport events in Turkey, although there was no woman manager in the middle or senior position at GDS at the time of the study. Additionally GDS has never had a woman president since its foundation in 1938.

TSFs are autonomous foundations which are subjected to the supervision of General Directorate of Sport (GDS), which is the head of all sport organisations and officiates under the Ministry of Youth and Sport. The president of an autonomous federation is elected among the candidates by the executive board members, sport clubs, and some athletes successful in the international arena. Before the autonomy, the president and general secretary of federations were appointed by GDS. But after the autonomy, the federation president began appointing the general secretary. At the time of the study, only 2 out of 59 federation presidents (Turkish Sailing Federation and Turkish Tennis Federation) and 7 out of 59 general secretaries (11.7 percent) were women.

TOC is a non-governmental organisation which aims to spread the spirit of Olympism throughout the country by collaborating with all institutions related to sport. As it is a voluntary organisation, the president and general secretary are elected by the executive board of TOC. The president of the TOC has always been male since its foundation in 1908. There is only one woman who has served in the senior position, general secretary, in the history of the TOC; she has been on duty since 2003.

Interviewees

In this chapter, we draw on data from a wider study which was conducted between March 2010 and March 2011, exploring gender inequity in sport organisations in Turkey. The wider study is composed of both sexes, but for the purpose of this chapter we applied the data particularly derived from the in-depth interviews with nine women sport managers. These nine women managers were the only women who occupied the middle and senior manager positions in TSFs and TOC at the time of the study. Purposive sampling was used to select interviewees with experience and knowledge (Patton, 2002). Demographic profiles of the interviewees appear in Table 10.1.

Women in this study work at two different TSOs; eight of them are at TSFs and one is at TOC. One of them, Gönül, is the president of the federation, and six of them are general secretaries, the highest position after the presidency. Yeşim and Özge have middle manager positions at Turkish Football Federation. All women have higher levels of education. Seven women are married and two are single. All women have a history of involvement in sports. In addition, only Fatma was appointed to a general secretary position by GDS, while the other women were elected or proposed to their current positions.

Table 10.1 Interviewee profiles

Interviewees	Positions	Education	Marital Status	Involvement in Sport
Yeşim	Coordinator TSF	Business Bachelor	Married	Athlete Track and Field, Volleyball, Kickboxing
Özge	Director TSF	Economics MA	Single	National Athlete Handball
Hazel	General Secretary TOC	Management PHD	Single	National Athlete and Coach Track and Field
Gülay	General Secretary TSF	Public and Media Relations Bachelor	Married 1 kid	Athlete Skiing, Tennis, Water-Skiing, Gymnastic
Fatma	General Secretary TSF	Economics Bachelor	Married 2 kids	Athlete Track and Field
Gülnaz	General Secretary TSF	Sport Science PhD	Married 1 kid	Athlete Volleyball
Yankı	General Secretary TSF	International Relations Bachelor	Married 1 kid	National Athlete Handball
Çiçek	General Secretary TSF	Public Administration MA	Married	Athlete Judo
Gönül	President TSF	Business Bachelor	Married	Athlete Sailing

Data Collection

We developed a semi-structured interview guide which did not represent a rigid document, but rather a flexible evolutionary set of questions (Corbin and Strauss, 2008) in order to gather in-depth knowledge of women's experiences. Interviews aimed at exploring women sport manager's gendered experiences, their thought about gender equity in sport organisations, their carrier path to current positions, barriers which women faced, and strategies implemented by women to achieve middle or senior positions or to remain in their position, as well as to survive in sport management, which is still primarily a male preserve. Women were interviewed at a location of their choice. Interviews lasted for around one hour and were tape-recorded. Each woman was asked to sign a consent form that explained conditions of confidentiality and the interview procedure.

Data Analysis

We transcribed all interviews verbatim and analysed raw data inductively via individual case and content analysis (Patton, 1990). We followed the steps of content analysis: identifying, coding, categorising, classifying, and labelling the primary pattern in data, proposed by Patton (2002). We firstly read all data by making comments and taking shorthand codes in the margins with the aim of developing the coding categories. Then, we reread the data to start the formal coding in a systematic way, depending on the theoretical framework of study. We manually coded the transcriptions independently and compared and discussed similarities and differences. We arrived at a series of codes and categories, and collapsed them into themes. To contribute to the overall credibility of findings, we used an analyst triangulation technique to analyse the same data and compared the findings (Patton, 2002). We also employed a member checking technique and sent the interview transcripts to the women for their review to corroborate/ensure the correctness of the content (Lincoln and Guba, 1985). We employed pseudonyms to protect the identity of the women in this study.

RESULTS AND DISCUSSION

We will discuss the findings under two themes: (1) a gendered field: Turkish sport organisations (TSOs) and (2) strategies implemented by women sport managers at the TSOs. Under the first theme, we will identify the gendered practices, capitals at stake, and women's positions at the TSOs. Under the second theme, we will discuss the women managers' strategies in order to understand how the women could endure within the TSOs.

A Gendered Field: Turkish Sport Organisations (TSOs)

As aforementioned, TSOs are culturally and numerically preserved by men from the past to today. GDS, as the head organisation, has much sharper gender inequity, particularly in senior positions, as Hazel (TOC) and Gülnaz (TSFs) indicate:

> GDS is heavily dominated by men.
> (Hazel, General Secretary)

> You can't see any woman at the GDS. All managers are almost men.
> (Gülnaz, General Secretary)

Besides GDS, interviews reveal that women are the minority at TSFs and TOC, particularly in senior positions. Gönül, president of the Turkish Sailing Federation (TSF), has never seen a woman president throughout her long history in sport management. On the other hand, the majority of stakeholders of TSOs, such as sport club managers, athletes, and coaches, are men. Hazel, who worked as a coach in track and field for seven years, says, "When I wanted to be a coach, people said, 'What are you going to do among so many men?'" because "only 1 of 10 coaches were women". Accordingly Yankı, general secretary of the Wrestling Federation, also says, "There is no woman role-model in wrestling. Besides, the coaches are mostly men."

Gendered Practices at TSOs: "You Would Prepare Meal and Do the Laundry, Madam!"

TSOs, as a field, are composed of practices (Bourdieu, 1992): discursive and material practices. Interviews show that women in the male-dominated TSOs are permanently exposed to discursive practices which emphasise their gendered domestic responsibilities and gendered stereotypes about women in Turkish society. Yeşim, who works at the Football Federation and is the only woman among 756 delegates, states, "*Men identify women with domestic work*" and states how her male colleagues talk to her at a long meeting late at night:

> Ms. Yeşim, it is too late. If you want, we can finish the meeting so you can go home. We can definitely stay longer but you would prepare meal and do the laundry.

In addition to gendered discursive practices, TSOs are intertwined with material practices. Particularly senior positions at TSOs demand long working hours on weekdays and weekends, frequent domestic and foreign trips for sport competitions and meetings, and even carrying heavy sport equipment.

Women we interviewed emphasised that a sport manager would be available at all times for important meetings and work trips. Gülnaz stated they are supposed to work 24/7, adding, "Executive board, supervisory board, and other boards hold the meetings out of working hours (in the weekends) since they use the time they spare from their current jobs".

These women were well aware of ways in which their managerial work could interfere with their domestic life. For example, Fatma, mother of two, was supposed to spend a couple of days out of town and therefore she could not perform her domestic responsibilities:

> Due to the federation travels, I find it difficult to spend the weekends with my family. Federation demands hard-working. I cannot perform my home responsibilities, I can't even cook and all that domestic stuff. My kids demand attention from me but sometimes I can't take care of them.

The expectation of spending many hours in the federation contributed to work-family conflict for women sport managers; however, three women (Hazel, Gönül, Yeşim) who also agreed on the fact that their job requires 24/7 availability did not mention any work-family conflict. Their experiences showed that a commitment to time-consuming work was possible only if they were single or married with no kids.

Despite these material practices within the organisations, TSOs may be seen as gender-neutral. However, we can argue that particularly this 24/7 availability strengthens and institutionalises the gendered division of labour in TSOs. According to the aforementioned gendered scripts prevailing in Turkish society, it is more difficult for women than men to achieve a work-life balance. Consequently, men are much more likely to meet these requirements and form the majority of potential candidates for a management position.

Competing Capitals at the TSOs: One Must Have a Higher Education Firstly and History of Involvement in Sport Secondly

Senior positions at TSOs and TOC, such as executive board membership and presidency, require occupants to have a deal of economic capital. These positions are voluntary, and accordingly Yeşim states, *"sport management is associated with economic power—thus men actively take part in it"*. For example, Gülay indicates the relationships between economic capital and senior positions at the Equestrian Federation:

> Executive board, supervisory board, disciplinary board, and sponsorship board consist of professionals. They all, including our federation president, are running a company.

Additionally, economic capital has great importance for not only presidency but also diverse positions at TSFs. Çiçek illustrates:

> Ice Skating Federation lacks sport complex; therefore sport clubs take into account whether a candidate can provide them with necessary facilities while selecting them for vacant positions. Executive board or president himself/herself is inclined to choose the candidates who can bring economic profits and revenue to federation, arrange sponsorships, make contacts with media and press in the short or long term.

Many researchers found that women's lack of fulfilling the requirement to hold economic capital can often cause them not to be considered as appropriate for managerial positions (Schell and Rodriguez, 2000; Sheridan and Milgate, 2003; Whisenant, Pederson, and Obenour, 2002).

Besides economic capital, cultural capital is the other vital capital at TSOs. As Hazel states, the most remarkable sorts of cultural capital functioning at TSFs and TOC are "having a higher education firstly and the history of involvement in sport secondly (being an insider)". The education levels of almost all women interviewed are quite high; for instance, four of the women managers had higher education degrees from abroad (see Table 10.1). Therefore, we can argue that no matter which TSOs they work for, women's cultural capital helped them get senior positions mostly occupied by men. In this sense, Gülnaz and Hazel are very special examples that show how both sorts of cultural capital function to a certain extent at TSFs and TOC. These two women have a long history of involvement in sport and a higher level of education in sport specifically. Gülnaz is the general secretary of the Turkish Volleyball Federation, which is immensely successful in the national and international arenas. She has a PhD degree in sport sciences as well as a history of involvement in volleyball for 12 years. Gülnaz explains why she was offered the general secretary position:

> I was chosen for the general secretary position due to primarily my education on sport, in other words, due to opportunities provided by my PhD. It was so important to have an education in one of the leading universities of Turkey. Also, it was crucial to be a former volleyball player.

Likewise, Hazel has a PhD degree in sport management in the US and a long history of involvement in sport as an athlete and a coach at the professional level. She explains why she was offered work at the TOC:

> I was offered to athletic director position at the TOC because I was doing my PhD on sport management and working as a member of organizing committee for 1996 Olympic Games. When members of TOC came to the US for 1996 Olympic Games, they saw my works there and said "would you like to work for us".

It is important to note that intensive commitment to sport is one of the most important qualities of sport managers. For example, Pfister and Radtke (2009) found that a commitment to sport and one's knowledge as an 'insider' seems to be an important precondition for a leadership position in the German sports system. In another study on sport organisations in Scandinavian countries, researchers also found that sport managers should have the necessary insights into "the rules of the game" (Ottesen et al., 2010).

In addition to economic capital and cultural capital, Gönül, the only woman president of the federation, shows that another capital operating at TSOs is social capital. Gönül has neither specific education in sport nor a long history of involvement in sport like others. However, she has a large social network in the national and international arenas. She has worked for the same federation in different positions for 16 years. Throughout these years, Gönül always teamed up with all stakeholders in the federation. She explains how her social capital brought her to the presidency position:

> I always had close relations with the sport club managers, coaches, and athletes. Our friendship has always continued even when I am not the president of the federation. I was elected to presidency of the federation just because we teamed up since 1994.

Gönül is also the vice-president of the International Sailing Federation (ISAF). She explains why she was elected:

> They voted for me because they know me in person. I have done lots of work at the international arena for years, such as organizing the European Sailing Championships in Turkey. Those years enabled me to create personal networks.

At this point, the interviews provide strong evidence of the conversion between capitals possessed by women. Capitals can be converted into one another as well as into valued resources, status, and positions. For instance, women who possess a high level of cultural capital converted it into social capital to a very certain extent. Their cultural capital, particularly involvement in/commitment to sport, allowed them to accumulate a social capital, enabling them to acquire a middle/senior position. Likewise, economic capital functioning as a symbolic capital was converted into social capital, as well as higher status and position, notably in TSFs. Therefore, when it was perceived that women possessed a lesser amount and fewer forms of capitals than men, they were excluded/marginalised within TSOs.

Women's Position at TSOs: A Woman Can Be a Secretary but Not a General Secretary

The interviews show that positions held by women at TSOs are mostly lower positions, such as secretariat and clerical positions. As Yeşim outlines,

"There are women at secretariat positions but not at the senior management positions at the football federation" because "management is not seen as a woman thing at this federation. If I ran for presidency, I would not be elected". Likewise, a real-life experience by Gülnaz materialised what Yeşim put forward and revealed how the common view of general secretary positions at TSOs favours men:

> Once I got a phone call and my fellow secretary transferred the call to me. When I picked up the phone, the voice asked me to transfer the call to the general secretary, thinking that the transfer failed. Because I am a woman.

According to Gülnaz, such a conversation took place due to the understanding that takes for granted that men hold general secretary positions (doxa), stating, "A woman can be a secretary but not a general secretary". It is quite striking because volleyball is one of the few federations where women athletes outnumber men. It should not be forgotten that the women senior managers interviewed represent only 5 percent of all management positions at TSOs. Besides, these women hold a high volume of economic, cultural, or social capitals. In view of the sociocultural context and women's position in Turkey, these women represent the minority of women in Turkey. Therefore, the majority of women are likely to be excluded/marginalised from senior positions in TSOs.

Strategies Implemented by Women Sport Managers at TSOs

Strategies implemented by agents depend on their positions in the field (Bourdieu and Wacquant, 1992); therefore, women, as subordinated/dominated in gendered TSOs, will face two options: *succession strategies* or *subversion strategies* (Bourdieu, 1993b). We will discuss the strategies of women managers at TSOs under two subheadings: succession strategies ("You have to work at least two times more than your male colleagues") and subversion strategies ("I consider myself as an activist").

Succession Strategies: "You Have to Work at Least Two Times More Than Your Male Colleagues"

Women interviewed mostly used a variety of succession strategies through their carriers for acceptance and competition for power within the field (Bourdieu, 1993b). As aforementioned, women managers hold a considerable amount of cultural capital. As Yankı points out, "all women sport managers are always highly educated. I have never seen women managers without bachelor's degree but saw men managers who were graduates of primary school". We can discuss women's higher education levels as a succession strategy implemented by women per se to survive in sport management; however, women still have to work much harder than men to have power in the field, to be accepted, and to prove themselves. Hazel (TOC) remarks,

> When I look at men and women managers, I can easily say that we need to be twice more well-qualified to achieve the same positions than men do. Even if we achieve those positions, we have to work at least two times more than our male colleagues and prove ourselves as women.

Yeşim, working as a director at the Football Federation, dominated numerically and culturally by men, states,

> I have to work twice harder than men. Because, I, as a woman, have no a chance to fail even once. If I do, men laugh up their sleeve.

Yeşim is in a relatively tougher position as the only woman among 756 delegates at the federation. She was frequently neglected and dropped out of conversations because she is perceived as an outsider to football culturally and historically and for her male colleagues, "football does not make sense to a woman". Thus Yeşim "started going to football matches" in order to get familiar with the field as her succession strategy. Moreover, she has to cope with gendered material practices within the federation, such as "having to work and attend meetings till late night":

> I started to bring along my husband to football matches and even to some meetings. So I can fix the balance between home and work with the help of my husband.

According to some women, they achieved managerial positions thanks to their personal qualities, which are in parallel with some managerial qualities, such as courage, risk-taking, action-orientation, and extensive social networks. When it is considered that these qualities are associated with masculinity (Hovden, 2000; Knoppers and Anthonissen, 2008), we can speculate that they were adopted by women managers as a kind of succession strategy to keep up with the requirements of their positions. Women state the following:

> If I am here today, it is only my courage and self-confidence that provided it.
>
> (Yeşim, Director, TSF)

> If you would like to improve your position, you need to make self-sacrifices and take risks when necessary. I am here today since I have took risks. If I had not done, I would have still been a coach in a sport club.
>
> (Hazel, General Secretary, TOC)

Some tasks assigned by the federation covers heavy/hard work for a woman. But it does not matter for me because I have a masculine nature, I can handle them.

(Çiçek, General Secretary, TSF)

Succession strategies adopted by women depend on women's positions (Bourdieu and Wacquant, 1992), and moving up the hierarchy of field positions (position-taking) allows an agent to adopt new strategies (Kitchin and David, 2013). Therefore Gönül, occupant of the highest senior position, implemented more than one strategy, such as toughness and developing a social network. For example, she states, while *table thumping*,

I don't leave anything I am in charge of unfinished. Some of my colleagues say I am too tough but I am not *that kind of man* who revolves around a problem and loses time. I don't know—maybe my colleagues have never seen me as a woman. I and my male colleagues have always worked together, shoulder to shoulder.

Gönül is aware of the importance of social networks. Therefore she developed close social networks with stakeholders such as sport club managers, coaches, and athletes and extended her networks for contestation of power in the field. Even though she was not the president of the federation, she always kept in touch with the stakeholders. Likewise, Gönül, as the vice-president of the ISAF, was responsible for the grassroots in emerging countries. Thus she had the chance to develop social networks in the international arena to support her future plans/careers in the long term, as she explains: "Due to my position at the ISAF, I had developed both local and regional networks. These networks started in sport but will continue in a different context in future".

In addition to various succession strategies used by women, Fatma implemented a distinct strategy which can be discussed as both a succession and subversion strategy. After Fatma worked as a typist at the GDS for a while, she decided to write a petition to her superior explaining her success in her position and demanding a promotion to the general secretary position. Her strategy succeeded and moved her to the general secretary position. Fatma says that "when I started to work at the federation, I had never thought I would become the general secretary" because 40 women, including Fatma, started work at the GDS at the same time, but only two of them could manage to make it to the general secretary position. According to Fatma, "It is not because they are incapable or lazy" but because of the gendered structure and male hegemony at TSOs which hardly allow women to occupy higher positions.

On the one hand, Fatma's strategy can be seen as a succession strategy because it brought more capitals and a higher position to her within the field. But when we consider that succession strategies are risk-free investments (Mander, 1987), her strategy can be seen as a subversion strategy for it challenges the legitimacy somehow and has a risk of failure.

Subversion Strategies: "I Consider Myself as an Activist"

Although the women managers interviewed may be seen as occupying dominant positions at TSOs, they are subordinated/marginalised heterogeneously within. Therefore women, as the dominated dominants of TSOs, are more liable to deploy subversion strategies (Wacquant, 1998, p. 222). In our study, subversion strategies were deployed by three women managers: Yankı, Gönül, and Hazel. These women are the most powerful women of the group.

Wrestling is accepted as the ancestor sport for men in Turkey and perceived as a male-appropriate sport. Male athletes, coaches, and managers overwhelmingly outnumber women in wrestling in Turkey. According to Yankı, "there is not any woman role model in wrestling", and she explains the reasons underlying this:

> Girls around 13–14 years old participate in wrestling but they drop out of wrestling when they turn around eighteen years old. We don't have any medal in senior women category because women wrestlers are getting married and quit wrestling. Also women's low participation level in wrestling is rooted in the religion. As well, none of Turkish fathers want their daughter to get hurt.

Therefore, Yankı employed a subversion strategy to modify the existing culture of wrestling and challenge the doxa: women don't wrestle or wrestling is not for a woman. She ran a campaign called 'Father, Send Me to Wrestling' for the federation:

> We started with coaches. Four or five coaches are coming to wrestling trainings with their daughters. Then we appointed wrestling coaches to some schools in eastern side of Turkey. Afterwards we get in contact with families to persuade them. Because none of them wants to send daughters to wrestling. However, we will overcome this mentality.

The subversion strategy adopted by Yankı presented a challenge to the naturalisation and arbitrariness in the established orders of wrestling and society in the broader extent. It may seem like her subversion strategy doesn't directly challenge the existing gender inequity in sport organisations, but it can be argued that it does indirectly because the subversion strategy can be seen as claiming to subvert the assumption of men's superior position (doxa) in wrestling and Turkish society.

Hazel employed several subversion strategies; one is related to the TOC and the other one is to promote women's sport participation in Turkey. Hazel thinks that she is somehow responsible for the gender equity. She states,

> When I started working at TOC, I was the only woman but there are two more women on the executive board now. I talked with the members of

commissions which has no women members about the importance of women representation. Now they are working to increase the numbers of women in their commissions.

However, according to Hazel, "if we cannot increase the numbers of women at the grassroots, then we cannot move them up to senior management positions". Therefore, the other subversion strategy she employed is to develop and strengthen the grassroots. She is working on social projects aiming at increasing girls' and women's participation in sports because she says, "I consider myself as an activist".

Hazel links under-representation of women at TSOs and in sports to the sociocultural context of Turkey. As she indicates, "there are barriers stemming from the culture and religion which prevent girls and women from participating in sports". She also noted that women are not raised to be powerful, dynamic, and passionate about making a career in Turkey. In this sense, Hazel's subversion strategies are more likely in order to challenge the taken-for-granted assumptions and beliefs associated with women in Turkish society (doxa) and transform the essence of the society. Likewise, Gönül employed variety of subversion strategies at the TSF. Whenever she came across or got together with the president of other federations, she questioned them about the gender inequity in their own federation by saying teasingly,

> Is not there even just a woman who can be assigned in your executive board? Have a heart!

Gönül is a strong supporter of gender quota regulation because according to her "as long as gender quota regulation was implemented mandatorily, nobody would open the sport organizations' door to women". As she says, "*male* chauvinism dominates the tradition of sailing (doxa) and girls are subject to discrimination at sport clubs". Therefore, Gönül implemented a subversion strategy to a great extent thanks to her high position (president): she changed the award regulation of the federation in order to push the local sport clubs to treat girls and boys equally. Before the new award regulation, the federation used to give a monetary award to female medal winners as long as there were at least five sailors in the female division. But afterwards, the federation started to give monetary awards to the female medal winners without a number requirement. She states how her subversion challenged the 'male chauvinism' at the sport clubs:

> Sailing clubs used to give the priority to boys and give the better equipment to boys. By doing so they used to marginalize girls. But when we decided to give monetary award to female medal winners, clubs started to bring girls to competitions.

CONCLUDING REMARKS

In this chapter, drawing on Bourdieu's approach, we examined the experiences of women managers at TSOs, with a particular focus on their strategies to accumulate more capital to gain legitimacy within the field, in order to understand the marginalisation of women in management positions of sport organisations. We applied a multilayered analysis that positions TSOs within their wider sociocultural and institutional context, while acknowledging their micro-level realities.

Although TSOs are seen as gender-neutral, interviews showed that TSOs are gendered social fields in favour of men, with elements such as discursive/material practices, capitals, and positions. Similar to the findings of previous sport studies (Knoppers and Anthonissen, 2008; Hovden, 2000), our research has shown that discursive and material practices at Turkish sport organisations are infused with masculine characteristics and they definitely restrict women's access to management positions. The 24/7 availability, which is the most emphasised material practice, has been shown by many sport scientists to be deeply rooted in sport organisations, has specific consequences for women, especially for women with families who are supposed to successfully integrate work and family obligations, and has led many women to leave their careers in sport organisations (Hovden, 2000; Pfister and Radtke, 2009).

The interviews revealed that economic capital is highly required for presidency due to it being a voluntary position. Since women don't possess economic capital for senior positions, they are not at that position, except for one. Cultural capital (education and involvement in sport) is the most robust capital for women managers in this study. However, cultural capital operates as a marginalising tool for women within the sociocultural context of Turkey because women managers are among the minority (5 percent) at TSOs and in the Turkish society (10 percent).

In conjunction with cultural capital, social capital is another striking power resource. Eight of the women were either chosen for or offered their current positions with the help of their social capital. As already mentioned, since women are usually not as deeply rooted in the world of sport in Turkey as men are, they do not have the same extensive networks. Therefore social capital can be more influential for men than women in sport organisations (Sagas and Cunningham, 2004).

The intersection between capitals held by and positions occupied by women managers determines the women's strategies in the field. The data analysis revealed that women managers at gendered TSOs employed different succession and subversion strategies of position-taking in the field. Some of the strategies pursued by women managers at TSOs may reproduce or transform the field-specific doxa—in Bourdieu's term, the point of view of the dominant, which represents and imposes itself as a universal point of view (Bourdieu, 1993b). However, the women interviewed mostly used a variety of succession strategies through their carriers for acceptance and competition for power within the field.

The experiences of women managers showed that women are widely considered to be outsiders to the field of sport, in particular to football, which in Bourdieu's terms relates to doxa, 'taken for granted' perceptions of power relations. Outsiders, or in Bourdieu's terms, those least endowed with capital, are inclined towards succession strategies, which result in reinforcing the doxa in the field. For example, as a manager in football, Yeşim employed succession strategies, such as trying to be an insider and balancing work-family responsibilities.

The type of agents' succession strategy depends on the gendered structure of sport organisations (sport-related gendered discursive/material practices). Many women managers at TSOs are also trying to perform the managerial duties associated with masculinity, such as being tough and carrying heavy equipment, as a succession strategy. With reference to several studies on women in male-dominated sports (Kay and Laberge, 2004; Sisjord, 2009), we argue that women attempt to improve their position within the field hierarchy by pursuing succession strategies to accumulate physical capital in the form of toughness.

Some of the strategies pursued by women managers at TSOs may transform the field-specific doxa which represents and imposes itself as a universal point of view (Bourdieu, 1993a). We found that only three women managers who are dominated, dominant actors adopted this type of subversion strategy to transform the field (in)directly. These women are inclined towards subversion strategies which result in challenging and transforming the existing gendered structure of the field (e.g. changing the award regulation of the federation in favour of women sailors, encouraging the commissions to include women members).

The indirect way of transforming the field is applying subversive strategies which result in challenging the taken-for-granted gendered beliefs about girls' and women's sport participation in Turkish society (doxa). Since the representation of women sport managers in sport organisations is highly associated with the level of women's sport participation, the subversion strategies of these women quite likely aimed at increasing the number of women athletes and coaches. For example, Yankı employed a subversion strategy (running a campaign to promote girls' participation in wrestling) to modify the existing culture of wrestling and challenge the doxa that women don't wrestle or wrestling is not for a woman. As aforementioned, this subversion strategy can be seen as claiming to subvert the assumption of men's superior position (doxa) in wrestling and Turkish society.

In conclusion, the theory of Bourdieu has allowed us to understand how macro-, meso-, and micro-level influences can impact the women managers' strategies to occupy positions in sport organisations where gender inequality is an institutionalised practice and how these strategies contribute to the reproduction and/or the transformation of gendered doxa in the field and society. This chapter gave a comprehensive insight into the literature on under-representation of women in management from the sociocultural context of Turkey, a non-European country, and strengthened the empirical investigations based on Bourdieu's theory of action by elucidating how the sport management field is the repercussion of broader social, cultural, and political circumstances. In addition, this chapter made considerable contributions to organisation studies and to the understanding of existing gender inequality in terms of the sport management context. Finally the chapter, bringing together Bourdieu's master concepts in a relational and multilayered sense, enriched the theoretical ground as well as relational sociology.

Under-representation of women in senior management positions in sport organisations as well as other management fields is a complex and intersectional issue which requires many relational and layered studies to cope with the inequalities within. Based on our study, we can suggest that gender inequalities in sport organisations should be challenged at the macro-meso-micro level. Policymakers should consider women's status to a greater extent to develop more inclusive and non-sexist equality policies so as to confront the taken-for-granted inequality/superiority embedded in the very core of daily life.

REFERENCES

Acar, F., and Altunok, G. (2013) The 'politics of intimate' at the intersection of neo-liberalism and neo-conservatism in contemporary Turkey. *Women's Studies International Forum*, 41, 14–23.

Acosta, R. V., and Carpenter, L. J. (2012) Women in intercollegiate sport: A longitudinal, national study, thirty five update 1977–2012. Available at: www.acostacarpenter.org. [Accessed 10 April 2014].

Aitchison, C. C. (2005) Feminist and gender research in sport and leisure management: Understanding the social-cultural nexus of gender-power relations. *Journal of Sport Management*, 19(4), 422–441.

Bourdieu, P. (1977) *Outline of a theory of practice*. Cambridge: Cambridge University Press.

Bourdieu, P. (1987). What makes a social class? On the theoretical and practical existence of groups. *Berkeley Journal of Sociology*, 32, 1–18.

Bourdieu, P. (1991) *Language and symbolic power*. Cambridge: Polity Press.

Bourdieu, P. (1992) The practice of reflexive sociology (the Paris workshop). In P. Bourdieu and L.J.D. Wacquant (eds.), *An invitation to reflexive sociology*, Chicago: University of Chicago Press, 216–260.

Bourdieu, P. (1993a) *The field of cultural production*. New York: Columbia University Press.

Bourdieu, P. (1993b) *Sociology in question*. London: SAGE.

Bourdieu, P. (1998) *Practical Reason: On theory of action*. Stanford: Stanford University Press.

Bourdieu, P., and Wacquant, L.J.D. (1992) *An invitation to reflexive sociology*. Chicago: University of Chicago Press.

Cinar, M. (Ed.) (2001) The economics of women and work in the Middle East and North Africa. *Research in the Middle East Economies*, Vol. 4. Greenwich, CT: JAI Press.

Connell, R. W. (1987) *Gender and power: Society, the person and sexual politics*. Cambridge: Polity Press.

Corbin, J., and Strauss, A. (Eds.) (2008) *Basics of qualitative research: Techniques and procedures for developing grounded theory*. 3rd ed. Thousand Oaks: SAGE.

Cunningham, G. B. (2008) Creating and sustaining gender diversity in sport organizations. *Sex Roles*, 58, 136–145.

Cunningham, G. B. (2010) Understanding the under-representation of African American coaches: A multilevel perspective. *Sport Management Review*, 13(4), 395–406.

Emirbayer, M., and Johnson, V. (2008) Bourdieu and organizational analysis. *Theory and Society*, 37(1), 1–44. doi:10.1007/s11186-007-9052-y

Growe, R., and Montgomery, P. (2000) Women and the leadership paradigm: Bridging the gender gap. *National Forum Journal*, 17E, 1–7.

Hall, M. A., Cullen, D., and Slack, T. (1990) The gender structure of national sport organisation. *Sport Canada Occasional Pages*, 12, 1–2.

Hovden, J. (2000) Gender and leadership selection processes in Norwegian sporting organizations. *International Review for the Sociology of Sport*, 35(1), 75–82.

Ilkkaracan, İ. (2012) Why so few women in the labor market in Turkey? *Feminist Economics*, 18(1), 1–37.

Kabasakal, H., Aycan, Z., Karakaş, F., and Maden, C. (2011) Women in management in Turkey. In M. J. Davidson and R. J. Burke (eds.), *Women in management worldwide*. 2nd ed. Surrey, UK: Gower, 317–338.

Kay, J., and Laberge, S. (2004) 'Mandatory equipment': Women in adventure racing. In B. Wheaton (ed.), *Understanding lifestyle sports: Consumption, identity and difference*. London: Routledge, 154–174.

Kitchin, P. J., and David Howe, P. (2013) How can the social theory of Pierre Bourdieu assist sport management research? *Sport Management Review*, 16(2), 123–134.

Knoppers, A., and Anthonissen, A. (2008) Gendered managerial discourses in sport organizations: Multiplicity and complexity. *Sex Roles*, 58(1–2), 93–103.

Koca, C., Arslan, B., and Aşçı, F. H. (2011) Attitudes towards women's work roles and women managers in a sports organization: The case of Turkey. *Gender, Work & Organization*, 18(6), 592–612.

Koca, C., and Hacisoftaoglu, I. (2010) Struggling for empowerment: Sport participation of women and girls in modern Turkey. In T. Benn, G. Pfister, and H. Jawad (eds.), *Muslim women in sport*. Abingdon, UK: Routledge, 154–165.

Lincoln, Y. S., and Guba, E. G. (1985) *Naturalistic inquiry*. Beverly Hills, CA: SAGE.

Mander, M. S. (1987) Bourdieu, the sociology of culture and cultural studies: A critique. *European Journal of Communication*, 2(4), 427–453.

Messner, M. A. (2002) *Taking the field: Women, men, and sports*. Minneapolis: University of Minnesota Press.

Ottesen, L., Skirstad, B., Pfister, G., and Habermann, U. (2010) Gender relations in Scandinavian sport organizations—A comparison of the situation and the policies in Denmark, Norway and Sweden. *Sport in Society*, 13(4), 657–675.

Özbilgin, M., and Tatli, A. (2005) Book review essay: Understanding Bourdieu's contribution to organization and management studies. *Academy of Management Review*, 30(4), 855–869.

Özbilgin, M. F., Tatlı, A., and Küskü, F. (2005) Gendered occupational outcomes: The case of professional training and work in Turkey. In J. Eccles and H. Watt (eds.), *Explaining gendered occupational outcomes*. Michigan: American Psychological Association (APA) Press, 406–449.

Patton, M. Q. (1990) *Qualitative evaluation and research methods*. Beverly Hills, CA: SAGE.

Patton, M. Q. (2002) *Qualitative research and evaluation methods*. 3rd ed. Thousand Oaks, CA: SAGE.

Pfister, G., and Radtke, S. (2009) Sport, women and leadership: Results of a project on executives in German sports organizations. *European Journal of Sports Sciences*, 9(4), 229–243.

Powell, G. N. (Ed.) (1999) *Handbook of gender and work*. Thousand Oaks, CA: SAGE.

Sagas, M., and Cunningham, G. (2004) Does having the right stuff matter? Gender differences in the determinants of career success among intercollegiate athletic administrators. *Sex Roles*, 50, 411–421.

Schell, L. A., and Rodriguez, S. (2000) Our sporting sisters: How male hegemony stratifies women in sport. *Women in Sport and Physical Activity Journal*, 9(1), 15–34.

Shaw, S. (2006) Scratching the back of 'Mr. X': Analyzing gendered social processes in sport organizations. *Journal of Sport Management*, 20(4), 510–534.

Sheridan, A., and Milgate, G. (2003) 'She says, he says': Women's and men's views of the composition of boards. *Women in Management Review*, 18(3), 147–154.

Sisjord, M. K. (2009) Fast-girls, babes and the invisible girls: Gender relations in snowboarding. *Sport in Society*, 12(10), 1299–1316.

Stelter, N. Z. (2002) Gender differences in leadership: Current social issues and future organizational implications. *Journal of Leadership Studies*, 8(4), 88–100.

Swartz, D. L. (2008) Bringing Bourdieu's master concepts into organizational analysis. *Theory and Society*, 37(1), 45–52.

Turkish Statistical Institute. (2013) Women in statistics 2012. Available from: www.tuik.gov.tr/Kitap.do?metod=KitapDetay&KT_ID=11&KITAP_ID=238. [Accessed 10 March 2014].

Wacquant, L.J.D. (1998) Pierre Bourdieu. In R. Stones (ed.), *Key sociological thinkers*. New York: New York University Press, 215–229.

Whisenant, W. A., Pederson, P. M., and Obenour, B. L. (2002) Success and gender: Determining the rate of advancement for intercollegiate athletic directors. *Sex Roles*, 47, 485–491.

World Economic Forum. (2013) The global gender gap report 2013. Available from: www3.weforum.org/docs/WEF_GenderGap_Report_2013.pdf [Accessed 7 March 2014].

Index

academics and tenure track model 152–3
accreditation standards in higher education 173–4
Adkins, L. 62
Alcaraz, J. 65
Allen, D. E. 63, 64, 67
Anderson, P. F. 63, 64, 67
Archer, M. S. 60
Australia *see* managerialism of higher education in Australia
Austria *see* gender equality in Austrian universities

Barnett, R. 166
Behnke, R. R. 164
board management 119
Boogaard, B. 27
Bourdieu, Pierre 2–3; *see also* capital; doxa; fields; habitus; *specific works*
Bourdieusian sociology, criticism of 210–11
Bradbury, H. 2
Brah, A. 39
Braun, Dietmar 144
Brown, P. 168
Brunsson, Nils 140
Buchholz, L. 55, 58–9, 60, 66
bureaucratic fields in universities 150, 155–6
Burkitt, I. 4

Calhoun, C. 127
capital: access to 191–2; advantages of capital-based approach 204–5; careers and 23–8; concept of 4, 5; conversion of 142, 218; in cultural and creative industries 196–205; embodied culture in organisations and 58–61; fields and 191–2; forms of 189–90; pension boards in UK and 125–7; political, in universities 152; power and 134, 190; relational theory of 9; role and importance of 187–8; scholars and 71–2; as social relation 188–9; universities and 141–3; value of 114, 192–6; *see also* cultural capital; social capital; symbolic capital
career capitals 25–6
careers: capital and 23–8; field and 21–3, 31; habitus and 28–30, 32; overview 19–20; power and 20–1; as sites of power 20, 30–2
carnal theorising: consumption and 63–5; culture and 58–61; gender dimension of 61–2; overview 55–6, 65–7; in sociology 56–8
Cartesian duality 56, 58
central and eastern European (CEE) migrant workers 38, 42, 45, 46, 49–50
Chandler, J. 179
Chell, E. 55
Clark, G. 133, 135
classes and cultural consumption 63–5
Cohen, L. 26
Colley, H. 167
commodification of migrant workers 38–40
conservation, as field strategy 211
consumption: carnal theorising and 63–5; difference and 188
cooperative learning 169, 175–6, 179
corporate boards, pension boards compared to 135

230 *Index*

Corsun, D. L. 121
Costen, W. M. 121
credentials and competence 168
Crenshaw, Kimberly 39
critical realist research 43
cultural and creative industries (CCI), capital in 196–205
cultural capital: in cultural and creative industries 198, 200–4; defined 24, 72; economic and social capital and 189–90; ethnicity as form of 26–7; forms of 61; gender as form of 26; managerialism of higher education and 168–9; pension boards and 126; as resource 60–1; in sport organisations 217, 219–20, 224; states of 189
culture, embodied, in organisations 58–61
Cunningham, G. B. 209

Darchen, S. 66
De Clercq, D. 134
Department of Health, Education and Welfare (DHEW, US) 104
Diaz Garcia, M. 62
dichotomies 1–2, 56–7
DiMaggio, P. J. 97, 99–100
dispositional habitus 129–30
dispositions, habitus as system of 74
Distinction (Bourdieu) 25, 64, 188
diversity managers, careers of 22
domestic life and managerial work 215–16, 224
doxa: of boardroom 129–33, 134; defined 73, 165, 211; language-games and 78
dualities: agency and structure 7–8; continuity and change 8; mind and body 8–9, 56–7; overview 5–6; subjectivism and objectivism 6–7
Duberley, J. 26
Durkheim, Emile 6

Earley, C. P. 60
economic capital: conversion rate for 26; in cultural and creative industries 198, 202; cultural and social capital and 189–90; defined 24, 71; overview 188–9; pension boards and 126; as resource 60; in sport organisations 216–17, 224

economic field, global 45–7
economy of practices 196, 197–8, 204
Egan, D. 101
elites, categories of 65
embodied capital 61, 64
embodied culture in organisations 58–61
embodiment: cultural consumption and 63–5; of habitus 73–4; organisational realities and 61–2
Emirbayer, M. 28, 139–40, 144–5
employability imperative in higher education: context for 172–4; groupwork assignments and 174–7; at macro level 166, 177–8; at meso level 178–9; overview 163–5, 181–2
energy, capital as 190
Erel, U. 26
ethnicity, as form of embodied cultural capital 26–7
EU, global economic field of 45–7
Evens, T. M. S. 70
Everett, J. 70
expressive interests, legitimising: within organisational communication studies 81–5; within other academic fields 85–90
external agents, influence of, in higher education 173–4, 177–8, 179

Fairclough, N. 47, 48
Falk, P. 57
FDA (Food and Drug Administration, US) 104–5, 109, 110
fields: academic, scholars as constituting relationships of ontological complicity with 71–9; boundaries and constituents of 115; capital and 191–2; careers and 21–3, 31; concept of 3–5, 44; construction of 97–8, 100–1, 114–15; features of 72–4; habitus and 73–4, 89–90, 180, 211; interaction between 91; language-games of 74–6; organisational 97–9, 114–15, 139–40; in organisational analysis 99–101; political, in universities 149–50, 155–6; reflecting on habitus of 89–90; of social forces 140, 141–3, 157–8; as social spaces 211; sport as 209–10; tenure track model and 149–50;

Index

transnational, discursive group formation across 44–7; university-as-field 144–5, 150–3, 165–6; *see also* ontological complicity between scholar and field; orphan drug (OD) field in US
Food and Drug Administration (FDA, US) 104–5, 109, 110
Forrier, A. 24
Foucault, Michel 21, 59, 71, 72
Fowler, B. 2
Freeman, J. H. 99

Gallagher, M. 166
game analogy: of boardrooms 121, 131–3; of fields 167; fields of social forces and 141; language-games, constituting ontological complicities through 74–6; of tenure track model 153–7; textwork-games, investigating constitution of complicities through 77–9, 81–90, 91–2
gender: carnal theorising and 61–2; as form of embodied cultural capital 26; linguistic differences and 133; *see also* women managers in sport organisations in Turkey
gender equality in Austrian universities: field, capital, and 141–3; game moves and manoeuvres 153–7; overview 139–41, 157–60; tenure track model 145–57; university-as-field 144–5, 150–3
General Directorate of Sport (GDS) 212
genres, governing 46–7
Gergen, K. J. 57
Giddens, A. 7, 74
global economic field 45–7
GLOBE Research Program 60
Gold, M. 132
Grenfell, M. 5–6
Gross, A. G. 85
group formation: across transnational fields 44–7; overview 41–2, 51
groupwork assignments 163–5, 174–7, 178–9

Habermas, J. 74
Habilmodel 147–8
habitus: of agents, evolution of through interactions between 114; assigned and performed, of migrant workers 48–50; careers and 28–30, 32; concept of 3–5; dispositional 129–30; duality of continuity and change and 8; embodied culture in organisations and 58–61; embodiment of 65; field and 73–4, 89–90, 180, 211; function of 29; linguistic 74–6, 88; managerialism of higher education and 167–8; at organisational level 159; overview 55–6; pension boards in UK and 127–30; power dynamics and 20; regenerative nature of boards and 120–2
Hannan, M. T. 99
Haraway, D. 62
Hatch, Orin 112
health professionals and rare diseases 105–6
heresy and field 23
higher education, managerialism of 162–5; *see also* universities in Austria, power struggles in
historical dimension of habitus 59
Hodkinson, P. 28
Hoffman, A. J. 97, 98, 101, 115
Hofstede, G. 60
Holtzman, Elizabeth 109
Homo Academicus (Bourdieu) 198
Huppatz, K. 22, 26, 62
Hutt, Peter 110–12

identities: discursive construction and transformation of 37–8, 42; social 48; workplace 41–2, 49
Iellatchitch, A. 22–3, 25
Ilkkaracan, İ. 209
illusio: of boardroom 131–3, 134; defined 121, 167
institutional environment, defined 99
intellectual capital 198, 199, 200, 201
international management and carnal theorising 66–7
intersectional analysis across spatial and temporal dimensions 43–4
intersectional commodification of migrant workers 39–40, 50–1
Invitation to Reflexive Sociology, An (Bourdieu and Wacquant) 55, 60
isotimy, principle of 29

James, D. 5–6
Jary, D. 162

Jenkins, R. 59, 64
Johnson, D. 169, 175
Johnson, R. T. 169, 175
Johnson, V. 28, 139–40, 144–5

Kakabadse, A. 65
Kakabadse, N. 65
Karatas-Ozkan, M. 59
Kefauver-Harris amendments 102
King, A. 70
King, P. E. 164
Klugman, Jack 109–10, 112
Klugman, Maurice 109, 112
knowing, ways of 23–4
Küskü, F. 209

labour organisations and pension schemes 123, 127
language-games, constituting ontological complicities through 74–6
Lash, S. 2
Latour, B. 91
Laumann, E. O. 99
Laybourn, P. 164
Layder, D. 43, 45
Lebaron, F. 187–8
Leblebici, H. 97
Levi-Strauss, C. 5
Levy, D. L. 101
Lichtenstein, B. M. B. 2
linguistic exchange 42
Logic of Practice, The (Bourdieu) 2
Lounsbury, M. 2–3

Maclean, M. 120–1, 134
macro level of analysis: field concept and 22, 30; of managerialism of higher education 165–6, 177–8; *see also* fields
Makrinioti, D. 58
managerialism in universities 143, 159
managerialism of higher education in Australia: context 172–4; groupwork assignments 174–7; limitations of research on 180–1; at macro level 165–6, 177–8; at meso level 167–8, 178–9; methodology 170–2; at micro level 168–9; overview 162–5, 181–2
marketing and consumer behaviour, and carnal theorising 67
material domains 9

Maton, K. 167–8, 180
Mauss, Marcel 59
McCall, L. 40
McDowell, L. 39, 40
'McUniversity' 166
meso level of analysis: career habitus and 28–30; of managerialism of higher education 167–8, 178–9; *see also* habitus
(meta)governance and global economic field 45–7
Meyer, J. W. 99
Meyers, Abbey 108
micro level of analysis: career capital and 23–8, 30; of managerialism of higher education 168–9; *see also* capital
migrant workers, commodification of across spatial and temporal dimensions 38–40
migrant workers' subjectivities: assigned and performed habitus and 48–50; (re)formation and commodification of 37–8; group formation across transnational fields 44–7; intersectional analysis of 43–4; overview 50–1; symbolic power, group formation, and 40–2
Miller, H. 162
Mills, A. J. 170–1
Mills, C. W. 2
Mills, J. H. 170–1
modern man 57
Moore, R. 190
Musselin, Christine 144

National Coalition for Rare Diseases 109
new institutionalism in organisational analysis: organisational field in 99–101; overview 97–8, 115
new public management (NPM) 143
Nice Treaty 47
Nicolini, D. 191
Nicolopoulou, K. 65
Nielsen, K. 65

occupational fields 22
ODA (Orphan Drug Act) 112–13
OD field *see* orphan drug (OD) field in US
OECD (Organisation for Economic Co-operation and Development) 162, 166

ontological complicity between scholar and field: field, features of 72–4; language-games and 74–6; methodology of research 79–80; within organisational communication studies 81–5; within other academic fields 85–90; overview 71–2; positioning in constitution of 76–7; practicing reflexivity through textwork-games 77–9
O'Reilly, D. 179
organisational analysis: concept of fields in 99–101; new institutionalism in 97–8, 99–101, 115
organisational communication studies: methodology for research on 79–80; results of research on 81–5
organisational fields: overview 97–9, 114–15; use of concept of 139–40
organisation and management studies: Bourdieusian theory in 3, 9; as discipline of social sciences 1–2; organisational communication studies within field of 85–6; relational epistemology for 67
Organisation for Economic Co-operation and Development (OECD) 162, 166
organisation habitus 159
Orphan Drug Act (ODA) 112–13
orphan drug (OD) field in US: construction of 98, 103–8; data collection and analysis of 102–3; origins of orphan drugs 101–2; overview 113–14; power and struggles within 108–13
orthodoxy and field 23
Ostrower, F. 65
Outline of a Theory of Practice (Bourdieu) 2, 59
outsiders: to boardroom activities 127–33; succession strategies of 225
Özbilgin, M. 59, 60, 134, 159, 209

Parker, M. 162
Parker, P. 24
Passeron, J. C. 64
Patton, M. Q. 214
pedagogical practices *see* groupwork assignments

Pension Act of 2004 122
pension boards in UK: capital and 125–7; habitus and 127–30; laws and trends affecting 122–3; methodology for research on 124–5; overview 119–20, 135–6; rules of game, and role of doxa and illusio 131–3; theoretical framework for examination of 120–2
Perrons, D. 49
Pfister, G. 218
pharmaceutical industry 103–4; *see also* orphan drug (OD) field in US
Pharmaceutical Manufacturers Association (PMA) 103, 110–11, 112, 114
Phoenix, A. 39
political, work of Bourdieu as 1–2
political capital in universities 152
political fields in universities 149–50, 155–6
political representation and legitimacy 133–5
positions in constituting ontological complicity 76–7
postcolonial condition and commodification of migrant workers' subjectivities 41–2, 51
postmodern man 57
Powell, W. W. 97, 99–100
power: capital and 134, 190; careers as sites of 20, 30–2; field construction and 101; within orphan drug field 108–14; overview 20–1; relational view on 139; symbolic 41–2; symbolic capital and 191; *see also* universities in Austria, power struggles in
Practical Reason (Bourdieu) 2
practice and power 21
Prichard, C. 162, 166, 178, 179
prism analogy 143, 156
Provost, G. P. 106
public authority and rare diseases 104–5
public service drugs 103–4

Radtke, S. 218
rare disease patient organisations 106–7, 112
rare diseases (RDs) 98, 101–2; *see also* orphan drug (OD) field in US

rectorate and tenure track model 151
Reed, M. 179
reflexivity 6
reflexivity in practice: expressive interests, legitimising 81–90; methodology 79–80; ontological complicity between scholar and field 71–9; overview 70–1, 90–2
relational epistemology 67
relational theory of practice 3–5; *see also* capital; fields; habitus
representational legitimacy and pension boards in UK: capital and 125–7; habitus and 127–30; methodology for research on 124–5; overview 119–20, 135–6; political representation and 133–5; requirements for 122; theoretical framework for 120–2; trends for 122–3
Reproduction in Education, Society and Culture (Bourdieu and Passeron) 64
Roggeband, C. 27
Ross-Smith, A. 62
Rowan, B. 99

Sakellariou, K. 65
Sartre, J.-P. 5
Savage, M. 25
Sayad, A. 45
Sayce, S. 132, 134
Scase, R. 168
Schneidhofer, T. M. 22
scholars, as constituting relationships of ontological complicity with academic fields 71–9
scholarship and commitment, duality between 2
scientific fields in universities 150
senate and tenure track model 151–2
Shilling, C. 56–7
Shirkey, H. C. 106
situated activity of transnational employment 47
Skeggs, B. 62
Smith, K. A. 169
social capital: in cultural and creative industries 198, 199–200, 201, 202; cultural and economic capital and 189–90; defined 24–5, 72, 189; in organisational communication studies 83; pension boards and 125–6; as resource 60; in sport organisations 218, 224; in universities 157
social class: concept of 40–1, 50; cultural capital and 61; cultural consumption and 63–5
social forces, fields of 140, 141–3, 157–8
social life, as game 140
social relation, capital as 188–9
social space: capital and 187; fields and 191, 211
social world, beyond dualities 5–9
sociology: Bourdieusian, criticism of 210–11; carnal theorising in 56–8; of culture 63–4; relational 3–5
Sousa, C. A. A. 179
spatial dimensions of intersectional analysis 39–40, 43–4, 50–1
sport, as social field 209–10
sports organisations *see* women managers in sport organisations in Turkey
staff of universities, categories of 147–8
state, functions of, in relation to migration 44–5
stereotype thread 30
Stilwell, F. 181
strategies, concept of 4, 5
struggles: field construction and 101; within orphan drug field 108–14; *see also* universities in Austria, power struggles in
style, defined 48
subversion, as field strategy 211, 221–3, 225
succession, as field strategy 211, 219–21, 224–5
Sulkunen, P. 7
Sweetman, P. 70
symbolic capital: in cultural and creative industries 202–3; defined 60, 72, 190–1; field and 25, 141–2; rules, probability of success, and 27
symbolic domains 9
symbolic power 41–2
symbolic violence 191

Tatli, A. 59, 60, 159, 209
teamwork skills 163–5, 174–7
temporal dimensions of intersectional analysis 39–40, 43–4, 50–1
tenure track model: fields, defining 149–50; game moves and

manoeuvres 153–7; gender equality and 158–9; implementation of 140, 147–8; power games around implementation of 145; research design and data collection on 145–7; university-as-field 150–3
textwork-games, investigating constitution of complicities through 77–9, 81–90, 91–2
Thanem, T. 166
time, and capital 189
Trade Union Congress 123
transitions within and across career fields 25–6
transnational labour migration processes 39
Tremblay, D. 66
Tretheway, A. 62
Turkey *see* women managers in sport organisations in Turkey
Turkish Olympic Committee (TOC) 212
Turkish Sport Federations (TSFs) 212
Turner, B. S. 56, 57, 58, 63–4

UK *see* pension boards in UK
under-representation of women in management *see* women managers in sport organisations in Turkey
universities in Austria, power struggles in: field, capital, and 141–3; game moves and manoeuvres 153–7; overview 139–41, 157–60; tenure track model 145–57

university-as-field 144–5, 150–3, 165–6
Urwin, R. 133, 135
US *see* orphan drug (OD) field in US

Ventresca, M. 2–3
voicing a text 78
Voronov, M. 134

Wacquant, L. 28, 39, 58, 59, 60, 70, 142, 165, 177
Wallenberg, L. 166
Walshe, J. M. 105–6
Waxman, Henry 105, 109, 111
Weick, Karl 73
Weininger, E. B. 63
Welter, F. 62
Whittaker, Bob 110–11
Willmott, H. 162, 166, 178, 179
Wills, J. 39
Wittgenstein, L. 75, 78
women managers in sport organisations in Turkey: competing capitals and 216–17; framework to investigate 210–12; gendered practices and 215–16; methodology of research on 212–14; overview 207–8, 224–6; positions held by 218–19; sociocultural context 208–9, 223; subversion strategies of 221–3, 225; succession strategies of 219–21, 224–5
Woolgar, S. 91

Yin, R. K. 170
Ylijoki, O.-H. 179